Sinclair
LEWIS
a reference guide

A
Reference
Publication
in
Literature

Ronald Gottesman
Editor

Sinclair LEWIS

a reference guide

ROBERT E. FLEMING
with
Esther Fleming

G.K. HALL & CO.

70 LINCOLN STREET, BOSTON, MASS.

Copyright © 1980 by Robert E. Fleming

Library of Congress Cataloging in Publication Data

Fleming, Robert E
  Sinclair Lewis, a reference guide.

  (Reference guides in literature)
  Includes index.
  1. Lewis, Sinclair, 1885-1951—Bibliography.
I. Fleming, Esther, 1936-   joint author.
II. Title. III. Series: Reference guide in
literature.
Z8504.38.F56   [PS3523.E94]   016.813′5′2   79-24048
ISBN 0-8161-8094-6

This publication is printed on permanent/durable acid-free paper
MANUFACTURED IN THE UNITED STATES OF AMERICA

Contents

INTRODUCTION vii

LEWIS'S MAJOR WORKS xvii

WRITINGS ABOUT SINCLAIR LEWIS, 1914-1978 1

INDEX . . . .

    A NOTE ON THE INDEX 213

    AUTHOR/TITLE INDEX 215

Introduction

For nearly sixty years now, Sinclair Lewis, the first American to win the Nobel Prize in Literature, has been well known in America and, for that matter, in most of the world. More than most authors, Lewis has been the subject of widespread disagreement and controversy and has suffered periods of neglect and critical attack unusual even if one makes allowances for the pendulum effect that often prevails in literary criticism. Perhaps the conflicting views of Lewis are epitomized by Mark Schorer, who ended his massive critical biography with the statement that Lewis "was one of the worst writers in modern American literature," and then added that "without his writing one cannot imagine modern American literature" (1961.15, p. 813).

Although it might have seemed to the American reading public that Lewis became an overnight success with the publication of Main Street in 1920, he had served his apprenticeship during the preceding six years, in which he had published five novels. Critical reaction to these early novels had been mixed: Our Mr. Wrenn (1914) was judged promising but more notable for the echoes of H. G. Wells and Charles Dickens than for its own merits. While The Trail of the Hawk (1915) was viewed by some as an advance on the first novel, others treated it as a decline. If the critics could not agree that The Innocents (1917) was a mere potboiler (as it was), at least they recognized that The Job (1917) was Lewis's most ambitious work thus far. Yet when Lewis reverted to a lighter and more commercial vein with Free Air (1919), which began as a serial for the Saturday Evening Post, only one reviewer registered disappointment. Lewis seemed to have established a niche for himself as an entertainer, a writer of light novels that touched and amused his readers but did not stimulate them intellectually.

Main Street changed all that. Whatever faults reviewers saw in the new novel--plotlessness, flat characters, lack of subtlety, monotony--nearly all agreed that it was one of the most significant books of its age. The more favorable reviewers compared Lewis to major contemporary figures such as Theodore Dreiser and Sherwood Anderson or to major writers of the past century such as Jane Austen and George Eliot. Those who disliked the book criticized it on social rather than on literary grounds: Lewis was seen as unfair to the inhabitants of small towns and unjust in his treatment of villagers so recently descended from pioneer stock.

Babbitt (1922) consolidated the reputation established by Main Street but surrounded Lewis with even greater controversy. Though the book was not praised without reservation, most reviewers considered it technically better than Main Street. The most vehement reactions, however, came not from the world of letters but from the world George F. Babbitt inhabited, as Rotarians expressed outrage and Nation's Business mounted an anti-Lewis campaign that went on for years. Nevertheless, Lewis advanced more solidly into literary respectability with the help of Stuart Pratt Sherman's pamphlet The Significance of Sinclair Lewis (1922). While some reviewers of the pamphlet protested its flattering conclusions and pointed out that it had been commissioned by Lewis's publishers, Sherman's reputation and the merits of Lewis's last two books assured him of treatment in early scholarly studies of twentieth century American literature.

During the remainder of the 1920s, Lewis became even more prominent, publishing three other major novels as well as two minor ones. Arrowsmith (1925) was regarded as a sign of Lewis's efforts to develop his art although some critics objected to the scientific material as too extensive, even tedious. The creation of a protagonist who, however flawed, had a positive sense of values was considered an improvement over his previous work. Joseph Wood Krutch noted that the satire in Arrowsmith was not as effective as that in Lewis's earlier books, but the novel was closer to life. The successes of Main Street, Babbitt, and Arrowsmith enabled most critics to forgive Lewis his two lighter works of the 1920s, Mantrap (1926) and The Man Who Knew Coolidge (1928). Each book was taken seriously by a few reviewers but most recognized them for what they were, a light commercial novel and a tour de force, respectively. A typical reaction to Mantrap was the assertion that Lewis had the right to toss off a minor work from time to time, whether he did it to make money or simply to amuse himself (1926.21).

Neither the general public nor the critics were so kind to Lewis when he refused the Pulitzer Prize in 1926. Lewis's gesture, probably stemming from pique at not having been offered the prize earlier as well as from a desire for publicity, met with general disapproval. Only a small minority, as represented by John Farrar of the Bookman (1926.22), believed that Lewis did have a valid point: the Pulitzer was not awarded to the best novel of the year, but to the "most wholesome," and therefore political considerations often affected literary judgments.

Elmer Gantry (1927) combined with the rejection of the Pulitzer Prize to give hostile critics ammunition against Lewis. The novel was considered bitter, obscene, and immoderate; even many of those who judged Lewis's criticisms of the clergy to be justifiable felt that his satire was too shrill and unrelieved to be effective. As might be expected, H. L. Mencken loved the book (1927.23), but so did the more moderate Joseph Wood Krutch (1927.19). They were distinctly in the minority. Lewis's last novel of the 1920s, Dodsworth (1929), did not fare much better with the critics, though not because of any scandal. Many reviewers objected to Lewis's reliance on journalistic descriptions of places, or mere "travelogue." Others looked for the kind of satire he had excelled in earlier and found it only in his treatment of the Dodsworth marriage. A few, like Henry Seidel Canby (1929.6), felt that Lewis had genuinely achieved a new maturity and had attempted to write a novel more challenging than his satires had been.

Besides Sherman's early pamphlet, three other book-length estimates of Lewis were published in the 1920s. Harrison Smith's Sinclair Lewis (1925.37) was, if anything, even more suspect than Sherman's work since the author was an old friend employed by Lewis's publisher. The other two works, however, Vernon L. Parrington's Sinclair Lewis: Our Own Diogenes (1927.26) and Hans Kriesi's Sinclair Lewis (1928.17) were both independent and quite favorable to Lewis.

The awarding of the Nobel Prize for Literature to Lewis in 1930 irritated many Americans and initiated considerable controversy that eventually embraced not only Lewis and his work but also the methods of the Nobel committee and the attitudes of Europe toward the United States. Extremely displeased with the award and with Lewis for accepting the prize, one faction recalled that Lewis had loftily rejected the Pulitzer Prize because prizes were an unwholesome influence on creative writers, and they saw his acceptance of the Nobel Prize as hypocrisy. Furthermore, Lewis's detractors felt that he had won the prize not for excellence as a writer of fiction but for his skill in reinforcing the stereotypes Europeans held concerning the American character. The most vicious of these detractors characterized Lewis as a "muckraker" who appealed merely because of the scandals he brought to light; others hinted that since he was only a satirist, he would be incapable of further development unless he learned to transcend satire and to write more balanced and realistic fiction. Some of the most vitriolic attacks were aimed at the Nobel Prize committee, on the grounds of its having deliberately insulted Americans by awarding the prize to one who had portrayed the United States in such negative terms.

Set against these hostile critics was a group that took a chauvinistic pleasure in the fact that an American had at last won the Nobel Prize; they were unconcerned about any possible negative implications in its being awarded to a critic of American society. Yet another faction responded to Lewis's detractors that although Lewis was not perfect, he had every right to the prize, for he had accomplished more than any other American novelist of his generation. Typical of this group was Henry Seidel Canby, who noted the tremendous achievement of Lewis in his five major novels of the 1920s and

asserted that no other American writer since World War I had produced
a comparable body of work (1931.16). Others observed that Lewis's
work was typically American not only because it captured the external
reality of the United States but because it embodied the spirit of
self-criticism that was a distinctly American tradition.

Finally, the Nobel Prize caused some serious scholars to examine
the body of Lewis's work before 1930 and to evaluate him as a major
writer. A short but perceptive essay by Howard Mumford Jones
(1931.26) typifies this approach. Reviewing the Nobel Prize Edition
of Lewis's novels, Jones concluded that Lewis showed little capacity
for growth over the years and that he tended to repeat successful
tricks throughout the 2000 pages comprising his five major novels.
This tendency toward repetition was to become a major stumbling block
for Lewis in the years that followed his winning of the Nobel Prize,
though some critics and reviewers were much slower to perceive it
than was Jones.

In 1933 Lewis's new publisher, Doubleday, brought out Ann Vickers
as well as Sinclair Lewis: A Biographical Sketch (1933.31), Carl Van
Doren's favorable view of their recently acquired author. Surprising-
ly, Ann Vickers was reviewed rather well, J. Donald Adams calling it
one of Lewis's best novels (1933.1). The book was also well received
by the Yale Review and the Saturday Review of London. Many critics,
among them H. L. Mencken (1933.24) and William Lyon Phelps (1933.25),
noted that Ann Vickers was not one of Lewis's best books although it
showed considerable merit. Two important critics voiced the opinion
that was to become the prevailing view: Ann Vickers was the beginning of a decline for Lewis. Malcolm Cowley, writing in the New Republic, compared the novel with Babbitt and Arrowsmith and found the
later Lewis wanting (1933.9), while Bernard De Voto, in an essay-
review on Ann Vickers and Van Doren's biography, asserted that
Lewis's latest novel proved that the author had been overrated, not
only by Van Doren, but by the critics of the 1920s in general
(1933.11). Lewis was the best novelist of his time, De Voto says,
only because his generation produced no real genius in fiction.

But Lewis's reputation died hard. Work of Art (1934), which recent criticism has accurately judged to be one of Lewis's weakest
books, received balanced or even favorable reviews, such as the one
by J. Donald Adams of the New York Times Book Review; Adams viewed
the novel as a sign that Lewis could still produce excellent fiction,
though he modified his previous endorsement of Ann Vickers (1934.1).
V. F. Calverton, however, saw Lewis's two latest novels as evidence
that Lewis had been unable to change with the times or to adapt his
art to the social concerns of the 1930s. Weaknesses that had been
overshadowed by Lewis's telling satire in the 1920s were now more ap-
parent, and the future as Calverton saw it was not bright (1934.19).
Meanwhile Lewis's attempt to develop a career as a dramatist with
Jayhawker was given only lukewarm encouragement.

Two Lewis books published in 1935 presented conflicting evidence to the critics. Selected Short Stories of Sinclair Lewis dredged up potboilers from Lewis's days as a literary hack, and Clifton Fadiman expressed the majority opinion in the New Yorker, where he said that it was hard to think of Lewis as a Nobel Prize winner when he read these stories (1935.16). On the other hand, Lewis demonstrated that he still had the ability to produce a major work with the publication of It Can't Happen Here. While they considered Lewis's attack on fascism a tract, not a novel, most critics thought it successful on its own terms. In the minority was R. P. Blackmur, who condemned the book as mere propaganda and raised doubts about its effectiveness even as a tract (1935.7). Clifton Fadiman, who called It Can't Happen Here one of the most important books ever written in America (1935.15), took an extreme view of its merits, but many agreed with his basic assumption that the intensity and significance of the book redeemed its obviously journalistic and hasty style. Unfortunately Lewis followed It Can't Happen Here with The Prodigal Parents (1938). Although a few reviewers were apparently still blinded by Lewis's former reputation, bad reviews outnumbered favorable ones and some of the more kindly reviewers were faint in their praise.

Lewis, who had begun the 1920s with the triumph of Main Street and the 1930s with the triumph of the Nobel Prize, began the 1940s as a man whose time seemed to have passed. Bethel Merriday (1940) was correctly appraised as slim or superficial; some few praised it for its mass of material on the theater or, at the least, for being a better book than The Prodigal Parents, a judgment that now appears debatable. Gideon Planish (1943), a better book than either, may have been treated too harshly since many characterized it as boring and heavy-handed. Those more sympathetic to Lewis noted that he seemed to show some of his old satiric fire, and Clifton Fadiman called Peony Planish Lewis's best female character since Leora Arrowsmith (1943.10). The string of poorly reviewed books continued with Cass Timberlane (1945), which was compared to women's magazine fiction and faulted for its ineffective satire. As always, some writers defended Lewis, but the halo effect that had caused even bad books such as Work of Art to be praised in the 1930s had clearly dissipated by this time. The serious scholarly critics Bernard De Voto and Warren Beck both published evaluations of Lewis during the 1940s. De Voto admitted that Lewis was the leading novelist of the 1920s but described him as a very limited writer, capable only of satire and unable to portray admirable characters (1944.6). Beck attacked Lewis's "inflated reputation" and warned critics and readers alike that they should stop waiting for Lewis to produce something as good as his best work, which itself was sadly flawed (1948.3).

The reading public, at least, was slow to catch up with the critics. Lewis's novels continued to sell very well, partly on the strength of his former reputation and partly because of factors such as book club selection. In a 1944 Saturday Review poll of its readers, Lewis came in fourth on the list of best novelists of the past

twenty years, and <u>Arrowsmith</u> headed the list of best novels for the
same period (1944.5). <u>Cass Timberlane</u> came to resemble <u>Main Street</u>
in one other respect than similarity of plot: Book-of-the-Month Club
selection caused it to climb rapidly on the best-seller lists.

<u>Kingsblood Royal</u> (1947), like <u>It Can't Happen Here</u> a decade ear-
lier, marked Lewis's return to critical favor. Lewis's novel on
racial discrimination was generally acknowledged to be a propaganda
tract rather than fiction, though some critics even argued that the
satire of American racial attitudes might be too overdone to accom-
plish its purpose. Unfortunately, it was to be Lewis's last major
work. Neither <u>The God-Seeker</u> (1949), Lewis's historical novel of
missionary activity in early Minnesota, nor <u>World So Wide</u> (1951), the
posthumously published international novel, belongs on the list of
his important works.

Lewis's death on January 10, 1951, provided the occasion for another round of general assessments, which ranged from an extremely
negative estimate in <u>Christian Century</u>, "Our Greatest Was Not Very
Great" (1951.7), to that of Marcel Brion, whose article in <u>Revue des
Deux Mondes</u> (1951.15) asserted that Lewis's works had the merits
needed to insure their survival. In between were the opinions of
Frederick J. Hoffman (1951.30) and Joseph Wood Krutch (1951.37), who
felt that Lewis had a secure though minor place in American literary
history, with Krutch wondering whether his works would continue to be
read.

America was not allowed to forget Lewis in the years that followed his death. <u>From Main Street to Stockholm</u> (1952.16) contained
letters written by Lewis from 1919 to 1930; 1952 also saw a New York
exhibition of Lewis papers and memorabilia sponsored by the American
Academy of Arts and Letters. In 1953 a collection of Lewis's non-
fiction and journalism, <u>The Man from Main Street</u> (1953.11), was well
received. <u>With Love from Gracie</u>, his first wife's account of their
courtship and marriage (1955.15), contributed to the biographical in-
formation available on Lewis.

Scholarly articles began to appear in significant numbers during
the first few years following his death. Deming Brown's article on
Lewis's Russian reputation (1953.6) and Lyon Richardson's on <u>The Man
Who Knew Coolidge</u> (1953.12) both appeared in <u>American Literature</u>,
while Franklin Walker published an article on Lewis and London in the
<u>Huntington Library Quarterly</u> (1953.15). These articles began a trend
that was to continue throughout the rest of the decade, marking a
steady, if limited, interest in Lewis and his work. The greatest
tribute to Lewis published during the 1950s came from novelist James
T. Farrell, who called Lewis a greater influence on his generation of
writers--those who began to publish during the 1930s--than either
Hemingway or Faulkner (1955.10). Farrell predicted that Lewis's work,
which was admittedly out of fashion at the moment, would eventually
win back a major place in American and world literature.

Just as the 1920s were the decade of Lewis's greatest achievement, the 1960s marked a resurgence of attention to the man and his work, led by Mark Schorer. In spite of the fact that Schorer's comprehensive biography, Sinclair Lewis: An American Life (1961.15), did not present Lewis in a flattering light, it was most highly regarded and encouraged scholarly activity that had been building since the author's death. Schorer followed the biography with his University of Minnesota pamphlet Sinclair Lewis (1963.21) and with Sinclair Lewis: A Collection of Critical Essays (1962.14) as well as with introductions and afterwords for a whole series of reprints of Lewis's works, including Lewis at Zenith (an omnibus volume containing Main Street, Babbitt, and Arrowsmith) and paperbound editions of Main Street, Babbitt, Arrowsmith, Elmer Gantry, Dodsworth, and Ann Vickers.

Other biographical and scholarly books appeared soon after the publication of Schorer's influential biography. Sheldon Grebstein's Sinclair Lewis (1962.6) was added to the Twayne United States Authors series, and was followed by Vincent Sheean's Dorothy and Red (1963.23), which concentrated on the marriage of Lewis and Dorothy Thompson. Although the latter book relied heavily on Thompson's diaries and other papers and was largely unsympathetic to Lewis, it did nothing to stem the growing interest among scholars. The next twelve years saw the publication of three book-length scholarly studies by American critics: D. J. Dooley's The Art of Sinclair Lewis (1967.2), James Lundquist's Sinclair Lewis (1973.8), and Martin Light's The Quixotic Vision of Sinclair Lewis (1975.5). During the same period Lundquist's brief Guide to Sinclair Lewis (1970.17) and Checklist of Sinclair Lewis (1970.16) and a reprinting of Carl Van Doren's Sinclair Lewis: A Biographical Sketch were added to the other studies. In addition, there were several collections of critical essays besides Schorer's. Robert J. Griffin edited Twentieth Century Interpretations of Arrowsmith (1968.4) and Martin Light collected essays and reviews to produce Studies in Babbitt (1971.13). The New York Times printed a portfolio of reviews of Lewis's books that had appeared in the New York Times Book Review over the years (1969.21).

Lewis was not overlooked in the journals during the 1960s and 1970s. In 1969 the Sinclair Lewis Newsletter was founded at St. Cloud State College, near Lewis's birth place, Sauk Centre, Minnesota, and a special issue of the South Dakota Review jointly honored Lewis and Frederick Manfred. Articles on Lewis continued to appear in respected journals such as American Literature, American Quarterly, Modern Language Quarterly, and Studies in Short Fiction.

Foreign interest in Lewis, which had been high in the 1920s and 1930s, returned in the 1960s and 1970s. Even before Schorer's biography, Russian critic Boris Gilenson and the head bibliographer at Moscow's Library of Foreign Literatures, Inna M. Levidova, had published their biobibliographical study Sinkler L'iuis (1959.6), which

contained the most complete Lewis bibliography to that date. Gilenson later treated Lewis at greater length in his Amerika Sinklera
L'iuisa (1972.13). German critic Wilfried Edener contributed a specialized study, Die Religionskritik in den Romanen von Sinclair Lewis
(1963.8), to the international canon, and the French scholar Robert
Silhol added Les Tyrans Tragiques: Un témoin pathétique de notre
temps: Sinclair Lewis (1969.30). Hiroshige Yoshida's massive study,
A Sinclair Lewis Lexicon with a Critical Study of His Style and Method (1976.12), suggests that the Far East has also discovered Lewis's
fiction.

Lewis was not one of the greatest novelists produced by America,
Placed beside other Nobel Prize winners such as Ernest Hemingway and
William Faulkner, he appears to be a minor writer, his work more dated than theirs. However, compared with American writers of fiction
in general, he stands out as an important satirist, a major social
historian of his times, a quick and shrewd delineator of character.
If he did not truly deserve the honor of the first American Nobel
Prize in Literature, neither does he deserve to be neglected, and the
continuing flow of interpretive and analytical criticism since his
death suggests that Sinclair Lewis will not be forgotten.

We have attempted to see all books and critical articles on Lewis
published in the United States from 1914 through 1978. Major works--
books and important critical articles--from England, continental Europe, Asia, and South America have also been included, though on a
less comprehensive basis than American materials; those interested in
foreign criticism of Lewis can consult the index for specialized bibliographies in languages other than English. When a work is published in a language other than English, we have so noted. Substantial reviews in American popular magazines and journals have been
included, along with important reviews in British magazines. A
sampling of reviews from major newspapers or their literary supple-
ments--the New York Times Book Review, the New York Herald Tribune
Books, and the Christian Science Monitor--have been included as representative newspaper reviews. Omitted are brief mentions in publications such as the Cleveland Open Shelf, Pittsburgh Monthly Bulletin,
and Wisconsin Library Bulletin and reviews in the daily press. News
stories reporting Lewis's frequent trips, public statements, and an-
tics are omitted unless they treat major incidents such as his famous
defiance of God in a Kansas City pulpit.

We have avoided the use of abbreviations except in the case of
three important collections of essays and one journal. Mark Schorer's
Sinclair Lewis: A Collection of Critical Essays (1962.14) is abbreviated SL:CCE; Robert J. Griffin's Twentieth Century Interpretations

of Arrowsmith (1968.4) is abbreviated TCIA; Martin Light's Studies in Babbitt (1971.13) is abbreviated SB; and the Sinclair Lewis Newsletter is SLN.

We wish to thank Alice Fidlar Fienning for her help with translation of foreign materials and with proofreading, and Dorothy Wonsmos of Interlibrary Loan, Zimmerman Library, University of New Mexico, for her industry in obtaining items not locally available.

Lewis's Major Works

Hike and the Aeroplane. New York: Stokes, 1912. Juvenile novel
    published under the pseudonym Tom Graham.
Our Mr. Wrenn. New York: Harper, 1914.
The Trail of the Hawk. New York: Harper, 1915.
The Job. New York: Harper, 1917.
The Innocents. New York: Harper, 1917.
Free Air. New York: Harcourt, Brace and Howe, 1919.
Main Street. New York: Harcourt, Brace and Howe, 1920.
Babbitt. New York: Harcourt, Brace, 1922.
Arrowsmith. New York: Harcourt, Brace, 1925.
Mantrap. New York: Harcourt, Brace, 1926.
Elmer Gantry. New York: Harcourt, Brace, 1927.
The Man Who Knew Coolidge. New York: Harcourt, Brace, 1928.
Cheap and Contented Labor. New York: United Feature Syndicate,
    1929.
Dodsworth. New York: Harcourt, Brace, 1929.
Ann Vickers. Garden City, N.Y.: Doubleday, Doran, 1933.
Work of Art. Garden City, N.Y.: Doubleday, Doran, 1934.
Selected Short Stories. Garden City, N.Y.: Doubleday, Doran, 1935.
Jayhawker. Garden City, N.Y.: Doubleday, Doran, 1935.
It Can't Happen Here. Garden City, N.Y.: Doubleday, Doran, 1935.
The Prodigal Parents. Garden City, N.Y.: Doubleday, Doran, 1938.
Bethel Merriday. Garden City, N.Y.: Doubleday, Doran, 1940.
Gideon Planish. New York: Random House, 1943.
Cass Timberlane. New York: Random House, 1945.
Kingsblood Royal. New York: Random House, 1947.
The God-Seeker. New York: Random House, 1949.
World So Wide. New York: Random House, 1951.
From Main Street to Stockholm: Letters of Sinclair Lewis, 1919-1930.
    Selected and with an introduction by Harrison Smith. New York:
    Harcourt, Brace, 1952.
The Man from Main Street: A Sinclair Lewis Reader. Selected Essays
    and Other Writings, 1904-1950. Edited by Harry Maule and Mel-
    ville Cane. New York: Random House, 1953.
I'm a Stranger Here Myself and Other Stories. New York: Dell, 1962.
Storm in the West. New York: Stein and Day, 1963.

Writings About Sinclair Lewis
1914-1978

1 ANON. "Chronicle and Comment." Bookman, 39 (May), 242, 248.
    Portrait and brief biographical sketch of Lewis, with
    emphasis on Our Mr. Wrenn.

2 ANON. "Fiction with a Purpose and Stories that Entertain."
    American Review of Reviews, 49 (14 May), 628.
    Our Mr. Wrenn, a "gently satirical novel," is an "amus-
    ing story" which Lewis seems to have "tossed off easily."

3 ANON. "News of Books." New York Times Review of Books,
    22 February, p. 92.
    Brief comment on Our Mr. Wrenn, noting its similarity to
    the work of H. G. Wells.

4 ANON. Review of Our Mr. Wrenn. A.L.A. Booklist, 10 (June),
    413.
    Lewis displays "understanding and humor" in this mixture
    of realism and romance.

5 ANON. Review of Our Mr. Wrenn. Nation, 98 (12 March), 266.
    This first novel is "better than average" and suggests
    that the author will produce "more telling work in the fu-
    ture." While Our Mr. Wrenn is a bit slow, the realism of
    setting and characterization makes up for plot deficiencies.

6 ANON. Review of Our Mr. Wrenn. New York Times Review of
    Books, 1 March, p. 100.
    This "whimsical little story," while showing the influ-
    ence of Dickens, is different enough from most fiction to
    make it appealing.

7 BRINSLEY, HENRY. "Three Harvard Novelists, and Others."
    Vanity Fair, 2 (June), 39, 96.
    Omnibus review including Our Mr. Wrenn, a charming book,
    "unimportant but decidedly agreeable."

1914

8   [TOWNSEND, R. D.]. "The New Books." Outlook, 107 (2 May),
      46.
         Lewis recalls both H. G. Wells and O. Henry with his
      first novel, Our Mr. Wrenn. While plot construction could
      be better, the book is "a promising story by a new writer."

1915

1   ANON. "The Modern Wanderlust." Independent, 84 (29 Novem-
      ber), 363.
         The Trail of the Hawk is disappointing after Our Mr.
      Wrenn. Lewis does not employ the "quiet humor" that
      strengthened his earlier novel.

2   ANON. Review of The Trail of the Hawk. A.L.A. Booklist, 12
      (December), 138.
         Adventurous story of a pioneer in aviation.

3   ANON. Review of The Trail of the Hawk. Nation, 101
      (28 October), 522.
         Key virtues of this interesting novel are its "exuber-
      ance" and realism. Lewis "has succeeded in giving a truer
      picture of our puzzling United States" than many more pre-
      tentious authors have managed.

4   ANON. Review of The Trail of the Hawk. New York Times Review
      of Books, 10 October, p. 362.
         While Our Mr. Wrenn was an appealing book, The Trail of
      the Hawk is many times better. This story really captures
      the spirit of modern America. Lewis has rare descriptive
      power, a "broad and kindly" sympathy, honesty, and an ob-
      vious wealth of experience to draw on.

5   COLBRON, GRACE ISABEL. Review of The Trail of the Hawk. Pub-
      lishers Weekly, 88 (11 December), 1961-62.
         An excellent and promising book. However, Lewis "has
      piled enough action, enough philosophy, enough character
      study into this book to fill several." If he can retain
      his "exuberance" while mastering the art of the novel, he
      will have a distinguished career.

6   COOPER, FREDERIC TABER. "Some Novels of the Month." Bookman,
      42 (October), 214-15.
         The Trail of the Hawk begins somewhat slowly but improves
      in Part 2, where Carl works at a series of odd jobs and be-
      comes a flier. "It would be hard to find anywhere else in
      current fiction any description that would give to the in-
      experienced a kindred thrill of breathless flight, of dan-

ger that is a fearful joy. . . ." The love story of the
third section is less successful, as is the story of Carl's
settling down in business.

1916

1 SOULE, GEORGE H., JR. "A Novelist with a Future." Book News
   Monthly, 34 (January), 208-10.
      Personal recollections of Lewis during his early days in
   New York, capsule biography from boyhood to 1915, and
   brief comments on The Trail of the Hawk and Our Mr. Wrenn.

1917

1 ANON. "Latest Works of Fiction." New York Times Review of
   Books, 11 March, p. 82.
      The Job is "in many ways . . . the best picture we have
   yet been given of the evolution of a successful business
   woman. . . ." Neither brutal nor sentimental, the book
   honestly and accurately examines the business world and a
   woman's opportunities in it.

2 ANON. "New Fiction by American Authors." New York Times Review of Books, 30 September, p. 365.
      Lewis, an optimist by nature, tells a cheerful story in
   a manner reminiscent of Dickens. The Innocents shows his
   capacity for sympathy with the little people of the world
   and his ability to make their lives interesting.

3 ANON. "Notes on New Fiction." Dial, 62 (5 April), 313.
      Lewis's The Job presents a "rather refreshing heroine,"
   Una Golden, in a plot and setting which accurately reflect
   the everyday business world and modern feminism.

4 ANON. "Notes on New Fiction." Dial, 63 (22 November), 531.
      The Innocents is disappointing, a "sweet little story"
   from an author who has shown he could do better in The
   Trail of the Hawk and The Job. This latest novel is a
   flimsy offering, disguised by Lewis's "facile smartness of
   phrase."

5 ANON. Review of The Innocents. Booklist, 14 (November), 60.
      The amusingly atypical love story of an old married
   couple.

1917

6   ANON. Review of The Innocents. New Republic, 13 (17 November), 16.
        Unlike The Trail of the Hawk or The Job, The Innocents
    is romantic, funny, and "sentimental." It is hard to fault
    a realist for writing a book which is so "amusing" even if
    it does not fit in with his previous work.

7   ANON. Review of The Job. A.L.A. Booklist, 13 (May), 355.
        The realistic story of a small-town girl who attempts to
    make a living in New York. While some may find it "sordid,"
    Lewis shows "honesty and vision."

8   ANON. "True Sentiment and False." Nation, 105 (15 November),
    540.
        Although The Innocents is ridiculously sentimental, it
    seems to be intended as a parody of such novels, for the
    reader is sure that Lewis is laughing at it as well.

9   ANON. "Women, Heroines, and Woman." Nation, 104 (12 April),
    432-33.
        Although Lewis preaches frequently in The Job, the book
    is redeemed by his earnestness and by the reality of Una
    Golden, his protagonist.

10 BOYNTON, H. W. "Some Stories of the Month." Bookman, 45
    (May), 316-17.
        The Job is "a feminist document" but makes an interest-
    ing novel anyway, although it might have been cut consider-
    ably. Its main virtue is the well-realized protagonist,
    Una Golden.

11 _____. "A Stroll Through the Fair of Fiction." Bookman, 46
    (November), 340-41.
        The Innocents is grouped with other "sentimental come-
    dies." It is surprising to find Lewis, a realist, turning
    out this sort of book.

12 H[ACKETT], F[RANCIS]. "A Stenographer." New Republic, 10
    (24 March), 234-35.
        Lewis's The Job compares favorably with Frank Norris's
    The Pit because Lewis examines business through the life of
    a single stenographer, while Norris looked at business too
    abstractly. Lewis shows great "sympathetic insight" in
    treating Una Golden. Characterization is a strong point
    except in the case of Una's husband, who is treated as a
    caricaturist might create him. The plot is too neatly and
    happily resolved, considering the realism of the book as a
    whole. On balance though the novel is an important contri-
    bution to modern American fiction.

<u>1919</u>

1   ANON. "Books of the Fortnight." <u>Dial</u>, 67 (1 November), 388.
        Lewis's <u>Free Air</u> "defends the new, unconventional America," which emphasizes the merit of the individual, rather than class and family.

2   ANON. "Latest Works of Fiction." <u>New York Times Review of Books</u>, 19 October, p. 580.
        Although Lewis does not spare America's faults, his love for the American people and landscape is evident in <u>Free Air</u>, a cheerful novel of love and adventure. He displays a gift for humor and an ability to transcribe real speech, sometimes all too accurately.

3   ANON. Review of <u>Free Air</u>. <u>Booklist</u>, 16 (December), 94.
        Lewis's latest adventure novel is "rather disappointing."

<u>1920</u>

1   ANON. "Latest Works of Fiction." <u>New York Times Book Review and Magazine</u>, 14 November, p. 18.
        Although <u>Main Street</u> contains some awkward writing and has almost no plot, some passages could not have been better and the book as a whole is "absorbing." Lewis sees the stuffiness of small towns through the eyes of youth, as if he had begun the book years ago and only recently finished it. At the same time, he is not hesitant about satirizing his young heroine Carol. Altogether, "a remarkable book."

2   ANON. Review of <u>Free Air</u>. <u>New Republic</u>, 21 (28 January), 275.
        In spite of its "commonplace" main characters, who could have stepped out of a dime novel, <u>Free Air</u> is charming, primarily because of Lewis's ability to create the western setting--the country, the small towns, and the people who inhabit both.

3   ANON. Review of <u>Main Street</u>. <u>Booklist</u>, 17 (December), 117.
        This balanced picture of a small town and its naive new citizen is "one of the few really good American novels of today."

1920

4   H[ACKETT], F[RANCIS]. "God's Country." <u>New Republic</u>, 25
     (1 December), 20-21.
        Although flawed by Lewis's tendency to create types
     rather than round characters, <u>Main Street</u> is not only his
     best novel so far, but "pioneer work." He has taken the
     American small town, seemingly thin raw material for fic-
     tion, and used its manners and foibles to produce a supe-
     rior American novel. Reprinted 1961.4.

5   [LEWISOHN, LUDWIG]. "The Epic of Dulness." <u>Nation</u>, 111
     (10 November), 536-37.
        Reviews <u>Main Street</u> and Sherwood Anderson's <u>Poor White</u>.
     While both novels deal with small midwestern towns, there
     can really be no comparison. Only Theodore Dreiser sur-
     passes the Lewis of <u>Main Street</u>, where Lewis shows that his
     greatest strength is to give "literary permanence to the
     speech of his time and section." "'Main Street' would add
     to the power and distinction of the contemporary literature
     of any country."

6   R., S. M. "Looking Ahead with the Publishers." <u>Bookman</u>, 52
     (December), 372.
        In spite of being "too long, rather tedious," <u>Main
     Street</u> is "the finest" of the new novels and should be a
     popular success as well as a serious study of the American
     small town.

7   SELIGMANN, HERBERT J. "The Tragi-Comedy of Main Street."
     <u>Freeman</u>, 2 (17 November), 237.
        <u>Main Street</u> is an uneasy blend of tragedy and comedy;
     however, Lewis's bigger problem is failure to be subtle
     enough in his depiction of Gopher Prairie. Not content
     with simply depicting its very real failings, he lambastes
     the town unmercifully, leaving nothing to the imagination
     of the reader. The novel is "both imperfect and important."

<u>1921</u>

1   ANON. "Brent Raps 'Main Street.'" <u>New York Times</u>, 14 July,
     p. 17.
        Episcopal Bishop Reverend Charles Brent criticized <u>Main
     Street</u> as a "pagan book" in an address delivered in Geneva,
     New York.

2   ANON. "Briefer Mention." Dial, 70 (January), [106].
         In Main Street, Lewis "mercilessly, brilliantly" sati-
      rizes the shallowness of small-town life in America. While
      the book "has more social than artistic implications," it
      is successful.

3   ANON. "The Gossip Shop." Bookman, 53 (June), 382.
         Brief account of the dramatization of Main Street by
      Harriet Ford and Harvey O'Higgins, with Lewis as consul-
      tant.

4   ANON. "We Nominate for the Hall of Fame." Vanity Fair, 16
         (June), 58.
         Lewis "has added a new word to the spoken language."
      Main Street "leaves no word unsaid" about the American
      small town.

5   COBLENTZ, STANTON A. "Main Street." Bookman, 52 (January),
         357-58 [457-58; issue misnumbered].
         While the plot of Main Street "might be condensed to
      five or six pages," character and setting make the novel
      significant. Lewis combines photographic realism with an
      ability to look "beneath the surface with a keenness that
      is more than photographic." He is compared with Jane
      Austen and George Eliot. Reprinted 1939.6.

6   D., K. "A New and Rather Revised 'Main Street.'" Vanity
         Fair, 16 (July), 17.
         Parody of Main Street.

7   ELY, CATHERINE BEACH. "A Belated Promenade on Main Street."
      New York Times Book Review and Magazine, 8 May, p. 16.
         Main Street is a monotonous book because of its dreary
      plot and "lumbering style." Modern realists like Lewis,
      who see only the surface, could learn from that great real-
      ist Balzac, who discloses significance beneath the surface
      details of his realistic novels.

8   LOVETT, ROBERT MORSS. "A Communication: The Pulitzer Prize."
      New Republic, 27 (22 June), 114.
         As a member of the committee to recommend a novel for
      the Pulitzer Prize, Lovett sets forth for the record the
      committee's unanimous choice of Lewis's Main Street and
      quotes a letter from Stuart Pratt Sherman detailing reasons
      for the choice. Columbia University ignored the recommen-
      dation and awarded the 1920 Pulitzer Prize to Edith Wharton
      for The Age of Innocence.

1921

9   LOWRY, HELEN BULLITT. "Mutual Admiration Society of Young In-
    tellectuals." New York Times Book Review and Magazine,
    8 May, pp. 6, 25.
        Satirizes the new group of "intellectual" writers such
    as Floyd Dell, Lewis, and F. Scott Fitzgerald, who achieve
    wealth and literary fame by attacking the American middle
    class. They share a tendency to promote each other's works
    and a dislike of the established critics.

10 MARSHALL, ARCHIBALD. "A Browse Among the Best Sellers."
    Bookman, 54 (September), 9-11.
        Main Street is an excellent realistic picture and in-
    dictment of small town life, but it is oddly limited as a
    novel. The characters fail to develop fully and never
    quite come alive.

11 MENCKEN, H. L. "Consolation." Smart Set, 64 (January),
    138-44.
        Lewis's great strengths are his ability to capture the
    externals of the lives of his fellow Americans and his re-
    fusal to oversimplify their problems by offering a prescip-
    tion. While he does not penetrate as deeply into their
    characters as does Dreiser, on the whole his work is a wel-
    come addition to American literature. Reprinted in SL:CCE,
    1962.14.

12 NICHOLS, BEVERLEY. Review of Main Street. Saturday Review
    (London), 132 (20 August), 230-31.
        "'Main Street' is perhaps one of the most wonderful lit-
    erary photographs that this generation has seen. And like
    most photographs, it is a libel." In depicting the mean-
    spirited people of an American village as seen by a rather
    "highly strung" girl, Lewis fails to do justice to the
    youthful spirit of the American Midwest.

13 NICHOLSON, MEREDITH. "Let Main Street Alone!" in his The Man
    in the Street: Papers on American Topics. New York:
    Charles Scribner's Sons, pp. 1-25.
        Defends small-town America against the satire in Main
    Street and contrasts Lewis's approach with that of writers
    who depict the small town fairly: Edward Eggleston, James
    Whitcomb Riley, Booth Tarkington, and Sarah Orne Jewett.
    First published in the New York Evening Post in 1921.

14 STEWART, DONALD OGDEN. "Main Street--Plymouth Mass." in his
    A Parody Outline of History. New York: George H. Doran,
    pp. 55-83.
        Story of early New England life, told "in the manner of
    Sinclair Lewis."

15   TOWNSEND, R. D.   "Hemmed in by Circumstance."   Outlook, 127
          (5 January), 31.
               Compares Main Street with Hugh Walpole's The Captives
          and Louis Couperus's The Inevitable. Main Street presents
          an unflattering and unfair picture of American small towns
          and of human nature. Its "excessive realism" may have some
          value for what it does show of small-town life, but the
          book is like a "half-complete photograph" which fails to
          show the whole.

16   VAN DOREN, CARL.   "The Revolt from the Village: 1920."
          Nation, 113 (12 October), 407-12.
               Discusses Edgar Lee Masters' Spoon River Anthology and
          suggests it has influenced authors such as Lewis, Sherwood
          Anderson, Zona Gale and Floyd Dell. Lewis's considerable
          strength as a novelist lies in his "photographic gifts of
          accuracy," his skill at "mimicry," and the "gusto" with
          which he presses his satiric attack. Like the other nov-
          elists treated, he attacks the village; his particular con-
          cern is its dullness, which he documents brilliantly. Re-
          printed 1922.31.

17   WAGSTAFFE, W. G.   "As Sinclair Lewis Sees the Rest of Them."
          New York Times Book Review and Magazine, 29 May, pp. 10,
          30.
               Lewis responds to an interview with an optimistic view
          of the new generation of novelists. They are for the most
          part excellent craftsmen, he says, who have read and
          learned from previous great literature. Most of the young-
          er writers he respects are much less concerned with popu-
          larity and money than with saying what they really want to
          say. Popular writers may be well rewarded at the time but
          are adding nothing to the growth of American literature.

18   WELLS, CAROLYN.   Ptomaine Street: The Tale of Warble Petti-
          coat. Philadelphia and London: J. B. Lippincott, 125 pp.
               Parody of Main Street.

                              1922

1   "AMERICANUS."   "Georgie from Main Street."   Spectator, 129
          (16 December), 928-29.
               Babbitt is both a sociological document dealing with the
          malaise of modern America and a well-written novel. It
          shows a great deal of development over Main Street, which
          was too much a collection of raw materials. Lewis is "one
          of the best of the younger generation of American writers."

1922

2   ANDERSON, SHERWOOD. "Four American Impressions: Gertrude
     Stein, Paul Rosenfeld, Ring Lardner, Sinclair Lewis." New
     Republic, 32 (11 October), 171-73.
         In spite of his careful observations of the surface of
     life in America, Lewis has missed something. He is too
     serious, too preoccupied with the ugliness of America, to
     see its good points, its beauty. Reprinted 1972.3. Sec-
     tion on Lewis reprinted in SL:CCE, 1962.14.

3   ANON. "Babbitt." Times Literary Supplement, 21 (12 October),
     647.
         Babbitt is an attack on the tyranny of conventions, spe-
     cifically in America. Lewis realistically creates both
     Babbitt and his "ugly environment." English readers will
     find that Lewis's attack on the barren quality of modern
     life applies to their lives as well.

4   ANON. "Babbitt, of Zenith, Searches in Vain for Happiness."
     Current Opinion, 73 (November), 591-92.
         Unlike Main Street, which dissipated its energy by be-
     coming too panoramic, Babbitt focuses sharply on one char-
     acter and thus succeeds more fully. Lewis depicts the
     "spiritual dissatisfaction" of an American businessman who
     would appear to be a complete success in his own eyes and
     in those of his fellows. Lewis offers no solution to the
     problem he poses, however.

5   ANON. "The Bookman's Literary Club Service: Sinclair Lewis."
     Bookman, 56 (November), 365.
         Brief excerpts from Carl Van Doren's Contemporary Ameri-
     can Novelists (see 1922.31) and Stuart Pratt Sherman's The
     Significance of Sinclair Lewis (see 1922.24). Intended as
     a study guide or discussion primer for literary clubs.

6   ANON. "Briefer Mention." Dial, 73 (October), [456].
         Lewis's Babbitt is a mixture of undigested raw material,
     sophomoric criticism of the American middle class, and, in
     the final third, some good fiction. "Mr. Sinclair's [sic]
     way of presenting surfaces is exceedingly persuasive. . . ."
     With all its faults, Babbitt is an improvement over Main
     Street.

7   ANON. "An English Countercheck Quarrelsome to Mr. Sinclair
     Lewis." Living Age, 314 (22 July), 244-46.
         Review of the controversy begun by Lewis when he accused
     British publishers of neglecting American authors. English
     literary men responded that American literature is so well
     distributed that it is driving some British authors out of
     business.

8   ANON. "The Literary Spotlight XII: Sinclair Lewis." Book-
     man, 56 (September), 54-59.
          Satirical sketch of Lewis, emphasizing his pride in Main
     Street and his tendency to drift from fiction to carica-
     ture. At the same time he ridicules Rotarians, Realtors,
     and Boomers, Lewis shares many of their attitudes about
     success. Reprinted 1924.1.

9   ANON. "A Reviewer's Notebook." Freeman, 6 (18 October),
     142-43.
          Stuart P. Sherman's pamphlet, "The Significance of Sin-
     clair Lewis" (see 1922.24), published by the same house
     that publishes Lewis's novels, is an obvious piece of
     salesmanship. Lewis may be a significant novelist someday,
     but he is not now. He has written a group of undistin-
     guished novels, then two, Main Street and Babbitt, that are
     gaining him a temporary notoriety. By suggesting that he
     has greater significance, Sherman and Harcourt, Brace have
     done Lewis more harm than good.

10   ANON. Review of Babbitt. Booklist, 19 (October), 21.
          "More amusing, more sure in its detail," and more satir-
     ical, Babbitt compares favorably with Main Street.

11   ANON. Review of Babbitt. North American Review, 216 (Novem-
     ber), 716-17.
          While Lewis is "the most phenomenally skillful exagger-
     ator in literature to-day," his fiction is not great fic-
     tion, as a comparison with that of H. G. Wells will show.
     The latter has a human sympathy not possessed by Lewis.

12   F[ARRAR], J[OHN]. "Hail Rotarians!" Bookman, 56 (October),
     216.
          Babbitt is even better than Main Street, partly because
     its characters seem more likable even though its satire is
     more scathing than that of the earlier book. There are no
     dry spots in Babbitt as there sometimes were in Main
     Street. George himself, in spite of his weaknesses, does
     manage to find "a certain part of his soul."

13   FLEISHER, FLORENCE. "Prophets in Their Own Country: A New
     Tendency in American Fiction." Survey, 49 (1 November),
     192, 201.
          Babbitt is one of several new books to take a searching
     look at American life and to find it wanting. Whatever the
     critics may think of this book as literature, its message
     must not be ignored.

1922

14 GAY, R. M. Review of <u>Babbitt</u>. <u>Atlantic Bookshelf</u>, 134
    (November), [3].
        Lewis successfully "portrays, without too much satirical
    exaggeration, the 'standardized American'. . . ." If Amer-
    icans heed the picture Lewis has painted, <u>Babbitt</u> "will do
    the Babbitts some good."

15 L[EWISOHN], L[UDWIG]. Review of <u>Babbitt</u>. <u>Nation</u>, 115
    (20 September), 284-85.
        In both content and art, <u>Babbitt</u> is even better than
    Lewis's earlier best-seller <u>Main Street</u>. While it is all
    ironic wit and "marvelously authentic talk" on the surface,
    Lewis shows the desperation that underlies the frenetic
    pace of American life. <u>Babbitt</u> is a book "of high cultural
    significance." Reprinted in <u>SB</u>, 1971.13.

16 LITTELL, ROBERT. "Babbitt." <u>New Republic</u>, 32 (4 October),
    152.
        Like <u>Main Street</u>, <u>Babbitt</u> is a brilliant attack on cer-
    tain elements in America, and its point is a great deal
    clearer. However, Lewis is not writing genuine fiction,
    skilled as he is at his game of social satire. His charac-
    ters lack fullness and are too obviously mere caricatures;
    his mood is so overwhelmingly pessimistic that it denies
    much of reality. Reprinted in <u>SB</u>, 1971.13.

17 McCORMICK, ANNE O'HARE. "Zenith Discusses 'Babbitt,' Epic of
    Pullmania." <u>New York Times Book Review</u>, 22 October, pp. 3,
    27.
        Satirical essay on the public reception of <u>Babbitt</u>, sug-
    gesting that those who are most opposed to the novel do not
    understand that Lewis is a satirist, not a realist.

18 MANSFIELD, J. B. "Babbitt." <u>National Real Estate Journal</u>, 23
    (18 December), 43.
        "Whatever may be the Realtor's estimate of 'Babbitt,' as
    one of the biggest sellers in the fiction of today, he will
    regret an analysis of his profession which eliminates, or
    apparently mocks at its ideals. . . ."

19 MARSHALL, ARCHIBALD. "Gopher Prairie." <u>North American Re-
    view</u>, 215 (March), [394]-402.
        <u>Main Street</u> is unfair to American small towns. While
    their architecture is ugly, they do have a natural beauty;
    and while their people are ignorant, they want to learn.
    Like many Americans, people in small towns are materialis-
    tic, and their conversation is too concerned with money.
    Yet Gopher Prairie is a young town and in "another genera-
    tion the reproach may be entirely removed."

20   MENCKEN, H. L.   "Portrait of an American Citizen."   Smart Set,
        69 (October), 138-40.
           Babbitt is both "a social document of a high order" and
        a bitingly funny novel. Lewis has captured the hollow soul
        of the American businessman as well as his false front. If
        some critics wondered whether Main Street was a lucky acci-
        dent, that suspicion will be dispelled by Babbitt. Re-
        printed in SL:CCE, 1962.14 and in SB, 1971.13.

21   _____. "Sinclair Lewis and 'Babbitt.'" Now and Then, no. 5
        (October), p. 22.
           The portrait of Babbitt, who is the first "wholly genu-
        ine American" to get into a book, is better than a photo-
        graph in that it is three dimensional. "A fine humanness
        clings to" Babbitt, and the novel is better than Main
        Street.

22   O'DELL, GEORGE E.   "The American Mind and 'Main Street.'" The
        Standard, 8 (July), 17-20.
           Main Street is popular because it appeals to the pecu-
        liarly American appetite for criticism. In time, as the
        nation matures, it will no longer need the sort of castiga-
        tion provided by Lewis.

23   RASCOE, BURTON.   "A Mirror of Mediocrity." New York Tribune,
        17 September, section 5, p. 8.
           Babbitt is "one of the finest social satires in the Eng-
        lish language." Its satire is more "delicate" than that of
        Main Street, its style shows much more care, and the tone
        is more "sympathetic." Overall the book makes a major con-
        tribution to "social history."

24   SHERMAN, STUART P.   The Significance of Sinclair Lewis.   New
        York: Harcourt, Brace, 22 pp.
           Pamphlet commissioned by Harcourt, Brace. Lewis is su-
        perior to any of his contemporaries, the heir of Twain,
        James, and Howells. The novels from Our Mr. Wrenn through
        Babbitt are analyzed, with emphasis on the last two.
        Lewis is compared with Tolstoy, Turgenev, Arnold Bennett,
        and Flaubert, and Main Street with Madame Bovary. Babbitt
        is proof of Lewis's continuing vitality, "not a sequel to
        Main Street but a parallel and coordinate extension," pro-
        duced by Lewis at the height of his powers as a satirist.
        If Lewis has a weakness, it is his pessimism. Perhaps
        some day he will create a positive hero who embodies the
        virtues implied in his satire. Reprinted 1927.33.

1922

25   SINCLAIR, MAY. "The Man From Main Street." New York Times
         Book Review, 24 September, pp. 1, 11.
              Babbitt is "an advance on its predecessor in style, con-
         struction and technique." While Main Street depicted a
         "provincial town," it suffered from lack of focus. Babbitt,
         on the other hand, is structured firmly around its protago-
         nist. One secret of Babbitt's success is that "though no-
         body will recognize himself in George F. Babbitt, everybody
         will recognize someone else." Reprinted in SB, 1971.13.

26   SINCLAIR, UPTON. "Standardized America." The Appeal to Rea-
         son [became Haldeman-Julius Weekly 11 November 1922],
         no. 1399 (23 September), p. 1.
              Personal memories of Lewis during the Helicon Hall days
         preface a review of Babbitt, which is found even better
         than Main Street. Sometimes the latest novel threatens to
         become caricature, "but then you stop and ask yourself, is
         is possible to caricature commercial America?" Reprinted
         in SB, 1971.13.

27   T., H. M. "The World of Books." Nation & Athenaeum, 32
         (21 October), 121.
              Babbitt depends largely on almost scientific observation
         of the American businessman: Lewis's "method is more like
         that of an enthusiastic entomologist in a monograph of the
         cockroach. . . ." Yet, unlike a scientist, Lewis is irri-
         tated by what he discovers about his subject. He would be
         a great writer if he were "moved by pity."

28   THOMAS, WILLIAM. Review of Babbitt. Double Dealer, 4
         (November), 245-47.
              Lewis's latest novel proves that he is "the greatest
         satirist in the history of American literature."

29   TOWNSEND, R. D. "Among the New Books." Outlook, 132
         (11 October), 253.
              While Babbitt is deficient in dramatic interest and
         plotting, it achieves a certain success as a novel of char-
         acter depicting "a whole class" which does exist in Amer-
         ica. Lewis has "technical skill" enough to keep Babbitt
         from becoming only a type. His realism will be a bit too
         meticulous for some tastes, and he seems to overlook the
         fact that "there are also plenty of non-Babbitts."

30   UNTERMEYER, LOUIS. "The Heaven of Mean Streets," in his Heav-
         ens. New York: Harcourt, Brace, pp. 63-81.
              Parody of Main Street, Poor White by Sherwood Anderson,
         Miss Lulu Bett by Zona Gale, and Moon Calf by Floyd Dell as
         works criticizing the small town.

31 VAN DOREN, CARL. "The Revolt from the Village," in his Con-
      temporary American Novelists: 1900-1920. New York: Mac-
      millan, pp. 146-71.
          Reprint of 1921.16.

32 WEST, REBECCA. "Notes on Novels: Babbitt." New Statesman,
      23 (21 October), 78, 80.
          Main Street was good, but Babbitt goes far beyond it,
      whether considered as satire or as art. Lewis's hatred of
      Zenith stems from his love of the place and people as they
      could be, and his methods of attack display both his
      craftsmanship and his unique personality as a writer. Re-
      printed in SL:CCE, 1962.14.

                            1923

1 ANON. "The Gossip Shop." Bookman, 56 (February), 789-90.
          Reprints a review identified only as by "Paul Adams of
      San Antonio, Texas." Adams, a realtor himself, thinks Bab-
      bitt is clever but shallow. While the book may fit the
      popular taste, it will never last because it is not really
      true to life and does not depict the American businessman
      accurately.

2 BECHHOFER, C. E. See Roberts, Carl Erik B., 1923.6.

3 MAIS, S[TUART] P. B. "Sinclair Lewis," in his Some Modern
      Authors. New York: Dodd, Mead, pp. 98-103.
          Lewis attacks modern materialism as Sherwood Anderson
      does, but he dwells more on the surface of things and is
      more vitriolic than Anderson. However, it must be admitted
      that Babbitt is more effective criticism than any of Ander-
      son's books.

4 MELVILLE, ARTHUR. "George Follansbee Babbitt--Realtor."
      Rotarian, 22 (February), 83-84.
          Babbitt "is a very readable book," but Lewis fails to
      examine "the favorable view of Babbittry." The book is too
      one-sided even though it points out real foibles in modern
      society.

5 PURE, SIMON (pseudonym). "The Londoner." Bookman, 56
      (January), 607-608.
          Babbitt has been much more popular in London than Main
      Street ever was, partly because of its "feast of authentic
      and convincing American slang."

1923

6 [ROBERTS, CARL ERIK B.] C. E. Bechhofer. Chapter 6 in his The
   Literary Renaissance in America. London: William Heine-
   mann, pp. 105-13.
       After a number of promising novels, Lewis captured the
   attention of America with Main Street and Babbitt, in which
   he depicts and satirizes the worst side of modern American
   culture. His popularity suggests that Americans are able
   to profit from criticism and that there may be hope for
   "the intellectual future of the country." Book is dedicated to "Sinclair Lewis: Most Romantic of Realists."

7 STUART, HENRY LONGAN. "Novels from the Grub Street Days of
   Sinclair Lewis." New York Times Book Review, 22 April,
   p. 3.
       Review-essay on the reissued Our Mr. Wrenn, The Trail of
   the Hawk, and The Job. While all three show promise, only
   the last escapes the formulaic pattern familiar to readers
   of the Saturday Evening Post. In The Job, however, Lewis
   begins to achieve both the realism and the satiric view of
   modern life which have made him famous. Una Golden is a
   memorable character and the dreariness of her work shows
   Lewis the social critic coming of age.

8 WARD, CHRISTOPHER. "Babbitt," in his The Triumph of the Nut
   and Other Parodies. New York: Henry Holt, pp. 59-69.
       Parody of a speech by George F. Babbitt.

                              1924

1 ANON. "Sinclair Lewis," in The Literary Spotlight. Edited by
   John C. Farrar. New York: George H. Doran, pp. 32-42.
       Reprint of 1922.8.

2 BALDWIN, CHARLES C. "Sinclair Lewis," in his The Men Who Make
   Our Novels. Revised edition. New York: Dodd, Mead,
   pp. 321-34.
       Short biography, depending substantially on information
   furnished by Lewis, and critical essay tracing Lewis's
   "steady and remarkable growth" from Our Mr. Wrenn through
   Arrowsmith. Main Street was an overrated book, but with
   Babbitt, a "comic masterpiece," and Arrowsmith Lewis has
   begun to achieve real excellence.

3 BELGION, MONTGOMERY. "How Sinclair Lewis Works." Bookman
   (London), 65 (January), 195-96.
       Emphasizes the research Lewis did for his fiction--
   checking the details of the people and places he was to
   use, choosing names, mapping out towns and floor plans--

and the long job of revision after writing the novel's first draft.

4   BOYD, ERNEST. "Sinclair Lewis," in his Portraits: Real and Imaginary. New York: George H. Doran, pp. 183-88.
      Sharply satirical portrait of Lewis, super-salesman. Lewis is aggressive, a go-getter who peddles a salable product--satire of everyone except the reader. Is it any wonder that he has compiled an enviable sales record and continues to bring in "repeat orders" from satisfied customers?

5   CABELL, JAMES BRANCH. "The Way of Wizardry," in his Straws and Prayer Books. New York: Robert M. McBride, pp. 50-51.
      Lists the suggestions he made to Lewis during the writing of Main Street: the marriage of Vida Sherwin and Raymie Wutherspoon, the death of Bea. Lewis ignored his suggestion that Carol have an affair with Erik Valborg.

*6   DE KRUIF, PAUL. "An Intimate Glimpse of a Great American Novel in the Making." Designer and the Woman's Magazine, 60, no. 2 (June), 64.
      According to Richardson, 1955.17, de Kruif introduces the serialization of Arrowsmith with a brief account of his collaboration with Lewis.

7   DELL, FLOYD. "Babbitt and my Russian Friend," in his Looking at Life. New York: Alfred A. Knopf, pp. 289-94.
      Babbitt is an excellent creation of a distinct American type. However, it is questionable whether Babbitt, once he became radical, could ever have returned so meekly to the fold.

8   FISK, EARL E. "The Chesterton-Drinkwater-Lewis Affair." Bookman, 58 (January), 538-40.
      Humorous account of a meeting and informal luncheon shared by the author, G. K. Chesterton, John Drinkwater, Lewis, and Chicago book collector Walter Hills, and of an elaborate joke involving a farcical play to be written by Chesterton, Drinkwater, and Lewis.

9   FRANK, WALDO. "The American Year," in his Salvos. New York: Boni and Liveright, pp. 201-206.
      Main Street was published at just the right time, when the American reading public was ready for "acute although not too searching criticism in the guise of comedy and satire." Although the book may cater to rather uncritical taste, it is at least better than the popular fiction Americans have read in the past.

17

1924

10 YOUNG, FILSON. "Antediluvian Lewis in England." New York
    Times Book Review, 13 April, p. 12.
        Review of Free Air, which is assumed to be Lewis's first
    novel. While "there is no doubt about Babbitt's being a
    masterpiece, . . . Free Air does not even seem like the
    journey work of a possible master." Characterization is
    weak and the plot "monotonous."

                            1925

1   ANON. "Babbitt Battles for his Rights." Nation's Business,
    13 (October), 38.
        Editorial denouncing Lewis and supporting the nation's
    Babbitts.

2   ANON. "Babbitt Boiling Hot." Literary Digest, 86 (19 Septem-
    ber), 30-31.
        Excerpts from the attacks on Babbitt which appeared in
    Nation's Business, the Chicago Tribune, and the Evening
    Standard.

3   ANON. "Books." New Yorker, 1 (21 March), 28.
        Arrowsmith is less perfect than Babbitt only because
    Lewis has attempted something more difficult. In spite of
    its imperfections, Arrowsmith is a "great American novel."

4   ANON. "John Bull and Sinclair Lewis." Living Age, 325
    (23 May), 429-30.
        Lewis has been popular in England largely because his
    satire in Main Street and Babbitt confirms the British
    opinion of crude Americans. Arrowsmith is encountering a
    more mixed response. Summarizes three English reviews of
    Arrowsmith.

5   ANON. "Martin Arrowsmith." Times Literary Supplement, 24
    (5 March), 153.
        Martin Arrowsmith is Lewis's "best work" so far, showing
    that he can achieve an "epic quality" that transcends the
    mere satire of Main Street and Babbitt. Not only Arrow-
    smith but Leora and Max Gottlieb are "as real as it is pos-
    sible for the written word to make them." Partially re-
    printed in TCIA, 1968.4.

6   ANON. "Mr. Sinclair Lewis." Spectator, 134 (7 March), 372,
    375.
        Martin Arrowsmith is "beyond doubt the best of Mr.
    Lewis's novels." Lewis's basic premises about science and
    his direct way of stating them flaw the novel and make it

                            18

technically a failure; however, the strength of its characterization and the drama in the choices Arrowsmith must
make as a man and as a scientist redeem the novel.

7 ANON. Review of <u>Arrowsmith</u>. <u>Booklist</u>, 21 (May), 303.
    "An absorbing book" about the medical profession and the
    problems faced by doctors.

8 ANON. "Sinclair Lewis--American Satirist and Novelist."
    <u>Vanity Fair</u>, 24 (May), 75.
    Man Ray photo of Lewis and a review of his career since
    <u>Main Street</u>, emphasizing <u>Arrowsmith</u>.

9 ANON. "We Nominate for the Hall of Fame." <u>Vanity Fair</u>, 25
    (October), 73.
    Lewis "has become the most popular novelist in America"
    since he followed <u>Babbitt</u> with <u>Arrowsmith</u>.

10 BALDENSPERGER, FERNAND. "Un romancier Américain d'aujourd'hui:
    M. Sinclair Lewis." <u>Le Correspondant</u>, 301 (25 December),
    [835]-54.
    Lewis's depiction of midwestern America and Americans in
    <u>Main Street</u> and <u>Babbitt</u> and of the medical profession in
    <u>Arrowsmith</u> reveals him to be not an artist but a sociolo-
    gist who demands a revision of values. He concentrates on
    exterior circumstances and details rather than on the inte-
    rior or soul of his characters. Abroad, he has been most
    favorably received in Great Britain because his realistic
    dialogue is a serious obstacle to translation; in France,
    his novels are viewed as "sans grâce."

11 BOYD, ERNEST. "Books and Other Hors Oeuvres [sic]." <u>Vanity
    Fair</u>, 24 (July), 57.
    <u>Arrowsmith</u> sounds dreadfully dull after "Mr. Sinclair's
    [sic]" earlier <u>Main Street</u> and <u>Babbitt</u>. Although H. L.
    Mencken and Stuart P. Sherman recommend it, Boyd has been
    unwilling to read it.

12 CANBY, HENRY SEIDEL. "Fighting Success." <u>Saturday Review of
    Literature</u>, 1 (7 March), 575.
    <u>Arrowsmith</u> may not be a great novel, but it is a great
    satire. Lewis goes beyond what he has done before, creat-
    ing not only caricatures who expose the follies of a seg-
    ment of American life but also a positive hero with ideals.
    Leora Arrowsmith is noteworthy as the first Lewis heroine
    to come to life fully. Reprinted 1927.11 and in <u>TCIA</u>,
    1968.4.

1925

13   COLLINS, JOSEPH. "Sinclair Lewis Diagnoses the Doctors."
      Literary Digest International Book Review, 3 (April),
      306-307, 367.
            Arrowsmith will not harm Lewis's reputation a great deal
      but it will add little to it. Overly long, the novel sen-
      sationalizes and caricatures certain faults of the medical
      profession. As a serious study of the profession, it is a
      failure.

14   DANIELSON, RICHARD. Review of Arrowsmith. Atlantic Bookshelf,
      April, p. [1].
            While Lewis showed himself to be a master at capturing
      the surface of his characters and the American scene in
      Main Street and Babbitt, in Arrowsmith he goes beyond sur-
      faces to probe the "spiritual" depths of a doctor and sci-
      entist. "A greater improvement on Babbitt than Babbitt was
      on Main Street. . . ."

*15   DAVIDSON, DONALD. "Sinclair Lewis." Nashville Tennesseean,
      15 March, n.p.
            Reprinted 1963.6.

16   DINWIDDIE, COURTENAY. Review of Arrowsmith. American Journal
      of Public Health, 15 (May), 448-49.
            Lewis praises the immunologist at the expense of the
      public health officer in Arrowsmith, which is otherwise an
      accurate picture of at least part of the medical profes-
      sion. The love story is moving.

17   EMERSON, HAVEN, M.D. "A Doctor Looks at Arrowsmith." Survey,
      54 (1 May), 180.
            Arrowsmith could have been a more realistic and thus a
      more valuable book had Lewis not distorted his treatment of
      the medical profession to make it the butt of his satire.
      "From an author of such ability we could wish a more typi-
      cal doctor for his hero." Reprinted in TCIA, 1968.4.

18   F[ISHBEIN], [MORRIS]. "Dr. Evans and Arrowsmith." Hygeia, 3
      (October), 588-89.
            Defends Lewis against the charge of inaccuracy on some
      technical medical treatment in Arrowsmith.

19   [FRANK, WALDO] Search-light. "Profiles: In America's Image."
      New Yorker, 1 (18 July), 10-11.
            Paradoxically Lewis was ignored as long as he pictured
      a blameless America but became famous when he criticized
      his country. America longs to read about itself, yet must
      have its literature presented as moral instruction. If
      Lewis ever writes the sort of book about America he really

wants to write, embodying his vision of his country, he will become a genuinely unpopular author. Reprinted 1926.23.

20 FRANKLIN, JOHN. "New Novels: Martin Arrowsmith." New Statesman, 24 (7 March), 629-30.
     The central theme is embodied by Gottlieb, "an incarnation of the scientific spirit, which, being a spirit of truth, is necessarily at tragic odds with a society based on moneymaking. . . ." Although the delightful "gallery of types" may be caricatures, the distortion is slight and "in America, the facts seem ever to caricature themselves." Lewis is compared to Wells, who can better "render the texture of life" but never presents science in such meticulous technical detail. Unlike Main Street and Babbitt, this novel expresses the power of a "higher order of experience."

21 GAINES, CLARENCE H. "Some Modern Novels." North American Review, 222 (September), 165-66.
     Arrowsmith is better than either Main Street or Babbitt, partly because Lewis finds positive values in science. However, he is still obsessed with discovering human failings. If Lewis could write more realistically and less satirically, his novels would improve greatly.

22 GOULD, GERALD. "New Fiction." Saturday Review (London), 139 (11 April), 389.
     Martin Arrowsmith is not so much overly long as it is tedious. Lewis is simply not selective enough to make science interesting, as he attempts to do in this novel. While a good deal better than most contemporary fiction, it lacks "the vital creative breath" that would make it a great work.

23 GREEN, PAUL and ELIZABETH LAY GREEN. "Sinclair Lewis," in their Contemporary American Literature: A Study of Fourteen Outstanding American Writers. University of North Carolina Extension Bulletin, 4, no. 14 (1 June), 19-20, 58. Chapel Hill: University of North Carolina Press.
     Discussion guide for women's clubs, short bibliography, and brief biographical note. Suggests three main topics: early works; Main Street and Babbitt; and Arrowsmith.

24 HARRISON, OLIVER. Pseudonym of Harrison Smith. See 1925.37.

25 H., R. S. "Go On and Be a Babbitt." Nation's Business, 13 (September), 34.
     Supports the achievements of the businessman and suggests that Lewis's Babbitt is no longer recognized when one is called "a Babbitt."

1925

26   K[ENNEDY], W. P. "Martin Arrowsmith." Nature, 115 (23 May),
      797.
            Lewis does a good job of showing how a man of science
      thinks and the book is recommended to scientists. Reprint-
      ed in TCIA, 1968.4.

27   KRUTCH, JOSEPH WOOD. "A Genius on Main Street." Nation, 120
      (1 April), 359-60.
            Unlike Main Street or Babbitt, Arrowsmith has a hero who
      at least partially transcends the limitations with which
      American society surrounds him. This novel is "not so re-
      markable as a pamphlet; but considered purely as a novel it
      is better than either . . . because it is essentially
      truer." Reprinted in TCIA, 1968.4.

28   LEBLANC, THOMAS J. "Scientific Books." Science, 61 (19 June),
      632-34.
            Arrowsmith is not only a good novel but an intelligent
      discussion of scientific research which does not talk down
      to the reader. Recommended to doctors, medical students,
      and scientists.

29   LEECH, HARPER. "Babbitt Pays for Babbitt-Baiting." Nation's
      Business, 13 (July), 13-15.
            Businessmen should "stand together" against the attacks
      of writers like Sinclair Lewis.

30   LOVETT, ROBERT MORSS. "An Interpreter of American Life."
      Dial, 78 (June), [515]-18.
            Once again Lewis has shattered the complacency of Ameri-
      can readers with an exposé, this time of the medical pro-
      fession. Arrowsmith, which utilizes the documentary form
      of Main Street rather than the "impressionistic" method of
      Babbitt, effectively satirizes all areas of medicine--from
      medical schools to general practice--in which fraud pre-
      vails. If some facets of the novel, such as Leora's death,
      seem too coincidental, all contribute to the effect Lewis
      was trying to create. Reprinted in SL:CCE, 1962.14; par-
      tially reprinted in TCIA, 1968.4.

31   MENCKEN, H. L. Review of Arrowsmith. American Mercury, 4
      (April), 507-509.
            This is a beautifully organized attack on the effects of
      materialism on science, sustaining reader interest through
      all of its nearly 500 pages. Some will say Lewis is preach-
      ing throughout: "Well, if this be preaching let us have
      more of it!" Arrowsmith himself may be a bit pale as a
      character, but the satirical portrait of Dr. Almus Picker-

baugh ranks with Lewis's best work. Reprinted 1926.31 and partially reprinted in TCIA, 1968.4.

32   MUIR, EDWIN. Review of Martin Arrowsmith. Nation & Athenaeum, 36 (14 March), 818.
Lewis's attempt at satirizing medical scientists as he earlier did businessmen is unsuccessful. In science, the truth will come out eventually in spite of the imperfec-tions of the men who do research. Reprinted in TCIA, 1968.4.

33   OVERTON, GRANT. "The Salvation of Sinclair Lewis." Bookman, 61 (April), 179-85.
After the publication of Main Street, many predicted that the novel's success would go to Lewis's head and he would never produce another work of significance. Babbitt confounded these critics, and now Arrowsmith should con-vince anyone that Lewis is firmly committed to serious lit-erary work. The book is a masterful and realistic examina-tion of modern medicine which should be equally interesting to doctors and to laymen.

34   RASCOE, BURTON. "Contemporary Reminiscences." Arts and Dec-
oration, 23 (May), 45, 85-87.
Arrowsmith is Lewis's best novel to date, and Max Gott-lieb his best character. In this book Lewis shows that he can treat certain characters and ideals positively. Brief background sketch of Lewis's collaboration with Paul de Kruif.

35   R., D. "Mr. Lewis Keeps on Growing." Independent, 114 (14 March), 302.
Although Arrowsmith may not be as popular as Babbitt, it is a better book because it sees more of life. Its charac-ters are fully rounded, not mere caricatures, and it has a really serious subject. "Here is an American writer grow-ing into his full stature."

36   SHERMAN, STUART P. "A Way Out: Sinclair Lewis Discovers a Hero." New York Herald Tribune Books, 8 March, pp. 1-2.
While Lewis's exposé of the foibles of doctors and medi-cal researchers is the most prominent feature of Arrow-smith, his skills with dialogue and characterization show new maturity in his art. Lewis has created a true hero with positive values; the result is "a far better book than 'Babbitt.'" Partially reprinted in TCIA, 1968.4.

1925

37   [SMITH, HARRISON] Oliver Harrison. <u>Sinclair Lewis</u>. New York:
       Harcourt, Brace, 28 pp.
          Publicity booklet for distribution at 1925 convention of
       American Booksellers. Summarizes Lewis's life and career
       through the writing of <u>Arrowsmith</u>. Written by an old
       friend, an editor at Harcourt, Brace, the pamphlet contains
       only positive judgments.

38   STRUNSKY, SIMEON. "About Books, <u>More or Less</u>: Men, Women,
       Etc." <u>New York Times Book Review</u>, 17 May, p. 4.
          Leora in <u>Arrowsmith</u>, in spite of her "slang and ciga-
       rettes," is anything but a liberated woman. She is an ad-
       junct to her man, an instrument, and resembles a heroine of
       the mid-nineteenth century more than a modern woman.

39   STUART, HENRY LONGAN. "Lewis Assails Our Medicine Men." <u>New
       York Times Book Review</u>, 8 March, pp. 1, 24.
          <u>Arrowsmith</u> "is an authentic step forward" for Lewis
       artistically, even though it shows no great intellectual
       advance. The satire is of the same high level we have come
       to expect from Lewis. It is in characterization that he
       improves: not only is Martin a believable protagonist but
       Leora, who is the sort of woman that even H. G. Wells could
       not have created, comes to "dominate" the book.

40   THORP, MERLE. "Dare to Be a Babbitt!" <u>Nation's Business</u>, 13
       (June), 40.
          Editorial deploring Lewis's treatment of American busi-
       nessmen.

41   _____. "Through the Editor's Spectacles." <u>Nation's Business</u>,
       13 (December), 37.
          Cartoon depicting a writer, not specifically Lewis, who
       uses desk, typewriter, and spectacles made by Babbitt com-
       panies to write a book against Babbitt.

42   TOWNSEND, R. D. "Babbitting the Doctors." <u>Outlook</u>, 139
       (25 March), 457-58.
          In <u>Arrowsmith</u> Lewis gives the illusion of fairness by
       showing some conscientious doctors, but he overdoes his
       criticism of the more selfish medical men, overloading the
       book with irony as well as with too much "technical knowl-
       edge." Leora is his most appealing and lifelike female
       character to date, and the presence of other likable char-
       acters suggests that Lewis may be growing more mellow.

43   VAN DOREN, CARL. "Sinclair Lewis and Sherwood Anderson: A
     Study of Two Moralists." Century Magazine, 110 (July),
     362-69.
          Dissimilar as they are in many ways, Lewis and Anderson
     share a "revolt against the standardized ways of thinking
     and feeling which have had the approval of the majority."
     Cites examples from Main Street, Babbitt, Arrowsmith and
     Windy McPherson's Son, Marching Men, Poor White, Many Mar-
     riages. Both authors have won national reputations because
     of their assault on dullness in American life and thought.

44   VAN DOREN, CARL and MARK VAN DOREN. "Prose Fiction," in their
     American and British Literature Since 1890. New York and
     London: Century, pp. 81-83.
          While dullness is the target of both Main Street and
     Babbitt, the latter is more perceptive "for it traces the
     discontents of its protagonists to their roots. . . ."
     Lewis's skill at comic writing makes his messages almost
     too palatable: some readers enjoy the comedy without get-
     ting the message.

45   WANN, LOUIS. "The 'Revolt from the Village' in American Fic-
     tion." Overland Monthly and Out West Magazine, 83 (August),
     298-99, 324-25.
          Traces the changing concept of the village from Oliver
     Goldsmith's "The Deserted Village" to the "revolt" school--
     Edgar Lee Masters, Zona Gale, Sherwood Anderson, and Lewis.
     Lewis carefully documents what is wrong with the midwestern
     village--and later with the midwestern city in Babbitt--but
     does so with love and sympathy, not hatred. What is still
     needed is a balanced picture of the village.

46   WHIPPLE, T. K. "Sinclair Lewis." New Republic, 42
     (15 April), Part 2, Spring Book Section, 3-5.
          Arrowsmith pictures a scientist who must overcome the
     obstacles his own country places before any seeker after
     the truth. Lewis has written his best novel yet because
     the satire makes its point but is less pronounced than in
     Main Street or Babbitt. Lewis seems to fear dropping his
     ironic mask completely, perhaps because he fears readers
     will discover his own philistinism. He is a telling critic
     but an incomplete artist due to his defensive use of irony.
     Reprinted in TCIA, 1968.4. Revised in 1928; see 1963.25.

1925

47   WOOLF, VIRGINIA. "American Fiction." Saturday Review of Lit-
         erature, 2 (1 August), 1-2.
            In technique "Babbitt is the equal of any novel written
         in English in the present century." However, Lewis is
         forced by the American poverty of traditions to "criticise
         rather than to explore . . . and the civilisation of
         Zenith . . . was unfortunately too meagre to sustain him."
         Reprinted 1949.24.

                                  1926

1   AIKMAN, DUNCAN. "The New Decadents: Babbitt Starts to Re-
         form." Harper's Magazine, 153 (September), [449]-56.
            Humorous essay suggesting that Lewis's Babbitt will soon
         make this the best of all possible worlds: businessmen are
         hesitant to join luncheon clubs lest they be identified as
         Babbitts, and members no longer allow themselves to be
         "standardized" but insist on being themselves.

2   ANON. "Arrowsmith in Germany." Living Age, 329 (15 May),
         381-82.
            The Germans, who earlier approved of Babbitt, have been
         at least as enthusiastic about Arrowsmith. Translates part
         of a review in Literarische Welt as an example of this re-
         sponse. Lewis is compared to Emile Zola.

3   ANON. "Briefer Mention." Dial, 81 (November), 444.
            Compared to Arrowsmith, Mantrap is a potboiler. In
         spite of occasional flashes of Lewis's satirical wit, the
         novel as a whole is a sentimental failure.

4   ANON. "Lewis Dares Deity to Strike Him Dead." New York
         Times, 20 April, p. 2.
            After a talk ridiculing Fundamentalist ministers for
         their contention that Luther Burbank's death was a sign of
         God's wrath, Lewis called on the Fundamentalist God to
         strike him dead in the next ten minutes.

5   ANON. "A Literary Main Street." Nation, 122 (19 May), 546.
            Although Lewis was honest enough in refusing the Pulitz-
         er Prize, his reasons were hardly valid. Neither the se-
         lection committee nor the National Institute of Arts and
         Letters, in which Lewis has refused membership, really con-
         trols American literature. Yet Lewis does call attention
         to the absurdity of awarding such prizes at all.

                                  26

6   ANON. "Mantrap." <u>Times Literary Supplement</u>, 25 (12 August), 536.
    <u>Mantrap</u> is "light-hearted but excellent" and shows that Lewis can tell a good story when he chooses. Even in this book satire is not absent, as Lewis plays with the American notion of rugged masculinity.

7   ANON. "Prizes and Principles." <u>Outlook</u>, 143 (19 May), 91-92.
    While Lewis's refusal of the Pulitzer Prize does call attention to the arbitrary nature of such awards, some of the statements he has made to explain his refusal are "too sweeping."

8   ANON. Review of <u>Mantrap</u>. <u>Booklist</u>, 23 (November), 81-82.
    "Entertaining" tale of a New Yorker in the Canadian woods.

9   ANON. Review of <u>Mantrap</u>. <u>Dial</u>, 81 (November), 444.
    <u>Mantrap</u> offers "occasional shrewd strokes of characterization and welcome flashes of humour," but after <u>Arrowsmith</u> it is a disappointing book, commercial and sentimental.

10   ANON. Review of <u>Mantrap</u>. <u>Spectator</u>, 137 (17 July), 105.
    <u>Mantrap</u> is not only a good adventure story but a social commentary as well--on the frontiersman fantasies of modern city-dwellers and on a certain type of modern young woman. But the book ranks far below <u>Martin Arrowsmith</u>.

11   ANON. "Signers of Our Literary Declaration of Independence." <u>Vanity Fair</u>, 26 (July), 70.
    Photos and brief descriptions of "independent" authors; Lewis is an "unsparing satirist."

12   ANON. "Sinclair Lewis's Gesture." <u>New Republic</u>, 46 (19 May), 397.
    The trustees of the Pulitzer Prize have the difficult task of selecting the novel "best presenting the wholesome atmosphere of American life and the highest standard of American manners and manhood." If Lewis does not agree with those principles, he may rightfully refuse the prize; however, the high moral tone he has taken has obscured the real issues.

13   ANON. "Sinclair Lewis's Hornet's Nest." <u>Literary Digest</u>, 89 (29 May), 27-28.
    Summarizes the reaction--largely negative--to Lewis's refusal of the Pulitzer Prize.

1926

14   BATES, ERNEST SUTHERLAND. "Lewis as Romantic." Saturday Re-
       view of Literature, 2 (26 June), 887.
             Mantrap is "a highly romantic rapid fire novel whose
       interest lies solely in plot, atmosphere, and characteriza-
       tion." But even in this adventure story suitable for the
       Saturday Evening Post or the movies, Lewis shows his ar-
       tistry. His characters are well drawn and there is social
       satire.

15   B[OYNTON], P[ERCY] H. Review of Mantrap. New Republic, 47
       (4 August), 316.
             Mantrap, "a tale of highly artificial people against a
       carefully pictured back-drop," ranks with such minor Lewis
       novels as The Innocents and Free Air.

16   B., R. A. "Mr. Sinclair Lewis." New Statesman, 27 (24 July),
       418, 420.
             Since Main Street the British literary world has closely
       watched Lewis, the most eminent American author since James.
       Mantrap will be disappointing to those watchers, as it is
       not one of Lewis's more careful efforts. "Nevertheless, it
       is better worth reading than any other novel we have seen
       this year. . . ."

17   DANIELSON, RICHARD. Review of Mantrap. Atlantic Bookshelf,
       August, pp. 10, 12.
             Unlike Lewis's other novels, Mantrap is a light-hearted
       piece of entertainment with no special social significance
       and depends on plot rather than on "observation and analy-
       sis," traits of the usual Lewis novel. Yet it is a good
       light novel and shows another side of a versatile author.

18   DONDORE, DOROTHY ANNE. "Recent Tendencies," in her The Prai-
       rie and the Making of Middle America: Four Centuries of
       Description. Cedar Rapids, Iowa: Torch Press, pp. 406-408.
             In Main Street and Babbitt Lewis satirizes the "narrow-
       ness" and provincialism of the midwestern small town and
       city. He exaggerates, often to the point of unfairness.

19   [DOUNCE, HARRY ESTY]. "New Books." New Yorker, 2 (5 June),
       87, 89.
             Mantrap is a mere "yarn," and not a very good one in
       spite of a few "patches" that remind us of Babbitt and
       Arrowsmith.

20   DREW, ELIZABETH A. The Modern Novel: Some Aspects of Contem-
      porary Fiction. New York: Harcourt, Brace, pp. 140-46.
            Lewis is the supreme critic of provincialism, from small
      towns like Gopher Prairie to larger ones like Zenith, but
      he captures externals only. He also seems unable, in most
      of his work, to view anything positively, the exception be-
      ing Arrowsmith, where science is treated sympathetically.

21   FARRAR, JOHN. "The Point of View: The Magazine Serial."
      Bookman, 64 (October), 132.
            Defends Mantrap as an "engaging . . . light fiction."
      Lewis has a right to toss off a light work now and then
      whether "for relaxation or cash."

22   _____. "The Point of View: Prizes." Bookman, 63 (July),
      513-14.
            Lewis's recent refusal of the Pulitzer Prize calls at-
      tention once more to the fact that the prize is not given,
      as the public supposes, to the best novel of the year, but
      to the "most wholesome." While most prize-winning novels
      have been well above the average, Lewis "is to be commended
      for his stand" even though he does seem to be overdramatiz-
      ing his attitude.

23   [FRANK, WALDO] Searchlight. "Sinclair Lewis: In America's
      Image," in his Time Exposures. New York: Boni and Live-
      right, pp. 131-37.
            Reprint of 1925.19.

24   HARKNESS, SAMUEL. "Sinclair Lewis' Sunday School Class."
      Christian Century, 43 (29 July), 938-39.
            Warm portrait of Lewis by a Kansas City minister who was
      a member of the discussion group Lewis held while doing re-
      search for Elmer Gantry. Maintains that if Lewis criti-
      cizes ministers harshly, it is because he is himself a
      religious man who has become sickened by the hypocrisy of
      the organized churches.

25   HARMON, WILLIAM E. "Lewis to Pulitzer: Harmon to Lewis."
      Survey, 56 (15 June), 392.
            Letter to the editor from president of the Harmon Foun-
      dation, criticizing Lewis for his public rejection of the
      Pulitzer Prize.

26   HARTLEY, L. P. "New Fiction." Saturday Review (London), 142
      (7 August), 156.
            Mantrap is different from most of Lewis's books--"irre-
      sponsible, lively and exhilarating." While it is not deep-
      ly significant, "it is intoxicating, all the same."

1926

27   KRUTCH, JOSEPH WOOD. "Babbitt Returns to Nature." <u>Nation</u>,
        122 (16 June), 672.
            Clearly a minor work in the Lewis canon, <u>Mantrap</u> does
        transcend its own limitations when Lewis gets onto the ab-
        surdity of urban man trying to save himself by returning to
        the wilderness.

28   MacAFEE, HELEN. "Some Novelists in Mid-Stream." <u>Yale Review</u>,
        15 (January), 338-40.
            Among current writers in mid-career, Lewis is exciting
        because his next satirical target is unpredictable. "A
        rough-rider among stylists," he showed "unexpected control"
        in <u>Arrowsmith</u>.

29   MANN, DOROTHEA LAURANCE. "Sinclair Lewis Pays Tribute to the
        He-Man." New York <u>Herald Tribune Books</u>, 4 July, p. 11.
            In <u>Mantrap</u> Lewis seems to be attempting to compete with
        Zane Grey. However, Lewis's satirical temperament makes
        him a poor writer of westerns: "Romance is outside Mr.
        Lewis's range. . . ."

30   MELVILLE, ARTHUR. "Heads or Tails? Two Current Estimates of
        Rotary and Kindred Organizations: Sinclair Lewis--Elmer T.
        Peterson." <u>Rotarian</u>, 28 (March), 14, 38, 40.
            Reviews the case for "boosterism" as stated by Peterson
        in <u>Saturday Evening Post</u> and by Lewis in a Kansas City
        speech to the Rotary Club. Lewis said the writer too is a
        sort of booster.

31   MENCKEN, H. L. "Arrowsmith," in <u>Readings from the American
        Mercury</u>. Edited by Grant C. Knight. New York: Alfred A.
        Knopf, pp. 129-34.
            Reprint of 1925.31.

32   MUIR, EDWIN. "Fiction." <u>Nation & Athenaeum</u>, 39 (31 July),
        506.
            <u>Mantrap</u> seems more like the work of a beginner than of
        Lewis. "The construction is slovenly, the dialogue flac-
        cid, the style weakly loquacious; the sentimentality is
        beyond characterization, and can only be deplored."

33   NEUMANN, HENRY. "Arrowsmith: A Study in Vocational Ethics."
        <u>American Review</u>, 4 (March-April), 184-92.
            <u>Arrowsmith</u> holds up high ethical standards for the medi-
        cal profession although Lewis is wrong to approve Gott-
        lieb's decision that half the plague victims should be left
        untreated. However, the novel's message should not be lim-
        ited to the medical profession: any human endeavor can be
        improved if it is motivated more by ethics than by profit-
        seeking.

34 PHELPS, WILLIAM LYON. "Sinclair Lewis Takes a Holiday in Canada." <u>Literary Digest International Book Review</u>, 4 (July), 485, 487.

    <u>Mantrap</u>, partially based on a Canadian vacation trip Lewis took, is not a bad novel but is clearly not up to the level of <u>Main Street</u>, <u>Babbitt</u>, and <u>Arrowsmith</u>. It is a disappointment, notable for weak characterization and a wild adventure plot.

35 R., D. "As Novelists See America." <u>Independent</u>, 116 (19 June), 721.

    <u>Mantrap</u> is a lesser work than <u>Arrowsmith</u> but Lewis employs his usual realistic method and tells the story with his typical "staccato progression." As usual, Lewis treats the "externals," not the psychological problems of his characters.

36 STUART, HENRY LONGAN. "Sinclair Lewis Hits the Trail." <u>New York Times Book Review</u>, 6 June, pp. 1, 25.

    <u>Mantrap</u> is less significant than <u>Main Street</u>, <u>Babbitt</u>, or <u>Arrowsmith</u>, and some may condemn Lewis for doing nothing more than telling a story in a popular manner. However, Lewis's skill as a novelist partially redeems even this slight work.

37 TOWNSEND, R. D. "Is It a Literary Sin to Please Readers?" <u>Outlook</u>, 143 (16 June), 256.

    <u>Mantrap</u>, unlike most of Lewis's novels, is meant mainly as entertainment, but seems sordid to this reader.

38 WALDMAN, MILTON. "Contemporary American Authors. III: Sinclair Lewis." <u>London Mercury</u>, 13 (January), 273-81.

    Reviews Lewis's career with major emphasis on <u>Main Street</u>, <u>Arrowsmith</u>, and <u>Babbitt</u>, the latter perhaps the best American novel of the twentieth century to date. Although his style can be faulty, Lewis is the most significant of all current American novelists because of his criticism of America's materialism, narrow-mindedness, and complacency. Reprinted 1928.34.

39 [WILSON, EDMUND]. "All-Star Literary Vaudeville." <u>New Republic</u>, 47 (30 June), 158-63.

    Although Lewis has a certain skill at satire in <u>Main Street</u> and <u>Babbitt</u>, he tells the reader "nothing new about life." Reprinted 1952.22 and 1956.10.

<u>1927</u>

1   ABBOTT, LAWRENCE F. "Honoré de Balzac and Sinclair Lewis."
      <u>Outlook</u>, 146 (6 July), 307–309.
         Lewis has much in common with Balzac, especially in his
      tendency to be fascinated by the worst in mankind. Like
      Balzac's books, Lewis's are works "that one <u>ought</u> to read
      but does not" except when motivated by "a sense of duty."
      A truly great writer should be able to examine life without
      becoming preoccupied by "its foulest abysses."

2   ANON. "Elmer Gantry." <u>Times Literary Supplement</u>, 26
      (31 March), 230.
         <u>Elmer Gantry</u> is too bitter to be a good work of art.
      The "amusing" satire of <u>Main Street</u> and <u>Babbitt</u> has given
      way to a merely clumsy attack on hypocritical clergymen.

3   ANON. "A New Scarlet Letter." <u>New Statesman</u>, 28 (26 March),
      737–38.
         "<u>Elmer Gantry</u> is a tract rather than a novel." It is
      hard to believe that the condition of American Fundamental-
      ist religion is as bad as Lewis paints it, though if it is,
      perhaps such a strong attack is necessary. <u>Elmer Gantry</u>
      is, however, a "horrible book," without a single "decent
      character who is not a fool" to redeem it.

4   ANON. Review of <u>Elmer Gantry</u>. <u>Booklist</u>, 23 (May), 344.
         Lewis's attack on hypocrisy in religion would have been
      more effective if it were more moderate and balanced.

5   ANON. Review of <u>Elmer Gantry</u>. <u>Independent</u>, 118 (9 April),
      392–93.
         In <u>Elmer Gantry</u>, which is overly long and tedious, Lewis
      shows that he is not a perceptive thinker, however skilled
      he may be at setting down superficial details. To attack
      religion by creating one roguish minister is a dubious
      technique.

6   ANON. "The Storm Over 'Elmer Gantry.'" <u>Literary Digest</u>, 93
      (16 April), 28–29.
         Brief review of <u>Elmer Gantry</u> and a survey of other re-
      views. Ministers such as John Roach Straton (<u>see</u> 1927.37)
      and a good many other reviewers have attacked the book as
      distortion while H. L. Mencken (<u>see</u> 1927.23) and a few
      others have praised it highly.

7   ANON. "Tearing Up 'Elmer Gantry.'" <u>Literary Digest</u>, 95
    (19 November), 29.
        Bayard Veiller, who received an advance for a dramatic
    version of <u>Elmer Gantry</u>, has torn up his script and re-
    turned the advance on moral grounds. He does not feel the
    book should be dramatized.

8   [BOYD, ERNEST]. "The New Books." <u>New Yorker</u>, 3 (19 March),
    98, 100.
        <u>Elmer Gantry</u> shows Lewis to be "a superb reporter, who
    cannot fail to hold his readers." The book will shock some
    Americans.

9   BOYNTON, PERCY H. "Sinclair Lewis." <u>English Journal</u>, 16
    (April), 251-60.
        Traces Lewis's career from <u>Our Mr. Wrenn</u> through <u>Elmer
    Gantry</u>. Lewis progressed as a writer through <u>Babbitt</u>, but
    with <u>Arrowsmith</u> his thesis began to overpower his art and
    he preached too much. <u>Elmer Gantry</u> continues in this false
    direction. Unless Lewis can return to real art, with its
    recognition of life's ambiguities and complexities, he will
    never again equal the best of his past work. Reprinted
    1927.10; revised version in 1940.10.

10 _____. "Sinclair Lewis," in his <u>More Contemporary Americans</u>.
    Chicago: University of Chicago Press, pp. 179-98.
        Reprint of 1927.9.

11 CANBY, HENRY SEIDEL. "Review of <u>Arrowsmith</u>," in <u>Essays of the
    Past and Present</u>. Edited by Warner Taylor. New York and
    London: Harper and Brothers, pp. 422-27.
        Reprint of 1925.12.

12 _____. "Vicious Ignorance." <u>Saturday Review of Literature</u>, 3
    (12 March), 637, 640.
        The uproar over <u>Elmer Gantry</u> should not obscure the fact
    that Lewis the journalist may have uncovered something
    wrong in the ministry. "Let us not ask then whether this
    pastor or that revivalist is like Elmer Gantry, but whether
    colleges, seminaries, congregations, people can be like
    that. If an Elmer Gantry is possible, then this book is
    justified."

13 _____. "Sinclair Lewis and Blasphemy: Two Views." <u>Bookman</u>,
    65 (April), 216.
        Finds <u>Elmer Gantry</u> "a poor novel but an admirable piece
    of journalism" though not blasphemous because Lewis is at-
    tacking only abuses among the clergy, much as Chaucer did.
    <u>See</u> Ferguson, 1927.16.

1927

14 COMPTON, CHARLES H. "The Librarian and the Novelist." South
    Atlantic Quarterly, 26 (October), 392-403.
        Librarians are often depicted in fiction as being rela-
    tively naive and flighty. Lewis's Carol Kennicott, for ex-
    ample, is "emotional, shallow, restless, and ineffectual."
    Works by Edith Wharton, Floyd Dell, and Hugh Walpole are
    also treated.

15 DAVIS, ELMER. "Mr. Lewis Attacks the Clergy." New York Times
    Book Review, 13 March, pp. 1, 22.
        Only about twenty pages of Elmer Gantry "have been writ-
    ten by Lewis the artist; the rest are preempted by Lewis
    the preacher. . . ." He preaches the gospel of the prophet
    H. L. Mencken and such is his power that he carries the
    reader along. However, the novel is an artistic failure
    with unreal monsters in place of its principal characters.

16 FERGUSON, CHARLES W. "Sinclair Lewis and Blasphemy: Two
    Views." Bookman, 65 (April), 216-18.
        Admits that the book may be blasphemous and that it is
    not a great work of art, but defends Elmer Gantry on the
    grounds that Lewis attacks very real abuses in the church
    and in American culture. See Canby, 1927.13.

17 HARTLEY, L. P. "New Fiction." Saturday Review (London), 143
    (9 April), 568-69.
        The protagonist of Elmer Gantry is a mere caricature,
    and the satire of religion is too unrelieved, but "as a
    story it has enough vitality to carry one over passages of
    extreme coarseness and a generally disagreeable flavour."

18 HAZARD, LUCY LOCKWOOD. The Frontier in American Literature.
    New York: Thomas Y. Crowell, xx + 308 pp., passim.
        Ties Lewis to the pioneering spirit in a number of ways,
    from Babbitt's yearning for wilderness to the pioneer an-
    cestors of Arrowsmith. In most of Lewis's works, however,
    the protagonist is finally dominated by society, since
    "after the passing of the frontier" individualism is impos-
    sible. Pages 283-85 reprinted in TCIA, 1968.4.

19 KRUTCH, JOSEPH WOOD. "Mr. Babbitt's Spiritual Guide." Na-
    tion, 124 (16 March), 291-92.
        After two atypical books, Arrowsmith and Mantrap, Lewis
    has returned to the sort of novel he does best. Elmer Gan-
    try, like Main Street and Babbitt, is marked by "a com-
    pleteness of documentation not less than amazing, a power
    of mimicry which, so far as I know, no living author can
    equal, and a gusto which . . . is all but inexplicable."
    Reprinted 1929.14 and in SL:CCE, 1962.14.

20 LIPPMAN, WALTER. "Sinclair Lewis," in his Men of Destiny.
    New York: Macmillan, pp. 71-92.
         Lewis is extraordinarily accurate in describing external
    details but in treating the real essence of people or
    groups, he often just replaces old stereotypes with new
    ones he has created. With Arrowsmith it looked as if he
    were developing a deeper art, but in Elmer Gantry he in-
    dulges again in distortion. Reprinted in SL:CCE, 1962.14.

21 LITTELL, ROBERT. "The Preacher Fried in Oil." New Republic,
    50 (16 March), 108-109.
         Elmer Gantry is the story of a Babbitt of religion, but
    one devoid of Babbitt's sympathetic qualities. Thus, Gan-
    try, like most of the other characters, seems flat and un-
    realistic. The book is far too long and fails even as
    propaganda.

22 McNALLY, WILLIAM J. "Americans We Like: Mr. Babbitt, Meet
    Sinclair Lewis." Nation, 125 (21 September), 278-81.
         Personality sketch on Lewis, stressing his mercurial and
    quixotic nature, his modesty about his writing, and his
    real love for Americans and the Midwest.

23 MENCKEN, H. L. "Man of God: American Style." American Mer-
    cury, 10 (April), 506-508.
         With Elmer Gantry Lewis has surpassed his own success in
    Main Street and Babbitt. Lewis avoids the obvious pitfall
    of making the novel "a mere lampoon" and gives the reader a
    believable main character and a host of accurately drawn
    minor characters. Those who thought Lewis's talent a minor
    one must by now concede that "the man actually has a tre-
    mendous talent."

24 MUIR, EDWIN. "Fiction." Nation & Athenaeum, 41 (23 April),
    85.
         Although it may be "the best [book] that its author has
    written," Elmer Gantry suffers from Lewis's determination
    to make it a novel, not a satire. Lewis "wants to sympa-
    thize with his hero and indict him at the same time."
    Thus, the book leaves the reader depressed rather than
    fortified against "the vices of the world" as unadulter-
    ated satire would leave him.

25 MUZZEY, DAVID SAVILLE. "Sinclair Lewis' Attack on the Cler-
    gy." Standard, 17 (July), 7-10.
         A cynical, pornographic book attacking the clergy by
    presenting a shallow caricature as its main character,
    Elmer Gantry manages to combine sordidness with monotony.

1927

26   PARRINGTON, VERNON L. <u>Sinclair Lewis: Our Own Diogenes</u>.
University of Washington Chapbooks, no. 5, edited by Glenn
Hughes. Seattle: University of Washington Book Stores,
27 pp.
   Lewis both fascinates and repels America as he satirizes
her self-satisfied, materially rich life. Paradoxically,
Lewis has been well paid for his attacks but he remains a
pariah. However, nobody has better captured contemporary
America--from its speech patterns to its spiritual empti-
ness. Reprinted 1930.20 and in <u>SL:CCE</u>, 1962.14.

27   P[EARSON], E[DMUND]. "Elmer Gantry." <u>Outlook</u>, 145
(16 March), 343.
   While many readers may misinterpret <u>Elmer Gantry</u> as an
attack on all clergy, Lewis is just exposing the spectrum
of hypocrisy in an admired profession, as he did in <u>Bab-
bitt</u> and <u>Arrowsmith</u>. In spite of Gantry's failings, Lewis
has sympathy for him as a man who has been pushed into a
calling for which he doesn't have the temperament. "An
important and valuable novel."

28   PETERKIN, JULIA. "Notes of a Rapid Reader." <u>Saturday Review
of Literature</u>, 3 (16 April), 725.
   Little of the controversy over <u>Elmer Gantry</u> has concerned the book as literature and few of those joining the
battle seem to realize that satire isn't supposed to be
evenhanded. Satire must contain enough truth to make it
meaningful, and <u>Elmer Gantry</u> does stay close enough to
reality to keep the book from going "flat."

29   ROSS, MARY. Review of <u>Elmer Gantry</u>. <u>Atlantic Bookshelf</u>, May,
p. [18].
   The uproar that has greeted the publication of <u>Elmer
Gantry</u> suggests that Lewis's satire has hit home. The book
is a novel, though, and not mere propaganda against religion as some imply.

30   SALPETER, HARRY. "Red-Tempered Novelist." New York <u>World</u>,
<u>Book World</u>, 13 March, p. 8M.
   Interview with Lewis in which he expounds on his favor-
ite among his own novels, <u>Arrowsmith</u>, the surprise he felt
when <u>Main Street</u> became a best-seller, and his continued
objections to prizes such as the Pulitzer Prize for fiction.

31   SCHROEDER, ERIC G. "The Other Side of Main Street: An Interview with William Allen White." <u>Rotarian</u>, 30 (June), 12-13.
   Although Lewis is "the greatest satirist America has
ever produced," he necessarily points out only the faults

of American institutions such as Rotary. However, Lewis
will ultimately strengthen America through his satire,
White feels.

32 SHAW, CHARLES G. "Three Americans: Exceedingly Personal
    Glimpses of Sinclair Lewis, Texas Guinan, and Clarence
    Darrow." Vanity Fair, 29 (November), 68.
        Character sketch of Lewis concentrating on personal ec-
    centricities and habits. Revised, 1928.30.

33 SHERMAN, STUART P. "The Significance of Sinclair Lewis," in
    his Points of View. New York, London: Charles Scribner's
    Sons, pp. [187]–217.
        Reprint of 1922.24.

34 SHILLITO, EDWARD. "'Elmer Gantry' and the Church in America."
    The Nineteenth Century and After, 101 (May), 739–48.
        Elmer Gantry bears no resemblance at all to any real
    Baptist or Methodist minister, and Lewis's frenzied attack
    on churches and seminaries is nearly devoid of value. El-
    mer Gantry would be more realistic if Lewis had not allowed
    his satiric purpose to prevail and had given a more bal-
    anced picture of church and clergy.

35 SINCLAIR, UPTON. "The Ex-Furnaceman," in his Money Writes!
    New York: Albert and Charles Boni, pp. 171–74.
        Lewis learned the principles of socialism as a young
    furnace-tender at Sinclair's socialist utopia Helicon Hall,
    but he fails to treat socialists or socialism in his fic-
    tion, apparently because he is afraid that the works will
    not sell. Perhaps when he writes his labor novel, Lewis
    will finally come to grips with the radical movement.
    Translated into German in 1927.36.

36 _____. "Sinclair Lewis." Weltbühne, 23:745–47.
        German translation of 1927.35.

37 STRATON, JOHN ROACH. "'Elmer Gantry' is Bunk, Vanity and Vul-
    garity." New York Evening Post Literary Review, 7
    (12 March), 1, 10.
        Lewis's powerfully advertised novel not only appeals to
    the lowest side of human nature, but fails to treat any of
    the genuine problems of modern Christianity. Furthermore,
    even apart from moral standards, the book is crude and in-
    artistic.

1927

38   TAYLOR, RACHEL ANNAND. "The Blatant Beast in America."
        Spectator, 138 (26 March), 566-67.
            At times Elmer Gantry is a compelling book as the reader
        follows the protagonist's picaresque adventures, but it is
        also a revolting book and ultimately "has only a documen-
        tary interest." One of Lewis's most serious errors was
        condemning the whole Christian church and not just Gantry.

39   VAN DOREN, CARL. "The Roving Critic." Century Magazine, 114
        (May), 123-24.
            Elmer Gantry will give the Babbitts of the nation an
        easier conscience when they drop their wives off at church
        and go to the golf course. Reprinted 1929.26.

40   _____. "St. George and the Parson." Saturday Review of Lit-
        erature, 3 (12 March), 639.
            Although marred by a loss of control when Lewis's anger
        distracts him from his carefully designed satire, Elmer
        Gantry is effective and timely, as it comes when the Funda-
        mentalists have brought resentment down upon themselves. As
        usual, Lewis captures the external reality of the world he
        depicts and gives a good view of church politics.

41   VAN DOREN, MARK. "First Glance at the Season's Books." Na-
        tion, 124 (20 April), 440.
            Elmer Gantry is the "sensation of the season," but all
        discussions concern the subject and not its value as
        literature.

42   WEST, REBECCA. "Sinclair Lewis Introduces Elmer Gantry." New
        York Herald Tribune Books, 13 March, p. 1.
            Lewis fails in Elmer Gantry partly because of ineptness
        in style and awkward plotting, but mostly because he fails
        to come to grips intellectually with religion. To satirize
        abuses among the clergy, one must have some notion of the
        ideals of the religious person, and this is beyond Lewis,
        who therefore contents himself with sniping at the colorful
        but petty failings of his clergymen. Reprinted 1928.35 and
        in SL:CCE, 1962.14.

43   WHARTON, EDITH. "The Great American Novel." Yale Review, 16
        (July), 646-56.
            One of the novels recently but mistakenly hailed as "the
        great American novel," Main Street is cited as an example
        of a work which becomes something different from what its
        author intended. Lewis "hacked away the sentimental vege-
        tation from the American small town," but the novel did not
        make its readers want to destroy Main Street "but only to
        read more" about it. Perhaps Main Street has received more

attention than such a theme can bear; it now "stands for
everything which does not rise above a very low average in
culture, situation, or intrinsic human interest. . . ."

44 WHIPPLE, LEON. "'Red' Lewis in a Red Rage." Survey, 58
    (1 May), 168, 170.
        Although Lewis let his rage overpower him and wrote a
    propaganda tract rather than a novel, Elmer Gantry will
    probably stir up a debate which will be helpful in the end.
    Lewis documents every possible failing of the clergy with-
    out understanding religion itself.

45 WILLIAMS, MICHAEL. "The Sinclair Lewis Industry." Common-
    weal, 5 (30 March), 577-79.
        It is ironic that Lewis, who satirizes American methods
    of advertising, should find his novels promoted in the same
    way as automobiles and movies. But in spite of the pub-
    licity preceding it, Elmer Gantry "is muck-raking journal-
    ism." In joining the current move against organized reli-
    gion, Lewis has written an almost unreadable novel. Re-
    printed 1928.38.

46 WOODWARD, WILLIAM E. "'Elmer Gantry' Is Truth As a Study of
    Hypocrisy." New York Evening Post Literary Review, 7
    (12 March), 1, 10.
        Lewis has written "the greatest, most vital and most
    penetrating study of religious hypocrisy that has been
    written since Voltaire." Those who will object to the
    book most violently are the real Elmer Gantrys, who will
    call Lewis a liar and invent scandalous rumors about him.

1928

1 ANON. "Bookman's Notes: Points of Accuracy." Bookman, 66
   (February), 663-66.
       Defends Lewis's depiction of the American businessman in
   the American Mercury version of The Man Who Knew Coolidge.
   It is not only an accurate criticism of American values,
   but "an exceptionally interesting and valuable tour de
   force."

2 ANON. "Books in Brief." Nation, 126 (18 April), 462.
       The Man Who Knew Coolidge is another of Lewis's "safe"
   books. While it is well done in its way, Lewis is simply
   repeating Babbitt rather than breaking any new ground.

1928

3   ANON. "The Man Who Knew Coolidge." <u>Times Literary Supple-</u>
<u>ment</u>, 27 (24 May), 394.
While Lewis probably "enjoyed" writing <u>The Man Who Knew</u>
<u>Coolidge</u>, not many readers will enjoy reading it. "It is
too easy an achievement" to be a good novel.

4   ANON. "A Monologue from Zenith." <u>New Statesman</u>, 31 (12 May),
162.
In <u>The Man Who Knew Coolidge</u> Lewis moves away from the
life story novel pattern in <u>Arrowsmith</u> and <u>Elmer Gantry</u> and
concentrates on what he does best--the satirical monologue.
The result is "brilliant and merciless."

5   ANON. Review of <u>The Man Who Knew Coolidge</u>. <u>Booklist</u>, 24
(July), 404.
This character study of an American bore is "tedious
reading at this length."

6   ANON. Review of <u>The Man Who Knew Coolidge</u>. <u>Independent</u>, 120
(12 May), 461.
Lewis has gone "from ironic portraiture to caricature"
and his work has declined seriously from the high point
reached in <u>Babbitt</u>.

7   BEARD, CHARLES A. "Is Babbitt's Case Hopeless?" <u>Menorah</u>
<u>Journal</u>, 14 (January), 21-28.
Defense of the American middle class with little reference to <u>Babbitt</u>. Babbitts of America should accept themselves as they are and not be shaken by satirists.

8   BELLAMY, FRANCIS R. "The Theatre." <u>Outlook</u>, 149 (22 August),
670.
Patrick Kearney's adaptation of <u>Elmer Gantry</u> is "as
spurious and amateurish a burlesque as we've ever wit-
nessed." Not only does it fail as art but even as propaganda. Gantry is a crude caricature of the main character
of Lewis's novel.

9   BIRKHEAD, L. M. <u>Is "Elmer Gantry" True?</u> Girard, Kansas:
Haldeman-Julius Publications, 64 pp.
Consists of five essays, two of which comment specifi-
cally on Lewis and <u>Elmer Gantry</u>. In "The Writing of
'Elmer Gantry,'" Birkhead, a liberal minister, tells how
Lewis asked him for help in writing the book and praises
Lewis's diligence and sincerity. "'Elmer Gantry' and What
Is Wrong with the Preachers," also by Birkhead, suggests
that Lewis was too mild in his denunciation of hypocritical
and incompetent preachers, that preachers who denounced
Lewis or the novel have often told deliberate lies, and

that it is time for the profession to reform. The other
three essays, on Aimee Semple McPherson, Undine Utly, and
revivals generally, by Birkhead, Raymond B. Brown, and Clay
Fulks, respectively, document abuses by the clergy to support the first two essays.

*10 BRICKELL, HERSCHEL. Review of The Man Who Knew Coolidge.
North American Review, 225 (June), advertising section.
Cited in Book Review Digest, 1928.

11 BURTON, BRADLEY. "Babbitt Ballads." Nation's Business, 16
(January), 28-29.
Lighthearted poem about Babbitts in all walks of life,
including literature. Lewis mentioned.

12 CANBY, HENRY SEIDEL. "Schmaltz, Babbitt & Co." Saturday Review of Literature, 4 (24 March), [697]-98.
Like Babbitt, The Man Who Knew Coolidge displays Lewis's
considerable ability at mimicry and satire and recalls the
work of Dickens and Twain; however, Lewis's work is not as
great as theirs because Lewis lacks pity and love for the
portion of mankind he depicts. His greatest failing is his
impatient contempt for the contemporary American. Lewis
loses sight of the good in modern man, and this short-
sightedness keeps him from real greatness as a novelist.

13 COWLEY, MALCOLM. "Babbilogues." New Republic, 54 (25 April),
302.
The Man Who Knew Coolidge consists of six "interminable
monologues" by a bore. While the book contains brilliant
passages on women and citizenship, 250 pages is too much,
and the satire that was fresh in Babbitt seems less interesting some five years later. Lewis must seek new material
and techniques.

14 HARTLEY, L. P. "New Fiction." Saturday Review (London), 145
(9 June), 738.
"'The Man Who Knew Coolidge' is a most entertaining
book." Lewis is not so venomous as he was in Elmer Gantry;
thus his satire is under better control. He manages to
characterize Schmaltz as a terrible bore without boring his
readers.

15 HUDDLESTON, SISLEY. Paris Salons, Cafés, Studios. Philadelphia and London: J. B. Lippincott, pp. 113-16.
Memories of Lewis: "he gave me the impression of a
country parson who was trying to look as sober as possible." He dressed in black English-cut clothes, wore spats
and a monocle, and carried a cane. He monopolized conver-

sation at a dinner, talked of his writing methods and be-
ginnings, was voluble but always sensible. Discusses
Lewis's quarrel with Harold Stearns.

16 KARSNER, DAVID. "Sinclair Lewis," in his <u>Sixteen Authors to</u>
<u>One</u>. New York: Lewis Copeland, pp. 65-80.
    Popular essay on Lewis as a prominent American person-
ality, briefly covering his life from boyhood to his posi-
tion as literary lion in the late 1920s. Parts originally
published in a variety of magazines and papers.

17 KRIESI, HANS. <u>Sinclair Lewis</u>. Frauenfeld and Leipzig: Von
Huber, 217 pp.
    Lewis is considered against the background of a short
history of the ethnic, political, religious and literary
development of the various parts of the United States.
Biography of Lewis (pp. 36-81) is followed by chapters on
the early works, <u>Our Mr. Wrenn</u>, <u>The Job</u>, <u>Main Street</u>, <u>Bab-</u>
<u>bitt</u>, <u>Arrowsmith</u>, and <u>Elmer Gantry</u>. Explores Lewis's po-
litical attitudes and satire. Praises the novels as "the
most effective that have been written in the fictional do-
main of American social criticism." In his characters we
see "the power of the free, strong personality, the ancient
truth of the superiority of the spiritual over the material. . . ." In German.

18 McALPIN, EDWIN A. "The Sordid or the Radiant Life," in his
<u>Old and New Books as Life Teachers</u>. Garden City, N.Y.:
Doubleday, Doran, pp. 96-108.
    In <u>Main Street</u> Lewis emphasizes the "sordid," "gloomy"
side of small-town life, but he distorts the truth in this
one-sided picture. He is similarly one-sided in <u>Elmer</u>
<u>Gantry</u>. Both books tell more about Lewis's limitations
than they do about their subject matter. In contrast, William Allen White's <u>In the Heart of a Fool</u> pictures the
pleasant side of Main Street.

19 MARBLE, ANNIE RUSSELL. "Sinclair Lewis," in her <u>A Study of</u>
<u>the Modern Novel: British and American Since 1900</u>. New
York and London: D. Appleton, pp. 377-81.
    Brief summary of Lewis's life and work up to 1927. Lewis
attempted to better his earlier work with <u>Arrowsmith</u> and
nearly succeeded, but the book grows weak near its end.
<u>Elmer Gantry</u> marks a distinct falling off of his power.

20   MENCKEN, H. L. "Babbitt Redivivus." <u>American Mercury</u>, 14
     (June), 253-54.
         <u>The Man Who Knew Coolidge</u> presents Lowell Schmaltz, who
     resembles Babbitt but is more content with his life. Lewis
     will again be attacked for presenting another caricature in
     Schmaltz, but that does not detract from his achievement.
     He has captured a large segment of American culture in his
     works, and if he has been cruel, he has also been fair and
     accurate.

21   MICHAUD, RÉGIS. "Sinclair Lewis and the Average Man," in his
     <u>The American Novel To-Day: A Social and Psychological</u>
     <u>Study</u>. Boston: Little, Brown, pp. [128]-53.
         Lewis as social critic. Carol Kennicott is seen as an
     average American woman living in an average American town.
     Babbitt is the average American man. Lewis shows, in their
     ineffectual rebellions, just how unhappy American culture
     really makes its apparently satisfied customers. In <u>Arrow-</u>
     <u>smith</u> and <u>Elmer Gantry</u> Lewis grows even more pessimistic
     about American society; nevertheless, he should ignore the
     criticism of the last book and continue his assault on
     hypocrisy.

22   MORTIMER, RAYMOND. "New Novels." <u>Nation & Athenaeum</u>, 43
     (26 May), 257.
         <u>The Man Who Knew Coolidge</u> illustrates "the difficulty of
     making a bore any more interesting on the stage or in a
     novel than he is in real life." Funny and pointed, but not
     one of Lewis's major books.

23   [PARKER, DOROTHY] "Constant Reader." "Reading and Writing:
     Mr. Lewis Lays It on with a Trowel." <u>New Yorker</u>, 4
     (7 April), 106-107.
         <u>The Man Who Knew Coolidge</u> is "rotten," whether consid-
     ered as "entertainment, a portrait, [or] a contribution to
     American letters." It is "heavy-handed, clumsy, and dis-
     honest." Lewis is historically important because of <u>Main</u>
     <u>Street</u> and <u>Babbitt</u>, and <u>Arrowsmith</u> is a great novel, but
     <u>The Man Who Knew Coolidge</u> is not even good as caricature.

24   PRINGLE, HENRY F. "George Babbitt's Best Friend." New York
     <u>Herald Tribune Books</u>, 15 April, pp. 3-4.
         <u>Elmer Gantry</u> suggests that Lewis "is becoming less sub-
     tle every year" and <u>The Man Who Knew Coolidge</u>, which is
     dull, confirms this judgment. While Lewis occasionally
     manages to be really funny, those passages do not justify
     so long a book.

1928

25 RASCOE, BURTON. "Bad Girls and Babbitts." Bookman, 67 (May), 306-307.
    Much of the attack on Lewis's latest book is inspired by the critics' propensity to attack successful authors. In The Man Who Knew Coolidge Lewis wisely emphasizes character and does a masterful job of depicting Schmaltz, who is sometimes likable, sometimes frightening.

26 RIDDELL, JOHN. "The Man Who Knew Lewis." Vanity Fair, 30 (July), 65.
    Parody of The Man Who Knew Coolidge.

27 ROBBINS, FRANCES LAMONT. "Speaking of Books." Outlook, 149 (16 May), 110-11.
    The Man Who Knew Coolidge follows much of Lewis's work in laughing at the American character, but does so only by distorting the average American.

28 RUSSELL, FRANCES THERESA. "The Young Mr. Lewis." University of California Chronicle, 30 (October), 417-27.
    By 1928 Lewis had gone through two periods in his art. The more famous works of the 1920s are marked by rather vitriolic satire which may cause critics to forget his early period, in which he displayed a zest for life not present in his later works. Perhaps a third period may see Lewis uniting the strong points of both periods to achieve "great art."

29 SHANKS, EDWAND [sic]. "Fiction." London Mercury, 18 (September), 538.
    Though its subject is not so rich as that of earlier Lewis novels, The Man Who Knew Coolidge shows that "Lewis's sheer skill is yearly increasing."

30 SHAW, CHARLES G. "Sinclair Lewis," in his The Low-Down. New York: Henry Holt, pp. 235-45.
    Revised version of Vanity Fair sketch of Lewis, 1927.32.

31 STRUNSKY, SIMEON. "About Books More or Less: the Truth About George." New York Times Book Review, 22 January, p. 4.
    Responds to article by Charles A. Beard (1928.7). Beard overlooks the real humanity of Babbitt to claim that he may be civilized someday. It would be a better defense to take him as he is and explore his strong points.

32   STUART, HENRY LONGAN. "Mr. Lewis Goes Back to Babbitt." New York Times Book Review, 8 April, pp. 1, 11.
        In The Man Who Knew Coolidge Lewis returns to a type he first created in Eddie Schwirtz (The Job) and returned to in Babbitt. However, this monologue by Schmaltz is too much of a good thing, and though Lewis carries it off with skill, it is hoped that he'll never try another such tour de force.

33   TAYLOR, RACHEL ANNAND. "Fiction." Spectator, 140 (19 May), 775-76.
        Lowell Schmaltz of The Man Who Knew Coolidge "is not a monumental portrait like Babbitt or the terrible Elmer Gantry. But he sketches himself very vividly. . . ."

34   WALDMAN, MILTON. "Sinclair Lewis," in Contemporary American Authors. Edited by J. C. Squire. New York: Henry Holt, pp. [70]-94.
        Reprint of 1926.38 with the addition of a note (pp. 92-94) on Elmer Gantry.

35   WEST, REBECCA. "Sinclair Lewis Introduces Elmer Gantry," in her The Strange Necessity. Garden City, N.Y.: Doubleday, Doran, pp. 295-308.
        Reprint of 1927.42.

*36 WHIPPLE, T. K. "Sinclair Lewis," in his Spokesmen: Modern Writers and American Life. New York: Appleton-Century-Crofts.
        See 1963.25, which is a reprint of this edition. Reprinted in SB, 1971.13.

37   [WHITE, E. B.] "The Theatre: Rough-House." New Yorker, 4 (18 August), 36, 38.
        The dramatic version of Elmer Gantry, by Patrick Kearney and Thompson Buchanan, is a bad play.

38   WILLIAMS, MICHAEL. "The Sinclair Lewis Industry," in his Catholicism and the Modern Mind. New York: Dial Press, pp. 239-50.
        Reprint of 1927.45.

1929

1   ANON. "Dodsworth." Times Literary Supplement, 28 (28 March), 258.
        In Sam and Fran Dodsworth, Lewis's characterization is at its best; and the settings, from New York to Europe,

are done well. "In spite of a certain monotony of structure and the usual excess of detail," the book makes good
reading. Reprinted 1957.2.

2 ANON. Review of <u>Dodsworth</u>. <u>Booklist</u>, 25 (April), 286.
<u>Dodsworth</u> is similar to Lewis's earlier work and adds
one more "portrait" to his American gallery.

3 BOGARDUS, EMORY S. "Social Distance in Fiction." <u>Sociology
and Social Research</u>, 14 (November-December), [174]-80.
Explores themes of "social distance" in <u>Main Street</u>--
between Carol and Will, Carol and the women of Gopher
Prairie, Carol and Bea, and between the Americanized citi-
zens of Gopher Prairie and the Swedish farmers.

4 BRENNECKE, ERNEST, JR. "A Man Between Worlds." <u>Commonweal</u>, 9
(17 April), 691-92.
<u>Dodsworth</u> suffers from a dull and ill-defined protago-
nist and although Lewis treats a number of themes, he does
justice to none of them. The novel is redeemed only by
Lewis's satiric portrait of Fran Dodsworth.

*5 BRICKELL, HERSCHEL. Review of <u>Dodsworth</u>. <u>North American Re-
view</u>, 227 (May), advertising section.
Cited in <u>Book Review Digest</u>, 1929.

6 CANBY, HENRY SEIDEL. "Sex War." <u>Saturday Review of Litera-
ture</u>, 5 (30 March), 821-22.
When he is at his best, as in <u>Main Street</u> and <u>Babbitt</u>,
Lewis pursues a single theme through an entire novel.
<u>Dodsworth</u> explores the war between the sexes in America,
the war which locks men into roles as stolid moneymakers
and makes women "esthetic Amazons with barbarians for husbands, protectors, and slaves." While Sam struggles, however clumsily, with culture for its own sake, Fran seeks it
as a social asset. In this book Lewis is perhaps most comparable to William Dean Howells, "less suave, but also less
inhibited" than Howells. <u>Dodsworth</u> establishes beyond
doubt that Lewis has "the gifts of a great social historian." Reprinted 1936.10.

7 DURTAIN, LUC. "Un Témoin des États-Unis: Le Romancier Sinclair Lewis." <u>La Revue Hebdomadaire</u>, 38, no. 11 (30 November), [554]-64.
Although it is difficult to understand a country through
its literature, two American writers give an impartial view
of the American people, both the sadness and truth of the
human comedy--Walt Whitman and Sinclair Lewis. Because

Lewis is little known to French readers, short analyses of
the major novels clarify how Lewis presents the contradic-
tions inherent in the American character as well as the
conflicts in American life. In French.

8   FORD, FORD MADOX. Review of Dodsworth. Bookman, 69 (April),
     191-92.
          As a novel, Dodsworth surpasses Elmer Gantry and its
     protagonist is considerably more likable than Babbitt. In
     his juxtaposition of a thinking American with European cul-
     ture, Lewis has written a book of considerable sociological
     significance. Lewis really makes the reader care about Sam
     and approach the ending with a sense of suspense. Reprint-
     ed in SL:CCE, 1962.14.

9   FORSTER, E. M. "A Camera Man." Life and Letters, 2 (May),
     336-43.
          Reprint of 1929.10.

10   _____. "Our Photography: Sinclair Lewis." New York Herald
     Tribune Books, 28 April, pp. 1, 6.
          Lewis in his early career was a skilled "spontaneous"
     photographer of American life and of certain types of char-
     acters. As his career progressed, the freshness left and
     has not been replaced with more mature skills. Reprinted
     1929.9, 1936.15 and in SL:CCE, 1962.14.

11   HARTLEY, L. P. "New Fiction." Saturday Review (London), 147
     (6 April), 482.
          Dodsworth "is a little too long," mostly because Lewis
     presents the Dodsworths' quarrels in minute detail. His
     satire of Fran is so thorough that the reader may wonder
     what Sam ever saw in her. Like most Lewis novels, Dods-
     worth holds the reader's interest, but here Lewis's talent
     seems "diluted."

*12 JOHNSON, A. T. "Realism in Contemporary American Literature:
     Notes on Dreiser, Anderson, Lewis." Southwestern Bulletin,
     September, pp. 3-16.
          Cited in Leary, 1954.10.

13   KRONENBERGER, LOUIS. "Sinclair Lewis Parts Company with Mr.
     Babbitt." New York Times Book Review, 17 March, p. 2.
          Although not up to Arrowsmith, Dodsworth is a fine book.
     Both Sam and Fran Dodsworth come to life as characters and
     Lewis's examination of the American abroad is a contribu-
     tion to the study of American manners. The style is flawed
     by Lewis's tendency to narrate more than he dramatizes, but
     the novel generally is his most successful in years.

1929

14 KRUTCH, JOSEPH WOOD. "Mr. Babbitt's Spiritual Guide: A Re-
    view of Sinclair Lewis's Elmer Gantry," in College Readings
    in Contemporary Thought. Edited by Kendall B. Taft, John
    Francis McDermott, and Dana O. Jensen. Boston: Houghton
    Mifflin, pp. [524]-26.
        Reprint of 1927.19.

15 MANLY, JOHN MATTHEWS and EDITH L. RICKERT. Contemporary Amer-
    ican Literature. New York: Harcourt, Brace, pp. 21-22,
    217-19.
        Biographical sketch, generalizations about Lewis as sat-
    irist, study questions on Main Street, Babbitt, Elmer Gan-
    try, and bibliography of works about Lewis.

16 MATTHEWS, T. S. "Spleen." New Republic, 58 (10 April), 232.
        Dodsworth takes a protagonist who resembles Babbitt in
    some respects and views him sympathetically, but Lewis's
    villain is Fran Dodsworth. Although Dodsworth is not as
    successful as his earlier work, Lewis's "journalistic fac-
    ulty" saves him from real failure. Where Lewis does return
    to the satiric mode, "his satire has become little more
    than spleen."

17 MAURICE, ARTHUR BARTLETT. "The History of Their Books: III.
    Sinclair Lewis." Bookman, 69 (March), 52-53.
        A collection of facts concerning Lewis's original plots,
    titles, and characters in Main Street, Babbitt, Elmer Gan-
    try, and Dodsworth contrasted with their final versions in
    the published novels.

18 MENCKEN, H. L. "Escape and Return." American Mercury, 16
    (April), 506-508.
        Dodsworth suffers from the unreality of both Sam and
    Fran Dodsworth and the artificial sound of their dialogue,
    but the book is redeemed by Lewis's inimitable observation
    and acid wit. "If he can produce a 'Babbitt,' a 'Main
    Street' or an 'Elmer Gantry' now and then, he is entitled
    to his intervening 'Dodsworths.'"

19 MORTIMER, RAYMOND. "New Novels." Nation & Athenaeum, 44
    (30 March), 915.
        In Dodsworth Lewis attempts the sort of thing that he
    does not do well, probing "delicate human relationships"
    instead of sticking to his forte, satire. However, "Lewis
    makes incidentally the truest comments I have ever read on
    the differences between Europeans and Americans. . . ."

20   [PARKER, DOROTHY] "Constant Reader." "Reading and Writing:
      And Again, Mr. Sinclair Lewis." New Yorker, 5 (16 March),
      106-107.
          Dodsworth is too often dull; there is too much of the
      travelogue about it and the "debates" among the characters
      are too long. Nevertheless, by the time the book ends, Sam
      Dodsworth does come to life.

21   PATERSON, ISABEL. "Babbitt Goes Abroad." New York Herald
      Tribune Books, 17 March, pp. 1-2.
          Dodsworth attempts to present an admirable American
      businessman to balance Babbitt. To that end, Lewis tells
      all sorts of favorable things about Dodsworth, who, when he
      appears, is painfully like Babbitt. Lewis's realism is
      again so relentless that parts of the book are tedious.

22   ROBBINS, FRANCES LAMONT. "Samson Agonistes." Outlook and In-
      dependent, 151 (20 March), 466-67.
          Dodsworth is a modern story of Samson and Delilah, told
      by a photographic realist. Lewis exposes the failure of
      modern marriage and the inability of modern society to of-
      fer fulfillment to mankind. There is little irony in the
      novel and there is a good deal of emotion--sympathy for
      Sam and hatred for Fran.

23   ROSS, MARY. "Travelog by Mr. Lewis." Survey, 62 (1 May),
      202-203.
          Sam Dodsworth is the best character Lewis has created so
      far. The rest of Dodsworth, like so much of Lewis's work,
      seems almost "too lifelike to be natural."

24   S., E. "New Novels." New Statesman, 33 (4 May), 119.
          Dodsworth is "not to be reckoned among the best of its
      author's recent books, because it is without those sudden
      gleams of beauty of which he is undeniably capable." Al-
      though his portrait of Sam Dodsworth is sympathetic, that
      of Fran is caricature. On the whole, Lewis has again shown
      himself to be "a great story-teller," whose skill unites
      the disparate parts of the novel.

25   TAYLOR, RACHEL ANNAND. "Fiction: The International Scene."
      Spectator, 142 (23 March), 485-86.
          Dodsworth is perhaps Lewis's most "readable" book so far
      and more good-natured than most of his previous novels. On
      the whole, it is "stimulating and mobile and tonic."

1929

26   VAN DOREN, CARL. "The Spring Lesson: A Review of Sinclair
        Lewis's Elmer Gantry," in College Readings in Contemporary
        Thought. Edited by Kendall B. Taft, John Francis McDermott,
        and Dana O. Jensen. Boston: Houghton Mifflin,
        pp. [521]-23.
              Reprint of 1927.39.

27   _____. "Zenith Meets Europe." Nation, 128 (3 April), 400-401.
              Following a long line of novels about Americans in Eu-
        rope, Dodsworth adds little to that tradition. What is new
        is that Lewis creates a protagonist with real "dignity" and
        clearly sympathizes with him. He has gone beyond his ear-
        lier satire to achieve "a depth and force which make [this
        novel] stand out from the comic documents. . . ."

1930

1   ANDERSON, MARGARET C. My Thirty Years' War. London: Knopf,
        pp. 76-79.
              Relates meeting Lewis in New York and later in Chicago.
        Lewis attacked Anderson's standards for the Little Review
        as too effete. Five years after its publication, Anderson
        read Main Street, which is "faithful and insignificant"
        photography completely lacking in art. "A great book is
        always based on the difference between its protagonist and
        the other characters" and Main Street fails this test.

2   ANDERSON, SHERWOOD. "Cotton Mill." Scribner's Magazine, 88
              Criticizes Lewis's one-sided reporting in his pamphlet
        Cheap and Contented Labor.

3   ANON. "Another Winner." Outlook and Independent, 156
        (19 November), 446-47.
              Lewis's refusal of the Pulitzer Prize and his acceptance
        of the Nobel Prize have caused some writers to suggest he
        is hypocritical. This controversy should not obscure his
        achievement as first American author to win the Nobel
        Prize.

4   ANON. "Babbitt Abroad." Commonweal, 13 (19 November), 61.
              "Satirists and muckrakers" such as Lewis, Theodore
        Dreiser, Upton Sinclair, and Jack London, stand out abroad
        among American creative writers, perhaps because they pre-
        sent a "seamy underside" of America that Europe would like
        to believe. Lewis's winning the Nobel Prize says little
        about his artistic success as a novelist.

5   ANON. "British View of Sinclair Lewis's Prize." <u>Literary</u>
     <u>Digest</u>, 107 (6 December), 19.
          Quotes <u>Manchester Guardian</u> to show that the British ap-
     prove Lewis's receiving the Nobel Prize.

6   ANON. "The Nobel Prize for Literature: Goes to Sinclair
     Lewis for 'Babbitt.'" <u>Publishers Weekly</u>, 118 (8 November),
     2197.
          Lewis's Nobel Prize reflects his great popularity in Eu-
     rope, where his works are available in German, Swedish,
     Polish, Hungarian, Danish, Norwegian, Czech, French, Dutch,
     Spanish, Italian, and Hebrew. Lewis rejected a Pulitzer
     Prize, which he did not respect, in 1926, but accepted the
     Nobel Prize because it marks genuine "excellence" and not
     narrow political considerations.

7   ANON. "Paul Morand Looks at Sinclair Lewis." <u>Living Age</u>, 338
     (15 April), [253]-54.
          Morand hails the translation of <u>Babbitt</u> into French,
     comparing Lewis to Flaubert. Lewis's goal is to liberate
     America from the constraints and prejudices that have held
     it back from achieving its maximum potential.

8   ANON. "Sinclair Lewis." <u>Nation</u>, 131 (19 November), 544.
          Lewis clearly deserves the Nobel Prize: "more than any
     other writer of equal or lesser eminence he has set down
     the spirit of America."

9   ANON. "Sinclair Lewis Struts his Stuff." <u>Literary Digest</u>,
     107 (27 December), 13-15.
          Excerpts from Lewis's Nobel Prize address and a sampling
     of favorable and unfavorable reactions to it in the Ameri-
     can press.

10   ANON. "Skoal for 'Red' Lewis." <u>Literary Digest</u>, 107
     (22 November), 16-17.
          Favorable comment on Lewis's being awarded the Nobel
     Prize and excerpts from favorable newspaper editorials.

11   BRACE, ERNEST. "Cock, Robin & Co., Publishers." <u>Commonweal</u>,
     13 (10 December), 147-49.
          <u>Main Street</u> was "as far reaching in the influence upon
     the popular ideals and ideas of the author's countrymen and
     upon publishing as 'Ulysses' has been upon the methods of
     contemporary fiction." Lewis produced a best-seller by
     finding scandals in the most homey American settings.
     Everyone had to read <u>Main Street</u> to assure himself he was
     not like its characters.

1930

12   CABELL, JAMES BRANCH. "Goblins in Winnemac: A Note as to
     Sinclair Lewis," in his Some of Us: An Essay in Epitaphs.
     New York: Robert M. McBride, pp. 59-73.
          Reprint, with minor textual variants, of 1930.13.

13   _____. "A Note as to Sinclair Lewis." American Mercury, 20
     (August), 394-97.
          Lewis does not accurately portray America, as some
     think, but presents a Dickensian view. Unlike Dickens,
     though, he gives us heroes who are unable to win out over
     the difficulties they encounter. Despite his distortions,
     Lewis creates enjoyable books, and his world is as real as
     that around us. Reprinted 1930.12.

14   [CANBY, HENRY SEIDEL]. "Sinclair Lewis." Saturday Review of
     Literature, 7 (22 November), [357].
          Considerable controversy has followed Lewis's Nobel
     Prize. While it would have been nice for an optimist like
     Emerson to be the first American to win the prize, postwar
     times call for a satirical reexamination of America, and
     Lewis "of all our writers has given the imagination brood-
     ing over those times the most to feed upon." Incorporated
     into 1931.16.

15   GIBBS, SIR PHILIP. "The Americans Best Known to Europe." New
     York Times Magazine, 79 (16 March), 7, 19.
          Lewis mentioned as the one American author with a world
     reputation.

16   KARLFELDT, ERIK AXEL. "Why Sinclair Lewis Got the Nobel
     Prize," in Why Sinclair Lewis Got the Nobel Prize and Ad-
     dress by Sinclair Lewis before the Swedish Academy. Trans-
     lated by Naboth Hedin. New York: Harcourt, Brace,
     pp. 1-8.
          Address by the Permanent Secretary of the Swedish Acad-
     emy at the Nobel Festival, 12 December 1930. Discusses
     Main Street, Babbitt, Arrowsmith, Elmer Gantry, and Dods-
     worth as evidence of Lewis's versatility. Though Lewis is
     a critic of America, he loves characters such as Babbitt,
     and his criticism is offered in the hope that his country
     will profit by it. Lewis is a "pioneer" in a land which is
     still in its "adolescence." Reprinted 1931.27, 1933.20,
     and in TCIA, 1968.4.

17   McCOLE, CAMILLE. "The Future Significance of Sinclair Lewis."
     Catholic World, 132 (December), [314]-22.
          Overview of Lewis's career from Our Mr. Wrenn to Dods-
     worth, concluding that Lewis has already done his best work

and seems destined for a decline unless he can transcend
his earlier dependence on satire and caricature.

18   MAINSARD, JOSEPH. "Les Américains d'après S. Lewis." Études,
      211 (14 April), 23-47.
          Discusses plot and characters of Babbitt, Arrowsmith,
      Elmer Gantry, and Dodsworth. "Lewis is, in reality, a
      prophet who reproves the aberrations of Israel; he over-
      turns the golden calf and searches, across deserts, for the
      road to a land of salvation." In French.

19   PALMER, RAYMOND H. "The Nobel Jury Judges America." Chris-
      tian Century, 47 (26 November), 1448-50.
          While Lewis has been honored by the Nobel Prize, America
      has not. In spite of Lewis's unpleasant manner, it is time
      the country listened to his valid criticism.

20   PARRINGTON, VERNON L. "Sinclair Lewis: Our Own Diogenes," in
      his Main Currents in American Thought: 1860-1920. Vol-
      ume 3. New York: Harcourt, Brace, pp. 360-69.
          Reprint of 1927.26.

21   PATTEE, FRED LEWIS. "Revolt from the Frontier," in his The
      New American Literature: 1890-1930. New York and London:
      Century, pp. 338-45.
          Lewis's career built up slowly from Our Mr. Wrenn to
      Main Street and Babbitt, where it reached a high point.
      After that Lewis began his decline, growing more mechanical
      in his satire and careless in his craftsmanship.

22   PHELPS, WILLIAM LYON. "Men Now Famous." Delineator, 117
      (September), 17, 94.
          Memories of Lewis (among others) as a Yale undergrad-
      uate by one of his former professors. Lewis changed little
      from his Yale days except for mellowing somewhat. "His
      satires are born of a passionate desire to make the world
      better. . . ."

23   RUSSELL, FRANCES THERESA. "The Growing Up of Sinclair Lewis."
      University of California Chronicle, 32 (July), 319-24.
          With Dodsworth "Lewis seems at last to have shed his
      literary adolescence." In "style, characterization, and
      theme," it is superior to anything he has done before. No
      longer content with facile satire, Lewis is calmer, more
      philosophical, as Sam Dodsworth attempts to find meaning
      in life.

1930

24 SLOSSON, PRESTON WILLIAM. "The Mind of a Nation," in his The
    Great Crusade and After. Volume 12 in A History of Ameri-
    can Life in Twelve Volumes. Edited by Arthur M. Schles-
    inger and Dixon Ryan Fox. New York: Macmillan, pp. 418-19.
        To a historian, Main Street is "the most important book
    written in the United States in the postwar decade," and
    Lewis followed this success with Babbitt. An excellent
    "journalist" who engaged in a literary version of "muck-
    raking," Lewis did make America examine its values.

25 STEINER, ARPAD. "Sinclair Lewis in German." Curme Volume of
    Linguistic Studies, Language Monographs of the Linguistic
    Society of America. Baltimore, Maryland: Waverly Press,
    pp. 134-40.
        Studies translation errors in German editions of Bab-
    bitt, Arrowsmith, The Job, and The Man Who Knew Coolidge.
    Translators are particularly weak in finding equivalents
    for Lewis's colloquialisms and slang.

                            1931

1   ANON. "'Arrowsmith' as a Movie." Outlook and Independent,
    159 (23 December), [515]-16.
        Lewis approves of the movie version of Arrowsmith.

2   ANON. "Do We Love Shaw's Abuse?" Literary Digest, 108
    (3 January), 17.
        Reprints George Bernard Shaw's letter defending Lewis's
    Nobel Prize speech. First printed in New York Times.

3   ANON. "In the Bookmarket." Publishers Weekly, 119 (4 April),
    1793.
        Doubleday, Doran will publish Lewis's next novel as he
    has left Harcourt, Brace.

4   ANON. "Lewis Declares Independence." Literary Digest, 109
    (9 May), 18-19.
        Reports a speech in which Lewis says American writers
    should sever ties with English literature. The London
    Morning Post disapproved and said the two literatures have
    a single tradition.

5   ANON. "Not on Fire." Commonweal, 15 (11 November), 32.
        Lewis's recent speech "A World on Fire" at Brooklyn In-
    stitute of Arts and Sciences certainly showed that he was
    not on fire himself. Where once he had "verve" and "fight-
    ing impact of expression," he now displays "tepid banality."

6   ANON. "Sinclair Lewis." Publishers Weekly, 119 (11 April),
      1900-1901.
            Lewis joins Doubleday. Details on royalties, adver-
      tising.

7   ANON. "Slap! Slap!" Literary Digest, 109 (11 April), 15-16.
            Reviews story of Dreiser's slapping Lewis's face and
      samples reactions of the press.

8   BECKER, MAY LAMBERTON. "The Reader's Guide." Saturday Re-
      view of Literature, 7 (16 May), 838.
            Lists Lewis's novels from Our Mr. Wrenn to The Man Who
      Knew Coolidge.

9   BELLESSORT, ANDRÉ. "Littérature Étrangère: États-unis:
      Sinclair Lewis." Le Correspondant, 324 (10 July),
      [119]-28.
            Lewis contradicts previous depictions of America (as in
      Wharton's House of Mirth and Age of Innocence) by present-
      ing a more realistic view. In Lewis novels, especially
      Babbitt, one gets the idea that in America, individualism
      is mass-produced like Ford cars. Dodsworth is a stronger
      novel and more irritating; it is a good picture of American
      life in the upper-class family. Arrowsmith is an accurate
      though satiric picture of medicine. In French.

10   BINSSE, HARRY LORIN and JOHN J. TROUNSTINE. "Europe Looks at
      Sinclair Lewis." Bookman, 72 (January), 453-57.
            While Americans recognize the Dickensian quality of many
      Lewis characters and situations, Europeans tend to take
      them literally. Because Lewis's picture of American char-
      acter and culture confirms the European view, Lewis has
      become immensely popular abroad and won the Nobel Prize.

11   BLANKENSHIP, RUSSELL. "Sinclair Lewis," in his American Lit-
      erature as an Expression of the National Mind. New York:
      Henry Holt, pp. 657-64.
            Capsule biography and critical survey of Lewis's work
      from Our Mr. Wrenn through Dodsworth. Lewis's weaknesses
      are his narrow range of literary devices and characters and
      his passion for causes. His strengths are keen intelli-
      gence and his ear for American idiom.

12   BOYD, ERNEST. "America's Nobel-Man." Vanity Fair, 36 (May),
      38.
            König-Rohde photo of Lewis in false whiskers, viewed as
      analogous to his hypocritical view of popular American au-
      thors. His true literary values are measured by royalty
      checks.

1931

13   BOYNTON, PERCY H.   The Rediscovery of the Frontier.   Chicago:
      University of Chicago Press, pp. 101-106, 182-[185].
          Lewis as critic of postfrontier America in Main Street
      and Babbitt, in which Babbitt wants to escape to a frontier-
      like existence.   However, in Dodsworth Lewis makes a posi-
      tive statement.   Dodsworth is a pioneer who survives, faces
      a new industrial and intellectual frontier, and will pre-
      vail over his difficulties.

14   BROUN, HEYWOOD.   "Hewing to the Line."   Woman's Home Companion,
      58 (February), 26.
          Reviews Lewis's career, emphasizing his methods of writ-
      ing.   His emphasis on facts makes him a realist, not a mere
      journalist.   In spite of superficial differences, his work
      derives from that of William Dean Howells.   Arrowsmith is
      Lewis's finest novel, for it penetrates the protagonist's
      character.

15   CALVERTON, V. F.   "Sinclair Lewis: An American Phenomenon."
      New Review (Paris), 1 (January-February), 46-52.
          Lewis cannot be compared with the great novelists of
      Europe.   He is a sort of photographer who received the
      Nobel Prize largely because of his country's growing polit-
      ical power and, paradoxically, because he made Americans
      the target of his sharpest satire.

16   CANBY, HENRY SEIDEL.   "Sinclair Lewis."   American-Scandinavian
      Review, 19 (February), [72]-76.
          Many Americans have resented Lewis's winning the Nobel
      Prize, but no other postwar American writer has produced a
      body of work to rank with Main Street, Babbitt, Arrowsmith,
      Elmer Gantry, and Dodsworth.   These five books "must be re-
      garded as one of the chief monuments of intellectual activ-
      ity in the post-war decade of the United States."   Article
      incorporates 1930.14.

17   DE CASSARES, BENJAMIN.   "Portraits en Brochette: Sinclair
      Lewis."   Bookman, 73 (July), 487-88.
          Humorous sketch of Lewis, concluding on a serious note:
      until now Lewis has "written the only authentic history ex-
      tant of the twentieth century American."

*18   DEMMIG, CHARLOTTE.   "Sinclair Lewis."   Der Gral, April,
      pp. 637-43.
          Cited in Leary, 1954.10.

19   ERSKINE, JOHN. "American Business in the American Novel."
      Bookman, 73 (July), 449-57.
          General discussion of American business in fiction with
      specific references to Main Street, Babbitt, and Booth
      Tarkington's The Plutocrat. Lewis impresses Europeans,
      most notably the Nobel Committee, because he perceives
      business as a European does, not as an American.

20   FISCHER, WALTHER. "Sinclair Lewis, der Nobelpreisdichter."
      Neue Jahrbücher für Wissenschaft und Jugendbildung. Vol-
      ume 7. Leipzig and Berlin: B. G. Teubner, pp. 700-709.
          "Lewis deserves to be the representative American author
      because he delineates contemporary America most fully."
      Short biography. Early works were characterized by the
      feeling that life itself is a great adventure. Babbitt,
      who embodies the collective traits of the middle class, is
      a broader and deeper Mr. Wrenn. Gantry is, like Dreiser's
      weak man in An American Tragedy, sensual and ignobly am-
      bitious. Lewis attempts to bring America out of its pro-
      vinciality. In German.

21   GAUSS, CHRISTIAN. "Sinclair Lewis vs. His Education." Satur-
      day Evening Post, 204 (26 December), 20-21, 54-56.
          Popular biography of Lewis. Reproduces two pages from
      his notebooks and discusses his method of building a novel
      from notes, floor plans, maps, and outlines.

22   GRAEVE, OSCAR. "The Living Delineator." Delineator, 118
      (April), 4.
          Famous writers once employed by Butterick, including
      Lewis, who worked on the staff of Adventure.

23   GUHA-THAKURTA, P. "Mr. Sinclair Lewis." Calcutta Review, 38
      (February), 206-10.
          Lewis may deserve the Nobel Prize for his picture of
      American society, but he is as much a philistine as any of
      the people he depicts, and his art is essentially akin to
      journalism or advertising. Thus, as a social critic he is
      likely to have little effect.

24   HOLT, EDGAR. "The Novels of Sinclair Lewis." Bookman (Lon-
      don), 79 (January), [233]-35.
          Lewis's Nobel Prize calls for an evaluation of his fic-
      tion. His strong points are selectivity as a realist,
      sense of humor, "descriptive powers," and ability to treat
      American civilization. His defects are occasional monotony
      and difficulty in plotting. Overall, Lewis stands "among
      the great writers of the modern world."

1931

25 HÜLSENBECK, RICHARD. "Sinclair Lewis." <u>Living Age</u>, 339
    (January), [479]-82.
        Translated from <u>Literarische Welt</u> (Berlin Literary Week-
    ly). Lewis's great power as a novelist is not style but
    extraordinarily keen observation and range and breadth of
    his fictional world. He treats all levels of America and
    its problems.

26 JONES, HOWARD MUMFORD. "Mr. Lewis's America." <u>Virginia Quar-
    terly Review</u>, 7 (July), [427]-32.
        The Nobel Prize Edition of his novels (<u>Main Street</u>, <u>Bab-
    bitt</u>, <u>Arrowsmith</u>, <u>Elmer Gantry</u>, <u>Dodsworth</u>) shows just how
    little growth Lewis exhibits. He repeats himself over and
    over in the 2000 pages, always in his distinctive "staccato
    style." "As documents these books are brilliant and su-
    perb. As great novels they trouble the literary con-
    science." Only in certain characters, which remind the
    reader of Dickens's characters, does Lewis really show an
    impressive ability.

27 KARLFELDT, ERIK AXEL. "Sinclair Lewis and the Nobel Prize."
    <u>Saturday Review of Literature</u>, 7 (10 January), 524-25.
        Reprint of 1930.16.

28 [KUNITZ, STANLEY J.] "Dilly Tante," editor. "Lewis, Sinclair."
    <u>Living Authors: A Book of Biographies</u>. New York: H. W.
    Wilson, pp. 224-26.
        Summarizes Lewis's background, biographical facts, ca-
    reer and personality.

29 LEWIS, GRACE HEGGER. <u>Half a Loaf</u>. New York: Horace Live-
    right, 392 pp.
        Novel based on Lewis's first marriage. Lewis is repre-
    sented by a character named Timothy Hale, Grace by Susan
    Brooke Hale.

30 MENCKEN, H. L. "Sinclair Lewis." <u>Vanity Fair</u>, 35 (January),
    48.
        Caricature of Lewis by William Cotton. Mencken gloats
    over Lewis's Nobel Prize.

31 MORGAN, LOUISE. "Sinclair Lewis," in her <u>Writers at Work</u>.
    London: Chatto and Windus, pp. 17-26.
        Lewis's work habits as he described them in an inter-
    view. He had to beware his "facile" writing and make him-
    self get beneath the surface; he described his planning,
    including the use of maps and floor plans, and claimed he

never took notes. When working on a novel, he did little else, but alternated these periods with periods of relative inactivity.

32 MUMFORD, LEWIS. "The America of Sinclair Lewis." Current History, 33 (January), 529-33.
   Lewis is one of "six or seven" Americans who might have been considered for the Nobel Prize, but not the most deserving. His work, though valuable in pointing out American foibles, is deficient in imagination. He is not capable of creating literature on the scale of Melville's, Hawthorne's, or James's works. However, his American characters correspond closely to the Europeans' concept of Americans, and the award thus has political overtones. Reprinted 1932.12 and in SL:CCE, 1962.14.

33 PHELPS, WILLIAM LYON. "As I Like It." Scribner's Magazine, 89 (March), 325-28.
   Although some very distinguished authors (Tolstoy, Ibsen, Strindberg, Hardy, Twain) have not been awarded the Nobel Prize, the choice of Lewis was a sound one. Lewis's acceptance speech, while hyperbolic in some statements, should be a positive influence on American literature.

34 ROURKE, CONSTANCE. "Round Up," in her American Humor. New York: Harcourt, Brace and World, pp. 283-86.
   Lewis is not so much a novelist as a "fabulist." He is almost alone among twentieth-century novelists in his creation of unique and colorful American types and scenes. Reprinted in SL:CCE, 1962.14.

35 ROZ, FIRMIN. "Les Littératures Étrangères: M. Sinclair Lewis et le Nouveau Roman Américain." Revue Bleue, politique et littéraire, 69 (17 January), 55-59.
   Lewis practices what might be called a new realism in that, instead of the smiling aspects of American life, he depicts the cruelties of industrial civilization. Illustrated by examples from Main Street, Babbitt, and, more briefly, Lewis's other works. In French.

36 SHERWOOD, R. E. "Literary Sign-Posts: Is the Nobel Prize an Insult?" Scribner's Magazine, 89 (January), 11-12.
   The Nobel Prize committee was wise to select Lewis, who is the most "representative" American author they could have chosen, though he may not be the most artistic.

1931

37   THOMPSON, DOROTHY. "At the Court of King Gustaf." Pictorial
      Review, 32 (April), 17, 45, 50, 52.
            Account and photos of the Lewises' trip to Sweden to ac-
      cept the Nobel Prize.

*38   VIERECK, GEORGE SYLVESTER. "The Ghost of Jack London." Lib-
      erty, 7 (10 October), 15-16, 18.
            According to Hendricks and Shepard (1965.8), a "sensa-
      tional" but "false" article which asserted that Lewis had
      served as a ghost-writer for London, based on the actual
      fact that Lewis had sold twenty-seven plots to London.

                              1932

1   ANON. "Elmer Gantry in French." Living Age, 342 (April),
      186.
            Translates part of a review of Elmer Gantry published
      in Candide. Lewis shows that American materialism is not
      so serious as the abuses practiced in the name of religion,
      yet materialism is the basis of Gantry's religion.

2   ANON. "'Red' Lewis." Vanity Fair, 39 (December), 21.
            Steichen photo and brief profile of Lewis: "bon vivant,
      mime," and author of "calculating novels on the graceless
      foibles of our domestic life."

3   ANON. "What is the Meaning of Life?" Literary Digest, 114
      (5 November), 20, 22.
            One of the celebrities responding, Lewis answers that
      religion is not needed to make life worthwhile.

4   BEACH, JOSEPH WARREN. The Twentieth Century Novel: Studies
      in Technique. New York: Appleton-Century-Crofts,
      pp. 263-66.
            Brief comparison of Babbitt with John Galsworthy's The
      Man of Property. Lewis's satire "is of a drier, purer
      brand" than Galsworthy's, not so elegant, yet "more sharp-
      edged."

5   BENNETT, ARNOLD. The Journal of Arnold Bennett. New York:
      Viking Press, pp. 755-56, 939-40, 1008.
            Memories of Lewis's impersonations and improvisations.
      Praise for Elmer Gantry.

*6   CABELL, JAMES BRANCH. Sinclair Lewis: A Critical Essay.
      With foreword by Harvey Taylor. New York: Author.
            Cited in Van Doren, 1933.30.

7   CALVERTON, V. F. "From Sectionalism to Nationalism," in his
     The Liberation of American Literature. New York: Charles
     Scribner's Sons, pp. 430-33.
         Although Lewis does not penetrate far beneath the sur-
     face, "in a minor sense he has written the saga of the
     American petty bourgeoisie of the small towns and upstart
     cities of the West." His novels are "American to the core."

8   [FISHBEIN, MORRIS]. "Arrowsmith: Medical Novel by Sinclair
     Lewis Satisfactorily Filmed." Hygeia, 10 (March), 225.
         Reviews the planning and writing of the novel and Paul
     de Kruif's part in it. Prints a letter from Lewis to Fish-
     bein. Well cast, the film covers the novel's high points.

9   FORSTER, E. M. Sinclair Lewis Interprets America. Harvard
     Press, 5 pp.
         Lewis has made the American Midwest live for many read-
     ers to whom America was previously a vast mystery with
     skyscrapers in New York and cowboys in the West. One hun-
     dred copies of this pamphlet were printed for Harvey Taylor
     for private distribution.

10   LEWISOHN, LUDWIG. "The Naturalist," in his Expression in
     America. New York, London: Harper and Brothers,
     pp. 492-513.
         Lewis should not have received the Nobel Prize because
     his work, which reached its peak with Arrowsmith, has de-
     clined so badly. While the author of Main Street and Bab-
     bitt might have deserved the prize, the author of Elmer
     Gantry, Mantrap, and Dodsworth did not. But at his best,
     Lewis captures his own "tragic age," and Babbitt and Arrow-
     smith are "two novels of manners, which ally him definitely
     and permanently with the masters in that kind." Reprinted
     1939.12.

11   MARBLE, ANNE RUSSELL. "Sinclair Lewis: The First American
     Winner of the Prize," in her The Nobel Prize Winners in
     Literature: 1901-1931. New York and London: D. Appleton,
     pp. 364-82.
         Treats Lewis's life and work (even Hike and the Aero-
     plane) up to 1930. Though Lewis may sometimes be unfair to
     the objects of his satire, his harshness stems from his
     earnestness.

12   MUMFORD, LEWIS. "The America of Sinclair Lewis," in Ventures
     in Contemporary Reading. Edited by Lewis Worthington
     Smith, Vincent Holland Ogburn, and Harold Francis Watson.
     New York, London: Longmans, Green, pp. 10-18.
         Reprint of 1931.32.

1932

13 NATHAN, GEORGE JEAN. "Literary Personalities: 1. Sinclair
Lewis," in The Intimate Notebooks of George Jean Nathan.
New York: Alfred A. Knopf, pp. 8-21.
Anecdotes emphasize Lewis as clown and mimic, trying out
roles and speeches he would later use in Babbitt and Elmer
Gantry. However, the usually manic Lewis could also be
"moody." Reprinted 1936.26 and 1952.12. Revised 1958.9.

*14 SALISBURY, WILLIAM. To Our Nobel Prize Winner; An Open Letter
to Mr. Sinclair Lewis. New Rochelle, N.Y.: Independent
Publishing, 20 pp.
Cited in Silhol, 1969.30.

15 WARD, A[LFRED] C[HARLES]. American Literature: 1880-1930.
New York: Lincoln Macveagh, Dial Press, pp. 117-20.
Lewis's work will live even after the abuses he satirized are forgotten. His best novel is Babbitt, where he
not only attacks the modern businessman's poverty of spirit, but creates his most unforgettable character.

16 WOOLF, S[AMUEL] J[OHNSON]. Chapter 24 in his Drawn from Life.
New York and London: Whitlesey House, pp. 312-20.
Reminiscence about Lewis, whom the author sketched in
1930. Lewis imitated a typical Main Street character.

1933

1 ADAMS, J. DONALD. "A New Novel by Sinclair Lewis." New York
Times Book Review, 29 January, p. 1.
Ann Vickers is one of Lewis's best novels mainly because
of the excellent portrayal of the title character, superior
to Carol Kennicott and Leora Arrowsmith. Unlike some Lewis
novels, this is not a tract, but a moving fictional
biography.

2 ANON. "Lewis Travels Far." Literary Digest, 115 (4 March),
18-19.
Samples reviews from mixed to unfavorable on Ann
Vickers.

3 ANON. "News of Books: Some of the Working Peculiarities of
Sinclair Lewis." New York Times, 9 March, p. 16.
Interview: Louis Florey, Lewis's secretary, tells how
Lewis outlines a novel, revises, and works, sometimes writ-
ing for days almost without stopping.

4   ANON. Review of Ann Vickers. Booklist, 29 (February), 181.
        A detailed picture of the modern woman--intellectually
    inclined and bold.

5   ARMSTRONG, ANNE. "New Novels." Saturday Review (London),
        155 (11 February), 143.
            In Ann Vickers Lewis successfully combines social criti-
    cism with the story of a modern woman: "one of the fairest,
    . . . most alive, . . . best books that I have read" for a
    long time.

6   BRANDE, DOROTHEA. "Four Novels." Bookman, 76 (February),
        188.
            Ann Vickers has so many feminist clichés that the reader
    may feel he's read it before. Lewis, who is at his best
    when he is satirical, admires his own character too much,
    but the book is redeemed by Ann, who eventually comes to
    life, and by Lewis's skill as a journalist, perhaps a great-
    er strength than has usually been recognized.

7   BRICKELL, HERSCHEL. "The Literary Landscape." North American
        Review, 325 (April), 383.
            Ann Vickers is a mixture of "vigor and zest" and "undi-
    gested lumps" of factual material on matters such as prison
    reform. Lewis is more a journalist than an artist, and
    only time will tell whether his reputation will endure.

8   C[OATES], R[OBERT] M. "Books: A Lady in Love." New Yorker,
        8 (28 January), 51-52.
            Sometimes a dull book, Ann Vickers has moments of bril-
    liance, and the character Lewis finally creates is "a pret-
    ty remarkable woman."

9   COWLEY, MALCOLM. "Tired Feminist." New Republic, 74
        (15 February), 22-23.
            Compared with Babbitt and Arrowsmith, Ann Vickers is
    fragmented and lacking unity. Lewis's protagonist fails to
    "move in a single direction" and Lewis doesn't know how to
    behave toward her. She "is a feminist and Lewis is really
    hostile toward feminism. Ann is a reformer and Lewis has
    learned to distrust reformers." The novel is a failure.

10 DELL, FLOYD. "Felix Fay," in his Homecoming: An Autobiogra-
        phy. New York: Farrar and Rinehart, pp. 343-44.
            Recalls how Moon-Calf was linked to Main Street by re-
    viewers but protests that, unlike Lewis, he meant to sati-
    rize his protagonist Felix, not the small town.

1933

11   DeVOTO, BERNARD. "Sinclair Lewis." Saturday Review of Liter-
      ature, 9 (28 January), [397]-98.
           Van Doren's reverent study Sinclair Lewis (1933.31) and
      Lewis's Ann Vickers have both been published by Doubleday,
      Doran. While Lewis may be, as Van Doren says, the best
      novelist of his time, Ann Vickers reminds us that he has
      been praised far more than he deserves. His supposed fi-
      delity to actual American speech is vastly overrated, and
      his novels are often clogged with long unrealistic speeches
      rather than conversation. Above all, the hate and anger in
      his books will keep them from achieving lasting fame. Re-
      printed 1934.24 and 1936.14.

12   DOWD, WILBUR J. "Morbid Sinclair Lewis." Forum, 89 (May),
      supplement, xiv-xv.
           Letter to editor agreeing with Hansen (1933.16) and
      further condemning Lewis as cynical, dreary.

13   EDGAR, PELHAM. "The Way of Irony and Satire," in his The Art
      of the Novel. New York: Macmillan, pp. 293-300.
           Babbitt is clearly organized, accurate, painstaking sat-
      ire, the sort of fiction Lewis writes best; it is his mas-
      terpiece, coming after the dull Main Street and before the
      less successful Arrowsmith. Dodsworth shows that Lewis may
      recover his old ability.

14   FISCHER, WALTHER. "Samuel Dodsworth bereist Europa." Nach-
      richten der Giessener Hochschulgesellschaft, 9 (June),
      31-42.
           For Lewis, interaction with a foreign country is an es-
      sential sociological element. Mr. Wrenn wanted to find his
      roots in England; Dodsworth goes to Europe to find himself
      and to lead his own life. Comments on earlier authors' and
      Lewis's observations of Europe and Europeans, especially of
      Germans. In German.

15   HAMILTON, COSMO. "Sinclair Lewis: The Anti-Elk," in his Peo-
      ple Worth Talking About. New York: Robert M. McBride,
      pp. [272]-79.
           Personal memories of Lewis dating to 1913, biographical
      summary from high school to 1920, and brief critical com-
      ments on novels from Main Street to Dodsworth. Lewis is
      not a satirist or caricaturist but a realist who shows
      "humbug" and "hypocrisy" as they really exist.

16   HANSEN, HARRY. "Fashions in Fiction." Forum, 89 (March),
      152-55.
           Lewis is more popular among readers than among the new
      generation of novelists, for he has not changed his art
      since Main Street. Younger writers are concerned with the
      art of the novel and with proletarian subject matter.
      Lewis has nothing to teach Faulkner, Virginia Woolf, or
      Dos Passos.

17   HAZLITT, HENRY. "Sinclair Lewis, Campaigner." Nation, 136
      (1 February), 125.
           Ann Vickers clearly surpasses Dodsworth. Like Arrow-
      smith it depends on a great deal of solid documentation,
      which is tied to a character more fully rounded than
      Lewis's "type" characters. Ann Vickers is also a "social
      document" on prison reform. His cause and fictional frame-
      work make this one of Lewis's better novels.

18   HICKS, GRANVILLE. The Great Tradition: An Interpretation of
      American Literature since the Civil War. New York: Mac-
      millan, pp. 230-31, 234-36.
           Lewis's biggest problem as novelist and thinker is that
      he "knows what he would like to destroy--provincialism,
      complacency, hypocrisy, intellectual timidity, and similar
      faults--but he has only the vaguest idea of what kind of
      society he would like to see in existence."

19   HOYT, BESSE T. "Sinclair Lewis, As Seen by an Average Read-
      er." MS.: A Magazine for Writers, 5 (December), 5.
           Lewis is disliked because he creates types rather than
      characters, and he feels contempt rather than sympathy (as
      does James Cozzens, for example), for Main Street and his
      fellow man.

20   KARLFELDT, ERIK AXEL. "Why Sinclair Lewis Got the Nobel
      Prize," in This Our Day. Edited by J. M. Gillis. New
      York: Paulist Press, pp. 236-39.
           Reprint of 1930.16.

21   LeVERRIER, CHARLES. "La Femme affranchie, d'après M. Sinclair
      Lewis: Ann Vickers." La Revue Hebdomadaire, 42, no. 5
      (13 May), [228]-37.
           Surveys women in past Lewis works, but views Ann Vickers,
      a study of the position of contemporary woman in the United
      States, as marking important progress for the feminist
      movement. The novel's value is in the pieces of the mosaic,
      the little portraits rather than in the whole. In French.

1933

22   MacAFEE, HELEN. "The Library of the Quarter: Outstanding
       Novels." Yale Review, n.s. 22 (March), vi.
            Ann Vickers, though displaying Lewis's "quick, sure at-
       tack" and "gift for caricature," is less harsh than Main
       Street, probes character more deeply, and "gives more gen-
       erous credit to the good."

23   McS., J. Review of Ann Vickers. Catholic World, 136 (Febru-
       ary), 622-24.
            In Ann Vickers Lewis again shows his ability to ferret
       out the corrupt and the rotten in society. Having demol-
       ished the American family, business, clergy, and medical
       profession, he now attacks the social worker. "Persons un-
       used to horrid and filthy things had therefore better stay
       at a safe distance from this book. . . ."

24   MENCKEN, H. L. "A Lady of Vision." American Mercury, 28
       (March), 382-83.
            Ann Vickers is "partly very good, but mainly bad."
       Lewis takes his heroine too seriously and even when she
       cries out for satire, he lets her get away with her be-
       havior. Lewis hasn't used his "really extraordinary tal-
       ents" to best advantage.

25   PHELPS, WILLIAM LYON. "As I Like It." Scribner's Magazine,
       93 (April), 256.
            Ann Vickers is primarily an attack on American prisons
       and, like most of Lewis's satires, it tends to exaggerate.
       It does not rank with his best, but it "glows with
       vitality."

26   QUENNELL, PETER. "New Novels." New Statesman and Nation, 5
       (4 February), 133.
            Ann Vickers is a craftsmanlike effort, unremarkable ex-
       cept where Lewis exposes the horrors of Copperhead Gap
       prison.

27   RASCOE, BURTON. "The Old Sinclair Lewis with his Great
       Gifts." New York Herald Tribune Books, 29 January,
       pp. 1-2.
            Ann Vickers combines Lewis's painstaking realism with
       the sort of "thoughtful or philosophical" approach used in
       Arrowsmith so that the novel is "beautiful and terrible
       and . . . true."

28   REDLICH, MONICA.   "Fiction."   Spectator, 150 (3 February),
        160.
             Ann Vickers is "a great story, brilliantly done."

29   ROBINSON, SELMA.   "Masterpieces for Fare."   Colliers, 91
        (13 May), 22, 24.
             Favorite foods of famous persons, including Lewis.
        Photo.

30   ROSS, MARY.   "Portrait of a Modern Woman."   Survey Graphic, 22
        (February), 114-15.
             Ann Vickers, "published simultaneously in fourteen coun-
        tries and nearly as many languages," cannot be ignored:
        Ann is so real a creation.   Lewis is "one of our most sen-
        sitive and just novelists--a man who becomes a social crit-
        ic through his understanding of individuals" but who also
        lauds courage and magnanimity.

31   VAN DOREN, CARL.   Sinclair Lewis: A Biographical Sketch.
        With a bibliography by Harvey Taylor (pp. [77]-205).
        Garden City, N.Y.: Doubleday, Doran, 205 pp.   Reprinted
        Port Washington, N.Y.: Kennikat Press, 1969.
             Colorful biographical sketch of Lewis from boyhood to
        the early 1930s, and an examination of the principles in
        his Nobel Prize acceptance speech.   Appraises Lewis's fic-
        tion from Our Mr. Wrenn to Ann Vickers, which is one of the
        best novels.   Descriptive bibliography of works from Hike
        and the Aeroplane to Dodsworth, and miscellaneous items
        such as pamphlets.   Lewis's contributions to books and pe-
        riodicals through 1931 plus a brief bibliography of second-
        ary materials are included.

32   VELTE, F. MOWBRAY.   "Sinclair Lewis."   Modern Librarian, 3,
        no. 3 (April), 129-34, 136.
             Lewis's Nobel Prize puzzled many who disagree with the
        European view of Lewis as "possibly the greatest literary
        interpreter . . . of the existing American scene."   A re-
        view of Lewis's social background, career, attitudes, and
        important works suggests that his "analysis of the American
        scene is one sided and inspired by ill-will."   His style is
        journalistic rather than artistic; his novels have scarcely
        any plot.

33   WALDMAN, MILTON.   "Tendencies of the Modern Novel: III--
        America."   Fortnightly Review, 134 (December), [717]-25.
             Lewis, like Dreiser, is extremely critical of America,
        yet loves the subjects of his satire.   Main Street depicts
        the ugliness of a small town, but also finds interesting
        realistic characters.   Reprinted 1934.47.

1933

34   [WHITE, E. B.] "The Current Cinema." New Yorker, 9
        (7 October), 57.
            The movie "Ann Vickers" tames a rather "hot" novel and
        renders it bland but amusing entertainment.

35   WILLIAMS, MICHAEL. "Babbittry into Vickery." Commonweal, 17
        (22 March), 567-69.
            Ann Vickers is more like popular romances than Lewis's
        satirical novels of the 1920s. Ann has elements of the
        "Feminist Woman" but is really the sentimental heroine in a
        new guise. The novel may sell many copies, but its shal-
        low, amoral nature should be immediately apparent to read-
        ers of taste.

                                1934

1   ADAMS, J. DONALD. "A New Novel by Sinclair Lewis." New York
        Times Book Review, 28 January, pp. 1, 19.
            Unlike Ann Vickers, which does not seem as good upon
        "reflection" as when first published, Work of Art is a new
        success which will rank with Babbitt, Arrowsmith, and Dods-
        worth. Lewis "has assimilated his material here to better
        advantage" than in Arrowsmith. If the literary world need-
        ed a sign that Lewis has a bright future, Work of Art is
        that sign.

2   ANNAND, GEORGE. "A Map of Sinclair Lewis' United States as It
        Appears in His Novels with Notes by Carl Van Doren."
        [Doubleday].
            Map (23-1/2" x 17-1/2") printed to promote Lewis novels,
        especially Work of Art, which is praised in a blurb on the
        back of the map. From thirteen novels, Van Doren notes
        seventeen locations on the map, along with Lewis's imagi-
        nary state of Winnemac.

3   ANON. "How Sinclair Lewis Writes a Novel." Author and Jour-
        nalist (Denver, Colorado), 19 (May), 6-8.
            Traces the growth of Work of Art from preliminary notes
        through final draft. Includes facsimiles of notebook pages
        with notes, catalog of names, map of setting, outline of
        first chapter, and first page of final typescript.

4   ANON. "Idealist: Innkeeper-Dreamer, Hero of Lewis's New
        Novel." News-Week, 3 (27 January), 35-36.
            Lewis is "more of a reporter than story teller" but in
        Work of Art he shows a sense of humor and "a sympathy so
        strong that it sometimes verges on sentimentality."

5 ANON. "The Lewises/ Reporters at Large." <u>Vanity Fair</u>, 42 (March), 48.
   Steichen photo of Lewis and Dorothy Thompson; profile of their current activities.

6 ANON. Review of <u>Work of Art</u>. <u>Booklist</u>, 30 (February), 181-82.
   This story of a model hotel manager thoroughly explores hotel-keeping in America.

7 ANON. Review of <u>Work of Art</u>. <u>Forum and Century</u>, 91 (March), v.
   Unlike most Lewis novels, <u>Work of Art</u> is not particularly satirical. Lewis uses his reporting skill, and "any diligent reader ought to be able to run the Waldorf-Astoria."

8 ANON. "Sinclair Lewis, Reformer." <u>Scholastic</u>, 25 (6 October), 7.
   Brief sketch of Lewis's career as introduction to excerpt from <u>Ann Vickers</u> (pp. 6-7, 9 of this issue).

9 ANON. "Stage: The Curtain Rings up on Mr. Lewis's 'Dodsworth.'" <u>News-Week</u>, 3 (3 March), 34.
   Sidney Howard's dramatization is "a triumph for the leading players."

10 ANON. "Two American Plays: Superficial Culture and Propaganda." <u>Literary Digest</u>, 117 (17 March), 22.
    Reviews <u>Dodsworth</u> dramatization favorably.

11 ANON. "Who's Who in the News: Red." <u>Scholastic</u>, 24 (10 February), 17.
    Character sketch of Lewis and brief remarks on <u>Work of Art</u>, for high school audience.

12 BACON, PEGGY. "Peggy Bacon's Guillotine." <u>New Republic</u>, 81 (12 December), 132.
    From her book <u>Off with Their Heads!</u> A drawing of Lewis and brief description, with graphic details on the ravaged appearance of his face.

13 BENCHLEY, ROBERT. "The Theatre: Like Old Times." <u>New Yorker</u>, 10 (24 November), 30, 32.
    "Jayhawker" has a good story but goes "to pieces toward the end."

1934

14 _____. "The Theatre: Playwriting and Propaganda." <u>New Yorker</u>, 10 (3 March), 30, 32.
Sidney Howard's dramatization of <u>Dodsworth</u> is "straightforward and honest," a "darned good" play.

15 BENÉT, WILLIAM ROSE. "The Earlier Lewis." <u>Saturday Review of Literature</u>, 10 (20 January), 421-22.
Account of Benét's friendship with Lewis: their days at Yale, at Carmel, and later when they lived near each other on Long Island. Reprinted 1957.3.

16 BRANDT, GEORGE. "Manhattan Offers: Outstanding Plays." <u>Review of Reviews</u>, 89 (April), 48.
"Intelligent adaptation, direction, and acting" make Sidney Howard's dramatization of <u>Dodsworth</u> succeed as well as its original.

17 BRICKELL, HERSCHEL. "The Literary Landscape." <u>North American Review</u>, 237 (April), 376-77.
<u>Work of Art</u> is currently more popular than it deserves to be, flawed as it is by "bad writing, the thinnest kind of characterization, and a manipulated plot."

18 CALDWELL, CY. "To See or Not to See." <u>New Outlook</u>, 163 (April), 44.
"Dodsworth" is interesting but not moving, primarily because the episodes are so numerous as to be too brief. The excellent cast overcomes this feature and the play is well worth seeing.

19 CALVERTON, V. F. "Sinclair Lewis: The Last of the Literary Liberals." <u>Modern Monthly</u>, 8 (March), 77-86.
<u>Ann Vickers</u> and <u>Work of Art</u> show that Lewis is unable to change with the times, to emphasize the social issues important now. Thus, he is working on dead issues in the last two novels. The superficial nature of his art was always apparent; he was too much the photographer, and his characterization was shallow. Lewis's strongest point was satire for its own sake, not for the sake of reform.

20 CANBY, HENRY SEIDEL. "Sinclair Lewis's Art of Work." <u>Saturday Review of Literature</u>, 10 (10 February), [465], 473.
"A piece of sheer virtuosity" similar to <u>The Man Who Knew Coolidge</u>, <u>Work of Art</u> depends not on character or plot, but on Lewis's ability to handle factual material about hotel-keeping. It is a tribute to his skill that the book is a success despite its difference from conventional fiction.

21   CODMAN, FLORENCE. "Objet d'Art." Nation, 138 (31 January),
        134-35.
            Work of Art is one of Lewis's "biographical romances"
        and, like most of its kind, is less successful than his
        satires. A great deal of factual material is incorporated
        but poorly digested, and the characters who could give it
        life never become believable.

22   C., S. M. Review of Work of Art. Canadian Forum, 14 (April),
        276-77.
            Work of Art is obviously the work of a master story-
        teller, but not as good as Dodsworth. Lewis is too heavy-
        handed in his satire of Ora Weagle, and relies more than
        ever on mere reproduction of slang.

23   DAVIS, ELMER. "Sinclair Lewis's Hick of Genius." Saturday
        Review of Literature, 10 (27 January), [433], 437.
            Work of Art is not as great as Arrowsmith yet "contains
        a maximum of the things Lewis does well and a minimum of
        the things he does badly." Lewis can afford to publish
        such lesser books because in the past he has done great
        work by which he may be judged.

24   DeVOTO, BERNARD. Review of Lewis's Ann Vickers and Carl Van
        Doren's Sinclair Lewis in Designed for Living: An Antholo-
        gy Drawn from the Saturday Review of Literature, 1924-1934.
        Edited by Henry Seidel Canby, et al. New York: Macmillan,
        pp. 213-21.
            Reprint of 1933.11.

25   DOBRÉE, BONAMY. "Fiction." Spectator, 152 (23 February),
        290.
            Work of Art is "entertaining reading" for its plot and
        its surprisingly interesting information on the hotel busi-
        ness. However, "every modern issue is completely evaded."

26   FADIMAN, CLIFTON. "Books: American Début of Ulysses--Mr.
        Lewis Takes His Ease in His Inn." New Yorker, 9 (27 Janu-
        ary), 61-63.
            Work of Art is interesting as fictionalized history of
        the American hotel, but will disappoint those looking for a
        novel as good as Arrowsmith or Babbitt.

27   FAY, BERNARD. "Portrait de Sinclair Lewis: L'Américain à
        Rebrousse-poil." La Revue de Paris, 41, part 3 (15 May),
        [401]-15.
            Lewis is himself "the American against the grain," the
        dissatisfied, malcontent American of whom he often writes.
        Book sales abroad show he is as popular in Europe as in the

1934

United States. Surveys Lewis's life, subjects of his major
novels, style and techniques. His goal is the impartial
view of the scientist as he faithfully reproduces American
people and their way of life and speaking. Questions Carl
Van Doren's biased opinion of Lewis's future significance
or literary reputation. In French.

28 GORDON, DONALD. "The Literary Lowbrow." <u>Saturday Evening
Post</u>, 206 (3 March), 86.
<u>Work of Art</u> is sometimes dull because of its unremark-
able protagonist and its excess detail about the hotel industry, but is worth reading because of Lewis's skill at
recording the American scene.

29 HARTWICK, HARRY. "The Village Virus," in his <u>The Foreground
of American Fiction</u>. New York: American Book Company,
pp. 250-81.
Relates <u>Main Street</u> to Lewis's earlier works and to its
tradition in English and American literature, most notably
<u>Damnation of Theron Ware</u>. Surveys Lewis's fiction after
<u>Main Street</u> up to <u>Work of Art</u>. The most frequent objects
of Lewis's satire are provincialism, materialism, "regi-
mentation," "dullness," and "smugness."

30 HAZLITT, HENRY. "Babbitt as Hero." <u>American Mercury</u>, 31
(March), 372-74.
<u>Work of Art</u> is better than <u>Dodsworth</u> or <u>Ann Vickers</u>.
Lewis depicts two brothers, an intellectual and a Babbitt,
and is clearly on the side of the latter. Unfortunately,
this novelty and Lewis's research into hotel-keeping do not
fully redeem the work, for its characters are too dull to
engage the reader throughout so long a novel.

*31 HICKS, GRANVILLE. Review of <u>Work of Art</u>. <u>New Masses</u>, 30 Jan-
uary, p. [25].
Reprinted in 1974.7. <u>Work of Art</u> is a pleasant book but
far less significant than Lewis's best works. Like <u>Free
Air</u>, it is largely aimed at entertaining the reader. Will
Lewis ever be able to write the labor novel he has planned
for the last five years?

32 HOWARD, SIDNEY. "A Postscript on Dramatization," in <u>Sinclair
Lewis's Dodsworth, Dramatized by Sidney Howard</u>. New York:
Harcourt, Brace, pp. vii-xvii.
Account of how Howard, who wrote a screenplay from
<u>Arrowsmith</u>, dramatized <u>Dodsworth</u>. The best part of the job
was working with Lewis.

33   ISAACS, EDITH J. R. "Swords Into Plowshares: Broadway in Re-
     view." Theatre Arts Monthly, 18 (May), 325-26.
          Sidney Howard's dramatization of Dodsworth is a "well-
     made, popular, realistic, unimportant drama" in which Fay
     Bainter as Fran cannot overcome the handicap of appearing
     in fourteen successive scenes from the Dodsworth marriage.

34   JONES, HOWARD MUMFORD. "Report on America." Virginia Quar-
     terly Review, 10 (April), 382-83.
          Artistically Work of Art is "no advance" over Lewis's
     earlier work, but thematically it is, for he writes sympa-
     thetically of a hard-working, average American and gives a
     hopeful view of life in America.

*35 KIMBROUGH, E. "Sinclair Lewis Place, Vermont." Home and
     Field, 44 (September), 44-45+.
          Cited in Reader's Guide to Periodical Literature, Vol-
     ume 9.

36   KRUTCH, JOSEPH WOOD. "Dodsworth." Nation, 138 (14 March),
     311-12, 314.
          Lewis's most successful novel makes an excellent play.
     While necessarily cutting a great deal from Dodsworth,
     Sidney Howard has "exercised an unfailing judgment in se-
     lecting the crucial moments."

37   _____. "Healthy Hawks and Sickly Eagles." Nation, 139
     (21 November), 600-601.
          Although badly constructed, "Jayhawker" is saved by
     Lewis's skill with dialogue and the strength of character-
     ization.

38   LUCCOCK, HALFORD E. "Post-War Realism," in his Contemporary
     American Literature and Religion. Chicago: Willett,
     Clark, pp. 72-81.
          The fact that Lewis does not present a balanced picture
     of life in Main Street or Babbitt should not obscure his
     achievement. The sociological study Middletown by Robert
     and Helen Lynd proves that Lewis knew what he was writing
     about in his satirical novel, Main Street. However, it is
     Lewis's rage that keeps him from becoming truly great, for
     his anger overcomes his artistic impulses.

39   LYNAM, HAZEL PALMER. "The Earliest Sinclair Lewis." Satur-
     day Review of Literature, 10 (14 April), 628.
          Letter to the editor, occasioned by Benét's article
     (1934.15). The writer knew Lewis in Sauk Centre when he
     was employed in her father's hotel. Lewis was a dreamy
     person who told the town children fascinating stories.

1934

40 MacAFEE, HELEN. "The Library of the Quarter: Outstanding
      Novels." Yale Review, n.s. 23 (March), x, xii.
        In Work of Art Lewis shows "lack of deftness" in han-
    dling the characters. Perhaps his feelings are too neutral
    compared with those toward Babbitt.

41 McS., J. Review of Work of Art. Catholic World, 138 (Febru-
      ary), 627-28.
        Work of Art is overly long; Lewis records every detail
    "yet does not pierce beneath the surface." The characters
    are "neither convincing nor attractive," and the book is
    "sordid and depressing."

42 MATTHEWS, T. S. "Including Sinclair Lewis." New Republic, 77
      (31 January), 343.
        As Lewis ages, his satire is losing its direction and he
    bears out the early opinion of this reviewer that "his rep-
    utation as a great American satirist was a great American
    joke." He has been dealing with Babbitt in different
    guises for so long that he defends the current version,
    Myron Weagle. Work of Art is "second rate" and "almost
    dull."

43 PATERSON, ISABEL. "Sinclair Lewis Writes in His Kindliest
      Mood." New York Herald Tribune Books, 28 January, pp. 1-2.
        A hotel-keeper who could be Babbitt's twin is treated
    sympathetically. Lewis's customary satire is absent, but
    his painstaking detail helps to make Work of Art interest-
    ing if not always lively.

44 PRITCHETT, V. S. "New Novels." New Statesman and Nation, 7
      (10 February), 194.
        Lewis offers "the low-down on art and hotels," but as
    fiction Work of Art is negligible.

45 SKINNER, RICHARD DANA. "Dodsworth." Commonweal, 19
      (16 March), 554.
        Although one must object to the approval of divorce,
    Sidney Howard has done an excellent job of adapting Dods-
    worth for the stage.

46 S., R. Review of Work of Art. Vanity Fair, 41 (February),
      60.
        Work of Art is dull and "pedestrian." Lewis follows a
    "formula" he has used often, with large amounts of factual
    journalism thrown in.

47 WALDMAN, MILTON. "America," in <u>Tendencies of the Modern Nov-</u>
      <u>el</u>. London: George Allen and Unwin, pp. 50-55.
            Reprint of 1933.33.

48 WOODWARD, W. E. "Profiles: The World and Sauk Center [sic]."
      <u>New Yorker</u>, 9 (27 January), 24-27; 9 (3 February), 24-27.
            Traces Lewis's career from small town doctor's son to
      the publication of <u>Main Street</u>. The more sensational stor-
      ries--daring God to strike him dead, Dreiser's slap, Lewis
      as mimic--are included.

49 WYATT, EUPHEMIA VAN RENSSELAER. "The Drama: Dodsworth."
      <u>Catholic World</u>, 139 (April), 86-87.
            Lewis's novel is effectively condensed into an "absorb-
      ing" play full of suspense; the cast, especially Walter
      Huston as Dodsworth, is excellent.

50 _____. "The Drama: Jayhawker." <u>Catholic World</u>, 140 (Decem-
      ber), 342.
            Brief summary of the play, which begins well but becomes
      "fairly static" in midpoint. No mention of Lewis.

51 YOUNG, STARK. "Three Serious Plays." <u>New Republic</u>, 78
      (14 March), 134.
            In dramatizing <u>Dodsworth</u>, Sidney Howard wisely cut much,
      yet the play's fourteen scenes convey the novel's essence.
      A notable difference is the absence of Lewis's ear for
      idiom.

1935

1 ADAMS, J. DONALD. "America Under the Iron Heel." <u>New York</u>
      <u>Times Book Review</u>, 20 October, pp. 1, 31.
            Although <u>It Can't Happen Here</u> sometimes strains the
      credulity of the reader, who may not believe how easily
      fascism can take over, it is meaningful and frightening.
      It may add little to Lewis's literary reputation, but shows
      he can still catch his readers up in excitement.

2 ANON. "Fascism: Nightmarish History that Hasn't Even Hap-
      pened Yet." <u>News-Week</u>, 6 (26 October), 38-39.
            While Lewis writes well on matters he has researched,
      "only nightmares can be held responsible" for <u>It Can't Hap-</u>
      <u>pen Here</u>.

1935

3   ANON. Review of <u>It Can't Happen Here</u>. <u>Booklist</u>, 32 (December), 110.
    "An angry, satirical picture" of American fascism, set slightly in the future.

4   ANON. Review of <u>Jayhawker</u>. <u>Booklist</u>, 31 (May), 293-94.
    A Civil War play set in Kansas.

5   ANON. Review of <u>Selected Short Stories of Sinclair Lewis</u>. <u>Booklist</u>, 32 (October), 42-43.
    Uneven collection, varying in "quality and interest."

6   ANON. "Transition: Honored." <u>News-Week</u>, 5 (26 January), 18, 19.
    Photo and brief note on Lewis's election to National Institute of Arts and Letters, which he denounced nine years previously.

7   BLACKMUR, R[ICHARD] P. "Utopia, or Uncle Tom's Cabin." <u>Nation</u>, 141 (30 October), 516.
    <u>It Can't Happen Here</u> is propaganda, not fiction, depending on "the urgency of the theme and the emotion of the author" to succeed. The book may not succeed even as propaganda--the reader may not believe it can happen here--largely because the liberals to whom it is addressed are too theoretical, too slow to take action. Reprinted in SL:CCE, 1962.14.

8   BRICKELL, HERSCHEL. "It Can't Happen Here." <u>North American Review</u>, 240 (December), 543-46.
    This propaganda novel was obviously written in haste and shows little imagination. Lewis has drawn heavily on the growth of fascism in Europe for his plot and on the biography of Huey Long for the character of his chief villain. Lewis too often speaks his own mind directly instead of dramatizing.

9   _____. "The Literary Landscape." <u>Review of Reviews</u>, 93 (January), 6-7.
    It Can't Happen Here is artistically flawed, but as a journalistic tract it is a "vivid" book.

10 CANTWELL, ROBERT. Review of <u>It Can't Happen Here</u>. <u>New Republic</u>, 85 (11 December), 152.
    Lewis oversimplifies fascism in <u>It Can't Happen Here</u>. If it were so blatant and repulsive, everyone would oppose it.

11   CROCKER, LIONEL. "Sinclair Lewis on Public Speaking." <u>Quar-</u>
     <u>terly Journal of Speech</u>, 21 (April), [232]-37.
          Lewis frequently uses a character's performance as a
     public speaker or his thoughts on public speaking to show
     something significant about his nature, as with Babbitt,
     Arrowsmith, Gantry, and Ann Vickers. "Is there not a dan-
     ger that public speaking may symbolize the emptiness of
     much of our culture, . . . our emphasis on form . . .
     rather than on substance?"

12   DAVIS, ELMER. "Ode to Liberty." <u>Saturday Review of Litera-</u>
     <u>ture</u>, 12 (19 October), 5.
          <u>It Can't Happen Here</u> is a frightening story though it
     starts very slowly. Lewis "shows you exactly the sort of
     people . . . who would find in fascism the outlet they have
     always wanted for envy, hatred, and malice." Newspaper
     stories today show that Lewis is not exaggerating the dan-
     ger of fascism much, only speeding up the timetable. Re-
     printed 1974.5.

13   DUFFUS, R. L. "Reviews of Recent Books: Free or Fascist."
     <u>Survey Graphic</u>, 24 (December), 620-22.
          <u>It Can't Happen Here</u> is "a book of power" which reminds
     readers that values now taken for granted are "worth fight-
     ing for." It shows "an Americanism trying to reassert it-
     self in terms of liberal democracy. . . ."

14   EATON, WALTER PRICHARD. "Clifford Odets and Others." New
     York <u>Herald Tribune Books</u>, 28 July, p. 15.
          <u>Jayhawker</u> reads well although it was a failure on the
     stage apparently because the playwrights attempted to com-
     bine "a huge canvas and a character study. . . ."

15   FADIMAN, CLIFTON. "Books: Red Lewis." <u>New Yorker</u>, 11
     (26 October), 83-84.
          <u>It Can't Happen Here</u> is "not only [Lewis's] most impor-
     tant book but one of the most important books ever produced
     in this country." While <u>Arrowsmith</u> was better written,
     this book is of much greater social import. Reading it is
     a "public duty."

16   _____. "Nobel Prizewinner." <u>New Yorker</u>, 11 (13 July), 56-58.
          Reading <u>Selected Short Stories of Sinclair Lewis</u>, it is
     hard to remember that Lewis won the Nobel Prize and actual-
     ly deserved it. It is bad enough to waste readers' time,
     but "it's hard to forgive him for wasting his own."

1935

17   GODFREY, ELEANOR. "Sinclair Lewis: Selected Short Stories."
       <u>Canadian Forum</u>, 15 (August), 333-34.
          Lewis's stories can only be described as "banal," but
       they might show scholars a Lewis who is, as he has some-
       times said, a "romantic." These stories, his earliest nov-
       el <u>Our Mr. Wrenn</u>, and his latest such as <u>Work of Art</u> sug-
       gest that perhaps the Lewis of the twenties was suffering a
       temporary disgust with mankind.

18   HAIGHT, ANNE LYON. <u>Banned Books: Informal Notes on Some
       Books Banned for Various Reasons at Various Times and in
       Various Places</u>. New York: R. R. Bowker, p. 71.
          The banning of <u>Elmer Gantry</u> in America and abroad.

19   HATCHER, HARLAN. "Sinclair Lewis," in his <u>Creating the Modern
       American Novel</u>. New York: Farrar and Rinehart, pp. 109-26.
          Discusses Lewis's career with emphasis on <u>Main Street</u>,
       which is treated in detail as a "revolt against the vil-
       lage" allied to E. W. Howe's <u>Story of a Country Town</u> and
       contradicting Zona Gale's <u>Friendship Village</u>. Other works
       by Lewis are surveyed briefly. While Lewis spoke effec-
       tively to the 1920s, he seems unable to find "the right
       tone or material to speak to the 1930's."

20   HICKS, GRANVILLE. "Sinclair Lewis--Anti-Fascist." <u>New
       Masses</u>, 14 (29 October), 22-23.
          "Lewis has discovered the great issue of his day and he
       has not been afraid to tackle it." A political tract, <u>It
       Can't Happen Here</u> "can no more be judged by ordinary stand-
       ards than could <u>Looking Backward</u> or <u>The Iron Heel</u>." How-
       ever, Lewis does not sufficiently emphasize "the capitalist
       basis of fascism," has needlessly limited the book's scope,
       and "demonstrates the helplessness of the liberal in the
       face of capitalist terror." Reprinted 1974.7.

21   ISAACS, EDITH J. R. "Without Benefit of Ingenue: Broadway in
       Review/ <u>Jayhawker</u>." <u>Theatre Arts Monthly</u>, 19 (January),
       9-10.
          A weak second act and "a spineless third" mar <u>Jayhawker</u>
       despite the playwrights' "fine play material and theme."

22   JACK, PETER MONRO. "Sinclair Lewis's First Collection of
       Short Stories." <u>New York Times Book Review</u>, 30 June,
       pp. 3, 17.
          These "baroque" stories will not enhance Lewis's reputa-
       tion. The collection was hastily edited, for Lewis had not
       even reread the stories until reading proof for the book.

23 JONES, HOWARD MUMFORD. "Mr. Lewis and the Primitive Ameri-
    can." <u>Saturday Review of Literature</u>, 12 (6 July), 7.
        Although <u>Selected Short Stories</u> shows Lewis "content
    with a simple and conventional technique," in his stories
    as in his longer fiction, Lewis's lively attitude and
    underlying optimism about life set him apart from most con-
    temporary writers. The volume is a success and shows Lewis
    "incapable of hate" and curiously romantic despite his sa-
    tiric bent.

24 LOVETT, ROBERT MORSS. "Mr. Lewis Says It Can." <u>New Republic</u>,
    84 (6 November), 366-67.
        While Lewis fails to make a fascist takeover seem proba-
    ble, he strikes some telling blows in <u>It Can't Happen Here</u>.
    Characterization is uneven: the group of important charac-
    ters that surround Jessup, who is believable and sympathet-
    ic, seem carelessly conceived, as are Jessup's daughter and
    mistress. For all its faults, the book is significant and
    timely.

25 NICHOLS, LEWIS. "The Recent Plays." <u>New York Times Book Re-
    view</u>, 28 July, p. 17.
        <u>Jayhawker</u>, recently published in book form, will please
    readers more than it pleased theater audiences.

26 PLOMER, WILLIAM. "Fiction." <u>Spectator</u>, 155 (8 November),
    790.
        <u>It Can't Happen Here</u> is a vigorous but "crude" warning
    about the dangerous possibility of American fascism. Lewis
    "does not write for people with any taste."

27 QUENNELL, PETER. "New Novels." <u>New Statesman and Nation</u>, 10
    (2 November), 644, 646.
        <u>It Can't Happen Here</u> is significant for its social con-
    tent but appears to have been written in great haste. It
    "lacks the clever craftsmanship that we should expect from
    the author of <u>Babbitt</u>. . . ."

28 RIDGWAY, WILLIAM H. "Sinclair Lewis, 'Fundamentalist,'" in
    his <u>"In God We Trust" (Cries the Little Red Cent) and Why
    Not!</u> Boston: W. A. Wilde, pp. 56-66.
        Ridgway, a Fundamentalist to whom Lewis alludes ironi-
    cally in <u>Babbitt</u>, tells of meeting Lewis in Los Angeles.
    Lewis asked him to reclaim his secretary, who had fallen
    from his religion. Ridgway obliged, and was rewarded by
    seeing "moisture under the [secretary's] eyes."

1935

29   ROBERTS, KATHARINE. "It Takes Experience." Colliers, 95
      (12 January), 16, 34.
           How the wardrobe of Fran, played by Fay Bainter in the
      play "Dodsworth," contributes to her characterization.

30   ROSS, MARY. "Hopeful Earnestness in Sinclair Lewis." New
      York Herald Tribune Books, 7 July, p. 4.
           Lewis's Selected Short Stories do not reflect the
      thoughtful Lewis of the novels, but as entertainment, they
      succeed admirably.

31   SHEEAN, VINCENT. Personal History. Garden City, N.Y.:
      Doubleday, Doran, pp. 279, 320-22, 331.
           Memories of Lewis's parodies at parties, writing habits,
      and willingness to help a younger writer.

32   S[LOPER], L. A. "Fascism in America: Book News of the Day."
      Christian Science Monitor (Atlantic Edition), 21 October,
      p. 18.
           It Can't Happen Here is not good literature. Lewis's
      irony is too heavy-handed and his characters fall into
      types. Yet as an attack on fascism, the book has a certain
      usefulness and power.

33   STOLBERG, BENJAMIN. "Sinclair Lewis Faces Fascism in the
      U.S." New York Herald Tribune Books, 20 October, pp. 1-2.
           It Can't Happen Here is Lewis's "best since Dodsworth."
      Even though he does not seem to understand the fine points
      of fascist ideology, he makes the picture of American fas-
      cism frightening.

34   STONE, GEOFFREY. "An Ironical Tract." Commonweal, 23
      (22 November), 107-108.
           It Can't Happen Here should be judged as propaganda not
      as art, but even on those terms, the book is disappointing.
      Lewis fails to "see into the actual issues concerned."

35   TAGGARD, ERNESTINE KEALOHA. "Sinclair Lewis, the Man Who Knew
      Main Street." Scholastic, 27 (21 September), 5, 12.
           Reviews Lewis's life and career through the 1930s, notes
      that since Arrowsmith his only major novel has been Dods-
      worth, and looks forward to It Can't Happen Here.

36   VAN DOREN, CARL. "Lewis," in his What Is American Literature?
      New York: William Morrow, pp. 118-22.
           Lewis is the most typical of American novelists although
      his books have stirred controversy. He is often ahead of
      his time, and when America catches up, it usually is forced
      to admit that he was right. Characterization is his strong
      point.

*37 _____. "The Real Sinclair Lewis." New York Herald Tribune
      Magazine, 17 February, pp. 5, 22.
         Unlocatable. Cited in Leary, 1954.10.

 38 VON HIBLER, LEO. "Sinclair Lewis und die amerikanische Wirt-
      schaft." Anglia, 59 (July), [448]-60.
         The romantic view of life which prevailed in America be-
      fore the Civil War has been replaced by a realistic and
      scientific view, and the new hero is the businessman. As a
      recorder of truth, Lewis reflects these views of the impor-
      tance of money and business. The Job, in particular, pre-
      sents the relationships between bosses and employees al-
      though Lewis is not a socialist or labor activist. Briefly
      surveys the types of business people in the other novels.
      In German.

 39 WALTON, EDITH H. "The Book Parade." Forum and Century, 94
      (December), vi.
         It Can't Happen Here is "about the most arresting and
      exciting book" Lewis has written. Despite a "vague and un-
      satisfactory" solution, Lewis makes the possibility of fas-
      cism in America real and terrifying.

 40 WEEKS, EDWARD. "The Meaning of Literary Prizes." Atlantic
      Monthly, 156 (October), 470-77.
         Reviews the history of literary prizes and summarizes
      Lewis's rejection of the Pulitzer and acceptance of the
      Nobel Prize. More often than not, prizes are awarded to
      deserving authors and inform the public about significant
      works.

*41 _____. Review of It Can't Happen Here. Atlantic Bookshelf,
      156 (December), 40.
         Listed in Book Review Digest, 1935. According to that
      annotation, It Can't Happen Here is judged mentally stimu-
      lating though not good fiction.

                               1936

  1 ANON. "Authors' League Protests Ban." Publishers Weekly, 129
      (7 March), 1076.
         Authors' League of America protests the movie industry's
      refusal to film It Can't Happen Here because it is contro-
      versial.

1936

2 ANON. "Four Best-Selling Personalities." <u>Literary Digest</u>,
       121 (11 January), 28.
           Personality sketch of Lewis and three other authors.

3 ANON. "Hollywood Tempest Breaks on 'It Can't Happen Here.'"
       <u>Publishers Weekly</u>, 129 (22 February), 900.
           Metro-Goldwyn-Mayer bought rights to <u>It Can't Happen
       Here</u>, but postponed filming, supposedly because of cost.
       Lewis claims MGM is suppressing the book because it fears
       controversy.

4 ANON. "'It Can't Happen Here' on the Stage." <u>Publishers
       Weekly</u>, 130 (5 September), 829.
           The Works Progress Administration Federal Theater Project
       plans to stage <u>It Can't Happen Here</u> in twenty-eight the-
       aters in thirteen American cities. Lewis and John C. Mof-
       fitt are adapting the novel, which has sold 100,000 copies.

5 ANON. "'It Can't Happen Here' Storm Continues Unabated."
       <u>Publishers Weekly</u>, 129 (14 March), 1174.
           Protests against MGM's failure to film <u>It Can't Happen
       Here</u> have made the book "almost a national by-word."

6 ANON. "Screen: 'Dodsworth' in Films As Good As the Novel and
       Play." <u>News-Week</u>, 8 (3 October), 34.
           Walter Huston is "flawless" as Dodsworth in this well-
       directed film.

7 ANON. "Stage: Lewis Drama Produced Simultaneously in 21 The-
       aters." <u>News-Week</u>, 8 (7 November), 40-41.
           Review of Lewis's career up to the Works Progress Admin-
       istration Federal Theater Project of "It Can't Happen
       Here," which is "a confused, disconnected job of play-
       writing."

8 ANON. "WPA, Lewis & Co." <u>Time</u>, 28 (9 November), 21.
           Traces development of <u>It Can't Happen Here</u> from novel to
       a play which is "serviceable and occasionally terrifying."

9 BOYNTON, PERCY H. <u>Literature and American Life</u>. Boston and
       New York: Ginn, pp. 769-71, 837-39, 851-52.
           Considers Lewis as critic of the intellectual narrowness
       of the Midwest in <u>Main Street</u> and <u>Babbitt</u>. With <u>Dodsworth</u>
       Lewis explores the positive side of the American character
       as Sam, unable to find new frontiers to conquer, finds "a
       new America within himself."

10 CANBY, HENRY SEIDEL. "Sex War," in his <u>Seven Years' Harvest:</u>
    <u>Notes on Contemporary Literature</u>. New York: Farrar and
    Rinehart, pp. 133-39.
       Reprint of 1929.6.

11 CANTWELL, ROBERT. "Sinclair Lewis." <u>New Republic</u>, 88
    (21 October), 298-301.
       Lewis has been amazingly prolific but also most uneven.
    If <u>Babbitt</u> is the best novel about American business, <u>Work</u>
    <u>of Art</u> is the worst. Lewis has done what other American
    writers have failed to do: he has set out to write a real
    cycle of novels. "For Lewis is the historian of America's
    catastrophic going-to-pieces--or at least of the going-to-
    pieces of her middle class--with no remedy to offer for the
    decline that he records; and he has dramatized the process
    of disintegration . . . in the outlines of his novels, in
    the progress of his characters, and sometimes . . . in the
    lapses of taste and precision that periodically weaken the
    structure of his prose." Reprinted 1937.2; in <u>SL:CCE</u>,
    1962.14; and 1964.6.

12 COLUM, MARY M. "Literature of Today and Tomorrow." <u>Scrib-</u>
    <u>ner's Magazine</u>, 100 (October), 66-69, 100.
       Lewis as realist in general discussion of changing nov-
    el. Portrait by E. H. Baker.

13 COWLEY, MALCOLM. "Nobel Prize Oration." <u>New Republic</u>, 88
    (19 August), 36-38.
       In giving the Nobel Prize to an American, the Academy
    recognized not only Lewis, but the growing importance of
    the United States. Like the award, Lewis's acceptance
    speech was a political document, praising those who had
    helped to end the genteel tradition and to declare the "new
    literary nationalism" of American literature. Lewis's in-
    sights about literature were remarkably sound.

14 DeVOTO, BERNARD. "<u>Ann Vickers</u> by Sinclair Lewis," in his
    <u>Forays and Rebuttals</u>. Boston: Little Brown, pp. [305]-314.
       Reprint of 1933.11.

15 FORSTER, E. M. "Sinclair Lewis," in his <u>Abinger Harvest</u>. New
    York: Harcourt, Brace, pp. 129-36.
       Reprint of 1929.10.

1936

16   FORSYTHE, ROBERT. "Let It Happen No More." <u>New Masses</u>, 18
        (10 March), 27-28.
            Protests the shelving of the film version of <u>It Can't</u>
        <u>Happen Here</u>. If it is ever filmed, "it will be the most
        blatantly patriotic, nationalistic" defense of democracy
        because Hollywood prefers innocuous films devoid of social
        consciousness.

17   GILLIS, ADOLPH and ROLAND KETCHUM. "Sinclair Lewis: Sati-
        rist," in their <u>Our America</u>. Boston: Little, Brown,
        pp. [34]-47.
            Brief biography and discussion of works from <u>Main Street</u>
        through <u>The Man Who Knew Coolidge</u>, for high school students.

18   HICKS, GRANVILLE. "Sinclair Lewis and the Good Life." <u>Eng-</u>
        <u>lish Journal</u>, 25 (April), 265-73.
            In the 1920s Lewis was preoccupied with the question of
        rebellion vs. conformity, a relevant topic for that decade,
        but he has failed to change with the times. Only <u>It Can't</u>
        <u>Happen Here</u>, which suggests that Lewis is regaining his
        former power, shows him to be aware of the real reasons why
        Americans cannot attain the good life: the capitalist sys-
        tem, to which fascism is related.

19   HUTCHINGS, WINIFRED. "Some Fiction of the Past Year." <u>Li-</u>
        <u>brary Journal</u>, 61 (15 November), 864-65.
            <u>It Can't Happen Here</u> effectively shows the stultifying
        results of regimentation under a dictatorship. Lewis's use
        of "homely detail" makes the situation seem all too pos-
        sible.

20   ISAACS, EDITH J. R. "Unwritten Plays: Broadway in Review."
        <u>Theatre Arts Monthly</u>, 20 (December), 930-31.
            "It Can't Happen Here" might have been a "stirring play"
        but is "a two-hour speech" and a "terrifying prophecy,"
        which ultimately does not move the audience.

21   JOHNSON, MERLE. <u>American First Editions: Bibliographic Check</u>
        <u>Lists of the Works of 199 American Authors</u>. Third edition.
        Revised by Jacob Blanck. New York: R. R. Bowker,
        pp. 287-89.
            Brief description of eighteen Lewis first editions,
        eighteen books and pamphlets which are in part by Lewis,
        and six items about Lewis.

22   LERNER, MAX. "Caliban on Main Street." Stage, 14 (December),
      78.
          "It Can't Happen Here" is "with minor qualifications,
      credible enough," though not as strong as the novel. While
      some question the wisdom of the Federal Theater's present-
      ing such a political play, fascism is dangerous enough to
      warrant strong countermeasures. Reprinted 1939.11.

23   MOSHER, JOHN. "The Current Cinema: The Man from Zenith."
      New Yorker, 12 (3 October), 61.
          Walter Huston's acting and Sidney Howard's screenplay
      provide a fine adaptation of Dodsworth.

24   MURRY, JOHN MIDDLETON. "The Hell It Can't." Adelphi, 11
      (March), 321-27.
          It Can't Happen Here effectively points out a serious
      danger to the world. Lewis seems to be the only writer in
      Anglo-American letters capable of seeing and depicting the
      fascist threat. "If only we had a man in England who could
      do the same for us!"

25   NATHAN, GEORGE JEAN. "Art of the Night." Saturday Review of
      Literature, 15 (28 November), 20.
          Lewis refuses to take the theater seriously though The
      Jayhawker and It Can't Happen Here suggest that he has
      promise as a playwright. Lewis has more ability "than
      nine-tenths" of contemporary American playwrights, but he
      needs to attend the theater, read modern drama, and study
      the principles of playwriting.

26   _____. "Three Friends: Lewis, O'Neill, Dreiser," in The
      Borzoi Reader. Edited by Carl Van Doren. New York:
      Alfred A. Knopf, pp. 579-89.
          Reprint of 1932.13.

27   PHELPS, WILLIAM LYON. "As I Like It: Mr. Lewis's Fourteenth
      Novel." Scribner's Magazine, 99 (January), 59-60.
          It Can't Happen Here is different from any of Lewis's
      earlier novels in that it is pure propaganda, skillful,
      but not truly moving.

28   QUINN, ARTHUR HOBSON. "Critics and Satirists--The Radicals,"
      in his American Fiction: An Historical and Critical Sur-
      vey. New York and London: D. Appleton-Century,
      pp. 660-69.
          Main Street and Babbitt show Lewis's strengths and weak-
      nesses as he piles up details and creates clever carica-
      tures but no lasting characters. In Arrowsmith he achieves
      a signficant character, and Dodsworth offers a sympathetic

1936

believable protagonist, but he descended to the use of
cheap sex in Ann Vickers and political sensationalism in
It Can't Happen Here. Lewis does not rank with other winners of the Nobel Prize.

29 SCHREIBER, GEORGES. Portraits and Self-Portraits. Boston:
    Houghton Mifflin, pp. 59-61.
        One paragraph biography, sketch by Schreiber, and
    Lewis's characterization of himself as essentially a
    "story-teller."

30 TAYLOR, WALTER FULLER. "Nationalism and the Cultural Battle:
    H. L. Mencken . . . and Sinclair Lewis . . .," in his A
    History of American Letters. American Literature Series.
    Edited by Harry Hayden Clark. Boston and New York: Ameri-
    can Book Company, pp. 382-90.
        Lewis's artistic development. In Main Street Lewis
    achieved satire but the novel's structure was weak. Bab-
    bitt was even more satirical but better planned. Arrow-
    smith continued Lewis's satiric vein and also showed where
    he put his faith--in science. In Dodsworth Lewis produced
    an international novel, his most mature work. Elmer Gantry
    and Ann Vickers represent steps backward.

31 THIERRY, JAMES F. When Roosevelt is Dictator--and How! A
    Fascist Prophecy . . . A Reply to "Red" Lewis's Novel "It
    Can't Happen Here." Brooklyn, N.Y.: Author, 16 pp.
        Responds to Lewis with a futuristic fable. Argues that
    it can happen here and suggests that Roosevelt can proclaim
    himself military dictator; makes specific predictions about
    how the dictatorship might operate.

32 VAN DOREN, CARL. Three Worlds. New York and London: Harper
    and Brothers, 317 pp. passim.
        Memories of Lewis in Van Doren's autobiography.

33 VERNON, GRENVILLE. Review of "It Can't Happen Here." Common-
    weal, 25 (13 November), 76.
        The novel had "some merit" but the play "It Can't Happen
    Here" is "unreal, undramatic, too long, and a bore." It
    shows the basic weaknesses of Lewis as creator of charac-
    ter once his witty narration is removed.

34 WYATT, EUPHEMIA VAN RENSSELAER. "The Drama: It Can't Happen
    Here." Catholic World, 144 (December), 338.
        Review of Federal Theater Project production of the
    play. Lewis's script creates incredible tension.

35 YOUNG, STARK. "Booth, Adelphi, Music Box." New Republic, 89
      (11 November), 50.
         While it is sometimes entertaining theater, "It Can't
      Happen Here" is too melodramatic, and as a sample of Ameri-
      can thought, "it is indeed damping." Lewis and John C.
      Moffitt should have done far more with intellectual issues.

<h2 style="text-align:center">1937</h2>

1   CALVERTON, V. F. "The Cultural Barometer." Current History,
      47 (October), 82-87.
         When "Dodsworth" was to be staged in Berlin, Lewis and
      Sidney Howard were asked to testify to their "Aryan puri-
      ty." Both replied that they were not sure they were Aryan
      and signed the reply "Sidney Horowitz and Sinclair Levy."

2   CANTWELL, ROBERT. "Sinclair Lewis," in Literary Opinion in
      America. Edited by Morton Dauwen Zabel. New York: Harper
      and Brothers, pp. 494-501.
         Reprint of 1936.11.

3   CLEATON, IRENE and ALLEN CLEATON. "A Reformer from Main
      Street" and "Fitzgerald, 7; Lewis, 7; Cabell, 12," in their
      Books and Battles: American Literature, 1920-1930. Bos-
      ton: Houghton Mifflin, pp. 14-18, 235-40.
         The genesis and reception of Main Street and the contro-
      versy which greeted Babbitt. Outlines Lewis's writing for
      the remainder of the decade and notes that he won the Nobel
      Prize after refusing the Pulitzer Prize for Dodsworth
      [sic].

4   DE VILLENEUVE, R. "Le Nationalisme de Sinclair Lewis." Mer-
      cure de France, 280 (1 December), 286-307.
         Lewis stands above other novelists in treating American
      society of the past fifty years. To know the Middle West,
      one must study the nine or ten novels of Lewis, "the su-
      perb chronicle, throbbing with life." Surveys the differ-
      ent American types represented in the novels. Carol Kenni-
      cott does not recognize the spirit of the midwesterners,
      who will increase the power and greatness of the country.
      In French.

5   FORD, EDWIN H. A Bibliography of Literary Journalism in
      America. Second edition. Minneapolis: Burgess Publish-
      ing, pp. 23-24.
         Lists Lewis's novels to 1934 and some critical and bio-
      graphical references.

1937

6   FORSYTHE, ROBERT. "Forsythe's Page: Mr. and Mrs. Sinclair
Lewis at Home." New Masses, 26 (28 December), 16.
    Satirical piece on the conflict of egos in the Lewis-
Thompson marriage. Reprinted as "Dottie and Red,"
1938.15.

7   _____. "Sinclair Lewis's Good Intentions." New Masses, 25
(30 November), 12.
    Lewis's recent lectures suggest that we need not choose
between communism and fascism. Like most lukewarm liberals, Lewis fails to see how serious the fascist threat is.

8   GRAY, JAMES. "The Minnesota Muse." Saturday Review of Literature, 16 (12 June), [3]-4, 14.
    Recent Minnesota writers have rejected narrow regional-
ism and proved themselves amazingly catholic. Writers such
as Lewis, F. Scott Fitzgerald, and Grace Flandrau have followed the lead of Charles Macomb Flandrau in producing
truly cosmopolitan works.

9   LOGGINS, VERNON. "Sinclair Lewis," in his I Hear
America. . . . New York: Thomas Y. Crowell, pp. 239-47.
    Examines Main Street, Babbitt, and Arrowsmith, and
classifies Lewis as a scientist like Arrowsmith. Lewis
diagnoses America's ills and hopes the country will cure
itself. His most severe fault is a tendency to interrupt
his serious writing for hack pieces such as Mantrap.

10   MULLER, HERBERT J. Modern Fiction: A Study of Values. New
York: Funk and Wagnalls, pp. 125-26, 225-26.
    Most of Lewis's novels display superficial realism, not
genuine insight. Thus, Main Street, unlike Madame Bovary,
is tied to its specific time and place. Only Arrowsmith
comes close to transcending this limitation.

11   PATTEE, FRED LEWIS. "The Nobel Lewis," in Essays in Honor of
A. Howry Espenshade: Contributed by His Colleagues. . . .
New York: Thomas Nelson and Sons, pp. 7-20.
    Reviews the tempest that followed Lewis's Nobel Prize
and attempts to explain why Lewis was selected, when so
many others had been passed over, by examining the criteria
implied in Karlfeldt's presentation speech (see 1930.16).
Lewis is a romanticist who envisions the world as it might
be; he and Eugene O'Neill, who received the 1936 Nobel
Prize, are leaders in a new American literature.

12   PAUL, ELIOT. "Hemingway and the Critics." Saturday Review of
     Literature, 17 (6 November), 3.
          Defends Hemingway against those who reviewed To Have and
     Have Not unfavorably, including Lewis, who "has never done
     anything mildly approaching Hemingway's least work."

13   WHARTON, DON. "Dorothy Thompson." Scribner's Magazine, 101
     (May), 9-14.
          Illustrated biographical article on Thompson, treating
     her courtship by and marriage to Lewis, and suggesting that
     she inspired him to write Ann Vickers and influenced It
     Can't Happen Here.

14   WHITE, GEORGE LEROY, JR. Scandinavian Themes in American Fic-
     tion. Philadelphia: University of Pennsylvania,
     pp. 85-87, 131, 135-38, 161, 168.
          Lewis depicts Scandinavian characters sympathetically,
     defends their right to their ethnic heritage, and shows the
     attitudes of other ethnic groups toward them in The Trail
     of the Hawk and Main Street.

                              1938

1   ADAMIC, LOUIS. "'Red' Lewis," in his My America. New York
     and London: Harper and Brothers, pp. 96-104.
          Lewis tentatively planned to write his labor novel using
     Adamic as technical advisor on the labor movement. Person-
     al reminiscences of Lewis at parties and in private, empha-
     sizing his insecurity.

2   ADAMS, J. DONALD. "A New Novel by Sinclair Lewis." New York
     Times Book Review, 23 January, p. 1.
          While It Can't Happen Here was not art, at least it was
     a stirring book, but The Prodigal Parents has wooden char-
     acters set in a plot that centers on an ineffective satire
     of the younger generation. Except for "an occasional sharp
     thrust," the book is an unalloyed failure.

3   ANON. "Authors of the Week." Saturday Review of Literature,
     17 (22 January), 21.
          Brief biographical note.

4   ANON. "People." Time, 32 (8 August), 33.
          Note on Lewis's first performance as Doremus Jessup in
     "It Can't Happen Here," Cohasset, Massachusetts.

1938

5   ANON. "Red Menace." Time, 31 (24 January), 61–62.
     The Prodigal Parents reverses several Lewis stands. He
     now defends the businessman he lampooned in Babbitt, and he
     attacks the left, which he seemed to favor in It Can't Hap-
     pen Here. A tedious novel.

6   ANON. Review of The Prodigal Parents. Booklist, 34 (1 Feb-
     ruary), 211.
     Lewis's latest novel reverses the theme of Babbitt.
     Fred Cornplow is believable and sympathetic, but his chil-
     dren are "puppets."

7   BERESFORD, J. D. "Five Novels." Manchester Guardian, 21 Jan-
     uary, p. 7.
     The Prodigal Parents defends a Babbitt type and attacks
     the younger generation. "A splendid story and a powerful
     commentary on modern life."

8   BROWN, JOHN MASON. "Dodsworth Dramatized," in his Two on the
     Aisle: Ten Years of the American Theatre in Performance.
     New York: W. W. Norton, pp. 174–77.
     Although Sidney Howard could not bring the sheer weight
     of Lewis's "factual detail" to the stage, his dramatization
     catches the "main points of the narrative" and the essen-
     tial mood and theme of the book. First published in New
     York Evening Post, 26 February 1934.

9   CALVERTON, V. F. "The Prodigal Lewis." Modern Monthly, 10
     (February), 11–13, 16.
     The Prodigal Parents is disappointing because it is a
     bad novel and because Lewis, who once "knew what concerned
     us and wrote about it in a way that was unforgettable,"
     has completely lost touch with the concerns of his country.

10   CHAMBERLAIN, JOHN R. "Literature." America Now. Edited by
     Harold Edmund Stearns. New York: Charles Scribner's Sons,
     pp. 42–44.
     In The Prodigal Parents Lewis takes another look at the
     Babbitt type in Fred Cornplow, but unlike the earlier nov-
     el, this one is a mere "tract" against the younger genera-
     tion and the left. Cornplow as hero and Gene Silga, the
     communist, as villain are equally shallow and unconvincing.
     The novel does document a disenchantment with the left that
     America was experiencing by 1938.

11   COLUM, MARY M. "Life and Literature." Forum and Century, 99
      (March), 146-47.
         The Prodigal Parents is an amusing book but is amusing
      as a comic strip rather than as a serious discussion of
      youth and communism.

12   COWLEY, MALCOLM. "George F. Babbitt's Revenge." New Repub-
      lic, 93 (26 January), 342-43.
         From Arrowsmith on, Lewis has been declining as a novel-
      ist. The Prodigal Parents has a Saturday Evening Post plot
      and wooden characters, and even Lewis's old gift of repro-
      ducing American speech seems to have failed him. The pro-
      tagonist is basically identical with Babbitt, but Lewis can
      no longer see Babbitt's failings. "A novel so stupid that
      the middle class won't read it."

13   DAVIS, ELMER. "From Babbitt to Cornplow." Saturday Review of
      Literature, 17 (22 January), 6.
         The Prodigal Parents shows marked falling off in Lewis's
      power as a novelist. Where once his satire was effective
      despite its extravagance, here it simply does not work.
      The novel contains some good ideas about the war between
      the generations, but most of them could have been better
      presented in essays.

14   FADIMAN, CLIFTON. "Books: Sinclair Lewis Sets 'Em Up and
      Knocks 'Em Down." New Yorker, 13 (22 January), 61.
         Although Lewis is the "most important novelist now work-
      ing in America," The Prodigal Parents is simply not worth
      reading. It is similar to Mantrap or Work of Art.

15   FORSYTHE, ROBERT. "Dottie and Red," in his Reading from Left
      to Right. New York: Covici, Friede, pp. 9-17.
         Reprint of 1937.6.

16   GRUBE, G. M. A. "Cornplow--Babbitt." Canadian Forum, 17
      (March), 426-27.
         In The Prodigal Parents Lewis, who has "always loved his
      Babbitts and his Dodsworths," takes the side of middle-
      class Fred Cornplow, who shares traits of both earlier fig-
      ures, against the radical younger generation. Not one of
      Lewis's great works but a good novel.

17   HICKS, GRANVILLE. "Sinclair Lewis's Stink Bomb." New Masses,
      26 (25 January), 19-21.
         The Prodigal Parents is Lewis's worst novel. Its char-
      acterization is "thin to the point of invisibility" and its
      workmanship careless. His attack on the communists shows

1938

no sign of his former patient, thorough research. He seems
never to have talked to a communist organizer before creating Eugene Silga. Reprinted 1974.7.

18   HOPKINS, F. M. "Rare Book Notes." Publishers Weekly, 133
     (21 May), 2025.
         Lewis has presented Yale University Library his note-
     books, manuscripts, and proofs of most of his novels.

19   HOWARD, BRIAN. "New Novels." New Statesman and Nation, 15
     (22 January), 128, 130.
         The Prodigal Parents fails because Lewis "has neglected
     the vehicle for the idea, the person for the propaganda."

20   HUNT, FRAZIER. "London Years," in his One American and His
     Attempt at Education. New York: Simon and Schuster,
     pp. 248-56.
         Personal memories of Lewis in England--drinking, per-
     forming at parties, and giving lectures.

21   JORDAN, ELIZABETH. "Enter Sinclair Lewis," in her Three Rous-
     ing Cheers. New York: D. Appleton-Century, pp. 339-47.
         Recalls editing Lewis's first adult novel Our Mr. Wrenn
     and his next two novels. Views Lewis as a charming person
     socially, a good worker, and a writer who took criticism of
     his work well.

22   KIRK, CLARA MARBURG. "'Reality' in the Novel." Survey
     Graphic, 27 (April), 238.
         The characters in Prodigal Parents lack psychological
     development and inner life. The novel is taken up with
     external details like radio programs and dress.

23   KRONENBERGER, LOUIS. "The Prodigal Lewis." Nation, 146
     (22 January), 101.
         The Prodigal Parents seems to be a gesture of concilia-
     tion to the middle-class anti-intellectuals Lewis attacked
     in the 1920s, but it is a very poor novel, shallow in both
     thought and characterization.

24   LOISEAU, JEAN. "La Croisade de Sinclair Lewis." Études
     Anglaises, 2 (April-June), [120]-33.
         Lewis's works are constructed around a single idea, and
     together they make up a vehement criticism of American
     life, especially the life of the middle class. His heroes
     are idealistic and struggle against the spirit of commerce,
     utilitarianism, materialism, and puritanical rigidity.
     Lewis is identified with Victorian muckrakers. His major

theme is that a man's value is not measured by his bank account; reason and individual sacrifice can defeat utilitarianism. Although Lewis is an accurate and observant journalist, his novels suffer from the ideas that inspire them so that they will be of only historical value in the future. In French.

25 MacCALLUM, T. W. and STEPHEN TAYLOR. "Sinclair Lewis," in their The Nobel Prize-Winners and the Nobel Foundation. Zürich: Central European Times Publishing, pp. 313-15; portrait, p. 550.
Brief biographical sketch, compiled from materials furnished by Lewis, covers his career up to 1930.

26 MORRIS, LLOYD. "Sinclair Lewis--His Critics and the Public." North American Review, 245 (Summer), 381-90.
Defends Lewis against critics who condemned The Prodigal Parents. Lewis is selling well anyway. He is connected with the mainstream of American literature: his "reforming spirit" ties him to Emerson, Thoreau, Hawthorne, and Twain, and his humor to Twain. Lewis's satire restricts his range narrowly, but within that range he is a master.

27 NATHAN, GEORGE JEAN. "The Red Menace." Newsweek, 12 (22 August), 22.
Lewis as an actor stimulates audience interest and critical curiosity; however, "It Can't Happen Here," in which he stars, needs further improvement.

28 REID, FORREST. "Fiction." Spectator, 160 (21 January), 104.
The Prodigal Parents is an excellent humorous treatment of the younger generation, full of irony and resembling the work of Twain. Lewis combines serious social commentary with a readable bit of fiction.

29 [SCHNITTKIND], HENRY THOMAS. "Sinclair Lewis, the Voice of the New Age," in his The Story of the United States: A Biographical History of America. New York: Doubleday, Doran, pp. 383-88.
Brief biography of Lewis, the sort of satirist needed during the materialistic, unspiritual period of the 1920s.

30 S[LOPER], L. A. "It Couldn't Happen: Book News of the Day." Christian Science Monitor, 22 January, p. 18.
Definitely one of Lewis's failures, The Prodigal Parents combines mere caricatures with an unbelievable plot.

1938

31 SOSKIN, WILLIAM. "When Parents Revolt Against Rebel Youth."
New York Herald Tribune Books, 23 January, p. 1.
    Not one of Lewis's best novels, The Prodigal Parents
aims merciless satire at the foibles of "dilettante
radicalism."

32 STORCH, WILLY. Sinclair Lewis und das amerikanische Kultur-
und Sprachbild. Marburg: Joh. Hamel, 96 pp.
    Surveys Lewis's popular and critical American reputation
and significance as well as European judgments. Examines
his style, including his use of simile, metaphor, onomato-
poeia, "word-magic," and names. Studies the artistic pur-
poses and effects of his reproduction of idiomatic speech,
especially slang, and the inseparability of speech and
culture. Bibliography, pp. 94-95. In German.

33 THOMAS, HENRY. See Schnittkind, 1938.29.

34 WEEKS, EDWARD. Review of The Prodigal Parents. Atlantic
Bookshelf, 161 (March), [11], [13].
    Recently Lewis has been more interested in ideas than in
character. In The Prodigal Parents he attacks the current
"collegiate rebel," but his characters are "exaggerated beyond belief."

1939

1 ANON. "Cartwheel Girl." Time, 33 (12 June), 47-51.
    Feature story on Dorothy Thompson, mentioning Lewis.

2 ANON. "Sinclair Lewis, Actor." Newsweek, 13 (9 January),
33-34.
    On Lewis's leading role in his play "Angela Is Twenty-
Two," written with Fay Wray. The Columbus Citizen said
Lewis "is a better writer than he is an actor, a better
novelist than he is a playwright."

3 BACON, LEONARD. "Yale '09." Saturday Review of Literature,
19 (4 February), 13-14.
    Reminiscences of Lewis as an upperclassman at Yale when
Bacon was a student there.

4 BAKER, JOSEPH E. "Sinclair Lewis, Plato, and the Regional
Escape." English Journal: College Edition, 28 (June),
460-68.
    Three stages in the rise of tyranny as described in
Plato's Republic are reflected in Lewis's novels: Babbitt

shows the rise of the "plutocracy," Prodigal Parents the
coming of "democracy," perhaps better termed "socialism,"
and It Can't Happen Here tyranny itself. Although Lewis
calls himself a "storyteller," his social ideas are his
greatest asset.

5   BARNETT, JAMES HARWOOD. "Divorce and the American Divorce
    Novel, 1858-1937." Ph.D. dissertation, University of
    Pennsylvania. Pp. 109-10, 119-22.
        Briefly discusses divorces in The Job, Dodsworth, and
    Grace Hegger Lewis's Half a Loaf. The latter two stem from
    the same experience, but Lewis transmutes it into art,
    while his former wife produces only veiled autobiography.

6   COBLENTZ, STANTON A. "Main Street," in Essays of Three Decades.
    Edited by Arno L. Bader and Carlton F. Wells. New York and
    London: Harper and Brothers, pp. 459-61.
        Reprint of 1921.5.

7   DAVID, SIMONE. "Carol Kennicott de 'Main Street' et sa lignée
    Européenne." Revue de Littérature Comparée, 19:407-16.
        Carol Kennicott is another incarnation of Emma Bovary,
    but she seems to have even more in common with Nora Helmer
    of A Doll's House by Ibsen, whose socio-critical outlook is
    similar to Lewis's. In French.

*8 EICKE, GUSTAV. Der Wirtschaftsgeist des Amerikaners im Spie-
    gel von Sinclair Lewis Romanen. Leipzig: Akademischer
    Verlag. 167 pp.
        Cited in Silhol, 1969.30.

9   HERRON, IMA HONAKER. "Crusaders and Skeptics," in her The
    Small Town in American Literature. Durham, N.C.: Duke
    University Press, pp. 377-90.
        Lewis began his career as a critic of the small town as
    in The Trail of the Hawk, the early part of The Job, and
    Main Street. He later broadened his attack to encompass
    many phases of American life.

10 HORTON, THOMAS D. "Sinclair Lewis: The Symbol of an Era."
    North American Review, 248 (Winter), 374-93.
        No writer understood the wild decade of the 1920s more
    fully than Lewis. His novels before Main Street show all
    his failures (inability to achieve depth of character,
    sentimentality, manic humor, and "sloppiness") alongside
    his virtues (his "fine ear" for speech and his feeling for
    "the sensitive failures of the middle class"). In the
    twenties Lewis exploited his strengths--sociological accu-
    racy and satire--and the public ignored his weaknesses.

1939

> For his social achievement, he deserves a place of respect in American literature.

11 LERNER, MAX. "Sinclair Lewis, Caliban, and the Federal Power," in his Ideas Are Weapons. New York: Viking Press, pp. 280-84.
> Reprint of 1936.22.

12 LEWISOHN, LUDWIG. "The Naturalists," in his The Story of American Literature. New York: Random House, pp. 465, 502-13.
> Originally published in Expression in America, 1932.10.

13 LUNDKVIST, ARTUR. Tre Amerikaner: Dreiser--Lewis--Anderson. Stockholm: Albert Bonniers Förlag, pp. 28-45, 64.
> Discusses Lewis as "social idealist" from Our Mr. Wrenn through The Prodigal Parents, emphasizing Main Street, Babbitt, Arrowsmith, and Elmer Gantry. In Swedish.

14 OSBORNE, LUCY E. "Sinclair Lewis: The Innocents. N.Y. Harper. 1917." Bibliographical Notes and Queries, 2, no. 12, p. 10, item 328.
> Bibliographical description of two copies of The Innocents. Query about a third binding and original frontispiece.

15 PHELPS, WILLIAM LYON. Autobiography, with Letters. New York, London: Oxford University Press, pp. 568, 658-59, 845, 898.
> Memories of Lewis, mostly as a student at Yale.

1940

1 ALEXANDER, JACK. "Rover Girl in Europe: The Story of Problem Girl Dorothy Thompson." Saturday Evening Post, 212 (25 May), 20-21, 107, 109-10, 113-16.
> Biography of Dorothy Thompson. Relates the story of Lewis's courtship and briefly discusses their marriage. Part 1, "The Girl from Syracuse," 212 (18 May), 9-11, 123-26, 128-29, concerns only Thompson.

2 ANON. "In Brief." Nation, 150 (23 March), 401.
> Bethel Merriday is probably accurate enough in describing the theater, but its characters, especially the protagonist, are hopelessly dull and Lewis's examination of them is shallow.

3   ANON. "'Professor' Lewis." Time, 36 (18 November), 56.
    Lewis taught for two months at the University of Wis-
    consin but left because of snubs by the faculty.

4   ANON. Review of Bethel Merriday. "Atlantic Bookshelf,"
    Atlantic Monthly, 165 (April), [1].
    Lewis's latest novel attacks no institution, but is an
    enjoyable story, a good picture of the workings of the
    theater with "the most convincing heroine Mr. Lewis has
    ever drawn."

5   ANON. Review of Bethel Merriday. Booklist, 36 (15 March),
    284.
    Bethel Merriday explores the theater world thoroughly
    but is "superficial."

6   ANON. Review of Bethel Merriday. Catholic World, 151 (May),
    250.
    Bethel Merriday lacks Lewis's usual satire but is "hon-
    est and human and cheerful."

7   ANON. "Road Work." Time, 35 (25 March), 97.
    Bethel Merriday is much better than The Prodigal Par-
    ents. Lewis gives a good idea of the American theater and
    tells a reasonably interesting, though sometimes "maudlin"
    story.

8   BINSSE, HARRY LORIN. "Two Novels." Commonweal, 31
    (22 March), 477-78.
    Bethel Merriday follows Lewis's usual journalistic pat-
    tern of presenting a large amount of factual information,
    this time about the theater. The plot is feeble, but the
    book is more "mellow" and the characters more human be-
    cause Lewis doesn't feel his customary hatred for the peo-
    ple and institution he is writing about.

9   BOAS, RALPH PHILIP and KATHERINE BURTON. Social Backgrounds
    of American Literature. Boston: Little, Brown, pp. 255,
    259-62.
    A recurring theme in Lewis is "the implacable dominance
    of environment"; thus, readers console "themselves with
    the hopelessness of the struggle they were unable or un-
    ready to undertake." In Main Street "narrative interest
    is distinctly subordinated to the pleasures of recogni-
    tion" since readers foresee Carol's failure. Babbitt's
    theme is as outdated as its details, and the later works
    are uneven.

10   BOYNTON, PERCY H. "Sinclair Lewis," in his America in Con-
         temporary Fiction. Chicago: University of Chicago Press,
         pp. 164-84.
              Revision of 1927.9, brought up to date with comments on
         Lewis's work since 1927. Dodsworth showed signs that Lewis
         wanted to return to real fiction, but subsequent books such
         as It Can't Happen Here and The Prodigal Parents show him
         reverting to his role as propagandist or journalist.

11   CARPENTER, HARLAND A. Review of Bethel Merriday. Library
         Journal, 65 (15 March), 257.
              "One of Lewis' poorer books."

12   FADIMAN, CLIFTON. "Mr. Lewis and the Stage--Catalogue." New
         Yorker, 16 (23 March), 71-72.
              As light reading, Bethel Merriday is a good novel. In
         addition to the diverting story, Lewis presents a huge body
         of facts about the theater.

13   FLANAGAN, HALLIE. "States United: It Can't Happen Here," in
         her Arena. New York: Duell, Sloan and Pearce, pp. 115-29.
              Account of the writing and staging of the play "It Can't
         Happen Here" in twenty-one cities simultaneously, sponsored
         by the Federal Theater of the Works Progress Administration
         in 1936.

14   GIBSON, WILFRID. "Three New Novels." Manchester Guardian,
         29 March, p. 3.
              Bethel Merriday is overly long and rather prosaic, with-
         out Lewis's usual biting satire. "The whole thing is lack-
         ing in distinction for a writer of Mr. Lewis's calibre."

15   "IGNOTO." "Babbitt: A Mysterious Inscription." Notes and
         Queries, 179 (6 July), 11.
              Query about Babbitt's notebook and inscription
         D.S.S.D.M.Y.P.D.F. What does it mean?

16   JACK, PETER MUNRO. "Sinclair Lewis on Holiday in the The-
         atre." New York Times Book Review, 24 March, p. 2.
              Bethel Merriday reflects Lewis's recent interest in the
         theater. As a "lightweight, amusing affair," it is not
         bad, but it makes no pretense of coming up to the level of
         Lewis's better novels.

17   JOHNSON, EDGAR. "Sinclair Lewis' Understudy." New Republic,
         102 (25 March), 413.
              The author of books such as Free Air is finally back,
         this time with an entertaining tale, Bethel Merriday, which
         will please readers of the Saturday Evening Post. "His

return coincides with the disappearance of Sinclair Lewis, the Nobel Prize winner, whose tricks of style and structural devices this book oddly parodies." Lewis's story of a girl making good in the theater mingles "all the shapes and sounds of real life with grease paint and treacle" to produce exactly the kind of American novel the old Lewis condemned in his Nobel Prize acceptance speech.

18   MARKS, JOHN. "New Novels." Spectator, 164 (5 April), 496, 498.
     Bethel Merriday is a good novel of the theater, told with "great verve, humour and understanding."

19   MUIR, JOHN. "New Novels." New Statesman and Nation, 19 (30 March), 436, 438.
     Bethel Merriday is a disappointing book, filled with stock characters and lacking the satire which made Lewis famous. Even Lewis's considerable skill as storyteller only partially redeems this novel.

20   REDMAN, BEN RAY. "Mr. Lewis's Suppressed Desire." Saturday Review of Literature, 21 (23 March), 7.
     Bethel Merriday "is one of the least successful and least satisfying novels that have ever come from an author of deservedly high reputation." While the novel captures the mechanics of the theater, it never gets beneath the surface of its characters and Lewis's acid wit never comes into play.

21   ROSS, MARY. "Sinclair Lewis Views Life in the Theatre." New York Herald Tribune Books, 24 March, p. 3.
     Bethel Merriday is not so much the story of its heroine as a study of the theater and its attraction for actors. Lewis has studied his material like an actor preparing for a role.

22   S[LOPER], L. A. "The Bookshelf: The Stage and Mr. Lewis." Christian Science Monitor, 22 March, p. 20.
     Bethel Merriday is one of Lewis's better books, although like even his best it tends to dwell too much on the surfaces of his subject matter. A warm book, it is perhaps most reminiscent of Dodsworth.

23   VAN DOREN, CARL. "Sinclair Lewis," in his The American Novel: 1789-1939. Revised and enlarged edition. New York: Macmillan, pp. 303-14.
     Lewis was not only a sensitive perceiver of public opinion, but its molder as well during his heyday. His works will remain important to the social historian, and the best

1940

will endure as art. Discusses works from <u>Main Street</u> through <u>It Can't Happen Here</u>. Partially reprinted in <u>TCIA</u>, 1968.4.

24   VAN GELDER, ROBERT. "Sinclair Lewis Talks of Writing--And Acting." <u>New York Times Book Review</u>, 30 June, p. 2.
      Interview with Lewis when he was appearing in "Ah, Wilderness" in Maplewood, N.J. Lewis said he likes the "professionalism" and the "gregariousness" of the theater. He became a writer perhaps because of his active imagination. He sneers at people who believe there must be a "system" for writing: it's just hard work. Reprinted 1946.9.

                                1941

1   BENÉT, WILLIAM ROSE. <u>The Dust Which Is God</u>. New York: Dodd, Mead, 559 pp., passim.
      Poeticized autobiography in verse by an old friend of Lewis, who appears as "Larry Harris," particularly during the poet's early years.

2   BLOOM, MURRAY TEIGH. "Literary Propheteering." <u>Saturday Review of Literature</u>, 23 (1 February), 3-4, 12, 14.
      Overview of prophecies in literature, including <u>It Can't Happen Here</u>.

3   PATRICK, WILLIAM HENRY. "A Study of Sinclair Lewis." Master's thesis, University of Illinois, 109 pp.
      Treats at length <u>Main Street</u>, <u>Babbitt</u>, <u>Arrowsmith</u>, and <u>Elmer Gantry</u>; these exemplify Lewis's greatest strengths: photographic realism, unparalleled dialogue, and keen satire. Although the best American novelist in capturing the 1920s Lewis was unable to adjust to the changes during the next two decades.

4   STOLBERG, BENJAMIN. "Sinclair Lewis." <u>American Mercury</u>, 53 (October), 450-60.
      Popular essay on Lewis's personality and work habits. Lewis is perhaps most comparable to Mark Twain, with whom he shares a distrust of pomposity and a basic satirical bent. Like Twain, he has become as much an American institution as an American author, valued for his personality as well as his work.

1942

1 JOHNSON, MERLE. American First Editions. Fourth edition.
   Revised and enlarged by Jacob Blanck. New York: R. R.
   Bowker, pp. 311-14.
       See third edition (1936.21); some additions, primarily
   to books or pamphlets to which Lewis contributed.

2 KAZIN, ALFRED. "The New Realism: Sherwood Anderson and Sinclair Lewis," in his On Native Grounds: An Interpretation
   of Modern American Prose Literature. New York: Reynal and
   Hitchcock, pp. 217-26.
       Lewis fitted in perfectly with the spirit of the twen-
   ties--satirical and iconoclastic--but as his career progressed, he continued to use the same techniques even when
   he had little to say. At his best Lewis skillfully captured the externals of America--its towns, homes, and
   people--and pilloried the folly that he perceived. Reprinted in SB, 1971.13 and SL:CCE, 1962.14. Pp. 219-21 reprinted 1961.5.

3 KUNITZ, STANLEY J. and HOWARD HAYCRAFT. "Lewis, Sinclair,"
   in their Twentieth Century Authors. New York: H. W.
   Wilson, pp. 821-23.
       Biographical details and evaluation of work: "an uneven
   writer" who is "genuinely uncritical of his own work." Includes description of work habits, excerpts from critical
   reactions, bibliographies of principal works and major
   criticism.

1943

1 ANON. "Fun With Fund-Raising." Time, 41 (19 April), 98.
       Gideon Planish is Lewis at his best again as he relent-
   lessly satirizes professional fund-raisers and their dubious philanthropic organizations.

2 ANON. "More Babbitry [sic]." Times Literary Supplement, 42
   (23 October), 509.
       Gideon Planish attacks the "philanthropical" organiza-
   tions that benefit only their organizers. At times Lewis
   overdoes his satire, but generally maintains enough humor
   to carry the novel effectively.

1943

3   ANON. "Off the Deep End." Commonweal, 38 (7 May), 78.
         Gideon Planish is not effective satire because too few
     real Planishes exist and the reader will not have a sense
     of recognizing a familiar character. However, his wife
     Peony is a realistic picture of a certain kind of middle-
     class woman. As a whole, the novel is disappointing.

4   ANON. "Plus and Minus: A Survey of Reviews." Story, 22
         (May-June), 8.
         Reprints partial reviews of Gideon Planish, one favor-
     able, one unfavorable, four mixed.

5   ANON. Review of Gideon Planish. Booklist, 39 (1 May), 354.
         Story is heavy-handed "and occasionally dull."

6   ANON. "Shorter Notices." Catholic World, 157 (July), 447-48.
         Gideon Planish fails because its satire is "exaggerated
     to the point of being ridiculous."

7   BARNES, HARRY ELMER. "Getting Back to 'Gideon Planish.'"
         Saturday Review of Literature, 26 (26 June), 13.
         Letter to the editor on Howard Mumford Jones's review
     (see 1943.13). Defends Lewis at length. The satire is so
     apt that it redeems Lewis's "old-fashioned" approach in
     Gideon Planish.

8   BRIGHOUSE, HAROLD. "New Novels." Manchester Guardian,
         29 October, p. 3.
         Gideon Planish is somewhat more gentle than most Lewis
     novels and is sometimes monotonous, but on the whole it is
     saved by its humor.

9   DuBOIS, WILLIAM. "The Artist from Sauk Center [sic]." New
         York Times Book Review, 18 April, pp. 1, 27.
         Gideon Planish is second-rate Lewis, better than The
     Prodigal Parents, not as good as Lewis's major novels. But
     in certain satiric passages, the old Lewis shines through,
     and it is a pleasure to welcome him back.

10   FADIMAN, CLIFTON. "Return of Mr. Lewis." New Yorker, 19
         (24 April), 76.
         Gideon Planish is the best novel Lewis has written for a
     long time. Again we see him as a satirist though sometimes
     too vigorous and again he creates characters the reader
     will really respond to, particularly Peony Planish, his
     best female character since Leora Arrowsmith.

11   GEISMAR, MAXWELL. "Young Sinclair Lewis and Old Dos Passos."
      American Mercury, 56 (May), 624-28.
          Lewis's career has appeared to be near its end since
      Elmer Gantry, yet Lewis keeps writing books that make it
      necessary to modify that judgment. Gideon Planish again
      shows the youthful energy and wit that characterized Lewis
      at his peak. The novel is flawed by the aimless progres-
      sion of the protagonist from college professor to national
      fund-raiser, but Lewis remains "our foremost youthful
      iconoclast."

12   GURKO, LEO and MIRIAM GURKO. "The Two Main Streets of Sinc-
      clair Lewis." College English, 4 (February), 288-92.
          Lewis's forte is satire, the backbone of his great works
      of the 1920s. However, his ambivalence toward Zenith and
      Gopher Prairie and their inhabitants caused him to shift
      from satire to a sympathetic portrayal of the Babbitt type.
      The ambivalence that was to end Lewis's period as a major
      writer is apparent in Dodsworth, where he sympathizes with
      Sam, the businessman, not Fran, the rebel.

13   JONES, HOWARD MUMFORD. "Sinclair Lewis and the Do-Gooders."
      Saturday Review of Literature, 26 (24 April), 6.
          Readers have been waiting for Lewis to go back to his
      exposé type of novel. In Gideon Planish he does so, but it
      doesn't work. His technique as a novelist is badly out of
      date and his thinking seems shallow. Despite a few bright
      passages, the book is a failure. See response, 1943.7.

14   KELLEY, H. GILBERT. Review of Gideon Planish. Library Jour-
      nal, 68 (15 March), 248.
          One of Lewis's successes, Gideon Planish shows "excel-
      lent satire" and should be a best-seller.

15   MAYBERRY, GEORGE. "Too Late for Herpicide." New Republic,
      108 (26 April), 570.
          Gideon Planish is "certainly one of the poorest books by
      an American writer of genuine talent." In it, Lewis is
      guilty of political naiveté, overdone caricature, "and
      downright bad writing." Even Lewis's good ear seems to
      have deserted him, since the slang seems "ten years out of
      date." The book is "enough to make H. L. Mencken turn over
      in his literary grave."

16   O'BRIEN, KATE. "Fiction." Spectator, 171 (29 October), 416.
          Gideon Planish is a good novel, humorous and yet pointed
      in its denunciation of professional fund-raisers, but not
      as good as Babbitt or even Elmer Gantry, and some parts are
      boring.

1943

17 S[LOPER], L. A. "The Bookshelf: Sinclair Lewis' Latest Vic-
    tim." Christian Science Monitor, 19 April, p. 18.
        Gideon Planish is not an effective satire because Lewis
    is so heavy-handed that the book becomes mere "burlesque."

18 SOSKIN, WILLIAM. "Sinclair Lewis's Satire on Organized Vir-
    tue." New York Herald Tribune Weekly Book Review,
    18 April, p. 3.
        Gideon Planish depicts "a newer and more streamlined
    Elmer Gantry." It is not one of Lewis's best novels, but
    the average American will read it and laugh at its satire.

19 STOVALL, FLOYD. "Contemporary Fiction," in his American
    Idealism. Norman: University of Oklahoma Press,
    pp. 143-47.
        Lewis shows the faults of America in Main Street and
    Babbitt, but in Arrowsmith and Dodsworth he creates ideal-
    istic characters whom the reader can admire. "Probe the
    depths of Lewis's best characters and you find something
    very much like Emerson's self-reliance."

20 T., M. I. Review of Gideon Planish. Canadian Forum, 23
    (July), 94-95.
        Lewis's attack on "philanthrobbers" is "by no means a
    novel of the caliber of Dodsworth or Babbitt," but the
    exuberance of its satire "makes it very entertaining."

21 TOYNBEE, PHILIP. "New Novels." New Statesman and Nation, 26
    (4 December), 371-72.
        Gideon Planish is both pointed and funny. "Perhaps
    the jokes are repeated too often, but they are good
    jokes. . . ."

22 TRILLING, DIANA. "Fiction in Review." Nation, 156 (8 May),
    675-76.
        Gideon Planish is "unimportant, sloppy, and even dull."
    Lewis sacrifices character to his love of satire, and un-
    like Babbitt, who comes to life through the satire, Planish
    never breathes. Reprinted 1978.3.

23 WEEKS, EDWARD. Review of Gideon Planish. Atlantic Monthly,
    171 (May), 127.
        If this exposure of the evils of organized philanthropy
    "is less exciting than it ought to be, the blame may lie
    with a world which has moved faster than Mr. Lewis."

1944

1   ADAMS, J. DONALD. "Main Street and the Dust Bowl," in his
     The Shape of Books to Come. New York: Viking Press,
     pp. 131-43.
        Considers Lewis and Steinbeck as realists who look "out-
     side and beyond themselves." Both document social problems
     realistically, without seeing life through "a naturalistic
     bias." Both emphasize the humor in life. There is love
     and concern for mankind in Lewis's satire, and though his
     work has fallen off recently, he accomplished a great deal
     during the 1920s.

2   _____. "Speaking of Books." New York Times Book Review,
     30 April, p. 2.
        Lewis's attack on Bernard DeVoto in "Fools, Liars, and
     Mr. DeVoto" (Saturday Review, 27 [15 April 1944], 9-12) may
     be well deserved, but both writers are acting like "two
     small boys thumbing their noses and hurling indiscriminate
     insults."

3   _____. "Speaking of Books." New York Times Book Review,
     14 May, p. 2.
        By this time Lewis and Bernard DeVoto should regret
     their harsh words about each other. While Lewis has a
     temper, he is quick to make up after fights.

4   ANON. "DeVoto Sets Off Hot Literary Feud With Attack on
     Writers of 1920's." Newsweek, 23 (1 May), 68-69.
        DeVoto's Literary Fallacy (1944.6) is "a Menckenesque
     crusade against those novelists and poets whom DeVoto dis-
     likes most" for misrepresenting their culture and divorcing
     themselves from life experiences that give "validity to
     art." Lewis's rejoinder (Saturday Review, 27 [15 April
     1944], 9-12) is a "two-fisted assault" which is "the first
     real critical mauling the outspoken DeVoto has received."

5   ANON. "SRL Poll on Novels and Novelists." Saturday Review of
     Literature, 27 (5 August), 61.
        Asked to name best novelist and best novel of the last
     twenty years, readers named Lewis fourth behind Ernest
     Hemingway, Willa Cather, and John Dos Passos. Arrowsmith
     was best novel, Farewell to Arms second and U.S.A. third.

1944

6   DeVOTO, BERNARD. "Waste Land," in his The Literary Fallacy.
    Boston: Little, Brown, pp. 95-102.
        Although Lewis may be the leading novelist of the 1920s
    by virtue of Main Street, Babbitt, Arrowsmith, and Elmer
    Gantry, he has severe limitations. He is at his best only
    when attacking characters with satire; when he attempts to
    depict admirable characters they are invariably "adoles-
    cent" or "emotionally undeveloped."

7   MILLETT, FRED B. "The Novel" and "Sinclair Lewis," in his
    Contemporary American Authors: A Critical Survey and 219
    Bio-Bibliographies. New York: Harcourt, Brace, pp. 79-80,
    436-41.
        Lewis is excellent at producing realistic and satiric
    pictures of the American of his day, but is clearly limited
    by his emphasis on external accuracy. Brief comments on
    principal novels, biography, list of works, and extensive
    bibliography of early secondary studies of Lewis.

1945

1   ANON. Biographical note to "The Artist, the Scientist, and
    the Peace" by Sinclair Lewis. Scholastic, 47 (12 Novem-
    ber), 17-18.
        Brief identification of Lewis as "first American to re-
    ceive Nobel Prize for literature." Mentions major works.

2   ANON. "Laureate of the Booboisie." Time, 46 (8 October),
    100, 103-104, 106, 108.
        Cass Timberlane is much better than Ann Vickers or Dods-
    worth though not as important as Babbitt. Lewis dwells far
    more on the love story than in his earlier novels, where
    his main purpose is satire. Popular account of Lewis's ca-
    reer and life. Lewis is on the cover of this issue.

3   ANON. Review of Cass Timberlane. Booklist, 42 (1 October),
    37.
        Lewis tells the story of a marriage and satirically re-
    flects on modern marriage.

4   ANON. Review of Cass Timberlane. Kirkus, 13 (15 August),
    344.
        Cass Timberlane is Lewis's best book in years. Unlike
    many of his novels, it treats realistic characters, and
    satire is a secondary concern.

5 ANON. "Shorter Notices." <u>Catholic World</u>, 162 (November), 187.
  <u>Cass Timberlane</u> seems to have been intended as a satire on marriage but is superficial as propaganda or as art.

6 CERF, BENNETT. "Trade Winds." <u>Saturday Review of Literature</u>, 28 (3 November), 20.
  Retells a story about the origin of "Harry Sinclair" as Lewis's first and middle names. Also comments on <u>Cass Timberlane</u>, which is likely to outsell <u>Main Street</u> and <u>Arrowsmith</u>.

7 COLUM, MARY M. "Sinclair Lewis's New Thesis Novel." <u>Saturday Review of Literature</u>, 28 (6 October), 8-9.
  In <u>Cass Timberlane</u> Lewis again reminds us that he is more the caricaturist than the satirist, that he is good at creating exteriors but deficient at portraying his characters' inner lives. Only Jinny Timberlane comes alive in this thesis novel about modern American marriage. Despite its shortcomings, it "is an able and even a brilliant book." Lewis is on the cover of this issue.

8 DICKSON, JAMES K. "Lewis, Sinclair (1885-). The Innocents, 1917." <u>Papers of the Bibliographical Society of America</u>, 39 (Second quarter), 167-68.
  Describes five variant bindings of <u>The Innocents</u>.

9 DUFFY, CHARLES. Review of <u>Cass Timberlane</u>. <u>Commonweal</u>, 43 (9 November), 100-101.
  Not as good as <u>Arrowsmith</u>, <u>Cass Timberlane</u> is a better book than Lewis has written for some time. His old skill in satirizing the American way of life and his deftness at caricature will remind readers of his novels of the 1920s.

10 ELGSTRÖM, ANNA LENAH. "Sinclair Lewis Gör Come Back." <u>Samtid och Framtid</u>, 2 (September), 428-35.
  Examines <u>Gideon Planish</u> and considers Lewis's earlier works. Views Lewis against the background of the Muckraking School and the Lost Generation, especially in relation to Dreiser, Hemingway, and Booth Tarkington. In Swedish.

11 FARBER, MARJORIE. "Recent Fiction." <u>New Republic</u>, 113 (22 October), 542.
  <u>Cass Timberlane</u> exhibits all of the worst characteristics of women's magazine fiction.

1945

12   GANNETT, LEWIS. "Sinclair Lewis Goes Home to Minnesota." New
      York <u>Herald Tribune Weekly Book Review</u>, 7 October, p. 1.
            <u>Cass Timberlane</u> returns to the Minnesota setting of
      Lewis's first triumph, <u>Main Street</u>. While the novel is
      mainly concerned with the problems of modern marriage, most
      readers will respond to it as a picture of life in a mid-
      western small city. Lewis has changed little since the
      1920s.

13   GARDINER, HAROLD C. "Neither Hot Nor Cold." <u>America</u>, 74
      (6 October), 19-20.
            In <u>Cass Timberlane</u>, as in most of his fiction, Lewis
      adopts no real viewpoint toward his characters, but simply
      makes easy cynical remarks about their lives. Especially
      in vignettes about marriages other than the Timberlanes',
      Lewis "shows too clearly the smallness of the mind that
      limits him." Reprinted 1972.11.

14   GIBBS, WOLCOTT. "Shad Ampersand: A Novel of Time and the
      Writer, Tentatively Based on 'Cass Timberlane, a Novel of
      Husbands and Wives.'" <u>New Yorker</u>, 21 (27 October), 21-23.
            Parody of <u>Cass Timberlane</u>.

15   HACKETT, ALICE PAYNE. <u>Fifty Years of Best Sellers: 1895-
      1945</u>. New York: R. R. Bowker, 140 pp., passim.
            Lists Lewis's best-sellers, from <u>Main Street</u>, number one
      in 1921, to <u>It Can't Happen Here</u>, number five in 1936.

16   MEALAND, RICHARD. "Books into Films." <u>Publishers Weekly</u>, 147
      (21 April), 1664.
            Metro-Goldwyn-Mayer bought <u>Cass Timberlane</u> for a minimum
      of $150,000. The price will rise if the book sells over
      400,000 copies or if a book club selects it.

17   NICHOLS, ELIZABETH P. Review of <u>Cass Timberlane</u>. <u>Library
      Journal</u>, 70 (1 October), 890.
            While <u>Cass Timberlane</u> is not as good as <u>Main Street</u>, it
      is far better than <u>Bethel Merriday</u>. Lewis seems to be mel-
      lowing with age.

18   POORE, CHARLES. "The Kingdom of Sinclair Lewis." <u>New York
      Times Book Review</u>, 7 October, pp. 1, 30.
            <u>Cass Timberlane</u> is "a fair novel but not one of Lewis'
      best." Jinny is like a modern Carol Kennicott, and Cass
      will remind some of Dodsworth. Lewis introduces no new
      ideas, but it is good at times to be transported back into
      Lewis's kingdom.

19 PRESCOTT, ORVILLE. "Outstanding Novels." <u>Yale Review</u>, n.s.
    35 (December), 381-82.
        <u>Cass Timberlane</u> is a thesis-ridden novel about the sorry
    state of marriage in America. Lewis includes "rage and
    scorn, good dialogue, and close observation of American
    mores," but the book is disappointing.

20 SLOPER, L. A. "Mr. Lewis Remains in the Rut: The Bookshelf."
    <u>Christian Science Monitor</u>, 3 October, p. 18.
        <u>Cass Timberlane</u> is another of Lewis's muckraking novels
    like <u>Elmer Gantry</u> or <u>Gideon Planish</u>. It is a pity that
    Lewis sees only despicable people when he looks about him;
    only Dodsworth is truly likable. The Timberlanes are "car-
    icatures," and the plot line is an old familiar Lewis
    "formula."

21 SPAYD, BARBARA G. "Sinclair Lewis: A Biographical Sketch"
    and "How Arrowsmith Was Written," in <u>Arrowsmith</u>. Modern
    Classics. New York: Harcourt, Brace, pp. v-xiv, xv-xxi.
        Brief biography mentioning most Lewis works. Even the
    least successful, such as <u>The Prodigal Parents</u>, are treated
    kindly although the slightness of Lewis's short stories is
    recognized. Lewis is motivated by the same creed that
    calls up Arrowsmith's scientific prayer for "unclouded
    eyes." The second essay treats the collaboration between
    Lewis and Paul de Kruif, whose educational and professional
    background is summarized. The research trip to the West
    Indies and the actual writing in London are described.
    <u>Arrowsmith</u> is often considered the best of Lewis's novels,
    not only for its scientific accuracy but for the depth of
    its characterization.

22 TRILLING, DIANA. "Of Husbands and Wives." <u>Nation</u>, 161
    (13 October), 381-[382].
        <u>Cass Timberlane</u> is a disappointing novel in which Lewis
    takes American marriage as his subject. The Timberlane
    marriage is unbelievable because of Cass's puppyish devo-
    tion to Jinny, and the lesser marriages give no sense of
    what marriage is really like, despite Lewis's documenta-
    tion of some "common marital pitfalls."

23 WEEKS, EDWARD. "The Peripatetic Reviewer." <u>Atlantic Monthly</u>,
    176 (October), 139, 141.
        Lewis shows a good deal of his old vitality in <u>Cass
    Timberlane</u>, especially when his "buzz-saw mind" attacks the
    current state of marriage in America. But Lewis's style
    and characterization show no advance.

1945

24   WILSON, EDMUND. "Salute to an Old Landmark: Sinclair Lewis."
      New Yorker, 21 (13 October), 94-97.
          Cass Timberlane shows that Lewis "in spite of his noto-
      rious faults, is one of the people in the literary field
      who do create interest and values, that he has still gone
      on working at this when many others have broken down or
      quit. . . ." Though this attempt to portray the emancipat-
      ed woman is not wholly successful, the book overall is
      good. Reprinted in SL:CCE, 1962.14.

25   WOOLF, S. J. "Sinclair Lewis is Back on Main Street." New
      York Times Magazine, 28 October, pp. 13, 41, 42.
          Lewis, who has gone back to a Minnesota setting for Cass
      Timberlane, talks about how Main Street has changed over
      the years, mostly in material and superficial ways. While
      a Gopher Prairie may have better architecture and more
      well-stocked stores, bigotry is still alive.

26   WYLIE, PHILIP. "Sinclair Lewis." American Mercury, 61
      (November), 629-32.
          Cass Timberlane "displays reel after reel of new film in
      the old [Lewis] technique." It has many similarities to
      Main Street but shows the passage of twenty-five years in
      the different relationships between husband and wife.
      Where Kennicott was calmly dominant, Timberlane is uncer-
      tain, insecure, even when he is in the right. Perhaps in
      the pseudo-happy ending Lewis is concealing a really sinis-
      ter barb and condemning the couple to a lifetime of misery.

                              1946

1   ANON. "The Best Sellers of 1945." Publishers Weekly, 149
      (19 January), 297-99.
          Cass Timberlane ranked fiftieth in sales for 1945,
      selling over 600,000 copies including Book-of-the-Month
      Club sales.

2   BRODIN, PIERRE. "Sinclair Lewis," in his Les Écrivains Amé-
      ricains de l'entre-deux-guerres. Paris: Horizons de
      France, pp. [45]-72, 272-74.
          Chronology of works. Biographical background. Discus-
      sion of all Lewis's novels with emphasis on Main Street
      (Carol is the "worthy American companion of Emma Bovary"),
      Babbitt (his "finest book"), Arrowsmith (Martin is "his
      only hero" and his finest character), Elmer Gantry (that
      "most odious of Lewis' characters" could only be an Ameri-
      can), and Dodsworth. Views Lewis as enlightened psycholo-
      gist, journalist, satirist, humorist, and reformer; his

"work remains deeply and essentially American." Bibliography. In French.

3   FEINBERG, LEONARD. "Sinclair Lewis as a Satirist." Ph.D. dissertation, University of Illinois. 257 pp.
      Analyzes Lewis's satiric method from the early 1920s to the late 1930s. Lewis adds three techniques to the normal repertoire of the satirist: the "mimicked monologue," the "illusion of realism," and "snob-appeal," which reassures the reader as to his superiority to the object of satire. In Main Street, Babbitt, and Arrowsmith Lewis created "perhaps the best satire produced by an American writer."

4   FEMALE ADMIRER, A. "Sinclair Lewis: A Comparison." Atlantic Monthly, 177 (February), 159-60.
      Reviews Cass Timberlane by comparing and contrasting it with Main Street. Ironically suggests that Lewis (and the society he treats) have progressed little.

5   GRAY, JAMES. "Sinclair Lewis," in his On Second Thought. Minneapolis: University of Minnesota Press, pp. 11-21.
      Gray quotes from and supplements reviews written for the St. Paul Pioneer Press and Dispatch. Comments on Babbitt and Bethel Merriday. Lewis looked as if he would transcend his limitations in Arrowsmith, but fell back into writing easy books of superficial cleverness. Only in It Can't Happen Here and Cass Timberlane does he regain some of his old integrity. At his best, he offered America honest and needed criticism.

6   LOISEAU, JEAN. "La Vie Conjugale aux États-Unis, d'après Sinclair Lewis." Cahiers des Langues Modernes: Romanciers Américains Contemporains. Paris: Librairie Didier, pp. [115]-31.
      Once more Lewis pleads for honesty, this time in marriage. In Cass Timberlane he presents the full picture of marriage from both sides; only one side was shown in Main Street and in Dodsworth. Primary bibliography, p. 318. In French.

7   SATS, IGOR. "A Controversy on Literature with our Foreign Friends." Soviet Literature, no. 12, pp. 40-47.
      Lewis's career and ideological development illustrate the case of a writer who "at the time of a social crisis sees the full profundity of the contradictions which separate the people from the ruling class to which the writer belongs and begins energetically defending the conservative position." His great novels of the '20s were "evidence of [his] profound devotion to the ideals of progress and

1946

humanity." Sensitive and perceptive, Lewis boldly "exposed
the defects of the capitalist system." Then he was so
shocked by the fascist coup in Germany that he became
afraid for himself and democracy so he wrote a "pamphlet"
that might have been "written by a Hearst hireling" in It
Can't Happen Here. A member of the threatened middle
class, Lewis reacts against the working class.

8   VAN DOREN, CARL. "Introduction" to Main Street. Cleveland
    and New York: World Publishing, pp. 7-9.
        History of the controversy surrounding initial publica-
    tion of Main Street. Perhaps the key "revolutionary ele-
    ment" of the novel is the fact that Carol refuses to admit
    that her rebellion was wrong. The book remains, deserved-
    ly, the work with which Lewis is most identified.

9   VAN GELDER, ROBERT. "Sinclair Lewis Talks of Writing--and
    Acting," in his Writers and Writing. New York: Charles
    Scribner's Sons, pp. 77-81.
        Reprint of 1940.24.

1947

1   ANON. "America's Angry Man." Newsweek, 29 (26 May), 98, 101,
    102.
        In Kingsblood Royal Lewis "is once again the honest,
    hard-hitting writer he started out to be 27 years ago."
    "Less a novel than a tract," it is nevertheless "a slashing
    and powerful book." Reviews the influence of Lewis's early
    years, his career and financial success, and his personal
    life. Photos.

2   ANON. "Black Mischief." Time, 49 (26 May), 104, 106.
        Kingsblood Royal may well be the most controversial book
    of an author noted for controversy. Unlike many of Lewis's
    earlier satires, however, Kingsblood deserts art for propa-
    ganda to such an extent that it is not even effective as
    propaganda.

3   ANON. "News of the Week: Ebony Award to 'Kingsblood Royal.'"
    Publishers Weekly, 152 (20 December), 2684.
        Ebony magazine chose Kingsblood Royal the book that did
    "the most to promote racial understanding in 1947."

4   ANON. Review of Kingsblood Royal. Booklist, 43 (15 May),
    290.
        Kingsblood Royal is not so much a novel as a fictional-
    ized social tract on race relations.

5   ANON. Review of <u>Kingsblood Royal</u>. <u>Kirkus</u>, 15 (15 March), 169-70.
     This thesis novel is so exaggerated that it can be read only as propaganda. Lewis uses "a sledge hammer, not a rapier."

6   ANON. "White Man Turns Negro." <u>Life</u>, 22 (9 June), 131-32, 134, 137.
     Reprints pictures from 1947.18 of dramatic reenactment of <u>Kingsblood Royal</u>. Discusses the dilemma of critics, who "knew that, as a literary work, Lewis' novel deserved straight panning," but hesitated to condemn a social tract which could do great good. Quotes eight reviewers, concluding with Malcolm Cowley's judgment that Babbitt would "be remembered longer than Neil Kingsblood."

7   CANBY, HENRY SEIDEL. "Who Was Who," in his <u>American Memoir</u>. Boston: Houghton Mifflin, pp. 306-309.
     Lewis has never been properly assessed for he was "too deep in social history to be valued rightly by the critics of belles-lettres, and too powerful an artist to be read . . . by the uncritical." He appeared to be just a debunker, but was always an idealist at heart.

8   COWLEY, MALCOLM. "Problem Novel." <u>New Yorker</u>, 23 (24 May), 100-101.
     "An effective tract," <u>Kingsblood Royal</u> is not nearly as successful as Lewis's better novels. Neither Neil nor his bigoted neighbors really come to life and the plot strains readers' credulity.

9   FADIMAN, CLIFTON. "The American Problem." <u>Saturday Review of Literature</u>, 30 (24 May), 9-10.
     Although <u>Kingsblood Royal</u> has faults--"not-too-believable dialogue, shaky motivation, and blunt instrument irony"--it still has the power to make Americans think about their own inconsistencies, hypocrisies, and attitudes regarding race. In becoming a "Negro," Neil Kingsblood learns new and appalling things about his own attitude and that of his nation. Lewis forces the lukewarm white liberal to look at himself. Boxed biographical note appended to review.

10   _____. "Foreword" to <u>Dodsworth</u>. New York: Modern Library, Random House, pp. v-vii.
     <u>Dodsworth</u> is not dated although some of its language may be. American businessmen are as far from finding themselves as when Lewis wrote the novel, and Fran, the "emo-

tional virgin," still exists. Despite his deficiencies as
a novelist, Lewis sees the real problems and issues of
American life. Reprinted 1955.9.

11   FLANAGAN, JOHN T. "A Long Way to Gopher Prairie: Sinclair
     Lewis's Apprenticeship." Southwest Review, 32 (Autumn),
     403-13.
         Surveys Lewis's first five novels in an attempt to find
     the roots of Main Street. Although his early plots are ro-
     mantic, his characters, settings, and style hint at the
     fiction that was to come. Especially in his descriptions
     of small midwestern towns, Lewis anticipates the realism of
     Main Street.

12   GEISMAR, MAXWELL. "Diarist of the Middle-Class Mind." Satur-
     day Review of Literature, 30 (1 November), 9-10, 42-45.
         Condensation of chapter from 1947.13. Revised in
     1958.3.

13   _____. "Sinclair Lewis: The Cosmic Bourjoyce," in his The
     Last of the Provincials: The American Novel, 1915-1925.
     Boston: Houghton Mifflin, pp. 69-150, 364-66.
         Discusses Lewis's works from Our Mr. Wrenn through Cass
     Timberlane. Lewis is perhaps the best example of a provin-
     cial writer and thinker, "a provincial who wanders, home-
     less, between a barren and deteriorating hinterland and an
     increasingly appalling industrial order. . . ." Although
     he "feels no ties" with the "hinterland," Lewis cannot
     treat the new "industrial order" artistically either. Like
     the middle-class bourgeoisie of his Midwest, Lewis was left
     behind by a changing America. Parts condensed in 1947.12.
     Pages 89-97 reprinted in SB, 1971.13. Pages 73-84, 135-50
     reprinted in SL:CCE, 1962.14.

14   GRUNWALD, HENRY ANATOLE. "Main Street 1947." Life, 22
     (23 June), 100-102, 104, 107-108, 110, 113-14.
         Picture story on Sauk Centre, which is "less isolated
     and less isolationist than it was when Sinclair Lewis lam-
     pooned his home town . . . 27 years ago."

15   HANSEN, HARRY. "The Fiction Shelf." Survey Graphic, 36
     (August), 449-50.
         Kingsblood Royal, "class B Lewis," is like Laura Z. Hob-
     son's Gentleman's Agreement. Both have "synthetic" plots
     and are journalism rather than deeply felt experience, as
     is a better novel, The Other Room by Worth Tuttle Heddon,
     which should have been chosen by the Literary Guild instead
     of Kingsblood.

16   HENDERSON, ROBERT W.   Review of <u>Kingsblood Royal</u>. <u>Library</u>
       <u>Journal</u>, 72 (15 May), 809.
              <u>Kingsblood Royal</u> is "Lewis' greatest book" and will have
       extensive social consequences.

17   MARSHALL, MARGARET.   "Notes by the Way." <u>Nation</u>, 164
       (7 June), [689].
              <u>Kingsblood Royal</u> not only is successful propaganda but
       also has one of the earmarks of real art: "It leaves one
       with the exhilarated sense of having had an actual and
       purging experience."

18   MILLER, WAYNE and THE EDITORS OF <u>EBONY</u>.   "<u>Kingsblood Royal</u>:
       Sinclair Lewis Writes a Best Seller on Negroes." <u>Ebony</u>, 2
       (June), 9-13.
              Favorable commentary on <u>Kingsblood</u> accompanied by thir-
       teen photographs by Miller, inspired by the novel. Re-
       printed in part in 1947.6.

19   MOON, BUCKLIN.   "Big Red." <u>New Republic</u>, 116 (26 May), 26-27.
              <u>Kingsblood Royal</u> is a better book than Lewis has written
       for a long time though by no means one of his best. Neil
       may act somewhat unrealistically, but the novel is a "hard-
       hitting" attack on the bigotry which exists in northern
       cities.

20   MORRIS, LLOYD.   "The National Gadfly," in his <u>Postscript to</u>
       <u>Yesterday, America: The Last Fifty Years</u>. New York:
       Random House, pp. 134-45.
              With <u>Main Street</u> Lewis became one of the principal crit-
       ics of American culture in the 1920s, especially of the
       standardization and anti-intellectualism in his native
       Midwest.

21   MOTT, FRANK LUTHER.   <u>Golden Multitudes: The Story of Best</u>
       <u>Sellers in the United States</u>. New York: Macmillan,
       pp. 253, 325, 326, 329, 330.
              Lewis's sales records, 1920-1945, attest to his
       popularity.

22   POORE, CHARLES.   "Trouble in Grand Republic, Minn." <u>New York</u>
       <u>Times Book Review</u>, 25 May, p. 1.
              Lewis's attack on racial prejudice in <u>Kingsblood Royal</u>
       is spirited but ineffective. The plot, particularly the
       ending, is melodramatic and the characters too often become
       caricatures.

1947

23   PRESCOTT, ORVILLE. "Outstanding Novels." <u>Yale Review</u>, n.s.
        37 (September), 189.
            While <u>Kingsblood Royal</u> is on a timely issue, it is a
        "melodramatic" book--"superficial, mechanical, and uncon-
        vincing." If it is to be respected, it is as propaganda,
        not art.

24   REDMAN, BEN RAY. "Sinclair Lewis on Intolerance." <u>American</u>
        <u>Mercury</u>, 65 (July), 111-17.
            Lewis was a remarkable novelist in the 1920s but <u>Kings-</u>
        <u>blood Royal</u> does not resemble his best novels although it
        is probably carefully researched. He attacks prejudice by
        using characters who are mere puppets. Finally, it is
        doubtful that really prejudiced people can be reached by an
        angry satirical book like this.

25   RYAN, ELIZABETH ANN. "The Heroines of Sinclair Lewis." Mas-
        ter's thesis, University of Illinois, 85 pp.
            Deals with general intellectual climate as well as spe-
        cific heroines such as Istra Nash (<u>Our Mr. Wrenn</u>), Una
        Golden (<u>The Job</u>), Claire Boltwood (<u>Free Air</u>), Carol Kenni-
        cott (<u>Main Street</u>), Alverna Easter (<u>Mantrap</u>), Ann Vickers,
        and Jinny Marshland (<u>Cass Timberland</u>). Fran Dodsworth and
        Leora Arrowsmith are two of his best, but like most of his
        characters, his women are often caricatures. His concept
        of the ideal woman changed during his career, growing in
        maturity.

26   SHEEAN, VINCENT. "Sinclair Lewis." <u>Commonweal</u>, 46 (6 June),
        191-92.
            <u>Kingsblood Royal</u> is comparable to Lewis's earlier suc-
        cesses. "Never has Mr. Lewis been more absolute master of
        his material; his very fury itself . . . is always superbly
        controlled, so that we believe the action from beginning to
        end. . . ."

27   S[LOPER], L. A. "Mr. Lewis's Latest Novel." <u>Christian Sci-</u>
        <u>ence Monitor Magazine</u>, 24 May, p. 14.
            In <u>Kingsblood Royal</u> Lewis's "literary ineptness defeats
        his laudable purpose." As usual Lewis sets up "carica-
        tures" and deals more in "sarcasm" than in irony.

28   STEVENS, ALDEN. Review of <u>Kingsblood Royal</u>. <u>Survey Graphic</u>,
        36 (July), 405-406.
            The novel's social impact can be more significant than
        its literary merits or demerits if it can only change
        readers' ways of thinking as have earlier powerful novels
        such as <u>Uncle Tom's Cabin</u> and <u>The Grapes of Wrath</u>.

29 STOUT, REX. "Learning What It Means To Be A Negro." New York
     Herald Tribune Weekly Book Review, 25 May, p. 1.
          Kingsblood Royal is "half novel" when Lewis dramatizes
     Neil's problems and "half tract" when he lets his charac-
     ters talk too much. But the book is important since it
     will probably teach every white reader something about
     racism.

30 WEEKS, EDWARD. "Atlantic Bookshelf: Dark Blood." Atlantic
     Monthly, 179 (June), 124.
          While Kingsblood Royal is not art, it is an effective
     attack on racism, Lewis's most powerful indictment of so-
     ciety since It Can't Happen Here.

31 WITHAM, W. TASKER. "Sinclair Lewis," in his Living American
     Literature: Book One, Panorama of American Literature.
     New York: Stephen Daye Press, pp. 264-70.
          Popular treatment of Lewis's career from Main Street to
     Kingsblood Royal, with heavy emphasis on Babbitt, which is
     quoted extensively. Five photographs.

32 WOODWARD, W. E. The Gift of Life. New York: E. P. Dutton,
     436 pp., passim.
          Account of a friendship with Lewis that began in 1912,
     when Woodward hired Lewis to run the Woodward and Van Slyke
     book review syndicate, and continued until 1930. Lewis's
     drinking habits during the 1920s are emphasized. Partially
     reprinted in 1947.33.

33 _____. "Strictly Personal: Sinclair Lewis Gets the Job."
     Saturday Review of Literature, 30 (1 November), 10-11.
          Account of Lewis's joining the book review syndicate of
     Woodward and Van Slyke as its first editor. See 1947.32.

                              1948

1   AMES, RUSSELL. "Sinclair Lewis Again." College English, 10
     (November), 77-80.
          Modern literary taste has grown precious and no longer
     appreciates the "coarse-textured realists, the story-
     tellers, the architects of our social consciousness," such
     as Lewis. Warren Beck (1948.3) is wrong in his assessment
     of Lewis, whose "honesty and rough truth" may outlast much
     of the self-consciously artistic fiction of the twentieth
     century.

1948

2 ANISIMOV, I. "Literature and the 'American Way of Life.'"
   Soviet Literature, no. 6, pp. 157-64.
      While many American writers have become cynics, writing
   only for money, Lewis shows, especially in Kingsblood Royal, that he is still interested in fighting America's tendencies toward fascism. By mercilessly exposing the racism
   of modern America, Lewis lays bare the entire nation's
   hypocrisy.

3 BECK, WARREN. "How Good Is Sinclair Lewis?" College English,
   9 (January), 173-80.
      Lewis uses "his old bag of tricks" in Kingsblood Royal.
   By now, critics should stop expecting another really good
   Lewis novel and start asking how good he was even at his
   best. He has always gotten by on superficial cleverness
   rather than on competent characterization, dramatic scenes,
   or an appeal to the reader's imagination. His reputation
   remains "the most extravagantly inflated" in American
   fiction.

4 CERF, BENNETT. "Trade Winds." Saturday Review of Literature,
   31 (4 December), 8.
      Before sailing for Europe, Lewis gave an interviewer the
   secret of literary success: work hard and stay away from
   distractions such as television.

5 LEWIS, JAY. "Sinclair Lewis," in his Other Men's Minds. Edited by Phyllis Hanson. New York: G. P. Putnam's Sons,
   pp. 30-34.
      Briefly reviews the high points of Lewis's career from
   Our Mr. Wrenn to Cass Timberlane. Although most critics
   feel that it is Babbitt for which Lewis will be remembered,
   It Can't Happen Here is "one of his most ambitious books"
   and will eventually go to "the head of the list."

6 SPITZ, LEON. "Sinclair Lewis' Professor Gottlieb." American
   Hebrew, 158 (3 December), 2, 10.
      Popular analysis of the "finest Jewish 'character' in
   American" fiction, Arrowsmith's mentor, Max Gottlieb, a Jew
   who replaces religion with science but nevertheless embodies
   many of the virtues of the biblical prophet.

                              1949

1 ANON. "Aaron Gadd." Time, 53 (14 March), 110.
      Unlike most frontier novels, The God-Seeker pictures a
   religious quest that is more important than frontier conflicts. However, it "wavers" between sympathy for Aaron's

                              118

religious feelings and ridicule of other religious characters, between realism and satire.

2   ANON. "American Mission." <u>Times Literary Supplement</u>, 48
     (5 August), 501.
        "Formless, facetious, and sadly lacking in . . . con-
     flict," <u>The God-Seeker</u> "will scarcely add to [Lewis's] rep-
     utation as a serious writer."

3   ANON. "Briefly Noted: Fiction." <u>New Yorker</u>, 25 (19 March),
     100.
        <u>The God-Seeker</u> is a "mediocre" historical novel lightened
     by touches of Lewis's type of humor.

4   ANON. "Lewis's Latest." <u>Newsweek</u>, 33 (14 March), 87.
        Lewis, "who has been somewhat on the downgrade these
     recent years, seems at last to have hit bottom with 'The
     God-Seeker.'"

5   ANON. Review of <u>The God-Seeker</u>. <u>Booklist</u>, 45 (15 February),
     202.
        "Uneven" historical novel of early Minnesota satirizes
     missionaries' attempts to convert Indians.

6   ANON. Review of <u>The God-Seeker</u>. <u>Catholic World</u>, 169 (May),
     158.
        Lewis's historical novel is less satirical than his
     novels of the 1920s, but he does indulge in irony when he
     treats hypocrisies of white missionaries, traders, and gov-
     ernment agents.

7   ANON. Review of <u>The God-Seeker</u>. <u>Kirkus</u>, 17 (1 January), 12.
        Neither the kind of "thesis novel" readers might expect
     nor a successful depiction of life on the frontier. In-
     stead, Lewis's story of early Minnesota "seems remote,
     lacking the impact of his approach to contemporary life."

8   BOYER, RICHARD O. "Downhill." <u>Masses and Mainstream</u>, 2
     (April), 79-81.
        <u>The God-Seeker</u> is an awkward and careless performance by
     Lewis, but even more shocking is Lewis's capitulation to
     the capitalistic system. The society Lewis used to sati-
     rize now seems to have "tamed" him.

1949

9   B[UTTERFIELD], R[OGER]. "From Babbitt to the Bomb." Saturday
    Review of Literature, 32 (6 August), 100-101.
        When Saturday Review began twenty-five years ago, Babbitt
    was the most famous literary character in America and Lewis
    was one of the leading writers in a protest tradition crit-
    ical of American life. Although much of the writing of the
    last ten years has been escape literature, Hersey's docu-
    mentary Hiroshima and such novels as Mailer's Naked and the
    Dead show a return to the impulse that motivated Lewis.
    Photo, p. 105.

10 DAICHES, DAVID. "Mr. Lewis' Accent on the Positive." New
    York Times Book Review, 6 March, pp. 5, 29.
        The God-Seeker appears to have been written by "an ear-
    nest young man, who has done a little research in the his-
    tory of Minnesota" or by a "competent hack." Lewis lacks
    the technique to be anything but a satirist, as he has been
    proving since he first tried to write a "positive" novel
    with Work of Art.

11 GANNETT, LEWIS. "Sinclair Lewis: Main Street." Saturday Re-
    view of Literature, 32 (6 August), 31-32.
        Main Street today may seem a period piece if we note the
    realistic details about small-town life. However, if we
    look at the typical American smugness it attacks, the novel
    hits just as hard as it did in 1920. Perhaps like Field-
    ing, Defoe, and Dickens, Lewis will endure far longer than
    some of the "self-conscious stylists" and "profound philos-
    ophers" among twentieth-century American novelists.

12 HANSEN, HARRY. "Cleaner Books Grow in Popularity." Rotarian,
    74 (May), 8-10, 55-56.
        The public demands less "vulgar" fiction. The God-
    Seeker marks a radical departure from Lewis's earlier, ir-
    reverent novel Elmer Gantry.

13 HART, H. W. Review of The God-Seeker. Library Journal, 74
    (1 February), 198.
        The God-Seeker is not one of Lewis's better novels, but
    Aaron Gadd is one of his better characters.

14 JONES, HOWARD MUMFORD. "Mission in Minnesota." Saturday Re-
    view of Literature, 32 (12 March), 11-12.
        Although "curiously uneven," The God-Seeker has "bounce
    and energy." Aaron Gadd's story is effective; less pala-
    table are Lewis's effusions about Minnesota as the cradle
    of democracy and some of his rather dated satire of small-
    town life. Nevertheless, this is a better novel than
    Kingsblood Royal.

15 MARSHALL, MARGARET. "Notes by the Way." Nation, 168
(2 April), 393-94.
The God-Seeker is built on an "interesting and moving"
theme but its protagonist is not interesting enough and its
plot slows down after a brisk beginning. Lewis treats history as honestly as possible, neither debunking nor glori-
fying the past.

16 MORRIS, LLOYD. "Spectacle of America in Search of a Soul."
New York Herald Tribune Book Review, 6 March, p. 3.
The God-Seeker, while flawed, is a welcome addition to
Lewis's novels because it shows he is capable of presenting
a "positive and eloquent affirmation" of the American
dream.

17 ORTIZ, ALICIA. Sinclair Lewis: Un Espiritu Libre Frente a la
Sociedad Norteamericana. Buenos Aires, Argentina:
Libreria Perlado, 172 pp.
Reviews Lewis's literary career from the perspective of
social criticism. Lewis's treatment of women and their
problems and the stratification of American society are
emphasized. In Spanish.

18 PARROTT, L. MARC, JR. "The Literary Scene: 1929." Theatre
Arts, 33 (September), 48-49, 105-107.
One major literary event of 1929 was Dodsworth, in which
Lewis "turned to George Babbitt's cousin german [sic] Sam
Dodsworth, and found much in him to commend."

19 REYNOLDS, HORACE. "The Bookshelf: Three New Spring Novels."
Christian Science Monitor, 17 March, p. 15.
The God-Seeker displays neither Lewis's gift for satire
nor his ability as a storyteller. The characters are
"types" and the plot seems "loose-jointed, disconnected and
padded. . . ."

20 SHRAPNEL, NORMAN. "New Novels." Manchester Guardian,
29 July, p. 4.
The God-Seeker proves that Lewis still has a good deal
of power left as a novelist. The book is a "robust addition to the literature of conversion."

21 STRONG, L. A. G. "Fiction." Spectator, 183 (12 August),
216, 218.
The God-Seeker marks a departure for Lewis as it is an
historical novel, but his satiric wit "has lost nothing of
its bite."

1949

22 WEEKS, EDWARD. "The Peripatetic Reviewer: Mission in Minne-
        sota." Atlantic Monthly, 183 (April), 78, 80.
        In The God-Seeker, Lewis is an historical novelist and we
    must ask "whether this is the old Red in fancy dress or
    whether he has disciplined himself in a different medium."
    He is at his best when writing of the Territory, using lo-
    cal lore and state history.

23 WOODBURN, JOHN. "Lament for a Novelist." New Republic, 120
        (16 May), 16-17.
        In the 1920s Lewis alternated between good and bad
    books, but the last six have been all bad. His latest, The
    God-Seeker, is comparable to one of Frank Yerby's histori-
    cal thrillers, seasoned with what Lewis thinks are touches
    of his old satire. On the whole, it's "an embarrassingly
    bad book by a reformed satirist."

24 WOOLF, VIRGINIA. "American Fiction," in her The Moment and
        Other Essays. London: Hogarth Press, pp. 98-101. First
    published 1947.
        Reprint of 1925.47.

                              1950

1   ANON. "Headliners of the 1920's." Life, 28 (2 January), 52.
        Photo of Lewis, 64, "vacationing in Italy."

2   BARRY, JOSEPH A. "Sinclair Lewis, 65 and Far from Main
        Street." New York Times Magazine, 5 February, pp. 13, 27.
        Describes Lewis's Florence establishment and solicits
    his opinions on his own earlier work. Lewis describes him-
    self as a "diagnostician" not a "reformer" though he admits
    Kingsblood Royal was an exception. Main Street has changed
    a great deal but people have not. Babbitt is still with
    us.

3   COMMAGER, HENRY STEELE. "The Literature of Revolt," in his
        The American Mind: An Interpretation of American Thought
        and Character Since the 1880's. New Haven: Yale Universi-
    ty Press, pp. 262-64.
        Compares and contrasts William Dean Howells and Lewis.
    Both were concerned with society and character but Lewis
    stayed always on the surface of things. The contrast is
    most obvious in The Rise of Silas Lapham and Babbitt, the
    former showing a genuine sense of values, the latter mir-
    roring confusion.

4   HART, JAMES D.   <u>The Popular Book: A History of America's
     Literary Taste</u>.   New York: Oxford University Press,
     pp. 236-37, 242, 269, 278.
        Accounts for Lewis's popularity by noting that his nov-
     els were simple "in form and idea" and were "concerned en-
     tirely with familiar contemporary scenes, and were boyishly
     vigorous in their obvious satire."   Documents his populari-
     ty by citing numbers of copies in print, copies held by ma-
     jor libraries, and selection by book clubs.

1951

1   ANDERSON, CARL.   "In Memoriam: Sinclair Lewis."   <u>Bonniers
     Litterära Magasin</u>, 20 (February), 163-64.
        Brief review of Lewis's career and laudatory survey of
     his skill as authoritative critic of aspects of American
     society, especially in <u>Main Street</u>, <u>Babbitt</u> (his "mäster-
     verk"), <u>Dodsworth</u>, and <u>Elmer Gantry</u>.   In Swedish.

2   ANON.   "Awards and Obituaries."   <u>Wilson Library Bulletin</u>, 25
     (March), 474.
        Brief obituary noting that Lewis was the first American
     Nobel Prize winner and listing best known works.

3   ANON.   "Craft and Contrivance."   <u>Times Literary Supplement</u>, 50
     (5 October), 625.
        "It is really rather a pity that [<u>World So Wide</u>] had to
     be published at all" since it is a weak novel full of wood-
     en characters and gives the impression that it was written
     only with the greatest effort.

4   ANON.   "Death of Lewis."   <u>Newsweek</u>, 37 (22 January), 84.
        Obituary tribute to Lewis, who typified his era and
     "responded so sensitively and quickly to changes in the
     cultural air that generalizations about him were out-of-
     date almost as soon as they were made."

5   ANON.   "Lewis on Labor."   <u>Newsweek</u>, 37 (5 February), 42.
        Dorothy Thompson reports that Lewis once tried to write
     a "proletarian" novel.

6   ANON.   "News of the Week: (Harry) Sinclair Lewis."   <u>Publish-
     ers Weekly</u>, 159 (27 January), 526-27.
        Obituary, reviewing Lewis's career, citing most of his
     novels with total publication figures for many.

1951

7   ANON. "Our Greatest Was Not Very Great." <u>Christian Century</u>,
     68 (24 January), 101.
         Lewis's real failure to achieve greatness was the result
     of his failure to care about finding the right answers to
     the questions and problems which he so mercilessly laid
     bare.

8   ANON. Review of <u>World So Wide</u>. <u>Booklist</u>, 47 (1 March), 230.
         The old satirical Lewis occasionally shines through in
     this last novel although it is not up to his earlier
     standard.

9   ANON. Review of <u>World So Wide</u>. <u>Kirkus</u>, 19 (15 January), 29.
         Lewis's characters are unconvincing and his story dull.
     He "has lost his skill. . . . But there's still magic in
     the Lewis name for dependable sales and rentals."

10   ANON. "Sinclair Lewis: 1885-1951." <u>Time</u>, 57 (22 January),
     36.
         Obituary. Reviews Lewis's career, in which he mostly
     created variations of his greatest character, Babbitt. Al-
     though a bad writer in many ways, "he made Americans on all
     main streets, including Babbitt, stop hustling long enough
     to wonder uneasily where they were going."

11   ANON. "Sinclair Lewis Dies in Italy." <u>Life</u>, 30 (22 January),
     69-70, 72.
         Though as a man Lewis died January 10, "as a writer, he
     may have died 15 years ago--or he may live for another 200
     years." Reviews career and personality. Twelve pictures,
     from childhood to shortly before his death.

12   ANON. "Sinclair Lewis's Executor." <u>New Yorker</u>, 27 (22 Sep-
     tember), 25-26.
         Melville Cane is working on an edition of Lewis's non-
     fiction (<u>Man from Main Street</u>, 1953.11).

13   ANON. "Valedictory." <u>Time</u>, 57 (26 March), 106, 108.
         Awkwardly written, <u>World So Wide</u> captures the new Ameri-
     can abroad, taken seriously by the world and perhaps too
     seriously by himself.

14   BARZUN, JACQUES. "<u>Elmer Gantry</u>," in <u>American Panorama:</u>
     <u>Essays by Fifteen American Critics on 350 Books</u>. . . .
     Edited by Eric Larrabee. New York: New York University
     Press, p. 201.
         Elmer Gantry, who is nearly an "epic character," belongs
     with Babbitt in the list of major modern literary charac-
     ters.

15   BRION, MARCEL.   "Sinclair Lewis."   Revue des Deux Mondes,
     15 February, pp. [723]-29.
          Traces the course of Lewis's reputation since Main
     Street. Lewis's fame during the 1920s surpassed his true
     merit, but the critical disfavor that followed has been an
     over-reaction. His work will survive on its merits. In
     French.

16   CAILLET, GÉRARD.   "Babbitt Méconnu."   France Illustration, 11
     (27 January), 106.
          Babbitt is an "extraordinary novel." The "unrecognized
     Babbitt" is the worried one, not the stereotyped caricature
     of the American who has sold his soul. There is a "veiled"
     part in all of Lewis's title characters. In French.

17   CLEMENS, CYRIL.   "Impressions of Sinclair Lewis with Some Let-
     ters."   Hobbies, 56 (April), 138-39.
          Popular treatment of Lewis's life and work, with brief
     quotations from several of his letters to Clemens.

18   CONRAD, BARNABY.   "Get to the Story!"   The Writer, 64 (June),
     188-89.
          Lewis helped Conrad to write his first novel, The Inno-
     cent Villa (1948), by telling him to throw away his first
     seventy-three pages of manuscript and get to the story. As
     a general rule, Lewis said he tried to catch the reader's
     attention in the first paragraph and fill in background
     later.

19   C[OUSINS], N[ORMAN].   "Sinclair Lewis."   Saturday Review of
     Literature, 34 (20 January), 20-21.
          It is ironic that Lewis, so American and so midwestern,
     should have died in Rome after having been abroad for most
     of his last two years. Lewis, "more than any other Ameri-
     can writer . . . brought about the renaissance of our lit-
     erature in the Twenties and Thirties." Although a satirist,
     Lewis was a kind man at heart and criticized because of a
     desire to reform America.

20   COWLEY, MALCOLM.   "Epilogue: New Year's Eve," in his Exile's
     Return. New York: Viking Press, pp. 296-97.
          Lewis's winning of the Nobel Prize marked the world's
     recognition of America's coming of age as a world power and
     a literary entity. Lewis is viewed as a transitional fig-
     ure between the older genteel writers and the new genera-
     tion he praised in his acceptance speech.

21 _____. "The Last Flight from Main Street." New York Times
   Book Review, 25 March, pp. 1, 16.
      Lewis's posthumous novel World So Wide reads like a pale
   reflection of Dodsworth. Lewis improved steadily from Our
   Mr. Wrenn through Arrowsmith, declined slowly with Elmer
   Gantry and Dodsworth, and then went into a serious decline.
   However, he will be remembered not for his failures of the
   last twenty years but for his great work of the 1920s. Re-
   printed in SL:CCE, 1962.14.

22 CRANDALL, C. F. "When Sinclair Lewis Wrote a Sonnet in Three
   Minutes, Fifty Seconds." New York Herald Tribune Book Review, 28 (2 September), 4.
      Account of Lewis's writing a sonnet, using end-rhymes
   furnished by Crandall, to win one pound during a London
   drinking party.

23 DEEGAN, DOROTHY YOST. The Stereotype of the Single Woman in
   American Novels. New York: King's Crown Press,
   xvi + 252 pp., passim.
      Briefly considers Lewis's portrayal of single women in
   The Job, Main Street, Elmer Gantry, and Ann Vickers.

24 DOWNING, FRANCIS. "Portraits of the Artist." Commonweal, 54
   (20 April), 36-37.
      An angry reaction to Alexander Manson's essay on Lewis's
   last days (see 1951.39) as an invasion of privacy and the
   worst sort of gossip.

25 EDITORS OF ROTARIAN. "Last Page Comment." Rotarian, 78
   (April), 64.
      Obituary note. Although Lewis ridiculed Rotary in Bab-
   bitt, after reading Rotarian, he wrote the editors admit-
   ting that he had misjudged the organization. He was essentially a fair-minded individual.

26 GANNETT, LEWIS. "Sinclair Lewis Never Doubted that America
   Was Home." New York Herald Tribune Book Review, 27
   (25 March), 1.
      World So Wide is well done for the first half, in which
   it "matches Dodsworth in insight," but the second half
   seems hastily written. However, the book reaffirms Lewis's
   basic love for America, in spite of all his criticism.

27 GARDINER, HAROLD C. "Sauk Centre Was Home Still." America,
   85 (7 April), 19-20.
      World So Wide displays not so much Lewis's love for
   America, as some have said, as his real "provincialism."
   There is a suspicion of the foreign and a self-satisfaction

with one's own ideas that mark Lewis as "like his characters, an innocent abroad." Reprinted 1972.11.

28   GRATTAN, C. HARTLEY. "Sinclair Lewis: The Work of a Life-
      time." New Republic, 124 (2 April), 19-20.
           World So Wide will neither help Lewis's reputation nor
      harm it. Like so many of his novels, it is simply a story
      Lewis tells because he can't help being a storyteller.
      Perhaps the real fault in Lewis's career is not in the
      writer but in the critics who saw him as so much more than
      a storyteller, who tried to make him "a major critic of
      American life."

29   HARCOURT, ALFRED. "A New Novelist," "S. L. Arrives," and
      "The Nobel Prize in Literature," in his Some Experiences.
      Riverside, Connecticut: Alfred and Ellen Harcourt,
      pp. 27-28, 54-59, 79-85.
           Memories of Lewis as a beginning novelist while he was
      still working at George Doran's, and an account of the bur-
      geoning of his career with Harcourt, Brace, his publisher
      from 1919 to 1929. Alfred Harcourt was responsible for the
      deletion of some 20,000 words from the manuscript of Main
      Street; this lost episode was destroyed. Sympathetic pic-
      ture of Lewis as a very lonely man in his later years.

30   HOFFMAN, FREDERICK J. "The American Novel Between Wars," in
      his The Modern Novel in America: 1900-1950. Chicago:
      Henry Regnery, pp. 110-17.
           Lewis's talent was a limited one, but he used it to full
      advantage in his works of the 1920s. At his best, Lewis
      creates "minor triumphs" in works such as Babbitt. At his
      worst, he can be as clumsy as "Sherwood Anderson at his
      feeble worst."

31   HOLLIS, C. CARROLL. "The American Novel Through Fifty Years:
      5. Sinclair Lewis." America, 85 (28 April), 99-102.
           Lewis's contribution to twentieth-century fiction was
      the revival of the Theophrastian Character as a genre and
      his attempt to merge its form with the novel. While he was
      not completely successful, at his best in Babbitt, he "came
      nearest to doing what is ultimately impossible." Judged
      only as novels, Lewis's works are disappointing except for
      Arrowsmith and Dodsworth, but approached from the stand-
      point of Character, his other works of the 1920s are more
      understandable. Expanded in 1968.6.

1951

32 HUGHES, SERGE. "From Main Street to the World So Wide."
    <u>Commonweal</u>, 53 (6 April), 648-50.
        Lewis, whose reputation is currently very low, is due
    eventually for a revival, which will rest on one single
    truth apparent in all his novels: Lewis is at his best
    when he treats "serious moral issues which remain unsolved"
    and at his worst when he tries to "present a solution"
    since his "solutions are either obviously inadequate or
    sentimental." Like <u>Babbitt</u>, <u>World So Wide</u> offers a simple
    solution and the illusion that a problem has been solved.

33 JENKINS, ELIZABETH. "New Novels." <u>Manchester Guardian</u>,
    31 August, p. 4.
        Although well paced and entertaining, <u>World So Wide</u> is a
    rather bland rewriting of <u>Dodsworth</u>.

34 JOHNSON, GERALD W. "Romance and Mr. Babbitt." <u>New Republic</u>,
    124 (29 January), 14-15.
        Among his twenty-one books are some bad ones, but Lewis
    deserves to be remembered for his best work, such as <u>Main
    Street</u>, <u>Babbitt</u>, and <u>Arrowsmith</u>. He was a realist, but a
    strain of romanticism in his nature made him angry about
    the imperfections he observed. Like most writers of the
    twenties, he revolted without moving outside of the Ameri-
    can literary tradition, and future generations may find a
    lot to empathize with in his best books. Reprinted 1954.9.

35 JONES, HOWARD MUMFORD. "Exiles in Florence." <u>Saturday Review
    of Literature</u>, 34 (31 March), 20.
        <u>World So Wide</u> could have been an important international
    novel, but its point of view is inconsistent, sometimes
    taking the characters seriously and sometimes subjecting
    them to the broadest satire. Lewis seems trapped "by his
    conception of himself as a preacher in comic prose" and
    buries his real insights beneath "noisy prose."

36 KASTNER, HAROLD. "On Losing a Friend." <u>Saturday Review of
    Literature</u>, 34 (3 March), 25.
        Letter to the editor: Although Kastner had little in
    common with Lewis, he felt he had lost a true friend.
    Lewis was superior to the critics who picked apart his
    work.

37 KRUTCH, JOSEPH WOOD. "Sinclair Lewis." <u>Nation</u>, 172
    (24 February), 179-80.
        During his lifetime, Lewis achieved a widespread liter-
    ary reputation, but what will become of it? If it lives,
    it will do so because of <u>Main Street</u> and <u>Babbitt</u>, and even

these novels, with their heavy reliance on mimicry and parody, are not great literature. Lewis will be remembered historically, but he may not be read. Reprinted in SL:CCE, 1962.14.

38 LEWIS, GRACE HEGGER. "Sinclair Lewis: A Fontainebleau Memory." Vogue, 117 (15 April), 102-103, 134.
    Personal recollections, by his first wife, of Lewis during the writing of Arrowsmith. Appears in chapter 28 of 1955.15.

39 MANSON, ALEXANDER, as told to Helen Camp. "The Last Days of Sinclair Lewis." Saturday Evening Post, 223 (31 March), 27, 110-12.
    Pictures Lewis during his last year of life as ill and alcoholic, working sometimes on poetry and overworking nearly to the point of collapse on World So Wide. Yet there were also good times when Lewis gave way to surprising generosity. Describes his final days in the hospital.

40 MATLOWSKY, BERNICE D. "Sinclair Lewis: 1885-1951." Semblanzas Literarias, 3. Washington, D.C.: Unión Panamericana, Departmento de Asuntos Culturales, 22 pp.
    Introductory essay on Lewis's life and work, stressing his treatment of American life and character. In Spanish. Bibliography of his works, including Spanish and Portuguese translations, and brief bibliography of secondary materials in English, Spanish, and Portuguese.

41 MILLER, PERRY. "The Incorruptible Sinclair Lewis." Atlantic Monthly, 187 (April), 30-34.
    Personal glimpses of Lewis during his last year of life. Confirms Lewis's interest in Dickens as a model for his own writing and quotes Lewis on the motive behind his satire: "I love [America] but I don't like it." Reprinted 1957.4.

42 MORRISON, ELTING E. "Babbitt," in American Panorama: Essays by Fifteen American Critics on 350 Books. . . . Edited by Eric Larrabee. New York: New York University Press, p. 200.
    Whether or not Lewis was a great novelist, in Babbitt he did what nobody had done before, organizing the materials surrounding American business into a coherent and understandable work of art.

1951

43 OSTERLING, ANDERS. "The Literary Prize," in Nobel: The Man
    and His Prizes. Edited by the Nobel Foundation. Norman:
    University of Oklahoma Press, pp. 123-24.
        Lewis received the Nobel Prize over Dreiser largely be-
    cause of his "gay virtuosity and flashing satire."

44 PAVESE, CESARE. "Sinclair Lewis," in his La letteratura
    americana e altri saggi. Torino: Giulio Einaudi,
    pp. 5-32.
        Discusses Lewis's works from Our Mr. Wrenn to Ann Vick-
    ers and Work of Art. His greatest strength is his use of
    slang and American vernacular; his weaknesses are the ten-
    dency to build novels around one topic or profession, his
    poverty of invention, and his emphasis on externals rather
    than the psychological aspects of his characters. It is
    best to enjoy Lewis for his vivid spectacle of a changeable
    reality and for his enthusiasm. First published in La Cul-
    tura in two essays, November 1930 and May 1934. In Ital-
    ian. Translated in 1970.21.

45 PICKREL, PAUL. "Outstanding Novels." Yale Review, n.s. 40
    (March), 575.
        World So Wide is a poor novel but represents Lewis's
    reconciliation with the America he so often criticized.

46 RAYMOND, JOHN. "New Novels." New Statesman and Nation, 42
    (22 September), 318.
        World So Wide is "astonishingly uneven," running from
    typical Lewis satire to an embarrassing treatment of the
    "hero's twin love affair, with Europe and with a lovely
    research scholar. . . ."

47 REYNOLDS, HORACE. "From the Bookshelf: Satire in the Lewis
    Manner." Christian Science Monitor, 2 April, p. 11.
        World So Wide is partially redeemed by a believable main
    character, but the rest of the characters are so wooden
    that the novel is no contribution to literature. Lewis, up
    to the last, could not transcend his tendency to dwell on
    the surface of life.

48 ROLO, CHARLES J. "Reader's Choice." Atlantic Monthly, 187
    (April), 75.
        World So Wide is sadly dated, though amusing at times.

49 SAUK CENTRE CIVIC AND COMMERCE ASSOCIATION. A Collection on
    Sinclair Lewis. Sauk Centre: Civic and Commerce Associa-
    tion, 9 pp.
        Mimeographed pamphlet includes bibliography of items
    published about Lewis in 1951 and a sketch of his life.

Reprints two articles (probably by Chuck Rathe) and an ed-
itorial from the Sauk Centre Herald (January 1951): "How
Close Was Sinclair Lewis to His Home? The Legend Is Taking
Root"; "The Private Papers of Chuck Rathe"; and "A Look at
Sinclair Lewis."

50 SMITH, HARRISON. "Sinclair Lewis: Remembrance of the Past."
Saturday Review of Literature, 34 (27 January), 7-9, 36-38.
Sentimental recollections of Lewis by a fellow graduate
of Yale who later became his close friend and publisher.
Dwells on Lewis as an outsider at Yale, his disastrous at-
tempt to present his Nobel Prize medal to an unappreciative
Yale Library administrator, his terrible loneliness, and
his sense of loss when his son Wells died in World War II.
Reprinted 1951.51.

51 _____. "Sinclair Lewis: Remembrance of the Past," in Satur-
day Review Reader. Edited by Harrison Smith. New York:
Bantam Books, pp. 12-22.
Reprint of 1951.50.

52 SWADOS, HARVEY. "Of Boors and Heroes." Nation, 172 (12 May),
446-47.
World So Wide is marred by the dated language of its
characters, all of whom "speak in the go-getter accents of
the twenties." This is just one symptom of Lewis's not being able to keep up with a changing world.

53 THOMPSON, DOROTHY. "Sinclair Lewis: A Postscript." Atlantic
Monthly, 187 (June), 73-74.
An appreciative reaction to Perry Miller's article
(1951.41). Stresses the sentiment and love in Lewis's
nature.

54 WALBRIDGE, EARLE F. Review of World So Wide. Library Jour-
nal, 76 (15 March), 514.
Although Lewis adds nothing new to his career with World
So Wide, there are flashes of his old skill at satire.

55 WARFEL, HARRY R. American Novelists of Today. New York:
American Book Company, pp. 266-67.
Brief biographical sketch and notes on subjects of in-
dividual novels.

56 WATERMAN, MARGARET. "Sinclair Lewis as Teacher." College
English, 13 (November), 87-90.
Portrait of Lewis as creative writing teacher based on
experience in short course he taught at University of Wisconsin in 1940.

1951

57 WEST, ANTHONY. "The Party Again." New Yorker, 27 (28 April),
    114-15.
        World So Wide occasionally shows flashes of the early
    Lewis but like most of his recent work, it is only a feeble
    reminder of Lewis at his best. In a few years Lewis's re-
    cent work will be forgotten and his work of the 1920s will
    be remembered so that there "will no longer be any mystery
    about how Sinclair Lewis got his reputation or his Nobel
    Prize."

58 WHARTON, FRED. "Sinclair Lewis." Masses and Mainstream, 4
    (April), 84-94.
        Retrospective survey of Lewis's career. He will be re-
    membered not for his worst works but for his best, in which
    he "lambasts the sterility of bourgeois culture, vividly
    portraying the chicanery and hypocrisy of the 'American
    way'. . . ." While he was never a true radical, he was a
    significant social critic.

59 WHICHER, GEORGE F. "Respectability Defied," in The Literature
    of the American People. Edited by Arthur Hobson Quinn.
    New York: Appleton-Century-Crofts, pp. 854-55.
        Lewis learned to use his skill at mimicry to achieve
    "ruthless" satire in Main Street and perfected the tech-
    nique in Babbitt. Arrowsmith continued the satire but also
    included more fully developed characters such as Martin and
    Max Gottlieb. After Arrowsmith Lewis began a decline.

                              1952

1   ANON. "The Lewis Letters." Newsweek, 40 (24 November),
    102-103.
        Review of From Main Street to Stockholm, "a blow-by-blow
    description" of Lewis's career.

2   ANON. "News of the Week: Sinclair Lewis Exhibition to Open
    in New York." Publishers Weekly, 161 (26 January), 476.
        A display of memorabilia, manuscripts, letters, and
    books sponsored by the American Academy of Arts and
    Letters.

3   BECKER, GEORGE J. "Sinclair Lewis: Apostle to the Phillis-
    tines." American Scholar, 21 (Autumn), 423-32.
        Overview of Lewis's career, emphasizing his "crusading
    zeal" in attacking contemporary American society. Dis-
    cusses specific targets of satire in Main Street, Babbitt,
    The Man Who Knew Coolidge, Elmer Gantry, Dodsworth, Kings-
    blood Royal, It Can't Happen Here.

4   BROOKS, VAN WYCK. The Confident Years: 1885-1915. New York:
       E. P. Dutton, pp. 502-11.
          Although he concentrated on content at a time when the
       "'art' of the novel" was more important to most critics,
       Lewis was a significant novelist, both for the large vari-
       ety of characters and topics he treated and for his zeal as
       a crusader against America's worst side.

5   DEMPSEY, DAVID. "In and Out of Books." New York Times Book
       Review, 10 February, p. 8.
          Mentions Lewis exhibit of American Academy of Arts and
       Letters and some items it contains.

6   _____. "In and Out of Books." New York Times Book Review,
       15 June, p. 8.
          Lewis's literary executors, the law firm of Cane and
       Berner, refuse to allow access to Lewis's papers to anyone
       but Mark Schorer.

7   GEISMAR, MAXWELL. "A Puritan for All." Saturday Review, 35
       (15 November), 24.
          Although the letters in From Main Street to Stockholm
       are all written to his publishers, Lewis's close associa-
       tion with the company and some of its members such as edi-
       tor Harrison Smith make this volume as revealing as any
       collection of personal letters. One impression is that
       Lewis seems obsessed with publicity, yet sometimes the
       reader also sees the artist. An appealing and sympathetic
       picture of Lewis emerges. Reprinted 1958.3.

8   GUTHRIE, RAMON. "The 'Labor Novel' that Sinclair Lewis Never
       Wrote." New York Herald Tribune Book Review, 28 (10 Febru-
       ary), 1, 6.
          Shorter version of 1952.10.

9   _____. "Restless, Lonely, Sensitive--'Red' Lewis' Letters Are
       a Self-Portrait." New York Herald Tribune Book Review, 29
       (16 November), 1.
          From Main Street to Stockholm reveals the complex man
       Lewis was--the mixture of generosity and irritability.

10   _____. "Sinclair Lewis and the 'Labor Novel.'" Proceedings
       of the American Academy of Arts and Letters and the Nation-
       al Institute of Arts and Letters. New York, pp. 68-82.
          Lewis planned to write a novel about the labor movement
       in America; he used Guthrie as technical advisor and sound-
       ing board while researching the book, which he never com-
       pleted. Shorter version in 1952.8.

1952

11   MILLER, PERRY. "Portrait of Sinclair Lewis." Nation, 175
        (6 December), 531-32.
            From Main Street to Stockholm provides not only materi-
        als for the study of Lewis but "for any discussion of the
        endless problem of the artist in America," torn between
        money and art.

12   NATHAN, GEORGE JEAN. "Literary Personalities: Sinclair
        Lewis," in The World of George Jean Nathan. Edited by
        Charles Angoff. New York: Alfred A. Knopf, pp. 19-29.
            Reprint of 1932.13.

13   PRESCOTT, ORVILLE. "Squandered Talents: Lewis, Steinbeck,
        Hemingway, O'Hara," in his In My Opinion: An Inquiry Into
        the Contemporary Novel. Indianapolis, New York: Bobbs-
        Merrill, pp. 50-58.
            Examines Lewis's last five novels and finds all disap-
        pointing. Probably the best are Cass Timberlane and Kings-
        blood Royal, but Lewis's lack of balance in hysterically
        attacking modern marriage and racism makes the novels far
        inferior to his impressive work of the 1920s.

14   ROUSSEAUX, ANDRÉ. "Le dernier roman de Sinclair Lewis." Le
        Figaro Littéraire, 7 (9 February), 2.
            Reviews French translation of World So Wide (Notre monde
        immense), relating it to Lewis's novels of the 1920s. Lewis
        does not finally resolve his ambivalent attitude toward
        America, but the novel is readable. In French.

15   SCHERMAN, DAVID E. and ROSEMARIE REDLICH. "Sinclair Lewis,"
        in their Literary America: A Chronicle of American Writers
        with Photographs of the American Scene that Inspired Them.
        New York: Dodd, Mead, pp. 126-27.
            Two photos of Main Street in Sauk Centre and discussion
        of Lewis's portrayal of American small towns.

16   SMITH, HARRISON. "Introduction" to From Main Street to
        Stockholm: Letters of Sinclair Lewis, 1919-1930. New
        York: Harcourt, Brace, pp. [ix]-xii.
            Account of Lewis's rise as a novelist and of his asso-
        ciation with Harcourt, Brace. Stresses the brilliance of
        Lewis's mind and the care with which he worked on his
        fiction.

17   T[INKER], C[HAUNCEY] B[REWSTER]. "The Lewis Exhibition."
        Proceedings of the American Academy of Arts and Letters and
        the National Institute of Arts and Letters. New York,
        pp. 63-64.

The planning behind the Lewis exhibition, opened 1 February 1952, with addresses by Tinker and Ramon Guthrie (see 1952.10 and 1952.18).

18 TINKER, CHAUNCEY BREWSTER. "Sinclair Lewis, a Few Reminiscences." Proceedings of the American Academy of Arts and Letters and the National Institute of Arts and Letters. New York, pp. 65-67.
    Memories of Lewis as an enthusiastic, excitable student at Yale, where Brewster taught him. Brief remarks on later meetings. Also printed in 1952.19.

19 ____. "Sinclair Lewis, a Few Reminiscences." Yale Alumni Magazine, June, p. 10.
    Address from opening of Lewis exhibition. See 1952.18.

20 WAGENKNECHT, EDWARD. "Sinclair Lewis and the Babbitt Warren," in his Cavalcade of the American Novel. New York: Henry Holt, pp. 354-67, 543-45.
    Survey of Lewis's career and an assessment: Lewis is not a realist but a satirist and his criticism of America and its citizens results not from hatred but from a friendly concern. Bibliography.

21 WILSON, ARTHUR HERMAN. "A Masterly Summation." American Scholar, 22 (Winter), 109-10.
    Letter praising George J. Becker article (see 1952.3), but defending Lewis's heavy use of propaganda by comparing his use of the comic to Dickens's.

22 WILSON, EDMUND. "The All-Star Literary Vaudeville," in his The Shores of Light: A Literary Chronicle of the Twenties and Thirties. New York: Farrar, Straus and Young, pp. 229-47.
    Reprint of 1926.39.

1953

1 AARON, DANIEL. "The Proud Prejudices of Sinclair Lewis." The Reporter, 9 (4 August), 37-39.
   Though at times the essays are dull--"as his conversation never was"--The Man from Main Street does a good job of recalling the real Lewis: his democratic attitudes, his respect for the truth, his "hatred for hypocrisy."

1953

2 ALDRIDGE, JOHN W. "Mr. Lewis as Essayist." New York Times
      Book Review, 15 February, pp. 6, 23.
          Some essays in The Man from Main Street are much better
      than one would expect. Overall, the book shows that Lewis
      had "a first-rate practical mind coupled with an arrested
      and largely third-rate creative sensibility." This book
      helps to explain both Lewis's great popularity and his
      "startling failure" as a novelist.

3 ANON. "Books: Briefly Noted." New Yorker, 28 (24 January),
      86, 88.
          From Main Street to Stockholm reveals Lewis's "odd mix-
      ture of vanity, irascibility, sentimentality, childishness,
      and talent."

4 ANON. "Books: Briefly Noted." New Yorker, 28 (14 February),
      116.
          The selections in The Man from Main Street range from
      good to bad but are never dull. The book is "like a series
      of newsreel shots of a man's intellect. . . ."

5 ANON. "Novelist as Critic." Time, 61 (16 February), 114,
      116.
          The Man from Main Street shows Lewis as a critic who de-
      fends his realistic principles even after he has won his
      battle against excessive gentility. Lewis "kept shadow-
      boxing at opponents he had knocked out years before" and
      kept himself from developing, but he retains his love for
      America and his ability to criticize himself.

6 BROWN, DEMING. "Sinclair Lewis: The Russian View." American
      Literature, 25 (March), [1]-12.
          Critical reaction to Lewis between 1924 and 1949. Lewis
      was popular with Russian critics during the 1920s, but in
      the 1930s his works were attacked for a lack of revolution-
      ary fervor and for a naive inability to distinguish the
      causes of the evils he depicts. As increasing emphasis on
      Marxist criticism demanded explicit ideological statements
      in art, even works which had been favored began to appear
      flawed. Lewis returned to limited approval with It Can't
      Happen Here, Gideon Planish, and Kingsblood Royal. Despite
      the extreme bias of Russian critics, many of their conclu-
      sions about the relative quality of Lewis's works agree
      with the judgments of American critics. Numerous Russian
      articles cited. Slightly revised in 1962.1.

1953

7   FADIMAN, CLIFTON. "Party of One: In Memory of a Man from
     Main Street." Holiday, 13 (March), 6, 8-9, 11.
         Memories and anecdotes about Lewis the man and a compar-
     ison of Lewis with Charles Dickens. Reprinted 1955.9.

8   FIGUEIRA, GASTON. "Perfiles: Dos escritores norteamericanos.
     1, Sinclair Lewis; 2, Langston Hughes." Revista Ibero-
     americana, 18 (September), [401]-404.
         Babbitt is Lewis's most representative work. Mentions
     Main Street, Elmer Gantry, and Arrowsmith as other major
     novels. In Spanish.

9   GEISMAR, MAXWELL. "Native Prizewinner." Saturday Review, 36
     (28 February), 17.
         Between the lines of The Man from Main Street one can
     see the "personal traits" that resulted in Lewis's success
     as a rebel in the twenties and his failure in the thirties.
     As a "popularizer . . . of literary revolt" Lewis needed "a
     strong tradition of authority to support [his] own revolt
     against it." Reprinted 1958.3.

10   GREENE, D. J. "With Sinclair Lewis in Darkest Saskatchewan:
     The Genesis of Mantrap." Saskatchewan History, 6, no. 2
     (Spring), 47-52.
         Careful historical account of Lewis's 1924 trip to Sas-
     katchewan, during which he gathered material later used in
     Mantrap. Includes map of his route.

11   MAULE, HARRY E. and MELVILLE H. CANE. "Introduction" to The
     Man from Main Street: A Sinclair Lewis Reader. New York:
     Random House, pp. xiii-xvi.
         The editors tried, not to determine Lewis's place in
     American literature, but to make additional evidence avail-
     able to those who will establish that place. Lewis's col-
     lected nonfiction, ranging from literary essays and auto-
     biography to journalism on social issues, emphasizes his
     "importance as a literary bridge" between fiction as writ-
     ten by William Dean Howells and as written in the 1920s and
     1930s.

12   RICHARDSON, LYON N. "Revision in Sinclair Lewis's The Man Who
     Knew Coolidge." American Literature, 25 (November),
     [326]-33.
         Comparing the first monologue printed in The Man Who
     Knew Coolidge with its text as printed in American Mercury
     (January 1928) reveals Lewis's extreme precision as a
     craftsman who altered his diction subtly and often expanded
     passages to achieve more telling satire.

1953

13   SCHORER, MARK. "Two Houses, Two Ways: The Florentine Villas
       of Lewis and Lawrence, Respectively." New World Writing:
       Fourth Mentor Selection. New York: New American Library,
       pp. 136–54.
            Describes visits to the Florence houses of Lewis and
       D. H. Lawrence. Includes interviews with several people
       who knew Lewis during his stay in Florence, near the end of
       his life. Lewis was ill--he suffered his first heart at-
       tack while living there--and either artificially gay or
       morose most of the time. Reprinted 1968.10.

14   _____. "The World of Sinclair Lewis." New Republic, 128
       (6 April), 18–20.
            Review-essay on Our Mr. Wrenn, World So Wide, and The
       Man From Main Street. Lewis's first and last novels are
       remarkably similar in plot, theme, and major characters.
       In both he examines the American character by placing it in
       a European setting. The Man From Main Street helps to
       clarify just how Lewis viewed America: The prose pieces
       show a mature, intellectual Lewis who has dropped the nov-
       elist's mask. When Americans were true to their own values,
       he loved them, but when they were false, he was ready to
       attack.

15   WALKER, FRANKLIN. "Jack London's Use of Sinclair Lewis Plots,
       Together with a Printing of Three of the Plots." Hunting-
       ton Library Quarterly, 17 (November), 59–74.
            Full account of the London-Lewis collaboration, employ-
       ing evidence from the Huntington Library Jack London col-
       lection: original copies of Lewis's letters to London,
       carbons of London's letters to Lewis, and manuscripts of
       three plots--"The House of Illusion," "The Guilt of John
       Avery," and "The Common Sense Jail"--none used by London.

16   WALLACH, IRA. "Sinclair Lewis." Masses and Mainstream, 6
       (May), 61–62.
            Editors of The Man from Main Street attempted "to emas-
       culate" Lewis, as when the reader is asked to consider the
       historical context in which Lewis delivered an anti-Nazi
       speech in 1944. A "fair picture of the man in his own
       words" despite the editors' attempt to "smudge the picture."

17   WEEKS, EDWARD. "The Peripatetic Reviewer: What Lewis Was
       Like." Atlantic Monthly, 191 (April), 78, 80.
            From Main Street to Stockholm contains "compelling
       letters."

1954

1   ANON. "People." <u>Time</u>, 64 (23 August), 36.
      Summarizes reminiscence by Charles Breasted (<u>see</u>
      1954.3).

2   ANON. "Powders and Jam." <u>Times Literary Supplement</u>, 53
      (2 April), 212.
      <u>The Man From Main Street</u> shows how good a novelist Lewis
      was, for his essays, in which he attacks problems directly,
      are far less effective than his novels.

3   BREASTED, CHARLES. "The 'Sauk-Centricities' of Sinclair
      Lewis." <u>Saturday Review</u>, 37 (14 August), 7-8, 33-36.
      Recalls some shared experiences with Lewis, including
      confidences from Lewis about his father's failure to under-
      stand his career as novelist, the breakup of his first mar-
      riage, the composition of the final part of <u>Elmer Gantry</u>
      and proofreading that book. In 1926 Lewis told Breasted
      that his best work was behind him, that <u>Babbitt</u> would prob-
      ably be thought his best work though <u>Arrowsmith</u> was his fa-
      vorite, that hereafter any book of his would sell 50,000 or
      so but neither he nor the critics would be fooled into
      thinking he was doing his best work. Reprinted 1959.2.

4   BROWN, GLENORA W. and DEMING B. BROWN. <u>A Guide to Soviet Rus-
      sian Translations of American Literature</u>. New York:
      King's Crown Press, Columbia University, pp. 15-16, 21, 24,
      106-108, [221].
      Lewis is one of the critical realists highly regarded by
      Soviet critics after 1924. Lists 30 separate publications
      (including excerpts and abridgments) up to 1947. Since
      then Lewis has been officially favored because <u>Kingsblood
      Royal</u> exposed American race prejudice.

5   GALLUP, DONALD. "Two Early Manuscripts of Sinclair Lewis."
      <u>Yale University Library Gazette</u>, 29 (July), 37-[41].
      Description of two Yale Library acquisitions: handbound
      pamphlet of twenty-five Lewis poems presented to the Wil-
      liam Rose Benét family for Christmas, 1909, and "Beautiful
      Bill of Beniciary" by Sigismun Slewis, a fifteen-page mock
      novel given to the Benéts in 1910. The holograph title
      page of the second is reproduced.

6   GREBSTEIN, SHELDON NORMAN. "Sinclair Lewis: American Social
      Critic." <u>Dissertation Abstracts</u>, 14:828-29 (Michigan
      State).

1954

> According to his abstract, Grebstein reviews Lewis's
> life, examines his role as a social critic, surveys the
> major criticism, and assesses his "place in modern litera-
> ture."

7 _____. "Sinclair Lewis' Minnesota Boyhood." Minnesota History, 34 (Autumn), 85-89.
   Thorough, authoritative biographical essay on Lewis's
   upbringing in Sauk Centre, drawing on virtually all the
   printed materials preceding it.

8 HOUSTON, PENELOPE. "Main Street." Spectator, 192 (11 June),
   721.
   The contents of The Man From Main Street, ranging from
   "transitory" journalism to thoughtful and significant essays, strike the reader as "more complex and . . . rather
   more positive than the novels. . . ."

9 JOHNSON, GERALD W. "Romance and Mr. Babbitt." New Republic
   (Fortieth Anniversary Issue), 131 (22 November), 29-30.
   Reprint of 1951.34.

10 LEARY, LEWIS. Articles on American Literature 1900-1950.
   Durham, N.C.: Duke University Press, pp. 180-82.
   Secondary sources on Lewis as well as some articles by
   him.

*11 LeCLAIRE, LUCIEN. "How It Was Done: Some Notes on a Sinclair
    Lewis Manuscript," in Seven Summers. Edited by David
    Denker. New Haven, Conn.: Yale University Press,
    pp. 18-28.
    Unlocatable. Listed in Silhol, 1969.30.

12 MANFRED, FREDERICK F. "Sinclair Lewis: A Portrait." American Scholar, 23 (Spring), 162-84.
   Personal account of friendship with Lewis, including ob-
   servation of Lewis's personal mannerisms and his opinions
   on writing, publishers, various competing authors.

13 PROTHRO, JAMES WARREN. Dollar Decade: Business Ideas in the
   1920's. Baton Rouge: Louisiana State University Press,
   pp. 62-64.
   The nation's businessmen object to Lewis's "patronizing
   contempt" and "the caricature quality" of Babbitt.

14   WARREN, DALE. "Notes on a Genius: Sinclair Lewis at his
          Best." Harper's Magazine, 208 (January), [61]-69.
             Memories of a friendship with Lewis that began in the
          middle 1930s and continued until his death. Comments on
          Lewis "on the wagon," drunk, and at his most charming as
          conversationalist and mimic.

1955

1   BRUNE, RUTH E. "Sinclair Lewis." English Journal, 44 (Novem-
          ber), 477-78.
             Account of Lewis's talk to a Bemidji, Minnesota, audi-
          ence in 1945. He advised aspiring writers to stay home and
          write about the environment they know best.

2   CABELL, JAMES BRANCH. "Remarks upon a Once Glorious Epoch,"
          in his As I Remember It. New York: Robert M. McBride,
          pp. 166-71.
             Personal memories of Lewis and an assessment of his
          work: Main Street was better as a general concept than as
          a book, for it was "too long, and the writing [was] strag-
          gly." Babbitt and Dodsworth were excellent novels, Mantrap
          and The Man Who Knew Coolidge mere potboilers. Lewis may
          have ruined himself by producing such frankly commercial
          books in an attempt to cash in on his fame.

3   CARPENTER, FREDERIC I. "Sinclair Lewis and the Fortress of
          Reality." College English, 16 (April), 416-23.
             In his novels of the 1920s Lewis shows characters fight-
          ing to maintain or achieve ideals in the face of harsh
          reality. In his later work Lewis "conceived of an American
          'reality' which excluded romance and idealism entirely."
          This shift explains the decline of his reputation. Reprint-
          ed, with slight revision in 1955.4.

4   _____. "Sinclair Lewis and the Fortress of Reality," in his
          American Literature and the Dream. New York: Philosophi-
          cal Library, pp. 116-25.
             Slightly revised version of 1955.3.

5   COLEMAN, ARTHUR B. "The Genesis of Social Ideas in Sinclair
          Lewis." Dissertation Abstracts, 15:1069 (New York Univer-
          sity).
             According to his abstract, Coleman treats Lewis's social
          philosophy, its sources in the works of H. G. Wells, Hamlin
          Garland, Thorstein Veblen, George Bernard Shaw, and H. L.
          Mencken, and its application to the three main periods of

1955

his work--from <u>Our Mr. Wrenn</u> to <u>Babbitt</u>, from <u>Arrowsmith</u> to <u>Ann Vickers</u>, and from <u>Work of Art</u> to <u>World So Wide</u>.

6 C[OUSINS], N[ORMAN]. "'Main Street' Comes into the Home." <u>Saturday Review</u>, 38 (17 December), 22.
Thirty-five years after its publication, <u>Main Street</u> no longer shocks; in fact, one is impressed by how much Lewis achieved without today's use of the "outhouse phrase." The book is still relevant not for its exposure of the small town's hypocrisies, but for what was then a secondary theme --the stifling effect of American life on the "new American woman."

7 DOOLEY, DAVID J. "The Impact of Satire on Fiction: Studies in Norman Douglas, Sinclair Lewis, Aldous Huxley, Evelyn Waugh, and George Orwell." <u>Dissertation Abstracts</u>, 15:2203-204   (State University of Iowa).
According to his abstract, since "satire can no longer be considered a distinct literary genre," satirists often use the novel as a vehicle. Lewis's works are torn between his desire to satirize and his desire to write good fiction.

8 DUFFUS, R. L. "Main Street Thirty-five Years Later." <u>New York Times Magazine</u>, 7 August, pp. 24, 62-63.
Essay and photos of Sauk Centre in 1955, emphasizing changes.

9 FADIMAN, CLIFTON. "No Knights in Minnesota" and "Dodsworth," in his <u>Party of One</u>. Cleveland, New York: World Publishing, pp. 47-53, 132-35.
Reprint of 1947.10 and of 1953.7.

10 FARRELL, JAMES T. "A Souvenir of Sinclair Lewis." <u>New Leader</u>, 38 (14 November), 23-25.
Personal anecdotes about Lewis, who was a "much more important and influential writer than Ernest Hemingway or William Faulkner" to Farrell and other writers of his generation. <u>Babbitt</u> was a profoundly liberating book. "At present, [Lewis's] books are not fashionable. . . . This will change, and Lewis's place in both American and world literature will be sure and firm." Reprinted 1976.5 with minor changes.

11 FYVEL, T. R. "Martin Arrowsmith and his Habitat." <u>New Republic</u>, 133 (18 July), 16-18.
While most modern critics dismiss Lewis as a journalist who achieved accidental popularity, a rereading of <u>Arrowsmith</u> suggests that Lewis merits reassessment. His zest for his subject, effective use of caricature, and sharp

vision of a nightmarish America made him outstanding. In
at least three novels (<u>Main Street</u>, <u>Babbitt</u>, and <u>Arrow-
smith</u>), "Lewis captured a glimpse of an American
age. . . ." Reprinted in <u>TCIA</u>, 1968.4.

12 GREBSTEIN, SHELDON. "The Education of a Rebel: Sinclair
Lewis at Yale." <u>New England Quarterly</u>, 28 (September),
372-82.
    Biographical treatment of Lewis's years at Yale (1903-
1908), with samples and citations of his contributions to
<u>Yale Literary Magazine</u> and <u>Yale Courant</u>.

13 HEINEY, DONALD W. "Sinclair Lewis," in his <u>Essentials of Contemporary Literature</u>. Great Neck, N.Y.: Barron's Educational Series, pp. 56-63.
    Brief biographical sketch and discussions of major
works. Lewis combines the detail of a naturalist with the
"scorn and wit of a born satirist."

14 HOFFMAN, FREDERICK J. "The Text: Sinclair Lewis's <u>Babbitt</u>,"
in his <u>The Twenties: American Writing in the Postwar Dec-
ade</u>. New York: Viking Press, pp. 364-70.
    <u>Babbitt</u> is both a parody of the era's American business-
man and a novel about the "sensitive, humane Babbitt" who
aspires to something more than his sterile life. Because
of this split, it is a flawed novel, but its criticism of
the middle class makes it a "representative" novel of the
1920s. Reprinted in <u>SB</u>, 1971.13.

15 LEWIS, GRACE HEGGER. <u>With Love From Gracie</u>. New York:
Harcourt, Brace, 345 pp.
    Subjective account of Lewis as a reserved husband and
an indifferent father by his first wife, covering the
years 1912 to 1925. Treats his need for travel and his
growing abuse of alcohol as well as his admirable work
habits as a writer.

16 O'DONNELL, NORBERT F. "Schorer and Satire." <u>New Republic</u>,
133 (28 November), 23.
    Schorer misreads <u>Elmer Gantry</u> (<u>see</u> 1955.18) because he
fails to read it as satire rather than "a contemporary novel of sensibility." It is supposed to be narrow and limited, but the result should be laughter rather than the sort
of total revulsion Schorer feels.

1955

17   RICHARDSON, LYON N. "Arrowsmith: Genesis, Development, Ver-
       sions." American Literature, 27 (May), [225]-44.
           Lewis's collaboration with Paul de Kruif is treated
       briefly. A textual comparison of Arrowsmith as serialized
       in The Designer and the Woman's Magazine and as published
       novel reveals that by omitting some excessively satirical
       sections, Lewis and the magazine editor actually produced
       a more readable story for the magazine. Partially reprint-
       ed in TCIA, 1968.4.

18   SCHORER, MARK. "The Monstrous Self-Deception of Elmer Gantry."
       New Republic, 133 (31 October), 13-15.
           Elmer Gantry, which has been considered less as a novel
       than as a social event, is analyzed as a sort of fictional
       world of total horror. It has power as a novel because the
       narrowness of its range forces the reader to recognize his
       own similarity to Gantry, to see that like Gantry we all
       deceive ourselves. Expanded in 1956.6.

19   SMITH, THELMA M. and WARD L. MINER. Transatlantic Migration:
       The Contemporary American Novel in France. Durham, N.C.:
       Duke University Press, pp. 9, 16, 17, 22.
           Documents Lewis's acceptance in France, with fourteen
       novels translated during the 1930s.

20   SPILLER, ROBERT E. "Second Renaissance," in his The Cycle of
       American Literature: An Essay in Historical Criticism.
       New York: Macmillan, pp. 222-24.
           Lewis's forte was exposing the foibles of the middle
       class through his "relentless and cruel" satire. Occasion-
       ally he produced a "memorable and living character" by
       tempering his satire with his "sense of humanity."

                              1956

1   AUBERY, PIERRE. "Les Industrial Workers of the World dans
       l'oeuvre d'Upton Sinclair." Revue Socialiste, no. 99,
       pp. 178-97.
           Erroneously cited in 1959.6 as "dans l'oeuvre de Sinclair
       Lewis."

2   CERF, BENNETT. "Trade Winds." Saturday Review, 39 (25 Feb-
       ruary), 7-8.
           Reader Rupert Hughes recalls Dreiser's slapping Lewis's
       face in public after Lewis accused him of incorporating
       3000 words by Dorothy Thompson in Dreiser Looks at Russia
       (1928). Quotes Ethel Barrymore's anecdote about Lewis in-
       terviewing (and browbeating) clergymen while researching
       Elmer Gantry.

3 DU BOIS, WILLIAM. "In and Out of Books." New York Times Book
   Review, 16 September, p. 8.
       A note on With Love from Gracie and the light it sheds
   on the composition of Main Street. Recounts the tremendous
   popularity of Main Street.

4 EDEL, LEON. "A Tragedy of Arrested Adolescence." New Republic, 135 (15 October), 29.
       In spite of its rather "trivial" title, Grace Hegger
   Lewis's With Love from Gracie gives new insights into the
   character of Sinclair Lewis and the basic insecurity that
   would not allow him to bear up under the reverses that followed his early success.

5 HACKETT, ALICE PAYNE. 60 Years of Best Sellers: 1895-1955.
   New York: R. R. Bowker, 260 pp., passim.
       To previous edition (1945.15) adds Cass Timberlane
   (fifth in 1945) and Kingsblood Royal (eighth in 1947).

6 SCHORER, MARK. "Sinclair Lewis and the Method of Half-
   Truths," in Society and Self in the Novel: English Institute Essays, 1955. Edited by Mark Schorer. New York:
   Columbia University Press, pp. 117-44.
       Incorporates and expands 1955.18. Unlike many novelists,
   Lewis is not concerned with presenting a coherent view of
   the world but with accomplishing a single objective. To do
   so, he screens out facts that do not illustrate his main
   point, thus telling a partial truth, as in Elmer Gantry,
   which is viewed as "a work of almost pure revulsion." No-
   where else does Lewis make it so clear how much he hates
   the subject of his satire. Reprinted in SL:CCE, 1962.14;
   1963.22; and 1968.10.

7 SMITH, HARRISON and DONALD BARR. "The Riddle of Sauk Centre."
   Saturday Review, 39 (6 October), 33, 48.
       Paired reviews offer the opinions of two different gen-
   erations on Lewis and on With Love from Gracie. Smith,
   contemporary and friend of Lewis, sees the book as answer-
   ing questions about Lewis and providing clues to the reasons for his spectacular rise and later drift toward ob-
   scurity. To Barr, a young Columbia professor, the book
   shows the insecurity, social and sexual, that motivated
   Lewis: the failure of his first marriage ended the fantasy
   Lewis created to enable him to deal with his insecurity,
   and he could no longer produce the kind of fiction that
   made him famous.

1956

8 STEVENS, BETTY. "A Village Radical Goes Home." Venture, 2,
   no. 2 (Summer), 17-26.
      Personal memories of Lewis in Duluth while he was writ-
   ing Kingsblood Royal. Lewis's opinions on hypocrites,
   communists, labor unions, and Negroes. See Part Two,
   1957.6.

9 TAYLOR, WALTER FULLER. "III. H. L. Mencken (1880-1956) and
   Sinclair Lewis (1885-1951)," in his The Story of American
   Letters. Chicago: Henry Regnery, pp. 349-56.
      Brief summaries of Lewis's apprenticeship and declining
   years. Emphasizes the better novels. Main Street and
   Babbitt employ "the technique of the novel of ideas" but
   are actually one-sided satires, while Arrowsmith is devoted
   to exposition of science as a faith for modern man. Dodsworth is a realistic character study and worthy addition to
   American international novels as written by Cooper, James,
   and William Dean Howells.

10 WILSON, EDMUND. "The All-Star Literary Vaudeville," in his
   A Literary Chronicle: 1920-1950. Garden City, N.Y.:
   Doubleday, pp. 78-80.
      Reprint of 1926.39.

                              1957

1 ANDERSON, CARL L. "Swedish Criticism 1920-1930: The Reception of Sinclair Lewis" and "The Award of the Nobel Prize
   to Sinclair Lewis," in his The Swedish Acceptance of American Literature. Philadelphia: University of Pennyslvania
   Press, pp. [45]-63, [84]-100, 142-44.
      Traces the growth of Lewis's reputation in Sweden in the
   1920s. While some critics felt reservations about Lewis
   because of his "photographic and phonographic" technique or
   because of his attack on organized religion in Elmer Gantry, by the end of the decade he was the best-known American novelist and had a secure critical reputation. His
   Nobel Prize was widely supported, but his reputation waned
   in the 1930s. Bibliography.

2 ANON. "Dodsworth," in American Writing Today: Its Independence and Vigor. Edited by Allan Angoff. New York: New
   York University Press, pp. 368-70.
      Reprint of 1929.1.

3   BENÉT, WILLIAM ROSE. "The Earlier Lewis," in The Saturday Re-
     view Treasury. Edited by John Haverstick. New York:
     Simon and Schuster, pp. 30-35.
          Reprint of 1934.15.

4   MILLER, PERRY. "Incorruptible Sinclair Lewis," in Atlantic
     Monthly Jubilee: One Hundred Years of the "Atlantic."
     Edited by Edward Weeks and Emily Flint. Boston: Little,
     Brown, pp. 332-40.
          Reprint of 1951.41.

5   MIZENER, ARTHUR. "The Pulitzer Prizes." Atlantic Monthly,
     200 (July), 42-45.
          Reviewing past Pulitzer Prizes, one can "understand how
     the judges came to think not only that The Age of Innocence
     was a better book than Main Street (which it probably is)
     but that it was superior in another, nonliterary way--it
     was a safer book to give the prize to." The judges seem to
     ignore an important writer's early and best books (as with
     Main Street and Babbitt) and choose his later and lesser
     work (as with Arrowsmith in 1926).

6   STEVENS, BETTY. "A Village Radical: His Last American Home."
     Venture, 2, no. 3 (Winter), 35-48.
          Memories of visit to Lewis's Williamstown house in 1947.
     Lewis spoke of Kingsblood Royal, politics, and his labor
     union work, which he thought he might do as a play. Pre-
     sents Lewis as charming and affable, as in Part One,
     1956.8.

7   SWINNERTON, FRANK. "Never Meet an Author." Saturday Review,
     40 (2 March), 7-9.
          Literary works are often spoiled if one knows the author
     too well, as was the case with H. G. Wells and Arnold Ben-
     nett, neither of whom could stand to read their friend
     Lewis. Includes a lively character sketch of Lewis as he
     often appeared at parties.

8   TAYLOR, ROBERT H. and HERMAN W. LIEBERT. Authors at Work.
     New York: The Grolier Club, pp. 22-23, 51, plate no. 67.
          Introduction and notes to manuscript materials on Bab-
     bitt exhibited at the Grolier Club, 18 October to 6 Decem-
     ber 1955. Plates reproduce first page of typescript with
     holograph corrections, a page of Lewis's plan of the novel,
     a list of characters and their biographies, and a page of
     notes on historical backgrounds.

1958

1 AUSTIN, ALLEN. "An Interview with Sinclair Lewis." University of Kansas City Review, 24 (Spring), [199]-210.
   In a 1948 interview Lewis was again speaking of writing his big labor novel. He favored socialism at the time and remembered Eugene Debs with fondness. On other writers, he acknowledged the influence of Wells, Dickens, and Thoreau, but not that of Flaubert. He respected the work of Hemingway, Wolfe, and Steinbeck, but not that of most writers of the 1940s except Mailer, whose Naked and the Dead he liked. Critics bored him; he claimed not to read criticism of his own work.

2 BRUCCOLI, MATTHEW J. "Textual Variants in Sinclair Lewis's Babbitt." Studies in Bibliography, volume 11. Charlottesville: Bibliographical Society of the University of Virginia, pp. 263-68.
   Bibliographical study of the first five printings of Babbitt, with special attention to two variants within the first printing. From the first to the fourth printing, the text was improved, but from the fifth printing on, earlier errors appeared as a second, uncorrected, set of plates was used. Any text printed after 1942 may be considered corrupt.

3 GEISMAR, MAXWELL. "Sinclair Lewis: Diarist of the Middle-Class Mind" and "A Postscript," in his American Moderns: From Rebellion to Conformity. New York: Hill and Wang, pp. 107-18.
   Revised version of 1947.12 and reprint of 1952.7 and 1953.9.

4 GREBSTEIN, SHELDON. "Sinclair Lewis's Unwritten Novel." Philological Quarterly, 37 (October), 400-409.
   As early as 1921 Lewis planned a novel on the labor movement in America. Examines Lewis's plans, bits of these plans used in other novels, and theories about practical and psychological reasons for his failure to write the book.

5 HEINEY, DONALD. "Sinclair Lewis," in his Recent American Literature. Woodbury, N.Y.: Barron's Educational Series, pp. 112-21.
   Brief introduction to Lewis as satirist, biographical sketch, and thumbnail analyses of Main Street, Babbitt, Arrowsmith, Dodsworth, and It Can't Happen Here.

6   LEWIS, GRACE HEGGER. "I Wrote a Biography." Virginia Quar-
      terly Review, 34 (Winter), [18]-25.
          Account of why and how With Love from Gracie was written
      after numerous scholars had asked for information on Lewis.
      She used not only her memory, photos, and notes, but inter-
      views and letters from old friends and acquaintances.

7   MAGILL, FRANK N. and DAYTON KOHLER. "Sinclair Lewis." Cyclo-
      pedia of World Authors. New York: Harper and Brothers,
      pp. 647-49.
          Biographical sketch and list of principal works. With
      Mencken, Lewis was one of the two dominant figures writing
      in the 1920s. Briefly discusses major novels.

8   MENCKEN, H. L. "Hints for Novelists," in The Bathtub Hoax,
      and other Blasts and Bravos from the Chicago Tribune. Ed-
      ited by Robert McHugh. New York: Alfred A. Knopf,
      pp. 67-71.
          Holds up Babbitt as a good example for the modern novel-
      ist. Lewis creates a distinctive character who also sati-
      rizes an entire class. Reprinted from Chicago Tribune,
      27 December 1925.

9   NATHAN, GEORGE JEAN. "Memories of Fitzgerald, Lewis, and
      Dreiser." Esquire, 50 (October), [148]-[54].
          Revised and updated version of 1932.13. Six paragraphs
      about Lewis and the theater are added at the beginning and
      two paragraphs about Lewis after 1932 are added at the end.

10 SCHORER, MARK, ed. "A Minnesota Diary: Second Thoughts on
      Babbitt, Main Street, the Search for Home." Esquire, 50
      (October), [160]-[62].
          Prints, with an introduction, portions of a journal
      Lewis kept between 1942 and 1946, when he attempted to make
      a home in Minnesota again. Documents his ambivalence to-
      ward Minnesota--the source of his inspiration, but a pro-
      vincial, unpleasant place as well.

                              1959

1   BOWERS, FREDSON. Textual and Literary Criticism. Cambridge:
      Cambridge University Press, pp. 18-20, 26-27.
          Discusses Louis N. Feipel's "list of about a hundred in-
      consistencies and errors in the first printing" of Babbitt,
      the types of errors Lewis made, and the reasons why only
      the fourth printing of Babbitt reflects "Lewis's revised
      intentions."

1959

2 BREASTED, CHARLES. "The Sauk-Centricities of Sinclair Lewis,"
   in The Saturday Review Gallery. Edited by Jerome Beatty,
   Jr., et al. New York: Simon and Schuster, pp. 231-42.
   Reprint of 1954.3.

3 DAVIES, HORTON. "Sinclair Lewis," in his A Mirror of the
   Ministry in Modern Novels. New York: Oxford University
   Press, pp. 23-40.
      In Elmer Gantry and The God-Seeker Lewis attacks empty
   rhetoric and hypocrisy, but his approach differs in each.
   In Elmer Gantry he emphasizes a roguish minister contrasted
   with a couple of admirable clergymen, while in The God-
   Seeker he depicts Aaron Gadd sympathetically and contrasts
   him with windy or pedantic missionaries.

4 DERLETH, AUGUST. "Three Literary Men: A Memoir of Sinclair
   Lewis, Sherwood Anderson, and Edgar Lee Masters." Arts in
   Society, [1] (Winter), 11-46.
      Tells of three meetings with Lewis and occasional corre-
   spondence, 1937-1944. Lewis was supportive to Derleth,
   partly because of the midwestern roots and subject matter
   of Derleth's fiction, and advised him to write less and
   more slowly. Reprinted in 1963.7.

5 FENTON, CHARLES. "The American Academy of Arts and Letters
   vs. All Comers: Literary Rags and Riches in the 1920's."
   South Atlantic Quarterly, 58 (Autumn), 572-86.
      History of the conservative Academy during the 1920s and
   Lewis's attack on the Academy in his Nobel Prize acceptance
   speech.

6 GILENSON, B. A. and I. M. LEVIDOVA. Sinkler L'iuis [Sinclair
   Lewis: Bio-bibliographical Index Commemorating the Seventy-
   Fifth Anniversary of his Birth]. Moscow: Vsesoyuznoi
   Knizhnoi Palaty, 88 pp.
      Gilenson reviews Lewis's life and career, including ex-
   cerpts from some of his works and speeches. Levidova's
   bibliographical sections include (1) articles, stories,
   books, letters, etc. by Lewis; (2) Russian editions of
   Lewis's works; (3) Russian articles and reviews; (4) literature on Lewis in other languages, including English;
   (5) obituaries; and (6) reviews.

7 GREBSTEIN, SHELDON. "Sinclair Lewis and the Nobel Prize."
   Western Humanities Review, 13 (Spring), 163-71.
      Review of Lewis's winning of the prize and the contro-
   versy surrounding it. Agrees with the majority of critics
   that Lewis deserved the prize, but it "marked the end" of
   his significant achievement as a major American novelist.

8   GREENE, DONALD and GEORGE KNOX, editors. <u>Treaty Trip: An</u>
     <u>Abridgment of Dr. Claude Lewis's Journal of an Expedition</u>
     <u>Made by Himself and His Brother, Sinclair Lewis, to North-</u>
     <u>ern Saskatchewan and Manitoba in 1924</u>. Minneapolis: Uni-
     versity of Minnesota Press, 42 pp.
          Account of the trip which furnished Lewis with the raw
     material for <u>Mantrap</u>. Dr. Lewis emphasizes his brother's
     drinking. Editors quote passages of <u>Mantrap</u> describing
     Indians, a hotel, a trading post, a square dance, and other
     details that parallel Dr. Lewis's factual observations of
     their sources on the trip.

9   LEWIS, CLAUDE. <u>See</u> 1959.8.

10   LOEB, HAROLD. <u>The Way It Was</u>. New York: Criterion Books,
     pp. 79-80, 84-86.
          Personal memories of Lewis and his first wife in Paris
     during the early 1920s.

11   MOORE, GEOFFREY. "Sinclair Lewis: A Lost Romantic," in <u>The</u>
     <u>Young Rebel in American Literature</u>. Edited by Carl Bode.
     London, Melbourne and Toronto: William Heinemann,
     pp. 51-76.
          Lewis began his career as a romantic, but after the re-
     ception of <u>Main Street</u> he realized that he could write
     serious satirical fiction. He then attempted to shape a
     reputation as an artist and critic of society. He failed
     after the 1920s because his talent was rather limited and
     he did not change enough with the times. Reprinted in
     SL:CCE, 1962.14.

12   OLDHAM, JANET. "<u>Dr. Zhivago</u> and <u>Babbitt</u>." <u>English Journal</u>,
     48 (May), 242-46.
          <u>Dr. Zhivago</u> and <u>Babbitt</u> have a great deal in common:
     each was probably the novel which won its author the Nobel
     Prize; both attack conformity and praise individualism;
     both emphasize ideas at the expense of plot; neither pre-
     sents "well-rounded characters." Finally, each author was
     attacked as unworthy in his own country when he won the
     Nobel Prize.

                          <u>1960</u>

1   ADAMS, J. DONALD. "Speaking of Books." <u>New York Times Book</u>
     <u>Review</u>, 31 July, p. 2.
          John P. Marquand and Lewis shared a love for the people
     and the country they satirized. Both had hot tempers,
     wrote excellent accurate dialogue, and had a "humor and

compassion shared by few of their contemporaries." Unfortunately both also continued to turn out "increasingly
paler carbon copies" of their best work as they grew older,
and both stayed essentially on the surface of the life
they wrote about. Reprinted 1965.2.

2   ANON. "Notes for Another Letter from Sauk Centre." Carleton
        Miscellany, 1, no. 2 (Spring), 110-11.
            Collection of small news items from Sauk Centre stress-
        ing the irony of the city's lionizing Lewis after he sati-
        rized the small town.

3   ANON. "People." Time, 75 (11 April), 48.
            Sauk Centre celebrates the seventy-fifth anniversary of
        Lewis's birth.

4   ANON. Sinclair Lewis: An Exhibition. Foreword by Grace
        Hegger Lewis. Austin, Texas: Humanities Research Center,
        28 pp.
            Catalog of special display from materials in the Grace
        Hegger Lewis-Sinclair Lewis Collection, University of
        Texas. Reprints facsimile of the first page of the type-
        script of Main Street with Lewis's handwritten corrections.

5   AUSMUS, MARTIN R. "Sinclair Lewis, Dodsworth, and the Fallacy
        of Reputation." Books Abroad, 34 (Autumn), [349]-55.
            The source of Lewis's literary reputation is not merely
        his biting satire or his photographic realism or even his
        specific comments on society, but his search for Truth.
        Dodsworth exemplifies that search. Discusses the novel as
        part of the Lewis canon and examines structure and themes.

6   BABCOCK, C. MERTON. "Americanisms in the Novels of Sinclair
        Lewis." American Speech, 35 (May), [110]-16.
            A list, with sources, of 100 examples of Americanisms re-
        corded by Lewis in Main Street, Babbitt, and Arrowsmith.

7   BRAND, PETER. "A Letter from Sauk Centre." Carleton Miscel-
        lany, 1, no. 2 (Spring), 103-10.
            Very personal account of trip to Sauk Centre during com-
        memoration of Lewis's seventy-fifth birthday anniversary.
        Sauk Centre observed 1960 as "Sinclair Lewis Main Street
        Year." Pokes fun at the town much in the manner of Lewis.

8   FLANAGAN, JOHN T. "The Minnesota Backgrounds of Sinclair
        Lewis's Fiction." Minnesota History, 37 (March), 1-13.
            Minnesota is the setting for six novels and a large
        number of Lewis's short stories. Fictional communities
        such as Gopher Prairie, Joralemon, Grand Republic, and

Northernapolis are based on real Minnesota places and pro-
ject Lewis's judgment of his home state. Some of Lewis's
best work draws on scenes remembered from his youth.

9   GEISMAR, MAXWELL. "Sinclair Lewis: Forgotten Hero." Satur-
    day Review, 43 (25 June), 29-30.
        Although Lewis's fiction declined badly after It Can't
    Happen Here, the neglect from which he suffers seems
    strange and undeserved. In the 1920s Lewis skillfully and
    prophetically traced the growing tendency of America to-
    ward materialism and uniformity. In the 1960s we could
    still use the correction of Lewis's satiric wit.

10 GUTHRIE, RAMON. "The Birth of a Myth, or How We Wrote 'Dods-
    worth.'" Dartmouth College Library Bulletin, n.s. 3,
    no. 3 (April-October), 50-54.
        Debunks a myth that Guthrie, an old friend of Lewis,
    wrote or helped to write Dodsworth. He provided Lewis with
    a brief history of automotive designing, most of which was
    omitted in the final draft, and he read the first draft for
    factual errors, mostly concerning European settings. In-
    cludes several homely anecdotes.

11 HOWARD, LEON. "Tradition in the Twenties," in his Literature
    and the American Tradition. Garden City, N.Y.: Doubleday,
    pp. 267-69.
        Lewis's reputation was deservedly short-lived because he
    lacked the ability to order his material and contented him-
    self with recording or shallowly satirizing it. In the in-
    dividualistic twenties, however, this seemed a strength as
    it allowed each reader to interpret the work for himself.

12 LEWIS, GRACE HEGGER. "When Lewis Walked Down Main Street."
    New York Times Magazine, 3 July, pp. 12, 28-29.
        Lewis's first wife reminisces about her first visit to
    Sauk Centre with Lewis. Published to mark 40th anniversary
    of publication of Main Street.

13 LIGHT, MARTIN. "A Study of Characterization in Sinclair
    Lewis's Fiction." Ph.D. dissertation, University of Illi-
    nois. 328 pp.
        Like Dickens's novels, Lewis's books are full of many
    characters and his minor characters are excellent. His
    best women are in the early novels. "Villains" such as
    Babbitt and Elmer Gantry are the "fulcrum of Lewis's work"
    and "the pivot of the humor in Lewis." Lewis has problems
    characterizing real heroes, since he envisions the American
    hero as less than completely heroic.

1960

14   MOORE, JAMES BENEDICT. "The Sources of 'Elmer Gantry.'" New
     Republic, 143 (8 August), 17-18.
         Lewis had two real-life models for Gantry--Dr. William
     L. Stidger of Kansas City and Dr. John Roach Straton of New
     York. Stidger, who became one of the leading denouncers of
     Elmer Gantry, described to Lewis his methods of selling
     Christianity and loaned Lewis some of his six books on
     "church-filling methods," many of which appeared in the
     novel. Straton's flamboyant anti-vice raids are imitated
     by Gantry in Zenith.

15   PRIESTLEY, J. B. "Between the Wars," in his Literature and
     Western Man. New York: Harper and Brothers, pp. 429-32.
         Lewis is at his best, like Mencken, when he plays the
     role of "satirical-clown." In his most successful novels
     he is not a realist or a true satirist for he has no "fixed
     set of values and standards." In Babbitt he manages to
     create a genuine American myth, on the level of Melville's
     or Twain's.

16   ROTHWELL, KENNETH S. "From Society to Babbittry: Lewis' Debt
     to Edith Wharton." Journal of the Central Mississippi Val-
     ley American Studies Association, 1 (Spring), 32-37.
         Babbitt is so closely based on Wharton's The Age of In-
     nocence that at times Lewis almost seems to parody the ear-
     lier novel. Lewis knew Wharton personally and dedicated
     the book to her. Cites numerous parallels in themes, plot,
     and characters.

17   SCHULBERG, BUDD. "Lewis: Big Wind from Sauk Centre."
     Esquire, 54 (December), [110]-[114].
         Account of friendship with Lewis begun in 1935, when
     Schulberg was a student at Dartmouth, where he talked Lewis
     into leading a discussion (fascism and the novel) and Lewis
     was "baited" by campus radicals, an experience alleged to
     be the genesis of The Prodigal Parents. Reprinted 1972.23.

18   SPRINGER, ANNE M. "Sinclair Lewis," in her The American Novel
     in Germany: A Study of the Critical Reception of Eight
     American Novelists Between the Two World Wars. Hamburg:
     Cram, de Gruyter, pp. 46-59.
         History of Lewis's publication and reputation in Germany
     from 1922 to the late 1940s. Lewis was never as popular as
     Jack London or Upton Sinclair, but in the 1920s and early
     1930s he did appeal to relatively liberal intellectuals.
     Detailed survey of critical reaction to the major novels.
     Lewis was blacklisted after It Can't Happen Here and re-
     gained only part of his following after World War II.

19   THOMAS, J. D. "Three American Tragedies: Notes on the Re-
     sponsibilities of Fiction." <u>South Central Bulletin</u>, 20
     (Winter), 11-15.
          <u>Kingsblood Royal</u>, Wharton's <u>Ethan Frome</u>, and Dreiser's
     <u>An American Tragedy</u> used as examples in general essay on
     the critic's right to make moral judgments about literature.

20   THOMPSON, DOROTHY. "The Boy and Man from Sauk Centre."
     <u>Atlantic Monthly</u>, 206 (November), [39]-48.
          Meditative essay on Lewis's ambivalent relationship with
     his family and home town.

21   THORP, WILLARD. <u>American Writing in the Twentieth Century</u>.
     Cambridge: Harvard University Press, pp. 51-52, 119-23.
          In his various thesis novels, Lewis is devoted to the
     single purpose of delineating the spiritual poverty of the
     American middle class, whether in the small town or the
     city, in business or in medicine.

22   VAN NOSTRAND, ALBERT. "Slick Nirvana," in his <u>The Denatured
     Novel</u>. Indianapolis, New York: Bobbs-Merrill, pp. 95-98.
          Lewis's acid wit was never congenially tuned to the
     slick magazines, and when he is not writing as a satirist,
     he has little to offer the reader. Examines <u>Mantrap</u> as
     example.

1961

1   BERG, ADELYNE. "Sinclair Lewis and Rules." <u>The Writer</u>, 74,
     no. 8 (August), 12-13, 37.
          Lewis felt a writer should observe six basic principles:
     write and not just talk about doing so; write regularly,
     every day; be curious about people, places, ways of life;
     avoid selling out to any one market such as confessions be-
     cause it might forever shape one's style; avoid slanting
     stories for a particular market; associate with other
     writers.

2   CONRAD, BARNABY. "Thompson on Lewis." <u>Atlantic Monthly</u>, 207
     (February), 32.
          Letter praising Dorothy Thompson's article (<u>see</u>
     1960.20) with a few reservations, from a former secretary
     to Lewis.

1961

3   GERSTENBERGER, DONNA and GEORGE HENDRICK. "Lewis, Sinclair,"
    in their The American Novel 1789-1959: A Checklist of
    Twentieth-Century Criticism. [Volume 1]. Denver: Allan
    Swallow, pp. 169-73.
        Bibliography of approximately one hundred major reviews
    or articles, primarily on Lewis's art in general rather
    than specific works.

4   HACKETT, FRANCIS. "Sinclair Lewis," in The Idea of an Ameri-
    can Novel. Edited by Louis D. Rubin, Jr. and John Rees
    Moore. New York: Thomas Y. Crowell, pp. 297-300.
        Reprint of 1920.4.

5   KAZIN, ALFRED. "Sinclair Lewis," in The Idea of an American
    Novel. Edited by Louis D. Rubin, Jr. and John Rees Moore.
    New York: Thomas Y. Crowell, pp. 301-303.
        Reprint of pp. 219-21 from 1942.2.

6   KNIGHT, GRANT C. "The Garment of Rebellion," in his The New
    Freedom in American Literature. Edited by Scott C. Osborn.
    Lexington, Kentucky: Mrs. Grant C. Knight, pp. 69-70.
        Our Mr. Wrenn stands out among the books of the period.
    It contains both Lewis's sharp observations of real life
    and his greatest weakness, the tendency to ridicule his ma-
    jor characters.

7   LIGHT, MARTIN. "A Further Word on Sinclair Lewis' Prize-
    Consciousness." Western Humanities Review, 15 (Autumn),
    368-71.
        Lewis evidently aspired to both the Pulitzer and Nobel
    Prizes early in his career, as documented by his letters to
    Harcourt, Brace. Thus, his show of surprise and modesty is
    sham. However, his failure to write great works after win-
    ning the Nobel Prize was due not to the prize but to the
    fact that Dodsworth "finished a cycle of novels" and he was
    unable to work into new ideas after that.

8   SCHORER, MARK. "Afterword" to Arrowsmith. Signet Classic
    Edition. New York: New American Library, pp. 431-38.
        Arrowsmith marked new directions for Lewis and for Amer-
    ican fiction: it was the first of his novels to have a
    true hero and heroine and to pursue a "spiritual" ideal,
    and in its exploration of science, it "brought almost en-
    tirely new subject matter into American fiction." Reprint-
    ed in TCIA, 1968.4.

9   _____. "Afterword" to Babbitt. Signet Classic Edition. New
       York: New American Library, pp. 320-27.
           Babbitt is a landmark in literature about American busi-
       ness, which includes novels by James, Howells, Norris,
       Dreiser, and Wharton. More than any of these, Lewis cap-
       tures the conformity and emptiness of the business world.
       Attacks on the novel center not on its real weaknesses
       (repetitiousness, overdone irony, "aimless" plot) but on
       its picture of American life, but it is one of the best
       documents of its milieu.

10   _____. "Afterword" to Main Street. Signet Classic Edition.
       New York: New American Library, pp. 433-39.
           As a picture of small town life, Main Street is an ef-
       fective historical novel, marking the end of one era and
       the beginning of another as Carol's life is traced from
       1912 to 1920.

11   _____. "Introduction" to It Can't Happen Here. New York:
       Dell, pp. 5-17.
           Places the novel in context of Lewis's life and career.
       While many Americans, especially "left-wing sympathizers,"
       felt that It Can't Happen Here was Lewis's greatest novel,
       it might better be described as "a tour de force in which
       he simply documented the transformation of traditional
       American political and social customs into their opposites."

12   _____. "Introduction" to Lewis at Zenith: A Three-Novel
       Omnibus. New York: Harcourt, Brace and World,
       pp. [vii]-xii.
           Reviews Lewis's career before Main Street as a rather
       romantic writer who perpetuated the myths of the goodness
       of American life. In Main Street and Babbitt Lewis criti-
       cized the failures of American life, but he was unable to
       articulate his idea of what the American character could
       achieve if it followed its ideals until, in Arrowsmith, he
       created a hero capable of transcending the limitations of
       America.

13   _____. "Main Street." American Heritage, 12 (October),
       28-31, 74-77.
           Excerpts from Sinclair Lewis (1961.15), dealing with the
       publication and reception of Main Street, and excerpts from
       H. L. Mencken's review (1921.11).

1961

14   _____. "My Life and Nine-Year Captivity with Sinclair Lewis."
         New York Times Book Review, 20 August, pp. 7, 26.
            Account of the researching and writing of Sinclair Lewis
         (1961.15). First conceived as a 350-page book, it became
         an obsession. Reprinted in 1964.19.

15   _____. Sinclair Lewis: An American Life. New York, Toronto,
         London: McGraw-Hill, xxiii + 867 pp.
            An official biography in the sense that Schorer had sole
         access to all of Lewis's papers, Schorer's massive and de-
         finitive work is nevertheless sharply critical of Lewis.
         Includes detailed commentary on all major works, though
         more attention is given to the history of composition and
         to reception than to literary analysis. A checklist of
         Lewis's novels, short stories, poems, and nonfiction, in-
         cluding over 400 entries covering 1902 to 1955, is appended.

16   _____. "Sinclair Lewis and the Nobel Prize." Atlantic Month-
         ly, 208 (October), 83-88.
            Detailed account of Lewis's reception of the Nobel
         Prize. Does not duplicate the account in Sinclair Lewis
         (1961.15).

17   _____. "Sinclair Lewis as a Young Publisher." Publishers
         Weekly, 180 (24 July), 36-39.
            Excerpts from 1961.15 on Lewis's contact with the busi-
         ness end of publishing.

18   SINCLAIR, UPTON. "Mr. Upton-Sinclair-Lewis." Harper's Maga-
         zine, 222 (March), 48.
            On readers' confusion over the names of Lewis and
         Sinclair.

19   STALLMAN, R. W. "Sinclair Lewis as Teacher." New York Times
         Book Review, 22 October, p. 53.
            Letter to the editor. Anecdotes on Lewis as creative
         writing teacher at the University of Wisconsin. Lewis was
         alternately humble and arrogant.

20   WALTERS, RAYMOND, JR. "In and Out of Books." New York Times
         Book Review, 27 August, p. 8.
            Suggests that publishers are contributing to a Lewis
         revival with the Schorer biography, the Lewis at Zenith
         omnibus, and paperback editions of several novels that have
         been out of print, such as Ann Vickers and It Can't Happen
         Here.

1962

1 BROWN, DEMING. "Sinclair Lewis and Theodore Dreiser," in his
Soviet Attitudes Toward American Writing. Princeton, N.J.:
Princeton University Press, pp. 239-71.
First half (pp. 239-51) is slightly revised version of
1953.6. The accuracy of the Russian translation of Kingsblood Royal is assessed (pp. 7-8). Lewis is frequently
mentioned throughout the book.

2 COARD, ROBERT L. "Names in the Fiction of Sinclair Lewis."
Georgia Review, 16 (Fall), 318-29.
Lewis was obsessed with getting just the right titles
for his novels and names for his characters. He collected
real names from tombstones. At his worst, Lewis uses humorous names that are too ridiculous, but at his best, his
choice of names is one of his strengths as a satirist.

3 COLUM, PADRAIC and MARGARET FREEMAN CABELL. Between Friends:
Letters of James Branch Cabell and Others. New York: Harcourt, Brace and World, xvi + 304 pp., passim.
Reprints numerous letters between Lewis and Cabell from
1915 to 1922, touching such subjects as Main Street, Babbitt, and Jurgen.

4 DE KRUIF, PAUL. The Sweeping Wind. New York: Harcourt,
Brace and World, pp. 54-105, 114-16, 126-27, 143.
Details of his collaboration with Lewis on Arrowsmith,
during which their relationship ranged from extremely close
to mutually suspicious, largely because of disagreements
over de Kruif's status. Recalls advice Lewis gave him on
writing.

5 GEISMAR, MAXWELL. "Society and the Novel," in A Time of Harvest: American Literature 1910-1960. Edited by Robert E.
Spiller. New York: Hill and Wang, pp. 37-39.
Lewis, especially in Babbitt, shows the failure of American society. Though it might have seemed realistic in its
day, we now see Babbitt as a surrealist "nightmare vision,"
as terrifying as Brave New World or 1984.

6 GREBSTEIN, SHELDON NORMAN. Sinclair Lewis. Twayne U.S. Authors Series. New York: Twayne Publishers, 192 pp.
Concentrates on the 1920s although other works are dis-
cussed for the light they shed on Lewis's career as a whole.
Although his shortcomings as thinker and artist are not
denied, his best novels should be recognized for their social criticism and history. Lewis helped America assess
its strengths and weaknesses and thus helped to reshape the

1962

American character. He also had a major part in maturing
the modern American novel. "Selected Bibliography,"
pp. 180-88. Pages 73-85 reprinted in SB, 1971.13.
Pages 86-96, except notes, reprinted in TCIA, 1968.4.

7   LIGHT, MARTIN. "H. G. Wells and Sinclair Lewis: Friendship,
    Literary Influences, and Letters." English Fiction in
    Transition, 5, no. 4: 1-20.
        Lewis was an acknowledged admirer of Wells and learned
    more from him than from any other writer. Our Mr. Wrenn
    was strongly influenced by Wells, and Lewis later liked to
    feel "that he was writing Wells' kind of novel." Reprints
    two letters by Wells and nine by Lewis.

8   MANFRED, FREDERICK. "Some Notes on Sinclair Lewis' Funeral."
    Minnesota Review, 3 (Fall), 87-90.
        Responds to Schorer's version of the memorial service
    (in 1961.15). Manfred was not overpraising Lewis in his
    eulogy, and the wind did not literally scatter Lewis's
    ashes.

9   MILLGATE, MICHAEL. "Sinclair Lewis and the Obscure Hero."
    Studi Americani, no. 8, pp. [111]-27.
        Contrasted with Dreiser's Frank Cowperwood, Babbitt is
    an obscure hero of the type more often treated by popular
    literature or films. The fact that Babbitt is less signif-
    icant as a character than as a representative of his cul-
    ture limits the value of the novel as work of art. Dods-
    worth, on the other hand, transcends his role as mere
    businessman. Much of this material appears in 1964.16.

*10 OHARA, HIROTADA. "Winesburg, Ohio and Main Street." Pursuit,
    no. 1 (December), pp. 57-66.
        Unlocatable. Cited in Leary, 1970.14.

11 SCHORER, MARK. "The Burdens of Biography." Michigan Quarter-
    ly Review, 1, 4 (Autumn), 249-58.
        On the writing of Sinclair Lewis (1961.15) and the prob-
    lems connected with it, ranging from interviews and the
    reading and rereading of Lewis's work to the choice of
    style and tone. Reprinted 1965.12 and 1968.10.

12 _____. "Introduction" to Ann Vickers. New York: Dell,
    pp. 5-17.
        Account of Lewis's life and work. Lewis based Ann
    largely on Dorothy Thompson, and in the novel he "put him-
    self in the position of describing sympathetically quali-
    ties that he was already resenting in life," such as
    Dorothy's interest in "liberal" and "radical" movements.

13 _____. "Introduction" to I'm a Stranger Here Myself and Other
Stories by Sinclair Lewis. New York: Dell, pp. [7]-16.
   Emphasizes Lewis's career from 1916 to 1920, when he
made his living writing short stories for magazines and
developed his characteristic style. During this period,
Lewis learned how to appeal to a mass audience and how to
use facts in his fiction.

14 _____, editor. Sinclair Lewis: A Collection of Critical Essays. Twentieth Century Views Series. Edited by Maynard
Mack. Englewood Cliffs, N.J.: Prentice-Hall, x + 174 pp.
   In his introduction (pp. 1-9; reprinted 1968.10)
Schorer surveys the critical reception of Lewis's novels
as well as the rise and decline of his reputation. Brief
bibliography and chronology of Lewis's life. Reprints 24
essays and critical reviews evaluating the novelist: Max-
well Geismar, "Origins of a Dynasty" (1947.13); H. L.
Mencken, "Portrait of an American Citizen" (1922.20) and
"Consolation" (1921.11); Rebecca West, "Babbitt" (1922.32);
Sherwood Anderson, "Sinclair Lewis" (1922.2); Constance
Rourke, "Round Up" (1931.34); Robert Morss Lovett, "An In-
terpreter of American Life" (1925.30); Joseph Wood Krutch,
"Mr. Babbitt's Spiritual Guide" (1927.19); Rebecca West,
"Sinclair Lewis Introduces Elmer Gantry" (1927.42); Mark
Schorer, "Sinclair Lewis and the Method of Half-Truths"
(1956.6); Vernon L. Parrington, "Sinclair Lewis: Our Own
Diogenes" (1927.26); T. K. Whipple, "Sinclair Lewis"
(1928.36); Walter Lippmann, "Sinclair Lewis" (1927.20);
E. M. Forster, "Our Photography: Sinclair Lewis" (1929.10);
Ford Madox Ford, "Dodsworth" (1929.8); Lewis Mumford, "The
America of Sinclair Lewis" (1931.32); Richard P. Blackmur,
"Utopia, or Uncle Tom's Cabin" (1935.7); Robert Cantwell,
"Sinclair Lewis" (1936.11); Alfred Kazin, "The New Realism:
Sherwood Anderson and Sinclair Lewis" (1942.2); Maxwell
Geismar, "The Land of Faery" (1947.13); Edmund Wilson,
"Salute to an Old Landmark: Sinclair Lewis" (1945.24);
Malcolm Cowley, "The Last Flight from Main Street"
(1951.21); Joseph Wood Krutch, "Sinclair Lewis" (1951.37);
Geoffrey Moore, "Sinclair Lewis: A Lost Romantic"
(1959.11).

1963

1 ANON. "The Old Frontier." Newsweek, 61 (15 April), 108-109.
   Storm in the West is a literary curiosity. An "allegory
of World War II," it nevertheless contains every Western
cliché.

1963

2   ARGOW, DOROTHY. "Dorothy and Red." Harper's Magazine, 227
    (December), 4.
        Letter reacting to Sheean's excerpted book, 1963.24.
    Approves Sheean's work and offers an additional anecdote
    about Thompson.

3   CANBY, HENRY SEIDEL. Part 6 of "Fiction Sums up a Century,"
    in Literary History of the United States. Third edition,
    revised. Edited by Robert E. Spiller, Willard Thorp,
    Thomas H. Johnson, Henry Seidel Canby, Richard M. Ludwig.
    New York: Macmillan, pp. 1222-29.
        Brief review of Lewis's development. Discusses Main
    Street, Babbitt, and Arrowsmith, and mentions others: "the
    best social history of the 'white collar' class of the
    United States at the high tide of its success is provided
    by these novels of Sinclair Lewis because of their almost
    naive honesty and their accurate focus upon typical
    experience."

4   CONTI, GIUSEPPI GADDA. "Sinclair Lewis." Studi Americani,
    no. 9, pp. 249-86.
        Evaluates Lewis's achievement as artist and social crit-
    ic by examining the degree of maturation evident in the
    novels from Free Air to World So Wide. His major fault was
    abandoning himself so completely to the formula which
    brought him success. Emphasizes his romanticism and ways
    in which he used the sentimental and romantic to illuminate
    American life. In Italian.

5   DANIEL, BENNE BERNICE. "Sinclair Lewis, Novelist and Speaker:
    A Comparison of the Themes and Rhetorical Methods Used in
    Three of His Public Addresses to the Themes and Methods
    Used in Six of His Novels." Dissertation Abstracts,
    23:1826-27 (University of Oklahoma, 1962).
        According to her abstract, themes and techniques in nov-
    els correlate closely with those in speeches. The tech-
    niques that gave Lewis appeal during his day--language of
    the common man, slang, and clichés--now cause his work to
    appear dated.

6   DAVIDSON, DONALD. "Sinclair Lewis," in The Spyglass: Views
    and Reviews, 1924-1930. Edited by John Tyree Fain. Nash-
    ville: Vanderbilt University Press, pp. 63-67.
        Although Lewis is more a popular novelist than a careful
    literary craftsman, Arrowsmith displays far more maturity
    than either Main Street or Babbitt and suggests that he is
    capable of writing fiction with some depth, not just satire.
    First appeared in Nashville Tennessean, 1925.15.

7   DERLETH, AUGUST W. "Sinclair Lewis," in his Three Literary
     Men: A Memoir of Sinclair Lewis, Sherwood Anderson, and
     Edgar Lee Masters. New York, Copenhagen: Candlelight
     Press, pp. 9-27.
          Reprint of 1959.4.

8   EDENER, WILFRIED. Die Religionskritik in den Romanen von
     Sinclair Lewis. Heidelberg: Carl Winter, Universitäts-
     verlag, 240 pp. Reprinted in Jahrbuch für Amerikastudien,
     no. 10, 1965.
          Surveys religious criticism in American literature from
     Benjamin Franklin to H. L. Mencken; these were the fore-
     runners of Lewis as well as sources of some techniques.
     Examines Lewis's life, religious criticism in early works,
     religion as a theme in specific novels, his place in Ameri-
     can literary history, his own spiritual situation and view
     of his life. In German.

9   FEINBERG, LEONARD. The Satirist: His Temperament, Motiva-
     tion, and Influence. Ames: Iowa State University Press,
     370 pp., passim.
          Lewis used as an example throughout.

10   KILLINGER, JOHN. "The Unredeemed Community" and "Earthen Ves-
     sels," in his The Failure of Theology in Modern Literature.
     New York and Nashville: Abingdon Press, pp. 95-100,
     150-55.
          Lewis satirized church and clergy somewhat in Main
     Street and Babbitt, but in Elmer Gantry this satire is the
     chief theme as he attacks unworthy clergymen, divinity
     schools, backward country churches, assembly-line city
     churches, and "the general decadence of Christianity."
     Though "a bit raw," Elmer Gantry is Lewis's "masterpiece."

11   LAND, MYRICK. "Mr. De Voto and Mr. Sinclair Lewis Call Each
     Other Fools and Liars," in his The Fine Art of Literary
     Mayhem: A Lively Account of Famous Writers and Their
     Feuds. New York: Holt, Rinehart and Winston, pp. 205-15.
          The feud began when De Voto belittled Lewis's fiction in
     The Literary Fallacy (see 1944.6) and ended when Lewis sec-
     onded the nomination of De Voto to the National Institute
     of Arts and Letters.

12   LIGHT, MARTIN. "Lewis' Finicky Girls and Faithful Workers."
     University Review, 30 (Winter), [151]-59.
          In Lewis's early fiction, he treats women sympathetical-
     ly as pleasant playmates for men; in Main Street his atti-
     tude is ambivalent; and in Arrowsmith and Dodsworth the

1963

playmate becomes the "Nagging Woman," who keeps the hero
from his work. Lewis's emphasis on the sacred nature of
work caused him to portray workers, even plodders like Fred
Cornplow, more sympathetically as his career progressed.

13 LÜDEKE, HENRY. "11. Der Massenstaat und die Erzählende Literatur," in his Geschichte der Amerikanischen Literatur.
Bern and München: Francke Verlag, pp. 407-409.
    Review of Lewis's literary career, with emphasis on the
major works of the 1920s. In German.

14 McDONALD, GERALD D. Review of Storm in the West. Library
Journal, 88 (15 March), 1179.
    A readable book which would have been effective as a
movie had Metro-Goldwyn-Mayer filmed it.

15 MARCUS, STEVEN. "An American Writer." New Statesman, n.s. 65
(29 March), 461-62.
    Review of Schorer's Sinclair Lewis (1961.15) and an
analysis of Lewis, who seems to be a man with no "inward-
ness" at all, a sort of machine who produced books as a
computer might. Ironically, Lewis made himself rich by
attacking commercial, materialistic America. Reprinted
1975.6.

16 NEVILLE, ROBERT. "A Talk with Vincent Sheean." New York
Times Book Review, 17 November, p. 63.
    Sheean justifies his decision to print diary entries in
Dorothy and Red (1963.23) because Dorothy had edited the
diary and presumably intended that it be published.

17 OBER, WILLIAM B., M.D. "Arrowsmith [and] The Last Adam."
Carleton Miscellany, 4, no. 4 (Fall), 101-106.
    In retrospect Arrowsmith is not really very "true to
life." Lewis's ear for dialogue is weak and his style un-
impressive; minor characters are poorly drawn and even
Martin seems unbelievable at times. James Gould Cozzens is
far more true to medical reality in The Last Adam, which is
a better example of craftsmanship. Reprinted, except two
paragraphs, in TCIA, 1968.4.

18 ROSENBERG, CHARLES E. "Martin Arrowsmith: The Scientist as
Hero." American Quarterly, 15 (Fall), [447]-58.
    On the details of the Lewis-de Kruif collaboration and
the accuracy of Lewis's depiction of abuses in the practice
of medicine. Emphasizes Jacques Loeb as a model for Max
Gottlieb and an example of what the man of medicine could
be. Reprinted, omitting all but last note, in TCIA,
1968.4.

19 SCHARY, DORE. "At Work with 'Red' Lewis: A Foreword by Dore
Schary," in Storm in the West. New York: Stein and Day,
pp. 5-18.
Account of Schary and Lewis writing a western allegor-
ically treating the rise of European fascism.

20 SCHIER, DONALD. "Main Street by Sinclair Lewis." Carleton
Miscellany, 4, no. 4 (Fall), 95-101.
Main Street, which seemed a ready-made modern classic in
1920, now seems shallow and dead. Lewis's satire is unsure
and unfocused, his realism external. Kennicott is dull and
Carol so flighty that the reader cannot sympathize with
her. Only the documentary aspect of the novel remains.

21 SCHORER, MARK. Sinclair Lewis. University of Minnesota
Pamphlets on American Writers, no. 27. Minneapolis:
University of Minnesota Press, 47 pp.
Overview and analysis of Lewis's life and career. In
spite of faults, his strengths ensure that his best work
will survive. He created characters powerful enough to become "archetypal figures." He recorded social life and
class distinctions in ways that no later novelist has done,
and pointed out to America "the terror immanent in the com-
monplace. Reprinted 1964.20.

22 _____. "Sinclair Lewis and the Method of Half-Truths," in
Modern American Fiction: Essays in Criticism. Edited by
A. Walton Litz. New York: Oxford University Press,
pp. 95-112.
Reprint of 1956.6.

23 SHEEAN, VINCENT. Dorothy and Red. Boston: Houghton Mifflin,
xii + 363 pp.
Detailed account of Lewis-Thompson marriage, drawing on
personal acquaintance with them and on the Dorothy Thompson
Papers at Syracuse University. Sheean illuminates Thompson's perceptions of the marriage and the reasons for its
failure more fully than Lewis's.

24 _____. "The Tangled Romance of Sinclair Lewis and Dorothy
Thompson." Harper's Magazine, 227 (October), 121-72.
Selections from 1963.23, including photos, diary entries,
and letters.

25 WHIPPLE, T. K. "Sinclair Lewis," in his Spokesmen: Modern
Writers and American Life. Reprint of 1928 edition. New
York and London: D. Appleton, pp. 208-29.
Revised and expanded version of 1925.46. Although his
irony is useful in satirizing American foibles, it prevents

Lewis from showing what he sincerely believes in and from developing the fully rounded characters hinted at in such creations as Leora Arrowsmith. Lewis cannot develop from competent satirist to genuine artist because he cannot drop his ironic mask. Reprinted in SL:CCE, 1962.14; first half reprinted in SB, 1971.13.

1964

1   ALLEN, WALTER. "The Twenties: American," in his Tradition and Dream: The English and American Novel from the Twenties to Our Time. London: J. M. Dent and Sons, pp. 65-71.
      How did Lewis capture the reading public so thoroughly with Main Street and Babbitt since today both seem so dated? Lewis remorselessly laid bare all the hypocrisies and weaknesses of his time in a way that Americans and Europeans could appreciate; his contribution is more social than literary.

2   ANON. "Hitler and the Posse." Times Literary Supplement, 63 (17 September), 864.
      Storm in the West is full of "familiar cowboy clichés" and would probably not have succeeded had it been filmed.

3   BLAKE, NELSON MANFRED. "How to Learn History from Sinclair Lewis and Other Uncommon Sources." Stetson University Bulletin, 64, no. 2 (July), 1-17.
      Although Elmer Gantry may be a "bad novel" it is a valuable social document. Despite Lewis's bias against the clergy, he researched the book carefully. The reader interested in social history may ignore Gantry, a caricature, and concentrate on the realistic portraits of other clergymen. Reprinted 1964.4.

4   _____. "How to Learn History from Sinclair Lewis and Other Uncommon Sources," in American Character and Culture: Some Twentieth Century Perspectives. Edited by John A. Hague. DeLand, Florida: Everett Edwards Press, pp. 33-47.
      Reprint of 1964.3.

5   BUCCO, MARTIN. "The Serialized Novels of Sinclair Lewis: A Comparative Analysis of Periodical and Book." Dissertation Abstracts, 24:4692-93 (Missouri).
      According to his abstract, Bucco treats differences in structure, theme, characterization, and style between the serial and the final novel of The Innocents, Free Air, Mantrap, Ann Vickers, Cass Timberlane, and World So Wide.

1964

Generally the final novel is more highly polished, but The Innocents became more melodramatic and weaker structurally. See 1969.8.

6   CANTWELL, ROBERT. "Sinclair Lewis," in After the Genteel Tradition. Edited by Malcolm Cowley. Originally published 1937. Carbondale: Southern Illinois University Press, pp. 92-102.
        Reprint of 1936.11.

7   COUCH, WILLIAM, JR. "Sinclair Lewis: Crisis in the American Dream." College Language Association Journal, 7 (March), 224-34.
        Most modern writers owe a considerable debt to Lewis, who helped turn the American novel from a formula of light amusement into which it had fallen in the early twentieth century. Emphasizes Lewis's belief in the perfectibility of American life and his critical reception in the 1920s.

8   COWLEY, MALCOLM. "Foreword: The Revolt Against Gentility" and "Postscript: Twenty Years of American Literature," in After the Genteel Tradition. Edited by Malcolm Cowley. Originally published 1937. Carbondale: Southern Illinois University Press, pp. [3]-20, [167]-82.
        Recapitulates the circumstances of Lewis's Nobel Prize and his acceptance speech, in which Lewis sees himself among the authors revolting against the genteel tradition. Considers that tradition and the revolt as viewed in 1937 and in 1964. Lewis's gift for assessing reputations in his Nobel Prize Address is taken up in the "postscript."

9   FULLER, JOHN. "Hick and Hep." New Statesman, 68 (4 September), 327-28.
        Storm in the West is terrible.

10   GENTHE, CHARLES V. "The Damnation of Theron Ware and Elmer Gantry." Research Studies of Washington State University, 32 (December), 334-43.
        Suggests that Lewis, who alludes to The Damnation in Main Street, knew the novel and used it in writing Elmer Gantry. Compares Harold Frederic's Celia Madden with Lewis's Sharon Falconer and Theron Ware with Frank Shallard of Elmer Gantry. Both novels also treat Higher Criticism and its influence on ministers.

1964

11   G[OHDES], C[LARENCE]. Review of Storm in the West. American
        Literature, 35 (January), 569.
            This allegorical treatment of World War II was written
        for Hollywood, but "luckily, the plans for production were
        shelved."

12   HAKUTANI, YOSHINOBU. "Sinclair Lewis and Dreiser: A Study in
        Continuity and Development." Discourse: A Review of the
        Liberal Arts, 7 (Summer), 254-76.
            Reviews biographical connections between Lewis and
        Dreiser from 1907 to 1944. Their work was connected by
        their common effort to "establish a fruitful and living
        contact with the American environment, to experience it,
        and express it to the full." In doing so, the two treated
        many of the same subjects, including the liberation of
        women and the American businessman.

13   LOCKERBIE, D. BRUCE. "Sinclair Lewis and William Ridgway."
        American Literature, 36 (March), 68-72.
            Identifies the Ridgway cited in Babbitt as a popular
        religious writer, a businessman turned fundamentalist.
        Quotes from Ridgway's account of a meeting with Lewis (see
        1935.28) and speculates that Lewis might have used the
        meeting as background for Elmer Gantry.

14   MARCUS, STEVEN. "American Gothic." New York Review of Books,
        1 (9 January), 3-5.
            Reviews Sheean's Dorothy and Red (1963.23) and comments
        on the Thompson-Lewis marriage. Although Sheean is far too
        "naive" to deal with it, the raw materials of his book give
        a view of the marriage that goes beyond Mark Schorer's.
        From Lewis's point of view, the marriage to Thompson, whose
        character was much like that of his father, was "ruinous."
        Reprinted 1975.6.

15   MILCH, ROBERT J. Babbitt Notes. Lincoln, Nebraska: Cliff's
        Notes, 56 pp.
            Study guide, including chapter by chapter summary, list
        of characters, brief discussion of techniques and biography.

16   MILLGATE, MICHAEL. "Sherwood Anderson and Sinclair Lewis,"
        in his American Social Fiction, James to Cozzens. Edin-
        burgh and London: Oliver and Boyd, pp. 93-106.
            Lewis's ambivalence toward American business and the
        middle class is clear when Babbitt is contrasted with Dods-
        worth, the former satirical toward the businessman, the
        latter sympathetic. A difference between them, however, is
        that Babbitt is only a middleman or seller and Dodsworth

is an inventor and creator. Much of this material appeared in 1962.9.

17   PUGLIATTI, PAOLA. "Il realismo di Babbitt." Studi Americani, no. 10, pp. 293-316.
     The verisimilitude of Babbitt has been exaggerated. Examination of the novel forty years after publication suggests that neither Lewis's crude exaggeration of ordinary language nor his apologia for conformity redeems the novel's lack of creative strength and of a valid controlling ideological concept. Nevertheless, Lewis's fragments of reality have made Babbitt part of the popular folklore of America. In Italian.

18   ROYSTER, SALIBELLE. Arrowsmith Notes. Lincoln, Nebraska: Cliff's Notes, 86 pp.
     Study guide, including brief biography, description of the Lewis-de Kruif collaboration, list of characters, plot summary, and brief critical analysis.

19   SCHORER, MARK. "My Life and Nine-Year Captivity with Sinclair Lewis," in Opinions and Perspectives from the New York Times Book Review. Edited by Francis Brown. Boston: Houghton Mifflin, pp. 346-52.
     Reprint of 1961.14.

20   _____. "Sinclair Lewis," in Seven Modern American Novelists: An Introduction. Edited by William Van O'Connor. Minneapolis: University of Minnesota Press, pp. 46-80.
     Reprint of 1963.21.

21   TANSELLE, G. THOMAS. "Sinclair Lewis and Floyd Dell: Two Views of the Midwest." Twentieth Century Literature, 9 (January), 175-84.
     Although both Lewis (in Main Street) and Dell (in Moon-Calf) are ambivalent about the Midwest, Dell's "idealistic dreamer" is a young man growing toward intellectual maturity in a small city while Lewis's is an adult woman stifled by a small town. Dell is concerned with depicting his hero in a setting, Lewis with satirizing his setting through his protagonist's reaction with it.

*22 WOLFE, LINDA and MARY ELINORE SMITH. A Critical Commentary: Main Street. New York: American R. D. M. Corporation.
     Unlocatable. Listed in 1970.16.

1965

1965

1   AARON, DANIEL. "Sinclair Lewis: Main Street," in The American Novel from James Fenimore Cooper to William Faulkner.
Edited by Wallace Stegner. New York, London: Basic Books,
pp. 166-79.
     Influences on Main Street. The ideas of H. L. Mencken,
Thorstein Veblen, and Henry David Thoreau united with
Lewis's own observations of the small town to produce a
book that shocked Americans but also showed them their
failings. Despite faults in plot and characterization,
Main Street is "of historical importance."

2   ADAMS, J. DONALD. "Lewis and Marquand" and "And Lewis Again,"
in his Speaking of Books--and Life. New York, Chicago, San
Francisco: Holt, Rinehart and Winston, pp. 158-62.
     Reprints 1960.1 and assesses Lewis: he may not have
been a great writer--"he was at once so powerful and so
limited"--but his best works of the 1920s are still great.

3   ALDER, BENNE B. "Sinclair Lewis: The Novelist Who 'Hated'
Lecturing." Quarterly Journal of Speech, 51 (October),
276-85.
     Examination of Lewis's practice as a public speaker from
his teens to shortly before his death suggests that Mark
Schorer was wrong to conclude that Lewis hated to lecture
and felt "only contempt for his audiences."

4   ANGOFF, CHARLES. "A Kansan in Westchester." University Review, 31 (Summer), [283]-88.
     Treats Dorothy Thompson and H. L. Mencken's analysis of
her--that she had a very bad effect on Lewis as writer and
as man. Reprinted 1966.1.

5   GRANT, DOUGLAS. "Sinclair Lewis: An American Life," in his
Purpose and Place: Essays on American Writers. New York:
Macmillan, pp. 163-68.
     Of Lewis's many novels, Babbitt is the best and most
idealistic. While the style and characterization might
have insured the book's survival, it is Lewis's creation
of a mythic figure that distinguishes Babbitt. Originally
published in Times Literary Supplement in 1961.

6   HART, JAMES D. "Lewis, [Harry] Sinclair," in his Oxford Companion to American Literature. Fourth edition. New York:
Oxford University Press, pp. 472-73.
     Brief review of Lewis's life and annotated list of his
works.

7   HASHIGUCHI, YASUO. "Arrowsmith and Escapism." Kyushu Ameri-
     can Literature, no. 8, pp. 14-18.
          In Arrowsmith Lewis attacks the traditional idea of suc-
     cess: as Martin becomes more successful, he is less ful-
     filled as an individual. His "escape" to pure science at
     the end of the novel is treated ambiguously: it may prove
     a frustrating illusion.

8   HENDRICKS, KING and IRVING SHEPARD, editors. "London-Lewis
     Letters," in their Letters from Jack London: Containing an
     Unpublished Correspondence Between London and Sinclair
     Lewis. New York: Odyssey Press, pp. 483-89.
          From Lewis, London bought 27 plots, three of which he
     used in published stories, two in novels. Prints four let-
     ters from Lewis to London and two from London to Lewis.

9   HUTCHENS, JOHN K. "Arrowsmith's American Dream." Saturday
     Review, 48 (3 July), 25.
          Rereading Arrowsmith today makes one realize how compe-
     tent Lewis was, especially compared with novelists of the
     1960s. In honesty, depth of characterization, and depic-
     tion of the American character, Arrowsmith remains Lewis's
     best work.

10   KISHLER, THOMAS C. "'The Sacred Rites of Pride': An Echo of
     'The Rape of the Lock' in Babbitt." Satire Newsletter, 3
     (Fall), 28-29.
          Compares the washroom scene in Babbitt (Chapter 5) with
     Belinda's toilet in "Rape of the Lock" (Canto 1, 2.
     121-28). Here Lewis is much less "heavy-handed" than
     usual. See response, 1968.8.

11   ROYSTER, SALIBELLE. Main Street Notes. Lincoln, Nebraska:
     Cliff's Notes, 61 pp.
          Study guide, including biographical sketch, list of
     characters, plot summary, discussions of structure, set-
     ting, technique, and satire.

12   SCHORER, MARK. "The Burdens of Biography," in To the Young
     Writer. Hopwood Lectures, Second Series. Edited by A. L.
     Bader. Ann Arbor: University of Michigan Press,
     pp. 147-65.
          Reprint of 1962.11

1965

13   STRAUMANN, HEINRICH. "The Power of Reality," in his <u>American</u>
      <u>Literature in the Twentieth Century</u>. Third revised edition.
      Originally published 1951. New York and Evanston: Harper
      Torch Books, pp. 17-22.
          Lewis's chief theme in his best novels--<u>Main Street</u>,
      <u>Babbitt</u>, and <u>Arrowsmith</u>--is "the struggle of one person to
      overcome the tribal opinions of his surroundings . . . to
      do something different." While plot and characterization
      are not his strong points, his books are powerful weapons
      against "prejudices and narrowmindedness."

14   WEST, PAUL. "A Mystique of Documentary," in his <u>The Modern</u>
      <u>Novel</u>. Volume 2: <u>The United States and Other Countries</u>.
      London: Hutchinson University Library, pp. 238-39.
          Lewis is "the creator of the novel as expert reportage."
      While he attacks various sectors of American society, sym-
      pathy for his targets undercuts his satire.

15   WINANS, EDWARD R. <u>Sinclair Lewis' Babbitt</u>. Monarch Litera-
      ture Review Notes, no. 683-3. New York: Monarch Press,
      79 pp.
          Study guide, including biography, notes on plot and
      characters, and critical discussion.

                            1966

1   ANGOFF, CHARLES. "Sinclair Lewis" and "Dorothy Thompson:
      Kansan in Westchester," in his <u>The Tone of the Twenties and</u>
      <u>Other Essays</u>. South Brunswick and New York: A. S. Barnes,
      pp. 69-73, 114-21.
          Informal anecdotes about Lewis's association with H. L.
      Mencken, George Jean Nathan, Philip Goodman, and Dorothy
      Thompson. Thompson chapter is a reprint of 1965.4.

2   BLOTNER, JOSEPH. "The Novel of the Future," in his <u>The Mod-</u>
      <u>ern American Political Novel: 1900-1960</u>. Austin and Lon-
      don: University of Texas Press, pp. 153-56.
          While it does not have the strength of earlier novels
      such as <u>Dodsworth</u> and <u>Arrowsmith</u>, <u>It Can't Happen Here</u> in-
      fluenced contemporary readers and impressed the critics
      because of its attack on fascism.

3   BROWN, DANIEL R. "Lewis's Satire--A Negative Emphasis."
      <u>Renascence</u>, 18 (Winter), 63-72.
          Although Lewis does not expect his satire to perfect
      mankind, he is optimistic about humanity's essential good-
      ness and thus pillories its foibles. Treats the subjects
      and techniques of Lewis's satire. His greatest fault is

                            172

his tendency to be heavy-handed, to underscore the satire. Reprinted in SB, 1971.13.

4 CHAPMAN, ARNOLD. "Sinclair Lewis: Mr. Babbitt's Dubious Victory," in his The Spanish American Reception of United States Fiction: 1920-1940. University of California Publications in Modern Philology, volume 77. Berkeley and Los Angeles: University of California Press, pp. 117-26.
    Survey of Lewis's critical reputation in Latin America from 1930 to the early 1950s, emphasizing the major critical disagreement over Lewis's Nobel Prize. Lewis has always been best known in Latin America for Main Street, Babbitt, and Arrowsmith; his later works are viewed as greatly inferior.

5 COLE, E. R. "George Babbitt: Mock-Hero of a Mock-Epic." Descant, 10 (Winter), 21-25.
    In Babbitt Lewis deliberately creates a mock-epic which parallels the Iliad. Classical references and names are abundant, and like Achilles, Babbitt goes into battle only after his close friend Paul Riesling is struck down by fate.

6 CONROY, STEPHEN SEBASTIAN. "The American Culture and the Individual in the Novels of Sinclair Lewis." Dissertation Abstracts International, 27:473A-474A (Iowa).
    According to the abstract, a sociological study of Lewis's novels to determine which institutions Lewis examines and which category the responses of his characters fall into: "Adjusted, anomic, or autonomous." By the time he published Dodsworth Lewis had "exhausted the responses open to the individual vis-à-vis his culture" and had nothing new to say.

7 FIFE, JIM L. "Two Views of the American West." Western American Literature, 1 (Spring), [34]-43.
    Lewis debunks the American West as a stultifying wasteland, while Eugene Manlove Rhodes attempts to defend it from that charge and from the sensationalism of the dime novelists and pulp writers. However, both share an idealistic notion of what the West could be if it were kept free of materialism and standardization.

8 FRIEDMAN, PHILIP ALLEN. "Babbitt: Satiric Realism in Form and Content." Satire Newsletter, 4 (Fall), 20-29.
    Though first determined not to make Babbitt a satire, Lewis eventually combined the techniques of satire with those of realism. Satiric epigrams and names, burlesques and parodies of serious meetings and speeches coexist with

1966

accurate observations of the externals of American life and
with sound use of psychology. The result is a work of
"satiric realism," "a mixed breed." Reprinted in SB,
1971.13.

9 HAND, HARRY E. "The Rise of a Modern American Hero." Laurel
Review, 6 (Spring), 14-20.
    The critics who call Kingsblood Royal good propaganda
but bad art ignore the stature of Neil Kingsblood, a modern
tragic hero who, like Howells's Silas Lapham, enjoys a
moral rise while he loses material goods and social
prominence.

10 KRAMER, MAURICE. "Sinclair Lewis and the Hollow Center," in
The Twenties, Poetry and Prose: 20 Critical Essays. Edited by Richard E. Langford and William E. Taylor. DeLand,
Florida: Everett Edwards Press, pp. 67-69.
    Lewis is at his best when he is dealing with external
facts rather than thinking deeply and when he is attacking
something, not praising or analyzing. He attempted to
transcend these limitations in Dodsworth, which suffers
from vagueness and an inconclusive ending. Lewis's other
shortcoming is inability to create a distinctive style.

11 MILNE, GORDON. "The Doctrinal Barrage (1920-1964)," in his
The American Political Novel. Norman: University of Oklahoma Press, pp. 127-32.
    Lewis's It Can't Happen Here, while popular among the
critics of the 1930s, doesn't hold up well intellectually
because it is superficial in its attack on fascism, about
which Lewis seems poorly informed. Characterization and
structure seem careless and inartistic, too.

12 NAPIER, JAMES J. "Letters of Sinclair Lewis to Joseph Hergesheimer, 1915-1922. American Literature, 38 (May),
236-46.
    Quotes from fourteen letters show that Lewis admires
Hergesheimer and that he is committed to treating the
Middle West in his own fiction.

13 PRICE, LAWRENCE MARSDEN. The Reception of United States Literature in Germany. Chapel Hill: University of North
Carolina Press, pp. 135-41, 220-21.
    Although "most of the German translations were exces-
sively bad," Lewis was popular for his depiction of everyday American life and his satiric criticism of American
society. Germans approved Lewis's Nobel Prize, but after
Dodsworth his reputation abroad declined. It Can't Happen

Here was viewed as "a direct declaration of war against National Socialism." Bibliography of articles in German.

14   ROGERS, KATHARINE M.   "The Fear of Mom: The Twentieth Century," in her The Troublesome Helpmate: A History of Misogyny in Literature.   Seattle and London: University of Washington Press, pp. 230-32.
       Lewis uses Fran Dodsworth, Jinny Timberlane and Winifred Homeward (of Gideon Planish) to suggest that women are intellectually inferior to men and that they seek to dominate their men. Especially through the last character, career women are disparaged.

15   STUCKEY, W. J.   The Pulitzer Prize Novels: A Critical Backward Look.   Norman: University of Oklahoma Press, 224 pp., passim.
       Covers the rejection of Main Street and Babbitt as contenders for the prize, Lewis's rejection of the prize awarded Arrowsmith, and finally his serving as member of the selection committee in 1936.

16   WALCUTT, CHARLES CHILD.   "Mud Huts of Intellect," in his Man's Changing Mask: Modes and Methods of Characterization in Fiction.   Minneapolis: University of Minnesota Press, pp. 240-47.
       Uses Babbitt to support the thesis that "ideas are more important to the success of a novel than character or plot." Babbitt's plot is "infantile" and its characterization "incredibly poor" but the book is a success because Lewis ridicules the American way of life with relentless multiplication of details.

17   YOSHIDA, HIROSHIGE.   "Satirical Techniques in Sinclair Lewis's Works: Contrastive and Contradictory Expressions." Studies in English Literature (English Literary Society of Japan, University of Tokyo), 42 (March), 209-22.
       Semantic analysis of Lewis's satirical effects in Main Street, Babbitt, Arrowsmith, Elmer Gantry, and Cass Timberlane. Not a master stylist, Lewis is careful to choose precise words to achieve the exact satirical tone.

18   _____.   "Some Devices and Techniques of Expression in the Works of Sinclair Lewis." Hiroshima University Studies, 24, no. 3 (Winter), 175-205.
       Detailed examination of Lewis's "piling up" of nouns or verbs to illuminate the characteristic detail of middle-class American life and his use of repetition for satirical purposes, as with Mrs. Babbitt's use of "That's so" and Babbitt's use of "That's a fact."

<u>1967</u>

1   COAN, OTIS W. and RICHARD G. LILLARD. <u>America in Fiction: An
     Annotated List of Novels That Interpret Aspects of Life in
     the United States. . . .</u> Palo Alto, California: Pacific
     Books, 232 pp., passim.
        Lewis's novels are annotated briefly under such headings
     as "Farm and Village Life," "City Life," "Business and
     Finance."

2   DOOLEY, D. J. <u>The Art of Sinclair Lewis.</u> Lincoln: Universi-
     ty of Nebraska Press, 286 pp.
        Discusses all Lewis's books. In spite of the novels'
     artistic weaknesses (shifts in tone and point of view, in-
     consistency in the creation of characters, weak structure,
     incomplete resolution of intellectual problems raised),
     Lewis still "went far beyond most of his more illustrious
     contemporaries in raising questions of enduring importance
     to the national life." Pages 106-17, except for one para-
     graph and all notes, are reprinted in <u>TCIA</u>, 1968.4.

3   DUFFY, CHARLES. "Sinclair Lewis Letter." <u>American Notes and
     Queries</u>, 5 (April), 118-19.
        Letter from Lewis about the names Dodsworth and Arrow-
     smith, which he says he did not get from two businessmen at
     the American Express office in Paris as Duffy had sus-
     pected.

4   FALKE, WAYNE C. "The Novel of Disentanglement: A Thematic
     Study of Lewis's <u>Babbitt</u>, Bromfield's <u>Mr. Smith</u>, and Up-
     dike's <u>Rabbit, Run</u>." <u>Dissertation Abstracts International</u>,
     28:194A (Michigan).
        According to his abstract, Falke examines a series of
     novels in which the protagonist tries unsuccessfully to
     escape a net or trap in which he is caught. Traces roots
     of the theme in nineteenth-century literature, but empha-
     sizes the three novels named in the title.

5   HACKETT, ALICE PAYNE. <u>70 Years of Best Sellers: 1895-1965</u>.
     New York: R. R. Bowker, 280 pp., passim.
        Includes same information on Lewis as 1956.5.

6   HINES, THOMAS S., JR. "Echoes from 'Zenith': Reactions of
     American Businessmen to <u>Babbitt</u>." <u>Business History Review</u>,
     41 (Summer), [123]-40.
        Although some businessmen responded to <u>Babbitt</u> with hos-
     tility, other accepted it as just criticism. <u>Nation's
     Business</u> carried attacks on Lewis, while the <u>Rotarian</u> ran
     the gamut from angry reactions to praise of Lewis for "an

accurate and long-overdue indictment" of some members.
Cites numerous articles from business magazines.

7 KALLAPUR, S. T. "Sinclair Lewis: Babbitt (A Reconsideration)." Journal of the Karnatak University (Humanities),
11:28-35.
Reviews the main satirical points of Babbitt--the criticism of cultural and spiritual emptiness, the assault on
standardization and conformity--and notes Lewis's amibiva-
lence toward Babbitt himself. One must concede the social
importance of the novel and may even enjoy reading it, but
it is not a great literary work.

8 LIGHT, MARTIN. "Lewis's 'Scarlet Sign': Accommodating to the
Popular Market." Journal of Popular Culture, 1 (Fall),
106-13.
Lewis's ten years as a "hack" before 1920 "endangered
rather than strengthened his skill." A typical story of
this period, "The Scarlet Sign," begins auspiciously like a
Hawthorne story, then is "deflated" and its tragic implications undercut. In his best novels, Lewis similarly "de-
flate[s] the size and potential dignity" of characters who
could be great and often approaches serious, admirable
characters in the "literary" style of the popular magazine.

9 PARK, SUE SIMPSON. "Satire of Characterization in the Fiction
of Sinclair Lewis." Dissertation Abstracts International,
27:2158A (Texas Tech).
According to the abstract, the key to Lewis's satiric
technique is characterization. Through the main characters
of the five major novels of the twenties, Lewis attacks the
false standards of his day as they relate to marriage,
business, art, and religion.

10 PETRULLO, HELEN BATCHELOR. "Satire and Freedom: Sinclair
Lewis, Nathanael West, and James Thurber." Dissertation
Abstracts International, 28:1445A (Syracuse).
According to her abstract, Petrullo compares the main
theme--the need for human freedom--and contrasts the satiric methods of the three authors. Main emphasis in Lewis is
on Babbitt and also It Can't Happen Here.

11 SCHORER, MARK. "Afterword" to Elmer Gantry. Signet Classic
Edition. New York: New American Library, pp. 419-30.
Details the research Lewis put into the writing of his
"preacher novel," analyzes its timeliness considering the
state of "decay" into which American religion had fallen in
the 1920s, and comments briefly on structure and characterization.

1967

12 SVENDSEN, WERNER. "Sinclair Lewis," in Fremmede Digtere i det
    20. århundrede [Foreign Writers in the Twentieth Century].
    Edited by Sven Møller Kristensen. Volume I. Copenhagen:
    G. E. C. Gads Förlag, pp. 463-78.
       Brief biography. Discusses Lewis's major works, largely
    in historical and social terms, and Lewis in relation to
    his contemporaries and later writers. Lewis's works should
    be read primarily for their historical value. In Danish.

13 WEST, THOMAS REED. "Sinclair Lewis: In Affirmation of Main
    Street," in his Flesh of Steel: Literature and the Machine
    in American Culture. Nashville: Vanderbilt University
    Press, pp. 116-31.
       Before Main Street, Lewis emphasized adventure and ro-
    mance and played them off against the routines of business.
    From Main Street through The Man Who Knew Coolidge, he
    rebelled against business and American bourgeois standards.
    With Dodsworth, however, he reconsiders his position, and
    he affirms the standards of the middle-class businessmen in
    Work of Art and The Prodigal Parents.

<u>1968</u>

1 DAVIS, JACK LaVERNE. "The Satire of Sinclair Lewis." Dis-
    sertation Abstracts International, 28:3666A-67A (University
    of New Mexico, 1967).
       Studies all twenty-two novels. According to his ab-
    stract, Davis finds that invective, diminution, and irony
    are chief satiric techniques, and Lewis's use of the sati-
    ric monologue was a major "contribution to the historical
    development of satire."

2 EARNEST, ERNEST P. Expatriates and Patriots: American Art-
    ists, Scholars, and Writers in Europe. Durham, N.C.: Duke
    University Press, pp. 248-49, 266-68, 271-73, 275, 277.
       As one of the expatriates of the 1920s in Paris, Lewis
    shared with others the sense of alienation evident in his
    novels' criticism of American life. Although he was once
    termed a "tourist," he used his experiences as expatriate
    in Dodsworth.

3 GRIFFIN, ROBERT J. "Sinclair Lewis," in American Winners of
    the Nobel Literary Prize. Edited by Warren G. French and
    Walter E. Kidd. Norman: University of Oklahoma Press,
    pp. 16-53.
       Survey of Lewis's career as a novelist, with special
    attention to books before Main Street as well as Mantrap,
    The Man Who Knew Coolidge, Arrowsmith, Elmer Gantry, and

178

<u>Dodsworth</u>. Lewis certainly deserved the Prize on the strength of his five best novels of the 1920s, and perhaps on the strength of <u>Babbitt</u> alone. He will be read for his social significance even though he contributed nothing to the art of the novel.

4 _____, editor. <u>Twentieth Century Interpretations of Arrow-smith: A Collection of Critical Essays</u>. Maynard Mack, series editor. Englewood Cliffs, N.J.: Prentice-Hall, viii + 119 pp.

    Griffin's introduction (pp. 1-17) traces Lewis's life and career with emphasis on the best work of the 1920s and comments on the rise, decline, and resurgence of Lewis's reputation. <u>Arrowsmith</u> is apparently uncomplicated but actually unites "two distinct though effectively inter-related levels, the personal and the social." It is novel and satire at the same time and thus one of Lewis's best works. Chronology of important dates and brief bibliography. Reviews and essays: Stuart P. Sherman, "A Way Out: Sinclair Lewis Discovers a Hero" (1925.36); Lyon N. Richardson, "<u>Arrowsmith</u>: Genesis, Development, Versions" (1955.17); T. K. Whipple, "Sinclair Lewis: <u>Arrowsmith</u>" (1925.46); Mark Schorer, "On <u>Arrowsmith</u>" (1961.8); Charles E. Rosenberg, "Martin Arrowsmith: The Scientist as Hero" (1963.18); William B. Ober, M.D., "<u>Arrowsmith</u> and <u>The Last Adam</u>" (1963.17); D. J. Dooley, "<u>Arrowsmith</u>" (1967.2); Sheldon N. Grebstein, "The Best of the Great Decade" (1962.6); Erik Axel Karlfeldt, "Why Sinclair Lewis Got the Nobel Prize" (1930.16); Carl Van Doren, "Sinclair Lewis and the Revolt from the Village" (1940.23); T. R. Fyvel, "Martin Arrowsmith and His Habitat" (1955.11); Anon., "<u>Martin Arrowsmith</u>" (1925.5); H. L. Mencken, "<u>Arrowsmith</u>" (1925.31); Robert Morss Lovett, "An Interpreter of American Life" (1925.30); Joseph Wood Krutch, "A Genius on Main Street" (1925.27); Haven Emerson, M.D., "A Doctor Looks at Arrowsmith" (1925.17); W. P. K., "<u>Martin Arrowsmith</u>" (1925.26); Edwin Muir, "Melodrama in America" (1925.32); Henry Seidel Canby, "Fighting Success" (1925.12); Lucy L. Hazard, "The Frontier in <u>Arrowsmith</u>" (1927.18).

5 HELLEBERG, MARILYN MORGAN. "The Paper-Doll Characters of Sinclair Lewis' <u>Arrowsmith</u>." <u>Mark Twain Journal</u>, 14, no. 2 (Summer), 17-21.

    <u>Arrowsmith</u>, like Lewis's other work, is marred by "paper doll" characters, divided into black and white. His failure to characterize more fully severely limits his fiction, for it forces readers to accept "half truths" and "stereo-types."

1968

6   HOLLIS, C. CARROLL. "Sinclair Lewis: Reviver of Character,"
     in Fifty Years of the American Novel: A Christian Apprais-
     al. Edited by Harold C. Gardiner. New York: Gordian
     Press, pp. 89-106.
          Expansion of 1951.31. Lewis's The Man Who Knew Coolidge
     is viewed not as a novel but as a Theophrastian Character,
     having as its point the creation of a "type." From Main
     Street through Elmer Gantry Lewis struggled to resolve a
     conflict between the Character and the novel, but in The
     Man Who Knew Coolidge he created "the nearest thing to pure
     Character that we have." His reputation rests on his work
     of the 1920s, when his use of the conventions of the Char-
     acter enabled readers to put complex questions into a mean-
     ingful perspective.

7   McCARTHY, JOHN F. "A New Look at an Old Street." English
     Journal, 57 (October), 985-87.
          Main Street is not just a historical novel of the 1920s
     but is still teachable and relevant in the 1960s. Young
     people still face the problems Carol faced and have to
     choose among the alternatives presented in the novel:
     revolution, flight, "dropping out," or trying to change
     things gradually.

8   NICHOLS, JAMES W. "Nathanael West, Sinclair Lewis, Alexander
     Pope and Satiric Contrasts." Satire Newsletter, 5
     (Spring), 119-22.
          Responds to 1965.10 and another article on West. A Cool
     Million, Babbitt, and The Rape of the Lock all employ a
     basic satiric device: "playing one set of ideas or values
     against another to insinuate that something is wrong,
     blameworthy, or ridiculous."

*9   SAITO, MITSURU. Sinclair Lewis (20 Seiki Eibei Bungaku Annai
     13 [Guide to Twentieth Century English and American Litera-
     ture 13]). Tokyo: Kenkusha.
          Cited in 1971 MLA International Bibliography, p. 153.
     According to 1976.12, this work contains a list of books
     and articles on Lewis written in Japan.

10   SCHORER, MARK. The World We Imagine: Selected Essays. New
     York: Farrar, Straus and Giroux, pp. [162]-218, [221]-39.
          "Elmer Gantry: The Method of Half-Truths" is a reprint
     of 1956.6. "Sinclair Lewis and His Critics" is a reprint
     of "Introduction" to SL:CCE, 1962.14. "Two Houses, Two
     Ways: The Florentine Villas of Lewis and Lawrence" is a
     reprint of 1953.13. "The Burdens of Biography" is a re-
     print of 1962.11.

11   WOODRESS, JAMES. <u>Dissertations in American Literature, 1891–
      1966</u>. Durham: Duke University Press, numbers 1673–92,
      3668–3741.
            Lists fifty-three M.A. theses on Lewis; nine Ph.D. dis-
      sertations in English and twelve in German.

<u>1969</u>

1   ALLEN, WALTER. "American Spokesmen," in his <u>The Urgent West:
     The American Dream and Modern Man</u>. New York: E. P. Dut-
     ton, pp. 197–200.
           Lewis's criticism of the small town in <u>Main Street</u> is
     "coarser and more superficial" than Anderson's in <u>Wines-
     burg, Ohio</u>. <u>Babbitt</u> is Lewis's best book though its satire
     is flawed by being only "intermittent," a flaw caused by
     Lewis's own similarity to Babbitt.

2   ANDERSON, HILTON. "A Whartonian Woman in <u>Dodsworth</u>." <u>SLN</u>, 1
     (Spring), 5–6.
           <u>Dodsworth</u>'s Edith Cortright seems to be based on Edith
     Wharton and three of her characters. All four were Ameri-
     can women who lived a long time in Europe but remained
     thoroughly American in their attitudes.

3   ANON. "Lewis Home Doubly Dedicated." <u>SLN</u>, 1 (Spring), 10.
           In 1968 Lewis's boyhood home was designated a historic
     site by the Minnesota Historical Society and a national
     landmark by the National Park Service.

4   ANON. "Photographs of Lewis, 1920–1944." <u>South Dakota Re-
     view</u>, 7, no. 4 (Winter), [65]–[71].
           Lewis in vicinity of Sauk Centre, at Yale University, in
     his house in Duluth.

5   BARRY, JAMES D. "<u>Dodsworth</u>: Sinclair Lewis' Novel of Charac-
     ter." <u>Ball State University Forum</u>, 10, no. 2 (Spring),
     8–14.
           <u>Dodsworth</u> has been too often read and criticized from a
     sociological standpoint. It emerges as Lewis's best novel
     if one reads it as a novel of character, showing how a man
     breaks with his past and achieves "a new awareness of him-
     self and his relation to society."

6   BLAKE, NELSON MANFRED. "Knockers and Boosters: Sinclair
     Lewis," in his <u>Novelists' America: Fiction as History,
     1910–1940</u>. Syracuse, N.Y.: Syracuse University Press,
     pp. 9–44.

1969

Discusses <u>Main Street</u>, <u>Babbitt</u>, <u>Dodsworth</u>, <u>Arrowsmith</u>,
and <u>Elmer Gantry</u> as very accurate presentations of the
United States from 1912 through the 1920s. Although Lewis
was far from objective, the student of history can learn
much from his "rich gifts for fact-gathering and mimicry."

7   BROWN, DANIEL RUSSELL. "The Cosmopolitan Novel: James and
     Lewis." <u>SLN</u>, 1 (Spring), 6-9.
        <u>The Ambassadors</u> and <u>Dodsworth</u> have many similarities,
     the most important being that both deal with "the question
     of how best to live" and explore this question "within the
     dramatic conflicts of the Old and New Worlds." In style
     and content <u>Dodsworth</u> is Lewis's finest novel.

8   BUCCO, MARTIN. "The Serialized Novels of Sinclair Lewis."
     <u>Western American Literature</u>, 4 (Spring), 29-37.
        Examination of the seven novels published both serially
     and in book form—among them <u>Arrowsmith</u>, <u>Ann Vickers</u>, and
     <u>Cass Timberlane</u>—shows that Lewis was capable of "cynical
     banality" when the price was attractive. He approved and
     often initiated editorial alterations which made his works
     less satirical and more polite. <u>See</u> 1964.5.

9   COARD, ROBERT L. "College and Schoolhouse in Main Street."
     <u>SLN</u>, 1 (Spring), 3-4.
        Lewis is not so sarcastic about formal education as some
     have thought: in <u>Main Street</u> he is actually even-handed.
     Carol, Vida Sherwin, and Guy Pollock all attended narrow
     denominational schools, but their horizons were broadened
     by them. The new high school is a hopeful symbol at the
     end of the novel.

10   CONRAD, BARNABY. <u>Fun While It Lasted</u>. New York: Random
     House, pp. 267-320, 336-39.
        Anecdotal account of meeting Lewis, a summer in Thorvale
     as Lewis's secretary-companion, and Lewis's comments on
     writing, his own novels, and other writers.

11   CURLEY, DOROTHY NYREN; MAURICE KRAMER; and ELAINE FIALKA,
     editors. "Lewis, Sinclair (1885-1951)." <u>A Library of Lit-
     erary Criticism: Modern American Literature</u>. Volume 2.
     Fourth edition. New York: Frederick Ungar, pp. 207-13.
        Brief, generally positive excerpts from twenty-two arti-
     cles and books on Lewis as man and author.

12 DUKE, MAURICE. "Sinclair Lewis on the Highway: An Unpub-
       lished Letter." SLN, 1 (Spring), 2.
         Prints, with brief introduction, a letter from Lewis to
       James Branch Cabell, dated 3 September 1919, concerning the
       Lewises' automobile trip from Virginia to West Chester,
       Pennsylvania.

13 HILFER, ANTHONY CHANNELL. "Sinclair Lewis: Caricaturist of
       the Village Mind" and "Elmer Gantry and That Old Time Re-
       ligion," in his The Revolt from the Village: 1915-1930.
       Chapel Hill: University of North Carolina Press,
       pp. 158-92.
         The best of Lewis's novels--Main Street, Babbitt, and
       Elmer Gantry--"are sociological in content and, to a large
       extent, in form." Lewis relies heavily on research to
       build up a corpus of knowledge, then sets it down, as in
       the first seven chapters of Babbitt, almost in the form of
       a case-study. Chief targets in his satires are threats to
       freedom in America from sources as diverse as narrow-minded
       religion and increasing mechanization. Pages 167-78 re-
       printed in SB, 1971.13.

14 HIND, C[HARLES] LEWIS. "Sinclair Lewis," in his More Authors
       and I. Originally published in 1922. Freeport, N.Y.:
       Books for Libraries Press, pp. 186-92.
         Lewis shows in Main Street, and to an extent in Free
       Air, that a new America will be heard from in literature.
       It recognizes no ancestors in New England or in England,
       but is original, brash, and refreshing. Reprinted from
       Christian Science Monitor.

15 KITTLESON, J. HAROLD. "Lewis." South Dakota Review, 7, no. 4
       (Winter), 19-20.
         Memoir of Lewis by publisher who met him only three or
       four times but who collected all his writings and presented
       them to Macalester College, St. Paul.

16 LIBMAN, VALENTINA A. Russian Studies of American Literature.
       Edited by Clarence Gohdes. Translated by Robert V. Allen.
       Chapel Hill: University of North Carolina Press, pp. 4,
       6, 9, 33, 113-18.
         Eighty-six bibliographical entries covering Russian
       criticism of Lewis from 1923 to 1963.

1969

17   LUNDQUIST, JAMES. "Acceptance and Assent." <u>SLN</u>, 1 (Spring),
      1.
          Lewis continues to influence American popular culture.
      The <u>Newsletter</u> is intended to "facilitate and intensify
      serious study of Lewis," which has been more thorough since
      1960 than it was during his lifetime.

18   MANFRED, FREDERICK. "Sinclair Lewis' Funeral." <u>South Dakota</u>
      <u>Review</u>, 7, no. 4 (Winter), 54-64, 77-78.
          Personal reflections on Lewis and the memorial address
      Manfred delivered at the burial ceremony in Sauk Centre.
      Stresses that Lewis was a satirist because he perceived the
      gap between things as they are and as they could be.

19   MARTHALER, SISTER M. ANDRE, O.S.B. "Ashes Come Home: The
      Funeral of Sinclair Lewis." <u>Minnesota English Journal</u>, 5
      (Spring), 17-18.
          Account of service held before burial of Lewis's ashes.
      Reprinted 1970.19.

20   [MILTON, JOHN R.]. "Literary or Not." <u>South Dakota Review</u>, 7
      no. 4 (Winter), 2, 132-33.
          Editor's note dedicating this issue of <u>SDR</u> to Lewis and
      to Frederick Manfred. Includes bibliography of each man's
      novels.

21   <u>New York Times Book Review</u>. <u>Critiques of Sinclair Lewis's</u>
      <u>Works</u>. New York: New York Times, 40 pp.
          A portfolio collection reproducing twenty-four reviews
      and articles on Lewis's works, from 1917 to 1951, as they
      appeared in the <u>New York Times Book Review</u>.

22   NIALL, BRENDA. "Salesman and Dream: Sinclair Lewis's <u>Bab-</u>
      <u>bitt</u>." <u>Twentieth Century</u> (Melbourne), 22 (September),
      24-32.
          Despite the satirical manner in which he is drawn, Bab-
      bitt has some characteristics of the heroic figure in the
      rebellious side of his nature. Ultimately, however, Lewis
      fails to develop this side of Babbitt, and what might have
      been tragedy becomes mere sentimentality.

23   PETRULLO, HELEN B. "<u>Babbitt</u> as Situational Satire." <u>Kansas</u>
      <u>Quarterly</u>, 1, no. 3 (Summer), 89-97.
          Examines formal satirical techniques in <u>Babbitt</u> and
      their effect. Babbitt is used as "central figure," with
      contrasting types in juxtaposition. He is exposed to
      "various satiric voices that present [different] points of
      view."

24 _____ . "Main Street, Cass Timberlane, and Determinism."
South Dakota Review, 7, no. 4 (Winter), 30-42.
Draws parallels between characters and situations in
Main Street and Cass Timberlane. Whereas determinism rules
Will Kennicott, Timberlane is able to break "the determin-
istic chain" that has bound his life so that in this way,
at least, the later novel surpasses Main Street.

25 QUIVEY, JAMES R. "George Babbitt's Quest for Masculinity."
Ball State University Forum, 10, no. 2 (Spring), 4-7.
To reinforce his masculinity Babbitt asserts himself in
business, has affairs, and attempts to play a rugged "manly" role on a fishing trip. Unlike Hemingway's Jake Barnes,
Babbitt finds no renewal in the wilderness, which merely
throws his ineffectual nature into relief.

26 _____ . "Release Motif and Its Impact in Babbitt." SLN, 1
(Spring), 4-5.
Babbitt is made up of a series of attempts by various
characters to find release from the tensions of their lives
through alcohol, illicit sex, or acts of rebellion. The
futility of their flight is repeatedly emphasized.

27 RATHE, C[HUCK]. "On the Occasion of Sinclair Lewis' Burial."
South Dakota Review, 7, no. 4 (Winter), 43-53.
Account of the burial of Lewis's ashes in Sauk Centre.
Reminisces about Lewis's 1947 visit to his home town.

28 ROTH, RUSSELL. "The Return of the Laureate: Sinclair Lewis
in 1942." South Dakota Review, 7, no. 4 (Winter), 3-10.
Lewis as creative writing teacher at the University of
Minnesota, by a former student.

29 SCHORER, MARK. "Sinclair Lewis: Babbitt," in Landmarks of
American Writing. Edited by Hennig Cohen. New York:
Basic Books, pp. 315-27.
Summarizes the history of Babbitt's composition. Although many of Lewis's novels are now dead, several proofs
of Babbitt's survival are advanced. The key to success in
this and Lewis's other best novels was the "mass of social
notation . . . that Lewis pursued with all the naturalist's
compulsiveness. . . ." Reprinted in SB, 1971.13. Trans-
lated into German, 1974.19.

1969

30 SILHOL, ROBERT. Les Tyrans Tragiques: Un Témoin pathétique
de notre temps: Sinclair Lewis. Paris: Presses Universi-
taires de France, 443 pp.
   Psychoanalytic approach to Lewis and his works suggests
that Lewis works out his private conflicts and obsessive
desires in his fiction. First the novels are viewed as un-
conscious autobiography (Main Street, Babbitt, Arrowsmith,
Elmer Gantry). The second part presents explicit evidence
from the novels: Babbitt is a representative tyrant, whose
tragedy is that he is a victim of the class structure. The
third part deals with implicit evidence in Arrowsmith and
Dodsworth. Very extensive bibliography (pp. [409]-32) includes many foreign publications. In French.

31 STAPLES, MARY E. "As I Remember Sinclair Lewis." South
Dakota Review, 7, no. 4 (Winter), 11-18.
   Reprints eight personal letters from Lewis to the author
and her husband, friends from Minnesota, 1942-1946.

32 SUDERMAN, ELMER. "Main Street Today." South Dakota Review,
7, no. 4 (Winter), 21-29.
   Despite unoriginal character, undistinguished style,
harsh tone, and an episodic plot, Main Street survives because Lewis provided a structured way of interpreting the
American scene and a fictional world so precisely and sa-
tirically drawn that even the present generation is led to
look critically upon its everyday life.

33 University of Virginia. "(Harry) Sinclair Lewis (1885-1951)."
The American Writer in England: An Exhibition Arranged in
Honor of the Sesquicentennial of the University of Vir-
ginia. With foreword by Gordon N. Ray and introduction by
C. Waller Barrett. Charlottesville: University Press of
Virginia, pp. 129-30.
   Catalogue. Lewis exhibits include first edition of
Babbitt, first English edition of Dodsworth, and four
"presumably unpublished" letters.

1970

1 ANON. "'Sinclair Lewis's Minnesota' Radio Grant Awarded."
SLN, 2 (Spring), 16.
   A grant will enable St. Cloud State College to produce
12 one-half hour radio programs on Lewis and his home
state. (See 1971.2.)

186

2　AUSTIN, JAMES C.　"Sinclair Lewis and Western Humor," in <u>Amer-ican Dreams, American Nightmares</u>.　Edited by David Madden. Carbondale and Edwardsville:　Southern Illinois University Press, pp. 94-105.

　　Lewis's humor, like that of folk humorists and humorous journalists, often "reflects the contradictory pulls of regional loyalty and realistic clear-sightedness" as seen in <u>The Man Who Knew Coolidge</u> and <u>Main Street</u>.

3　BURTON, DOLORES M.　"Intonation Patterns of Sermons in Seven Novels."　<u>Language and Style</u>, 3 (Summer), 205-20.

　　Includes one-paragraph analysis of a sermon in <u>Babbitt</u>.

4　COARD, ROBERT L.　"Arrowsmith and 'These Damn Profs.'"　<u>SLN</u>, 2 (Spring), 6-8.

　　<u>Arrowsmith</u> attacks the modern state university and its professors in anticipation of the student revolt of the sixties, but also shows positive elements.　Although the administration and most teachers at Winnemac are satirized, Gottlieb and Dean Silva are heroes.　Also, Martin dissents without support of any group movement.

5　CONROY, STEPHEN S.　"Sinclair Lewis's Sociological Imagina-tion."　<u>American Literature</u>, 42 (November), [348]-62.

　　Lewis's major works of the 1920s explore the individ-ual's reaction to the surrounding culture.　Carol Kenni-cott and Babbitt attempt to adjust; Arrowsmith is unable to adjust; both Gantry and Dodsworth achieve autonomy, though in opposite ways.　Unfortunately, Lewis was unable to transcend the "limitations of his sociological imagina-tion."

6　DOUGLAS, GEORGE H.　"<u>Main Street</u> after Fifty Years."　<u>Prairie Schooner</u>, 44 (Winter), 338-48.

　　<u>Main Street</u> has become a "mild and easy-going book" which presents praiseworthy features of Gopher Prairie when the reader views it from fifty years' perspective.

7　EARNEST, ERNEST P.　"The Sophomores," in his <u>The Single Vision:　The Alienation of American Intellectuals</u>.　New York:　New York University Press, pp. 123-30.

　　No intellectual but a sort of brash provincial, Lewis could satirize even people with whom he partially identi-fied, such as <u>Babbitt</u>.　Lewis's ideas "put no great strain upon the reader who . . . had also been repelled by some of the more obvious crudities of manners, advertising, business, and evangelical religion."

1970

8   FERRARA, COSMO F. "'Babbitt': What's Good and Bad in a
    Novel?" <u>Missouri English Bulletin</u>, 27 (March), 9-12.
       Pedagogical essay on the use of <u>Babbitt</u> in the high
    school classroom, emphasizing the contrast between Lewis's
    skill as an observer and satirist and his deficiencies as
    a creator of effective plots.

9   FLEISSNER, ROBERT F. "'Something Out of Dickens' in Sinclair
    Lewis." <u>Bulletin of the New York Public Library</u>, 74
    (November), 607-16.
       Attempt to establish which of Dickens's works Lewis knew
    or might have known. Traces parallels in characterization
    and incident between Dickens's works and <u>The Innocents</u> and
    <u>Bethel Merriday</u>.

10 _____. "Sinclair Lewis's Zenith--Once Again." <u>SLN</u>, 2
    (Spring), 10-11.
       The city Lewis had in mind when he created Zenith may
    have been Xenia, Ohio, with which Howells was associated
    in his youth. Lewis, who felt that Howells had established
    a timid standard for American literature, might have used
    Xenia ironically.

11 GERSTENBERGER, DONNA and GEORGE HENDRICK. "Lewis, Sinclair,"
    in their <u>The American Novel: A Checklist of Twentieth
    Century Criticism of Novels Written Since 1789</u>. Volume II,
    <u>Criticism Written 1960-1968</u>. Chicago: Swallow Press,
    pp. 225-29.
       Updates Lewis bibliography in volume I (1961.3), with
    emphasis on recent collections of essays on Lewis.

12 HILL, JOHN S. "Sinclair Lewis, <u>Dodsworth</u>, and the Nobel
    Prize." <u>Husson Review</u>, 3 (May), 105-11.
       Explores the possibility that <u>Dodsworth</u> was a signifi-
    cant factor in Lewis's winning the Nobel Prize. <u>Dodsworth</u>
    discloses a new Lewis, capable of compassion in his treat-
    ment of Fran and capable of more subtle and deep character-
    ization in Sam. Lewis left behind the practiced satirical
    tricks that he had mastered earlier in the 1920s and em-
    barked on a riper, more mature book in <u>Dodsworth</u>.

13 HUBBELL, JAY B. "1922: A Turning Point in American Literary
    History." <u>Texas Studies in Literature and Language</u>, 12
    (Fall), 481-92.
       Notes Lewis's rapid rise as an author with a major repu-
    tation in the early 1920s.

14   LEARY, LEWIS, with CAROLYN BATHOLET and CATHARINE ROTH.
      Articles on American Literature 1950-1967. Durham, N.C.:
      Duke University Press, pp. 338-41.
         Lists articles and some obituaries.

15   LUNDQUIST, JAMES. "Frederick Manfred Talks about Sinclair
      Lewis." SLN, 2 (Spring), 1-5.
         Interview. Manfred talked of Lewis as actor, of the ad-
      vice Lewis gave him on marketing his fiction, and of Lewis's
      ambivalence about Minnesota. Manfred thought Lewis a
      greater writer than critics recognized and felt that
      Schorer's biography was unjust.

16   _____. *The Merrill Checklist of Sinclair Lewis*. Charles E.
      Merrill Checklists, edited by Matthew J. Bruccoli and
      Joseph Katz. Columbus, Ohio: Charles E. Merrill,
      iv + 36 pp.
         Selective bibliography of primary and secondary sources,
      including some reviews, which are listed separately for the
      individual Lewis works.

17   _____. *The Merrill Guide to Sinclair Lewis*. Columbus, Ohio:
      Charles E. Merrill, 50 pp.
         Introduction to Lewis's life and work. Briefly treats
      novels before *Main Street*, then summarizes and analyzes ma-
      jor novels of the 1920s. Surveys the novels from 1930 to
      1951 and suggests that Lewis will survive on his merits:
      strong characterization, meaningful themes, and craftsman-
      ship.

18   _____. "*World So Wide* and Sinclair Lewis's Rewritten Life."
      SLN, 2 (Spring), 12-14.
         Although a bad novel, *World So Wide* shows insight into
      Lewis's own life. Like Hayden Chart, Lewis had spent his
      life seeking his identity in the wrong places, when he
      might have achieved self-knowledge by confronting himself,
      as Chart ultimately does.

19   MARTHALER, SISTER M. ANDRE, O.S.B. "Ashes Come Home: The
      Funeral of Sinclair Lewis." SLN, 2 (Spring), 11-12.
         Reprint of 1969.19.

20   NEVIUS, BLAKE. "Lewis, Sinclair (1885-1951)," in his *The
      American Novel: Sinclair Lewis to the Present*. Goldentree
      Bibliographies in Language and Literature. New York:
      Appleton-Century-Crofts, pp. 65-67.
         Approximately fifty important biographical and critical
      books and articles listed.

1970

21 PAVESE, CESARE. "An American Novelist, Sinclair Lewis" and
    "The Fictionalized Biographies of Sinclair Lewis," in his
    American Literature: Essays and Opinions. Translated by
    Edwin Fussell. Berkeley and London: University of Cali-
    fornia Press, pp. 3-29, 146-49.
        English translation of 1951.44.

22 ROSS, ISHBEL. The Expatriates. New York: Thomas Y. Crowell,
    pp. 260, 263-65.
        Patron of the best hotels and restaurants, Lewis was a
    "confirmed expatriate" but did not associate with the Left
    Bank Exiles, who considered him "just a best seller."
    Quotes critical remarks by Robert McAlmon.

23 RYLANDER, EDITH. "Two Minnesota Boys." SLN, 2 (Spring), 5-6.
        Short free verse poems dedicated to Fitzgerald and
    Lewis.

24 SARGENT, MARION S. "The Babbitt-Lapham Connection." SLN, 2
    (Spring), 8-9.
        Babbitt and The Rise of Silas Lapham both deal with a
    rise and fall, contrast moral with material standards, and
    study American business and manners. However, Lewis alters
    the rise and fall pattern so that the novel ends in an
    irony acceptable to his times. Reading the novels together
    illuminates both because of their differences.

25 STIRLING, NORA. "Sinclair Lewis," in her Who Wrote the Modern
    Classics? New York: John Day, pp. 43-79.
        Brief popular biography for young readers.

1971

1 ANGUS, DAVID ROBERTSON. "The Many Roles of Harry Lewis: A
   Study of Motive and Method in Creative Techniques." Dissertation Abstracts International, 31:3537A (Michigan
   State).
       According to his abstract, Angus examines Lewis's psycho-
   logical tendency to become a "moral martyr" by studying
   characterization in his first seven books (including Hike
   and the Aeroplane). Basically, Lewis's characters in these
   novels reflect his own personality as his later characters
   do not.

2   ANON. "'Sinclair Lewis's Minnesota: A State of Mind': Radio Series Accepted for National Distribution." SLN, 3 (Spring), 22-23.
        Lists twelve thirty-minute programs done at St. Cloud State College to be broadcast over some 190 stations. (See 1970.1)

3   BATCHELOR, HELEN. "A Sinclair Lewis Portfolio of Maps: Zenith to Winnemac." Modern Language Quarterly, 32 (December), 401-[408] plus 20 plates, pages unnumbered.
        Describes and prints a set of maps and diagrams Lewis drew while working on Babbitt. Includes diagrams of Babbitt's office and house as well as list of names used in the novel.

4   CADY, EDWIN H. The Light of Common Day: Realism in American Fiction. Bloomington: Indiana University Press, pp. 147-48.
        Notes the basic similarity between Lewis's treatment of race in Kingsblood Royal and Howells's in An Imperative Duty.

5   CHURCHILL, ALLEN. The Literary Decade. Englewood Cliffs, N.J.: Prentice-Hall, 346 pp., passim.
        Informal history of the literary life of the 1920s with numerous personal anecdotes about Lewis, brief discussions of novels, and summaries of critical and popular reactions to his work.

6   COARD, ROBERT L. "Dodsworth and the Question of Art." SLN, 3 (Spring), 16-18.
        Contrasts Dodsworth with Lewis's most successful novels to assess Lewis's strengths and weaknesses. His strengths are those of the popular novelist of the twenties--controversy, realism, strongly contrasted characters, easily followed plots. His attempt to treat a complicated subject and character in Dodsworth is only a limited success.

7   DANIELS, HOWELL. "Sinclair Lewis and the Drama of Dissociation," in The American Novel and the Nineteen Twenties. Stratford-upon-Avon Studies 13. Edited by Malcolm Bradbury and Palmer Davis. London: Edward Arnold, pp. 85-105.
        Lewis at his best captured the dissociation of newly urbanized America. Carol Kennicott, Babbitt, Arrowsmith, and Dodsworth escape a squalid reality by fleeing to a more primitive life or to the richer life of Europe, either in fact or imagination.

1971

8   DAVIS, JACK L. "Mark Schorer's Sinclair Lewis." <u>SLN</u>, 3
    (Spring), 3-9.
        His formalist bias as a critic and his personal envy of
    Lewis unsuited Schorer to write a critical biography of
    Lewis. It will remain useful for the facts collected, but
    must be read cautiously. As critic, Schorer viewed Lewis
    as one of the worst American writers in his full-length
    biography (1961.15), modified that position in his Minne-
    sota pamphlet on Lewis (1963.21) and then nearly capitu-
    lated in an essay on <u>Babbitt</u> (1969.29).

9   FLEISSNER, ROBERT F. "Charles Dickens and Sinclair Lewis: An
    Exordium." <u>SLN</u>, 3 (Spring), 10-13.
        Dickens was a major influence on Lewis. Characters such
    as Babbitt share qualities of Dickens's characters such as
    Micawber. Both authors wrote for the theater, experimented
    with acting and directing, dabbled in socialism, attacked
    hypocrisy in the clergy, used the idiom of real people in
    their fiction, and were interested in psychology.

10 FRIEDMAN, PHILIP ALLEN. "In Retrospect: Sinclair Lewis."
    <u>Twentieth Century</u>, 179, no. 1046, pp. 44-48.
        Overview of Lewis's career from <u>Our Mr. Wrenn</u> to <u>World
    So Wide</u>. Lewis will continue to be read by intellectuals,
    social historians, and even by Babbitts who see their
    neighbors mirrored in his satires.

11 GILENSON, BORIS. "Sinclair Lewis' Books in the Soviet Union."
    <u>Soviet Life</u>, no. 1 (January), pp. 50-51.
        Lewis was second only to Upton Sinclair among American
    writers read in Russia during the 1920s. A nine-volume
    edition of his works with explanatory notes was published
    in 1965. His works are estimated to have sold 4,000,000
    copies in Russia to date, and he is seen by Russian critics
    "as a worthy heir of Mark Twain." Illustrated.

12 IANNI, LAWRENCE. "Sinclair Lewis as a Prophet of Black Pride."
    <u>SLN</u>, 3 (Spring), 13-15, 21.
        Lewis was ahead of his time in <u>Kingsblood Royal</u>, which
    seems more believable and solid now. Its reputation suf-
    fered from critics' inability to believe that Neil Kings-
    blood would identify himself as black, but Lewis prepared
    carefully for Neil's announcement.

13 LIGHT, MARTIN, editor. <u>Studies in Babbitt</u>. Charles E. Mer-
    rill Studies, edited by Matthew J. Bruccoli and Joseph
    Katz. Columbus, Ohio: Charles E. Merrill, vi + 116 pp.
        Light's preface (pp. iii-vi) reviews critical questions
    posed by <u>Babbitt</u> and explains his selection of the five

contemporary reviews and nine critical essays reprinted
here in addition to letters from Lewis to his publishers
and Lewis's unpublished introduction to Babbitt. Contents:
May Sinclair, "The Man from Main Street" (1922.25); Ludwig
Lewisohn, "Babbitt" (1922.15); Robert Littell, "Babbitt"
(1922.16); H. L. Mencken, "Portrait of an American Citizen"
(1922.20); Upton Sinclair, "Standardized America" (1922.26);
Sheldon Norman Grebstein, "Babbitt: Synonym for a State of
Mind" (1962.6); Frederick J. Hoffman, "Critique of the Middle Class: Sinclair Lewis's Babbitt" (1955.14); Daniel R.
Brown, "Lewis's Satire--A Negative Emphasis" (1966.3);
Philip Allan Friedman, "Babbitt: Satiric Realism in Form
and Content" (1966.8); T. K. Whipple, "Sinclair Lewis"
(1928.36); Anthony Channell Hilfer, "Lost in a World of
Machines" (1969.13); Maxwell Geismar, "On Babbitt"
(1947.13); Alfred Kazin, "The New Realism: Sinclair Lewis"
(1942.2); Mark Schorer, "Sinclair Lewis: Babbitt (1969.29).

14 McCORMICK, JOHN. "5: Lewis and Svevo," in his The Middle
    Distance: A Comparative History of American Imaginative
    Literature: 1919-1932. New York: Free Press, pp. 75-85.
        Lewis was vastly over-rated, his Nobel Prize the result
    of "anti-Americanism on the part of the Swedish committee."
    Main Street is his "least embarrassing novel," but even it
    displays "intellectual quackery." Lewis's famous ear for
    colloquial speech is suspect, and his research is simply
    "a substitute for inventiveness." Italo Svevo of Trieste
    is a far better critic of the middle class.

15 MANFRED, FREDERICK. "Writers with Roots: A Salute to 'Stay-
    at-Homes.'" Minneapolis Sunday Tribune, 24 January, p. E 4.
        Review of August Derleth's Return to Walden West, sug-
    gesting that Derleth's uncomplimentary recollections of
    Mark Schorer as a boy help to explain the latter's attack
    on Lewis in his biography (1961.15). Reprinted 1971.16.

16 _____. "Derleth on Schorer and Staying at Home." SLN, 3
    (Spring), 21.
        Reprint under new title of 1971.15.

17 MOODIE, CLARA LEE REDWOOD. "The Shorter Fiction of Sinclair
    Lewis and the Novel-Anatomy." Dissertation Abstracts In-
    ternational, 32:1520A-21A (Michigan).
        According to the abstract, Lewis's books are a "hybrid"
    of two genres, the novel and the anatomy. His short sto-
    ries are a testing-ground for his development of the anato-
    my form, which is carried further in the novels.

1971

18   MOTTRAM, ERIC. "The Hostile Environment and the Survival
     Artist: A Note on the Twenties," in The American Novel and
     the Nineteen Twenties. Stratford-upon-Avon Studies 13.
     Edited by Malcolm Bradbury and Palmer Davis. London:
     Edward Arnold, pp. 258-60.
          Compares Lewis's characters in Main Street and Babbitt
     with Robinson Jeffers's poetic revelation of the "wide-
     spread nature of sickness, tension and decay" and the in-
     dividual's "self-consumption" in the twenties. "Babbitt is
     strictly a horror novel, an unconscious prophecy of a fu-
     ture America of drop-outs and organization men." Its ter-
     ror foreshadows that of Death of a Salesman.

19   NATHAN, GEORGE JEAN. The Morning After the First Night. Re-
     print of 1938 edition. Rutherford, Madison, Teaneck, N.J.:
     Fairleigh Dickinson University Press, pp. 142-45.
          Lewis is potentially "a valuable writer for the American
     stage" but he merely indulges his interest in the theater
     during slack intervals between novels. His prodigious re-
     search for novels is contrasted with his ignorance of the
     fundamentals of playwriting; his plays "have breathed much
     more of the bookstall than of the stage."

20   O'CONNOR, RICHARD. Sinclair Lewis. American Writers Series.
     New York: McGraw-Hill, 144 pp.
          Critical biography for young people. Treats Lewis's
     life, analyzes major novels, and comments briefly on most
     of his lesser works. Includes short bibliography.

21   PETRULLO, HELEN B. "Clichés and Three Political Satires of
     the Thirties." Satire Newsletter, 8 (Spring), 109-17.
          Although Nathanael West's A Cool Million, Lewis's It
     Can't Happen Here, and James Thurber's The Last Flower were
     addressed to audiences in the 1930s and warned of contempo-
     rary abuses, all have "permanent value" because they warn
     against emotional response to clichés.

22   _____. "Dorothy Thompson's Role in Sinclair Lewis' Break with
     Harcourt, Brace." Courier, 8, no. 3 (April), 50-58.
          Thompson "was probably more responsible for the termina-
     tion of [the] publishing relationship [with Harcourt,
     Brace] than Lewis himself." Quotes from Thompson's letters
     in the Syracuse University Library collection.

23   _____. "Sinclair Lewis's Condensation of Dickens's Bleak
     House." Yale University Library Gazette, 45 (January),
     85-87.
          Describes the "judicious" and "sensitive" condensation
     completed for the Readers Club but never published. Re-
     prints Lewis's introduction on pp. 88-92.

24 RATHE, CHUCK. "Sauk Centre Keeping Lewis Memory Warm." St.
    Cloud Daily Times, 28 January, p. 4.
        In the town once insulted to be the prototype of Gopher
    Prairie, Lewis souvenirs are sold, a street is named after
    him, and his former home is a historical landmark. Re-
    printed 1971.25.

25 _____. "Sinclair Lewis Was Buried Here 20 Years Ago Today."
    SLN, 3 (Spring), 19.
        Reprint under new title of 1971.24.

26 SCHMIDT, DOLORES BARRACANO. "The Great American Bitch." Col-
    lege English, 32 (May), 900-905.
        Some famous male writers--Hemingway, Fitzgerald, Lewis,
    and Anderson--have perpetuated the myth of the castrating
    wife in their novels. Briefly discusses Dodsworth, Cass
    Timberlane.

27 SCHRIBER, MARY SUE. "You've Come a Long Way, Babbitt! From
    Zenith to Ilium." Twentieth Century Literature, 17
    (April), 101-106.
        Draws parallels between Lewis's Babbitt and Kurt Vonne-
    gut's Player Piano. However, while Lewis blames the indi-
    vidual such as Babbitt for his plight, Vonnegut blames the
    increasing mechanization of the mid-twentieth century.

28 SHELTON, FRANK WILSEY. "Sinclair Lewis," in his "The Family
    in the Novels of Wharton, Faulkner, Cather, Lewis and
    Dreiser." Ph.D. dissertation, University of North Carolina
    at Chapel Hill, pp. 227-92.
        Lewis sees two sides of the family: it may be either a
    limiting force which prevents the protagonist from achiev-
    ing freedom or a "refuge and source of comfort."

1972

1   ADELMAN, IRVING and RITA DWORKIN. "Lewis, Sinclair, 1885-
    1951," in their The Contemporary Novel: A Checklist of
    Critical Literature on the British and American Novel since
    1945. Metuchen, N.J.: Scarecrow Press, pp. 312-26.
        Extensive bibliography of criticism on Lewis and on each
    of his works.

1972

2 ALDRIDGE, JOHN W. The Devil in the Fire: Retrospective Essays on American Literature and Culture, 1951-1971. New
   York: Harper's Magazine Press, 364 pp., passim.
      In spite of his failings as an artist and thinker, no
   one since Lewis has surpassed him in picturing the American
   small town or businessman. While Lewis and H. L. Mencken
   led a minority of intellectuals in "the war against barbarism," modern writers seem afraid to take a stand against
   the barbarism of the "liberal conformist."

3 ANDERSON, SHERWOOD. "Four American Impressions: Gertrude
   Stein, Paul Rosenfeld, Ring Lardner, Sinclair Lewis," in
   The Portable Sherwood Anderson. Edited by Horace Gregory.
   New York: Viking Press, pp. 428-33.
      Reprint of 1922.2.

4 BURLINGAME, DWIGHT and JEAN K. ARCHBALD. "Two Minnesota College Reports on Sinclair Lewis Collections." SLN, 4
   (Spring), 17-18.
      St. Cloud State College has all Lewis's novels, some
   early journalism, and over ninety poems and stories from
   1905-1912. Macalaster College has books by Lewis, foreign
   editions, books and magazines to which he contributed, a
   large collection of secondary sources, and seventy-six letters by Lewis.

5 BUTCHER, FANNY. "Sinclair Lewis," in her Many Lives--One Love.
   New York: Harper and Row, pp. 383-98.
      Amusing account of her friendship with Lewis from ap-
   proximately 1915 to 1950. Includes an acid portrait of
   Grace Hegger Lewis.

6 CHERNIAK, WILLIAM UDO. "An Analysis of Sinclair Lewis's Main
   Street and Its Relationships to Babbitt, Arrowsmith, Elmer
   Gantry, and Dodsworth." Dissertation Abstracts International, 32:3945A (Michigan).
      According to the abstract, Lewis's novels can be ap-
   proached as art, not merely as social criticism. His characterization is a strong point, and his photographic and
   phonographic skills are used to advance "character, theme
   and conflict."

7 COARD, ROBERT L. "Mark Twain's The Gilded Age and Sinclair
   Lewis's Babbitt." Midwest Quarterly, 13 (April), 319-33.
      Although Lewis owes no "specific indebtedness" to Twain,
   these two novels share a number of parallels. Both take
   place during corrupt administrations, attack contemporary
   politics and religion, have loosely woven plots, employ

irony, and use common idiom for humorous effect. Colonel
Sellers and Babbitt exhibit many common traits.

8   _____. "'Vulgar Barnyard Illustrations' in Elmer Gantry."
     SLN, 4 (Spring), 8-10.
          Studies Lewis's animal imagery, especially that charac-
     terizing Gantry, who is sometimes a hog and often a tomcat.
     Lewis uses animal images much as a caricaturist does, for
     humorous and satiric purposes.

9   DOUGLAS, GEORGE H. "Babbitt at Fifty--The Truth Still Hurts."
     Nation, 214 (22 May), 661-62.
          Lewis was not an artistic novelist or an accurate real-
     ist, but in Babbitt he captured a genuine American dilemma
     which still exists. Just as Babbitt dreamed of doing great
     things and compromised, Americans have always had great po-
     tential and settled for something less.

10   FLEISSNER, ROBERT F. "L'Affaire Sinclair Lewis: 'Anti-
     Semitism?' and Ancillary Matters." SLN, 4 (Spring), 14-16.
          Defends Lewis against the charge of anti-Semitism stem-
     ming from a report by Dorothy Thompson. Lewis often de-
     fended Jews and once thought of writing a novel about anti-
     Semitism. There are cases, as in Dodsworth, when Jewish
     financiers are mentioned unfavorably, but there are also
     allusions to superior Jews, and Arrowsmith's Gottlieb is
     one of Lewis's heroic figures.

11   GARDINER, HAROLD C. "Neither Hot Nor Cold" and "Sauk Centre
     Was Home Still," in his In All Conscience: Reflections on
     Books and Culture. Freeport, N.Y.: Books for Libraries
     Press, pp. 138-41.
          Reprint of 1945.13 and 1951.27.

12   GASTON, EDWIN W., JR. "'Hail, Hail, The Gang's All Here'--
     Twenty Years Late: Sinclair Lewis and the Revolt Against
     the 'Establishment.'" Journal of the American Studies As-
     sociation of Texas, 3:50-55.
          Although Lewis's reputation declined after the early
     1930s and was not significantly restored even by Mark
     Schorer's biography, his critical view of America has much
     in common with that of the "flower children" of the late
     1960s and early 1970s. The "youth rebellion" could learn
     from Lewis, and "might profitably borrow" from him "to
     articulate more clearly its complaints."

1972

13   GILENSON, B[ORIS] A.   Amerika Sinklera L'iuisa [The America of
     Sinclair Lewis].   Moscow: Nauka, 191 pp.
        Considers Lewis's life and reputation as "the angry
     American."   Chapters are devoted to discussion of Main
     Street, Babbitt, Arrowsmith, Elmer Gantry, It Can't Happen
     Here, and Gideon Planish.   Assessment of Lewis as artist.
     In Russian.

14   HUBBELL, JAY B.   Who Are the Major American Writers?   A Study
     of the Changing Literary Canon.   Durham, N.C.:   Duke Uni-
     versity Press, 344 pp., passim.
        Lewis's changing reputation from the 1920s through the
     late 1960s.

15   LEWIS, ROBERT W.   "Babbitt and the Dream of Romance."   North
     Dakota Quarterly, 40, no. 1 (Winter), 7-14.
        Like many writers of the twenties, Lewis treats romantic
     love.   Babbitt first loves an ideal, the "fairy child,"
     then experiments with extramarital love affairs before ac-
     cepting reality in a more mature attitude toward his mar-
     riage.   This theme gives the book a unity that critics of-
     ten ignore.

16   LUNDQUIST, JAMES.   "Old Dr. Alagash's Traveling Laboratory:
     Sinclair Lewis and the Bunko Artist."   SLN, 4 (Spring),
     13-14.
        In his novels Lewis frequently used bunko artists of two
     distinct classes: those like Buzz Windrip and Gantry who
     are "downright rascals," and those like Babbitt and Gideon
     Planish who deceive themselves as well as others and are
     probably more dangerous since they are more numerous.

17   McCULLOUGH, SARAH J.   "Kingsblood Royal: A Revaluation."
     SLN, 4 (Spring), 10-12.
        Kingsblood Royal has been undervalued for two reasons:
     it was ahead of its time in 1947, and modern critics have
     been interested in "subtle and . . . psychological" prob-
     lems rather than in social satire.   The novel should be
     read for its interesting plot and direct confrontation of
     racism.

18   MENDELSON, MORIS O.   "Social Criticism in the Works of Bellow,
     Updike, and Cheever," in Soviet Criticism of American Lit-
     erature in the Sixties.   Edited and translated by Carl R.
     Proffer.   Ann Arbor, Michigan: Ardis Publishers,
     pp. 68-70.
        Some of the motifs in Updike's Couples show the influ-
     ence of Lewis, especially the assaults on materialism,
     architectural ugliness, and the lack of spiritual values.

19 ROGAL, SAMUEL J. "The Hymns and Gospel-Songs in Elmer
   Gantry." SLN, 4 (Spring), 4-8.
      Identifies and classifies the twenty-four hymns and
   gospel songs in Elmer Gantry. Lewis made chronological
   errors on "The Church in the Wildwood" and "Jesus, I Am
   Coming Home." Hymns help to characterize Gantry as "entertainer" during his rise as a minister, but as he becomes
   more powerful and dangerous, the songs almost disappear
   from the novel.

20 ROWLETTE, ROBERT. "A Sinclair Lewis Letter to the Indianapolis News." English Language Notes (University of Colorado),
   9 (March), 193-95.
      Reprints 1921 letter in which Lewis protests being mis-
   quoted in the News. Lewis had praised Booth Tarkington in
   a lecture but was quoted as condemning Tarkington's fiction.

21 SAUER, PHILIP VON ROHR. "The 1945 Lectures: A Happy Episode
   in Sinclair Lewis's Life." SLN, 4 (Spring), 3-4.
      Account of Lewis lecture tour of smaller Minnesota col-
   leges during summer 1945, by his host, former chairman of
   Bemidji State College.

22 SCHORER, MARK. "Afterword" to Dodsworth. Signet Classic
   Edition. New York: New American Library, pp. 355-63.
      Like Lewis's first novel, Our Mr. Wrenn, and his last,
   World So Wide, Dodsworth exposes an incomplete American man
   to the sophisticated European scene. Better than either of
   these books, Dodsworth explores the weaknesses and strengths
   of the American character--its provincialism and naiveté,
   set against "self-reliance, candor, a decent modesty, and an
   absence of pretentiousness. . . ."

23 SCHULBERG, BUDD. "1. Sinclair Lewis: Big Noise from Sauk
   Centre," in his The Four Seasons of Success. Garden City,
   N.Y.: Doubleday, pp. 29-53.
      Reprint of 1960.17.

24 SIMON, TOBIN. "The Short Stories of Sinclair Lewis." Dissertation Abstracts International, 33:765A (New York
   University).
      According to the abstract, Simon takes a psychological
   approach to the stories, which have been unjustly neglected. Lewis's guilt about becoming a writer, his loneliness,
   sexual uneasiness, and relationship with his father are all
   reflected. As a short story writer, Lewis is solidly in
   the popular tradition.

1972

25 TUTTLETON, JAMES W. "Sinclair Lewis: The Romantic Comedian
    as Realist Mimic," in his The Novel of Manners in America.
    Chapel Hill: University of North Carolina Press,
    pp. [141]-61.
        In novels before Main Street, Lewis juxtaposes eastern
    and midwestern characters to defend the manners of the Mid-
    west, but with Main Street "he turned his guns around to
    attack the very village culture he had defended. . . ."

                            1973

1   CRANE, JOAN ST. C. "Rare or Seldom-Seen Dust Jackets of Amer-
    ican First Editions: XIII." Serif, 10, no. 4 (Winter),
    35-37.
        Bibliographical descriptions of jackets for first edi-
    tions of Hike and the Aeroplane, Our Mr. Wrenn, The Trail
    of the Hawk, and The Job.

2   FLEISSNER, R. F. "The Reincarnation of Holmes in Dr. Gott-
    lieb." Baker Street Journal, 23 (September), 176-79.
        Tongue-in-cheek discussion of parallels between Gottlieb
    and Holmes, Arrowsmith and Watson. Calls attention to
    Arrowsmith's metaphorical comparisons between doctors and
    detectives.

3   HOLMAN, C. HUGH. "Anodyne for the Village Virus," in The
    Comic Imagination in American Literature. Edited by Louis
    D. Rubin, Jr. New Brunswick, N.J.: Rutgers University
    Press, pp. 247-58.
        Places Lewis within a context of midwestern writers who
    react to their harsh environment with "self-mocking and
    sardonic laughter," a group which includes Twain, Edgar Lee
    Masters, and Ring Lardner. Lewis satirizes the people and
    institutions of the Midwest through simple invective, car-
    icature, and a technique of his own which ridicules by
    mimicking the speech of real people without apparent exag-
    geration.

4   KALLSEN, T. J. "The Undeserved Degeneration of 'Babbitt.'"
    Names, 21 (June), 124-25.
        Dictionary definitions of "Babbitt" or "babbitt" empha-
    size only the external reality of the novel's main charac-
    ter and completely overlook the side of Babbitt that wishes
    to escape the stereotyped role of the businessman.

5 LEA, JAMES. "Sinclair Lewis and the Implied America." Clio:
   An Interdisciplinary Journal of Literature, History, and
   the Philosophy of History, 3 (October), 21-34.
   Lewis's fiction not only shows a dissatisfaction with
   present-day America but implies approval for the earlier
   culture and values of his country. The God-Seeker shows
   Lewis's feeling for frontier America.

6 LIGHT, MARTIN. "The Quixotic Motifs of Main Street." Arizona
   Quarterly, 29 (Autumn), [221]-34.
   Like Don Quixote, Carol Kennicott is "maddened by books"
   and in the course of the novel "induce[s] a kind of maddened response in others, or at least unsettle[s] them
   enough to reveal their hypocrisies." Thus Carol is ironically undercut because she is a quixotic figure "more honest and more deceived than anyone around her, and thereby
   both more trapped and more alive."

7 LOVE, GLEN A. "New Pioneering on the Prairies: Nature,
   Progress and the Individual in the Novels of Sinclair
   Lewis." American Quarterly, 25 (December), [558]-77.
   Lewis explored new concepts of the pioneering West in
   The Trail of the Hawk, Free Air, Main Street, Babbitt, and
   Arrowsmith. Dodsworth is the culmination toward which
   Lewis has been building; he is "a Western idealist who has
   mastered the technology necessary to achieve his goal" of
   creating a better American city. Western dreamers and
   builders continue to appear in less impressive roles in
   Lewis's later work.

8 LUNDQUIST, JAMES. Sinclair Lewis. Modern Literature Mono-
   graphs. New York: Frederick Ungar, 150 pp.
   After a biographical chapter, discusses Lewis as social
   satirist or "moralist," as artist, and as essayist. Examines Lewis's failures from Ann Vickers to World So Wide but
   points out that even in these books Lewis had much to say.
   His novels will live in spite of artistic weaknesses because of his role as social critic.

9 McWILLIAMS, WILSON CAREY. "The Redhead," in his The Idea of
   Fraternity in America. Berkeley, Los Angeles, and London:
   University of California Press, pp. 518-26.
   Lewis treats "false fraternity" as a perversion of true
   brotherhood. In Babbitt, for example, he juxtaposes Babbitt's real friendship with Paul Riesling and the noisy
   camaraderie of Babbitt with his fellow boosters. "Lewis
   understood better than most of his contemporaries both the
   nature of fraternity and man's need for it," but never having found it himself, Lewis is unable to depict real
   fraternity.

1973

10   MAGLIN, NAN BAUER. "Women in Three Sinclair Lewis Novels."
      Massachusetts Review, 14 (Autumn), 783-801.
         The Job, Main Street, and Ann Vickers show Lewis "grap-
      pling with the problem of how women are to find meaningful
      lives within American society" and faithfully reflect his-
      torical conditions and social barriers.

11   MITGANG, HERBERT. "Babbitt in the White House." New York
      Times Book Review, 20 May, p. 63.
         Recent attacks on freedom of the press have once again
      made It Can't Happen Here a timely book.

12   SANDERS, MARION K. Dorothy Thompson: A Legend in Her Time.
      Boston: Houghton Mifflin, xv + 428 pp., passim.
         Biography including detailed study of Thompson's mar-
      riage to Lewis.

13   SEYMOUR-SMITH, MARTIN. Guide to Modern World Literature.
      London: Wolfe Publishers, pp. 98-99.
         Lewis was basically a journalist and "one of the worst
      writers to win a Nobel Prize"; nevertheless, he has a cer-
      tain "historical" importance because of his depiction of
      contemporary society.

14   SORKIN, ADAM J. "Booth Tarkington and Sinclair Lewis: Two
      Realists as Social Historians." Dissertation Abstracts
      International, 34:341A-42A (N.C.: Chapel Hill).
         According to Sorkin's abstract, Lewis's novels, like
      those of Tarkington, are flawed as social history. Lewis
      documents historical and social change, but he fails to
      show its major effects on characters' lives. While his
      achievement is notable, he is unable to do as much as Dos
      Passos, who transcends the realism Lewis practices.

1974

1   COARD, ROBERT L. "Babbitt: The Sound Track of a Satire."
     SLN, 5-6 (1973-1974), 1-4.
        Lewis emphasizes the noisiness of modern life in Babbitt
     by generous use of alliteration between consonants such as
     b, p, and g, all stops. He also employs repetition and at-
     tributes to his characters various animal noises--bellows,
     yelps, barks, and growls.

202

2   CONROY, STEPHEN S. "Popular Artists and Elite Standards: The
    Case of Sinclair Lewis." Forum (Houston), 12, no. 1
    (Spring), 28-32.
        Like Twain, Lewis was a popular writer, more concerned
    with reaching a large audience than with perfecting his
    art; yet he was clearly superior to hack writers who mere-
    ly cater to mass taste. Critics should devise different
    standards for writers like Lewis rather than apply the same
    standards to all.

3   _____. "Sinclair Lewis's Plot Paradigms." SLN, 5-6 (1973-
    1974), 4-6.
        Lewis's plots are of two basic types: a metaphorical
    journey in a straight line "toward some goal never quite
    reached" as in Arrowsmith, The Job, or Ann Vickers; or a
    temporary quest or escape from a setting and a return to
    that setting, as in Main Street, Babbitt, or Dodsworth.
    The latter structure characterizes his best novels, for it
    allows more complex and interesting juxtaposition of char-
    acters and environment.

4   CRANE, JOAN ST. C. "Rare or Seldom-Seen Dust Jackets of
    American First Editions: XIV." Serif, 11, no. 1 (Spring),
    34-38.
        Bibliographical descriptions of jackets of Main Street,
    Babbitt, Mantrap, Elmer Gantry, The Man Who Knew Coolidge,
    and Dodsworth.

5   DAVIS, ELMER. "Ode to Liberty," in The Golden Age: The Sat-
    urday Review 50th Anniversary Reader. Edited by Richard L.
    Tobin. New York: Bantam Books, pp. 30-32.
        Reprint of 1935.12.

6   HAWORTH, JANE L. "Revisions of Main Street; or, From 'Blood,
    Sweat, and Tears' to the Loss of a 'Literary Curiosity.'"
    SLN, 5-6 (1973-1974), 8-12.
        The writing of Main Street, from the first idea for the
    book in 1905 to the final cutting of a 20,000 word segment
    by Lewis and Alfred Harcourt in July 1920.

7   HICKS, GRANVILLE. "The Artful Dodger," "Sinclair Lewis--Anti-
    fascist," and "Sinclair Lewis's Stink Bomb," in Granville
    Hicks in the New Masses. Edited by Jack Alan Robbins.
    Port Washington, N.Y. and London: Kennikat Press,
    pp. 72-75, 93-97, 123-28.
        Reprints of 1934.31, 1935.20, and 1938.17.

1974

8   HOHENBERG, JOHN. <u>The Pulitzer Prizes</u>. New York and London:
     Columbia University Press, pp. 58-61, 85-87.
       Reviews Lewis's failure to win the fiction prize for
     <u>Main Street</u> or <u>Babbitt</u> and his subsequent rejection of the
     Pulitzer Prize for <u>Arrowsmith</u>.

9   MAGILL, FRANK N., editor. <u>Cyclopedia of World Authors</u>.
     Volume 2. Revised edition. Englewood Cliffs, N.J.: Salem
     Press, pp. 1067-69.
       Brief discussion of Lewis's techniques and significance,
     emphasizing his five major novels. Includes bibliography
     of selected major articles and books on Lewis.

10   MATHESON, TERENCE J. "H. L. Mencken's Reviews of Sinclair
     Lewis's Major Novels." <u>Menckeniana: A Quarterly Review</u>,
     no. 51 (Fall), pp. 2-7.
       Mencken was a failure as a reviewer of Lewis's novels
     because he allowed his own prejudices to blind him to what
     Lewis was actually attempting and accomplishing, especially
     when Lewis was most realistic, as in <u>Dodsworth</u>. When Lewis
     was obviously being satirical, Mencken responded sensitive-
     ly and thus does his best job on <u>Babbitt</u>. Reprinted
     1976.8.

11   _____. "Lewis's Assessment of Carol Kennicott." <u>SLN</u>, 5-6
     (1973-1974), 12-13.
       Lewis thought of Carol as a "shallow and self-deluded
     person" as he indicates when he burlesques her character
     in <u>Nation</u>, 119 (10 September 1924), 255-60. <u>Main Street</u>
     should be read, therefore, with the knowledge that Lewis
     is undercutting his protagonist.

12   _____. "The Unfortunate Failure of <u>Kingsblood Royal</u>." <u>SLN</u>,
     5-6 (1973-1974), 13-15.
       Although <u>Kingsblood Royal</u> is a socially significant
     document, its assault on racism is overstated, Neil's ad-
     mission of his ancestry is unrealistic, and Lewis gets
     caught in a logical trap, wavering between the assertion
     that there is no difference between black and white and
     the contradictory assumption that Negroes are superior.

13   MAYER, GARY H. "Idealism in the Novels of Sinclair Lewis."
     <u>Dissertation Abstracts International</u>, 34:4273A (Baylor).
       According to Mayer's abstract, Lewis displays romantic
     idealism in his first five novels, although his protago-
     nists reconcile themselves to reality. The later protago-
     nists from Dodsworth on, settle for "realistic goals,"
     usually connected with work.

14 MELTON, JOHN L. "Main Street in the Classroom: Another Approach." SLN, 5-6 (1973-1974), 8.
    Main Street was the basis for a graduate course in bibliography and research techniques at St. Cloud State. The class investigated 500 items ranging from songs to originals of Gopher Prairie stores in Sauk Centre.

15 PALEY, ALAN L. Sinclair Lewis: 20th Century American Author and Nobel Prize Winner. Outstanding Personalities Series, no. 67. Series edited by D. Steve Rahmas. Charlottesville, N.Y.: SamHar Press, division of Story House, 29 pp.
    Surveys Lewis's life, career, novels, and reputation. Speculates on "whether he was a major American novelist or merely a brilliant social critic like H. L. Mencken."

16 PANDEYA, S. M. "Form and Content in the Fiction of Sinclair Lewis," in Indian Studies in American Fiction. Edited by M. K. Naik, S. K. Desai, and S. Mokashi-Punekar. Delhi, Bombay, Calcutta, Madras: Macmillan Company of India, pp. [134]-52.
    Lewis is undervalued because his works are viewed as realistic novels not as satires. The nature of Lewis's protagonists, plots, settings, and tone are all determined by the inherent "artistic premises of the satiric form." Thus the naive character of a Carol Kennicott or the circular plots of the novels are not defects but natural parts of a satire, if not of a realistic novel.

17 POWNALL, DAVID E. "Lewis, Sinclair," in his Articles on Twentieth Century Literature: An Annotated Bibliography, 1954-1970. Volume 4. New York: Kraus-Thomson Organization, pp. 2331-42.
    Items L695 to L751 include general items on Lewis and on some specific novels.

18 SCHORER, MARK. "Sinclair Lewis." American Writers: A Collection of Literary Biographies. Volume 2. Editor-in-chief, Leonard Unger. New York: Charles Scribner's Sons, pp. 439-60.
    Material drawn from Sinclair Lewis (1961.15). Includes basic bibliography of major primary and secondary materials.

19 _____. "Sinclair Lewis' Babbitt," in Der Amerikanische Roman im 19. und 20. Jahrhundert: Interpretationen. Edited by Edgar Lohner. Berlin: Erich Schmidt, pp. 162-72.
    Translation into German by Marlene Lohner of essay, 1969.29.

1974

20   SHEPHERD, ALLEN. "A Fairly Hard Week's Work: <u>Main Street</u> in
        the Classroom." <u>SLN</u>, 5-6 (1973-1974), 6-7.
            On teaching <u>Main Street</u> in a modern American novel
        course. The greatest difficulty is getting students to ac-
        cept the novel as a work of art and not a collection of so-
        ciological records.

21   WOODRESS, JAMES. "Sinclair Lewis (1885-1951)." <u>American Fic-</u>
        <u>tion, 1900-1950: A Guide to Information Sources</u>. Vol-
        ume 1. American Literature, English Literature, and World
        Literature in English: An Information Guide Series.
        Detroit: Gale Research Company, pp. 139-43.
            Introductory material to the study of Lewis, including
        biographical note, bibliography and manuscript sources, and
        information on reprints and editions. Evaluates relative
        worth of biographical and critical materials and emphasizes
        those most accessible.

22   WURSTER, GRACE S. "The Hollow Note in Lewis's Satire." <u>SLN</u>,
        5-6 (1973-1974), 15-18.
            Lewis is not an effective satirist. Even his best nov-
        els do not analyze the situations they present in enough
        depth, and Lewis is too often ambivalent about the charac-
        ters and situations. There is simply not enough bite in
        his satire.

<u>1975</u>

1   CHIEL, ARTHUR A. "Sinclair Lewis--A Pro-Jewish Stance."
        <u>American Jewish Historical Quarterly</u>, 64 (March), 258-67.
            Traces Lewis's pro-Jewish sentiment from his Yale days
        when he explored the Russian-Jewish ghetto of New Haven
        through his sympathetic treatment of Max Gottlieb in <u>Arrow-</u>
        <u>smith</u> and his anti-Nazi stand in <u>It Can't Happen Here</u>. Re-
        prints 1905 Lewis story "That Passage in Isaiah" which
        treats Jewish protagonist sympathetically.

2   COONEY, CHARLES F. "Sinclair Lewis Manuscripts in the Library
        of Congress Manuscript Division." <u>Prospects: An Annual</u>
        <u>Journal of American Cultural Studies</u>. Volume 1. New York:
        Burt Franklin, pp. 75-79.
            Inventory of over fifty letters by Lewis in the Library
        of Congress.

3 _____. "Walter White and Sinclair Lewis: The History of a Literary Friendship." Prospects: An Annual Journal of American Cultural Studies. Volume 1. New York: Burt Franklin, pp. 63-75.

Traces the friendship between White and Lewis, from the time Lewis wrote a blurb for The Fire in the Flint (1924) and offered constructive criticism of the novel, to the writing of Kingsblood Royal, on which White offered advice.

4 CUNLIFFE, MARCUS. "Fiction since World War I," in his The Literature of the United States. Harmondsworth: Penguin Books, pp. 281-82.

Lewis made the novel "a branch of superior journalism." Although he satirized America, he loved it and its people; his sympathy sometimes works against his satire and blurs the total effect.

5 LIGHT, MARTIN. The Quixotic Vision of Sinclair Lewis. West Lafayette, Indiana: Purdue University Press, 176 pp.

Analyzes Lewis's "apprentice fiction" and the novels of the 1920s from the standpoint of the tension in those works --and in Lewis's mind--between realism and romanticism. Lewis "was quixotic in his approach to life and recreated in his fiction the stories of significant quixotic heroes."

6 MARCUS, STEVEN. "Sinclair Lewis," in his Representations: Essays on Literature and Society. New York: Random House, pp. 41-60.

Reprint of 1963.15 and 1964.14.

7 MONTEIRO, GEORGE. "Addenda to the Bibliographies of Conrad, Cooke, Damon, Ford, Glasgow, Holmes, Jewett, Lewis, Mumford, Robinson, and Scott." Papers of the Bibliographical Society of America, 69 (Second quarter), 273-75.

Adds a letter to the editor by Lewis to Schorer's "Sinclair Lewis Checklist" in 1961.15.

8 MOODIE, CLARA LEE. "The Short Stories and Sinclair Lewis' Literary Development." Studies in Short Fiction, 12 (Spring), 99-107.

During Lewis's apprenticeship as a writer of fiction in the sixteen years before Main Street, he wrote seventy-six stories. Themes, characters, and narrative techniques that appear first in the stories and later in the novels are identified. Bibliography of Lewis's short fiction.

1975

9   MORLEY-MOWER, GEOFFREY. "Sinclair Lewis's Attempts to Reform
     James Branch Cabell." Kalki: Studies in James Branch
     Cabell, 6:140-45.
         Biographical notes on the friendship between Lewis and
     Cabell, from 1915, when Lewis rejected Cabell's The Cream
     of the Jest, to 1927. Lewis offered advice to Cabell on
     his writing career, aimed at making Cabell more popular.
     Quotes two Lewis letters.

10   PUGH, DAVID G. "Baedekers, Babbittry, and Baudelaire," in
     The Twenties: Fiction, Poetry, Drama. Edited by Warren
     French. DeLand, Florida: Everett Edwards Press,
     pp. 87-99.
         While Babbitt or Main Street may need some background
     material and explanation for today's readers, much of their
     era comes through understandably even without footnotes.
     Explains a few topical references in both novels, espe-
     cially in Babbitt.

                              1976

1   BUNGE, NANCY. "Women as Social Critics in Sister Carrie,
     Winesburg, Ohio, and Main Street." MidAmerica III. Edited
     by David D. Anderson. East Lansing: Michigan State Uni-
     versity, Midwestern Press, pp. 46-55.
         Examines Carrie Meeber, various women in Winesburg,
     and Carol Kennicott as critics and rebels who fight against
     the "competitive, materialistic" standards of their society.
     Women see what is wrong with society but are often con-
     quered by it because the men they love are dominated by its
     standards.

2   CHILDS, MARQUIS. "The Guest Word: Prophecies." New York
     Times Book Review, 11 January, p. 31.
         Summarizes Lewis's speech to the Swedish Academy, noting
     that he accurately predicted the fall of the genteel tradi-
     tion. O'Neill and Hemingway, whom Lewis singled out for
     praise, both went on to win the Nobel Prize.

3   CLARK, WALTER H., JR. "Aspects of Tragedy in Babbitt."
     Michigan Academician, 8 (Winter), 277-85.
         Lewis frustrates the reader's expectations in Babbitt by
     building toward a tragedy which never develops. Babbitt
     and Paul Riesling both seem to be potential tragic figures,
     but Paul's attempt to kill his wife results in a flesh
     wound, and Babbitt's attempt to rebel ends in his sinking
     back into the status quo. Lewis thus shows the spiritual
     poverty of modern civilization, which is unable to support
     genuine tragedy.

                              208

1976

4   COARD, ROBERT L.   "Sinclair Lewis's Kingsblood Royal: A The-
       sis Novel for the Forties." SLN, 7-8 (1975-1976), 10-17.
          Thorough discussion of Kingsblood Royal's journalistic
       "newsmagazine" style, ties with the traditions of Mark
       Twain and others, timeliness, and popular and critical re-
       ception. Lewis may well have helped to change the racial
       climate of the United States.

5   FARRELL, JAMES T.   "Sinclair Lewis," in his Literary Essays:
       1954-1974. Edited by Jack Alan Robbins. Port Washington,
       N.Y.: Kennikat Press, pp. 65-69.
          Reprint of 1955.10, with minor textual changes.

6   GALE RESEARCH COMPANY.   "Lewis, Sinclair," in Who Was Who Among
       North American Authors: 1921-1939. Volume 2. Detroit:
       Gale Research Company, p. 883.
          Brief biographical sketch and list of works.

7   KERN, BEN.   "Original Main Street Honors Lewis Memory." SLN,
       7-8 (1975-1976), 22-24.
          Covers 15 June 1975 dedication of Sauk Centre's Sinclair
       Lewis Interpretive Center, containing dioramas, photostats
       of manuscript materials, and various autographed and for-
       eign editions of Lewis books. Reprinted from Minneapolis
       Sunday Tribune, 15 June 1975.

8   MATHESON, TERENCE J.   "H. L. Mencken's Reviews of Sinclair
       Lewis's Major Novels." SLN, 7-8 (1975-1976), 7-10.
          Reprint of 1974.10.

9   MEASELL, JAMES S.   "A Descriptive Catalogue of Sinclair Lewis's
       Novels." SLN, 7-8 (1975-1976), 2-5.
          Bibliographical essay identifying first editions and
       limited signed editions, with prices, of all Lewis novels.

10 PIACENTINO, EDWARD J.   "The Main Street Mode in Selected Minor
       Southern Novels of the 1920's." SLN, 7-8 (1975-1976),
       18-22.
          Lewis influenced several southerners to depict their own
       areas in tones reminiscent of Main Street. Edith Summers
       Kelley wrote of Kentucky in Weeds; Emanie N. Sachs, also of
       Kentucky, published Talk; T. S. Stribling wrote about Ten-
       nessee in Birthright, Teeftallow, and Bright Metal. These
       authors in turn influenced later southerners such as Erskine
       Caldwell, Thomas Wolfe, and William Faulkner.

1976

11 SEYMOUR-SMITH, MARTIN. Who's Who in Twentieth Century Litera-
      ture. London: Weidenfeld and Nicolson, pp. 209-10.
         "Lewis is only of socio-anthropological interest: as a
      writer he is almost worthless. . . ."

12 YOSHIDA, HIROSHIGE. A Sinclair Lewis Lexicon with a Critical
      Study of His Style and Method. Tokyo: Hoyu Press,
      viii + 653 pp.
         Linguistic examination of Lewis's work. Part 1 treats
      four satirical methods Lewis used: invective, caricature,
      parody, and mimicry. Part 2 catalogues colloquial and
      slang usages in the novels by part of speech or by special
      category ("Idioms of Greeting and Endearment" for example),
      defining each and commenting on its literary effect.
      Part 3 is an alphabetical lexicon of some 2500 terms--
      idioms, Americanisms, or slang--citing sources in the
      Lewis canon and defining.

1977

1 GROSS, BARRY. "In Another Country: The Revolt from the Vil-
      lage." MidAmerica IV. Edited by David D. Anderson. East
      Lansing: Michigan State University, Midwestern Press,
      pp. 101-11.
         Debunks the popular notion that midwestern writers such
      as Lewis and Anderson were whole-heartedly revolting against
      the area. In Main Street "Lewis devotes at least as much
      time and energy to ridiculing Carol as he does to ridicul-
      ing Gopher Prairie."

2 HACKETT, ALICE PAYNE and JAMES HENRY BURKE. 80 Years of
      Best Sellers, 1895-1975. New York and London: R. R.
      Bowker, 265 pp., passim.
         By 1975 Babbitt had sold 1,275,739 in hard cover; Main
      Street had sold 930,929.

3 MILNE, GORDON. "Practitioners, 1920-1960," in his The Sense
      of Society: A History of the American Novel of Manners.
      Rutherford, Madison, Teaneck, N.J.: Associated University
      Presses, pp. 205-11.
         Although Lewis recreated the "forms, rituals, and char-
      acterizing features" of middle-class society, he is not a
      good novelist of manners because of his pedestrian style
      and constant use of caricature.

4   ROBBINS, J. ALBERT, et al. "Lewis, Sinclair," in American
    Literary Manuscripts: A Checklist. Second edition.
    Athens: University of Georgia Press, pp. 192-93.
        Lists holdings of Lewis's papers.

                            1978

1   LINGEMAN, RICHARD R. "Home Town, U.S.A.: In the Footsteps of
    Four Novelists." New York Times, 29 January, Section 10,
    pp. [1], 14.
        Travel article on visits to home towns of Willa Cather,
    Edgar Lee Masters, Sherwood Anderson, and Lewis, whose boy-
    hood home has been restored and turned into a museum.

2   LUNDÉN, ROLF. "Theodore Dreiser and the Nobel Prize." Ameri-
    can Literature, 50 (May), 216-29.
        Analyzes the competition for the Nobel Prize between
    Dreiser and Lewis. Though both coveted the prize and tried
    to attract the attention of the Nobel committee, Lewis out-
    campaigned Dreiser. However, "the judgment of posterity
    tends to be that Dreiser was robbed of a prize that right-
    fully belonged to him."

3   TRILLING DIANA. "May 8, 1943," in her Reviewing the Forties.
    New York and London: Harcourt Brace Jovanovich, pp. 31-33.
        Reprint of 1943.22 with minor textual changes.

4   WAGENAAR, DICK. "The Knight and the Pioneer: Europe and
    America in the Fiction of Sinclair Lewis." American Liter-
    ature, 50 (May), 230-49.
        Though Lewis is noted for his depiction of American man-
    ners, he treats them principally by contrast with those of
    Europe. Our Mr. Wrenn, Dodsworth, and World So Wide exhibit
    an evolution in Lewis's idea of Europe, from youthful ro-
    manticizing to a "retreat where weary Americans like Sam
    Dodsworth (and himself) could drift toward death. . . ."
    American, with all its shortcomings, "remained for Lewis
    the land of promise."

A Note on the Index

In addition to authors, titles of books and articles (excluding reviews, news items, and brief mentions), the titles of Lewis's works, and the names of people, this index includes a number of subject entries. As in the case of Lewis's works, substantial treatments are indexed under the following topics:

Bibliography
Biography
Business
Characterization
Dramatization of novels
Exhibits
Feminism
General assessments
General critical studies
Interviews
Labor novel
Letters
Lewis and the theater
Lewis as lecturer
Lewis as popular novelist
Lewis as teacher
Linguistic analyses
Literary influences on Lewis
Manuscripts and typescripts
Maps and diagrams

Movies from novels
Nobel Prize
Obituaries
Parodies of Lewis's works
Photographs
Pulitzer Prize
Realism
Religion
Reputation
Romanticism
Satire
Sauk Centre
Serialization of novels
Short stories
Small town
Social criticism
Techniques
Thematic studies
Translations
Writing theory and practice

Author/Title Index

Aaron, Daniel, 1953.1; 1965.1
Abbott, Lawrence F., 1927.1
"Acceptance and Assent," 1969.17
Adamic, Louis, 1938.1
Adams, J. Donald, 1933.1; 1934.1;
    1935.1; 1938.1; 1944.1-3;
    1960.1; 1965.2
Adams, Paul, 1923.1
Adelman, Irving, 1972.1
"L'Affaire Sinclair Lewis:
    'Anti-Semitism?' and Ancil-
    lary Matters," 1972.10
"Afterword" to Arrowsmith,
    1961.8; 1968.4
"Afterword" to Babbitt, 1961.8
"Afterword" to Dodsworth, 1972.22
"Afterword" to Elmer Gantry,
    1967.11
"Afterword" to Main Street,
    1961.10
Aikman, Duncan, 1926.1
Alder, Benne B., 1965.3
Aldridge, John W., 1953.2; 1972.2
Alexander, Jack, 1940.1
Allen, Walter, 1964.1; 1969.1
"Les Américains d'après S.
    Lewis," 1930.18
"American Academy of Arts and
    Letters vs. All Comers:
    Literary Rags and Riches in
    the 1920's," 1959.5
"American Business in the
    American Novel," 1931.19
"The American Culture and the
    Individual in the Novels of
    Sinclair Lewis," 1966.6

"American Gothic," 1964.14;
    1975.6
"Americanisms in the Novels of
    Sinclair Lewis," 1960.6
"The American Mind and 'Main
    Street,'" 1922.22
"The American Novel Between
    Wars," 1951.30
"An American Novelist, Sinclair
    Lewis," 1970.21
"The American Novel Through Fifty
    Years: 5. Sinclair Lewis,"
    1951.31; 1968.6
"Americans We Like: Mr. Babbitt,
    Meet Sinclair Lewis," 1927.22
"Americanus," 1922.1
"An American Writer," 1963.15
"The America of Sinclair Lewis,"
    1931.32; 1932.12; 1962.14
"America's Nobel-Man," 1931.12
Amerika Sinklera L'iuisa, 1972.13
Ames, Russell, 1948.1
"An Analysis of Sinclair Lewis's
    Main Street and Its Relation-
    ship to Babbitt, Arrowsmith,
    Elmer Gantry, and Dodsworth,"
    1972.6
Anderson, Carl, 1951.1; 1957.1
Anderson, Hilton, 1969.2
Anderson, Margaret C., 1930.1
Anderson, Sherwood, 1920.5;
    1921.16; 1922.2, 30; 1923.3;
    1925.43, 45; 1930.2; 1962.14;
    1964.16; 1969.1; 1971.26;
    1972.3; 1976.1; 1977.1
"And Lewis Again," 1965.2

"Angela Is Twenty-Two," 1939.2
Angoff, Charles, 1965.4; 1966.1
Angus, David Robertson, 1971.1
Anisimov, I., 1948.2
Annand, George, 1934.2
Ann Vickers, 1933.1-2, 4-9, 11,
    17, 21-28, 30, 34-35;
    1934.19, 24; 1962.12; 1964.5
"Anodyne for the Village Virus,"
    1973.3
"Another Winner," 1930.3
Archbald, Jean K., 1972.4
Argow, Dorothy, 1963.2
Armstrong, Anne, 1933.5
Arrowsmith, 1924.2, 6; 1925.3-8,
    10-18, 20-23, 26-28, 30-39,
    42, 46; 1926.2, 28, 33;
    1927.11; 1928.17; 1930.18;
    1931.1; 1932.8; 1944.5;
    1945.21; 1946.2; 1955.11, 17;
    1961.8, 12; 1962.4; 1963.6,
    17-18; 1964.18; 1965.7, 9;
    1968.4; 1970.4; 1972.10;
    1973.2, 7
"Arrowsmith and Escapism," 1965.7
"Arrowsmith [and] The Last Adam,"
    1963.17; 1968.4
"Arrowsmith and 'These Damn
    Profs,'" 1970.4
"Arrowsmith: A Study in Voca-
    tional Ethics," 1926.33
"Arrowsmith: Genesis, Develop-
    ment, Versions," 1955.17;
    1968.4
Arrowsmith Notes, 1964.18
"Arrowsmith's American Dream,"
    1965.9
The Art of Sinclair Lewis, 1967.2
"Art of the Night," 1936.25
"Ashes Come Home: The Funeral of
    Sinclair Lewis," 1969.19;
    1970.19
"As I Like It," 1931.33; 1933.25;
    1936.27
"As I Remember Sinclair Lewis,"
    1969.31
"Aspects of Tragedy in Babbitt,"
    1976.3
"As Sinclair Lewis Sees the Rest
    of Them," 1921.17
"At the Court of King Gustaf,"
    1931.37

"At Work with 'Red' Lewis: A
    Foreword by Dore Schary,"
    1963.19
Aubery, P., 1956.1
Ausmus, Martin R., 1960.5
Austen, Jane, 1921.5
Austin, Allen, 1958.1
Austin, James C., 1970.2
"The Award of the Nobel Prize to
    Sinclair Lewis," 1957.1

Babbitt, 1922.1, 3-4, 6, 9-18,
    20-21, 23-29, 32; 1923.1,
    3-6, 8; 1924.2, 7; 1925.1-2,
    44, 47; 1926.1; 1928.7, 17;
    1930.7, 18; 1932.4, 15;
    1940.15; 1946.2; 1947.31;
    1949.9; 1951.16, 42; 1955.14;
    1957.8; 1958.2, 8, 10;
    1959.1, 12; 1960.16; 1961.9,
    12; 1962.9; 1964.13, 15-17;
    1965.5, 10, 15; 1966.5, 8,
    16; 1967.4, 6, 7; 1968.8;
    1969.22, 23, 25-26, 29;
    1970.24; 1971.3, 13, 18, 27;
    1972.7, 9, 15; 1973.4, 7-9;
    1974.1, 20; 1975.10; 1976.3
"Babbitt Abroad," 1930.4
"Babbitt: A Mysterious Inscrip-
    tion," 1940.15
"Babbitt and My Russian Friend,"
    1924.7
"Babbitt and the Dream of
    Romance," 1972.15
"Babbitt as Situational Satire,"
    1969.23
"Babbitt at Fifty--the Truth
    Still Hurts," 1972.9
"Babbitt Battles for his Rights,"
    1925.1
"Babbitt Boiling Hot," 1925.2
"Babbitt in the White House,"
    1973.11
"Babbitt-Lapham Connection,"
    1970.24
"Babbitt Méconnu," 1951.16
Babbitt Notes, 1964.15
"Babbitt: Satiric Realism in
    Form and Content," 1966.8
"Babbitt: The Sound Track of a
    Satire," 1974.1

Babcock, C. Merton, 1960.6
Bacon, Leonard, 1939.3
Bacon, Peggy, 1934.12
"Baedekers, Babbittry, and
Baudelaire," 1975.10
Baker, Joseph E., 1938.4
Baldensperger, Fernand, 1925.10
Baldwin, Charles C., 1924.2
Balzac, Honoré de, 1921.7;
1927.1
Barnes, Harry Elmer, 1943.7
Barnett, James Harwood, 1939.5
Barr, Donald, 1956.7
Barry, James D., 1969.5
Barry, Joseph A., 1950.2
Barrymore, Ethel, 1956.2
Bartholet, Carolyn, 1970.14
Barzun, Jacques, 1951.14
Batchelor, Helen, 1971.3
Bates, Ernest Sutherland, 1926.14
Beach, Joseph Warren, 1932.4
Beard, Charles A., 1928.7, 31
Bechhofer, C. E., 1923.2
Beck, Warren, 1948.1, 3
Becker, George J., 1952.3
Becker, May Lamberton, 1931.8
Belgion, Montgomery, 1924.3
Bellamy, Francis R., 1927.8
Bellessort, André, 1931.9
Benchley, Robert, 1934.13-14
Benét, William Rose, 1934.15,
39; 1941.1; 1954.5; 1957.3
Bennett, Arnold, 1922.24; 1932.5;
1957.7
Beresford, J. D., 1938.7
Berg, Adelyne, 1961.1
Bethel Merriday, 1940.2, 4-8,
11-12, 14, 16-22
Bibliography, 1925.23; 1929.15;
1933.31; 1937.5; 1938.32
(German); 1942.3; 1944.7;
1946.2 (French); 1951.40
(Spanish and Portuguese);
1951.49; 1952.20; 1954.10;
1957.1 (Swedish); 1959.6
(Russian); 1960.3; 1961.15;
1962.6, 14; 1966.13 (German);
1967.6; 1968.9 (Japanese);
1969.16 (Russian); 1969.20,
30 (French); 1970.11, 14, 16,
20; 1972.1; 1974.9, 17-18,
21; 1975.7-8; 1977.4

Bibliography: descriptive and
analytical, 1933.31; 1936.21;
1939.14; 1942.1; 1945.8;
1958.2; 1959.1; 1973.1;
1974.4; 1976.9
Binsse, Harry Lorin, 1931.10;
1940.8
Biography, 1914.1; 1916.1;
1922.8, 26; 1924.1-2, 4, 8;
1925.8, 37; 1926.4, 24;
1927.22, 32; 1928.15-17, 19;
1929.15; 1930.1, 22; 1931.11,
21, 28-29, 37; 1932.5, 13,
16; 1933.15, 29, 31-32;
1934.5, 8, 12, 15, 35, 39,
48; 1935.6, 31, 35; 1936.2,
17, 29, 32; 1937.1, 6, 13;
1938.1, 3, 20-21, 25, 29;
1939.1, 3, 15; 1940.1;
1941.4; 1942.3; 1944.7;
1945.2, 21; 1946.2; 1947.32-
33; 1950.2; 1951.11, 17, 22,
29, 38-39, 41, 49-51;
1952.18-19; 1953.7, 13;
1954.1, 3, 7, 12, 14;
1955.2, 10, 12, 15; 1956.2,
7-8; 1957.3, 6-7; 1958.7,
10; 1959.4, 6, 8, 10;
1960.17; 1961.15; 1963.7-8,
23-24; 1964.12-13; 1965.4;
1966.1; 1968.10; 1969.4, 10,
14, 18-19; 1970.15, 17, 19,
25; 1971.5, 19, 22; 1972.3,
5, 23; 1973.8, 12; 1974.15,
18; 1975.3, 9; 1976.6
Birkhead, L. M., 1928.9
"Birth of a Myth, or How We Wrote
'Dodsworth,'" 1960.10
Blackmur, R. P., 1935.7; 1962.14
Blake, Nelson Manfred, 1964.3-4;
1969.6
Blanck, Jacob, 1936.21; 1942.1
Blankenship, Russell, 1931.11
Bloom, Murray Teigh, 1941.2
Blotner, Joseph, 1966.2
Boas, Ralph Philip, 1940.9
Bogardus, Emory S., 1929.3
"Booth Tarkington and Sinclair
Lewis: Two Realists as So-
cial Historians," 1973.14
Bowers, Fredson, 1959.1

"The Boy and Man from Sauk
 Centre," 1960.20
Boyd, Ernest, 1924.4; 1925.11;
 1927.8; 1931.12
Boyer, Richard O., 1949.8
Boynton, H. W., 1917.10-11
Boynton, Percy H., 1926.15;
 1927.9-10; 1931.13; 1936.9;
 1940.10
B., R. A., 1926.16
Brace, Ernest, 1930.11
Brande, Dorothea, 1933.6
Brand, Peter, 1960.7
Brandt, George, 1934.16
Breasted, Charles, 1954.1, 3;
 1959.2
Brennecke, Ernest, Jr., 1929.4
Brent, Bishop Charles, 1921.1
Brickell, Herschel, 1928.10;
 1929.5; 1933.7; 1934.17;
 1935.8-9
Brighouse, Harold, 1943.8
Brinsley, Henry, 1914.7
Brion, Marcel, 1951.15
"British View of Sinclair Lewis's
 Prize," 1930.5
Brodin, Pierre, 1946.2
Bromfield, Louis, 1967.4
Brooks, Van Wyck, 1952.4
Broun, Heywood, 1931.14
Brown, Daniel, 1966.3; 1969.7;
 1971.13
Brown, Deming, 1953.6; 1954.4;
 1962.1
Brown, Glenora W., 1954.4
Brown, John Mason, 1938.8
Brown, Raymond B., 1928.9
Bruccoli, Matthew J., 1958.2
Brune, Ruth E., 1955.1
Bucco, Martin, 1964.5; 1969.8
Buchanan, Thompson, 1928.37
Bunge, Nancy, 1976.1
"The Burdens of Biography,"
 1962.11; 1965.12; 1968.10
Burke, James Henry, 1977.2
Burlingame, Dwight, 1972.4
Burton, Bradley, 1928.11
Burton, Dolores M., 1970.3
Burton, Katherine, 1940.9

Business, 1917.12; 1925.1-2, 25,
 29, 40-41; 1926.30; 1931.19;
 1935.38; 1954.13; 1967.6, 13.
 See Babbitt, Dodsworth,
 Prodigal Parents
Butcher, Fanny, 1972.5
Butterfield, Roger, 1949.9

Cabell, James Branch, 1924.5;
 1930.12-13; 1932.6; 1955.2;
 1969.12; 1975.9
Cabell, Margaret Freeman, 1962.3
Cady, Edwin H., 1971.4
Caillet, Gérard, 1951.16
Caldwell, Cy, 1934.18
Caldwell, Erskine, 1976.10
Calverton, V. F., 1931.15;
 1932.7; 1934.19; 1937.1;
 1938.9
"A Camera Man," 1929.9. See
 1929.10
Canby, Henry Seidel, 1925.12;
 1927.11-13; 1928.12; 1929.6;
 1930.14; 1931.16; 1934.20;
 1936.10; 1947.7; 1963.3;
 1968.4
Cane, Melville, 1951.12; 1953.11
Cantwell, Robert, 1935.10;
 1936.11; 1937.2; 1962.14;
 1964.6
"Carol Kennicott de 'Main Street'
 et sa lignée Européenne,"
 1939.7
Carpenter, Frederic I., 1955.3-4
Carpenter, Harland, 1940.11
Cass Timberlane, 1945.2-7, 9,
 11-14, 16-20, 22-26; 1946.1,
 4, 6; 1964.5; 1969.24
Cather, Willa, 1944.5
Cerf, Bennett, 1945.6; 1948.4;
 1956.2
Chamberlain, John R., 1938.10
Chapman, Arnold, 1966.4
Characterization, 1937.14;
 1947.25; 1948.6; 1951.31;
 1960.13; 1966.6; 1967.9;
 1968.5-6; 1969.5; 1970.5, 9;
 1971.1, 26; 1972.6, 8

"Charles Dickens and Sinclair Lewis: An Exordium," 1971.9
Cheap and Contented Labor, 1930.2
Cherniak, William Udo, 1972.6
"The Chesterton-Drinkwater-Lewis Affair," 1924.8
Chesterton, G. K., 1924.8
Chiel, Arthur A., 1975.1
Childs, Marquis, 1976.2
Churchill, Allen, 1971.5
Clark, Walter H., Jr., 1976.3
Cleaton, Allen, 1937.3
Cleaton, Irene, 1937.3
Clemens, Cyril, 1951.17
"Clichés and Three Political Satires of the Thirties," 1971.21
Coan, Otis W., 1967.1
Coard, Robert L., 1962.2; 1969.9; 1970.4; 1971.6; 1972.7-8; 1974.1; 1976.4
Coates, Robert M., 1933.8
Coblentz, Stanton A., 1921.5; 1939.6
"Cock, Robin & Co., Publishers," 1930.11
Codman, Florence, 1934.21
Colbron, Grace Isabel, 1915.5
Cole, E. R., 1966.5
Coleman, Arthur B., 1955.5
A Collection on Sinclair Lewis, 1951.49
"College and Schoolhouse in Main Street," 1969.9
Collins, Joseph, 1925.13
Colum, Mary M., 1936.12; 1938.11; 1945.7
Colum, Padraic, 1962.3
Commager, Henry Steele, 1950.3
"A Communication: The Pulitzer Prize," 1921.8
Compton, Charles H., 1927.14
Conrad, Barnaby, 1951.18; 1961.2; 1969.10
Conroy, Stephen Sebastian, 1966.6; 1970.5; 1974.2-3
"Consolation," 1921.11; 1962.14
"Contemporary American Authors. III: Sinclair Lewis," 1926.38; 1928.34
"Contemporary Fiction," 1943.19

"Contemporary Reminiscences," 1925.34
Conti, Giuseppi Gadda, 1963.4
"Controversy on Literature with our Foreign Friends," 1946.7
Cooney, Charles F., 1975.2-3
Cooper, Frederic Taber, 1915.6
Cooper, James Fenimore, 1956.9
"The Cosmopolitan Novel: James and Lewis," 1969.7
"Cotton Mill," 1930.2
Couch, William, Jr., 1964.7
Couperus, Louis, 1921.15
Cousins, Norman, 1951.19; 1955.6
Cowley, Malcolm, 1928.13; 1933.9; 1936.13; 1938.12; 1947.6, 8; 1951.20-21; 1962.14; 1964.8
Cozzens, James Gould, 1963.17
Crandall, C. F., 1951.22
Crane, Joan St. C., 1973.1; 1974.4
A Critical Commentary: Main Street, 1964.22
"Critics and Satirists--The Radicals," 1936.28
Critiques of Sinclair Lewis's Works, 1969.21
Crocker, Lionel, 1935.11
"La Croisade de Sinclair Lewis," 1938.24
"Crusaders and Skeptics," 1939.9
C., S. M., 1934.22
Cunliffe, Marcus, 1975.4
Curley, Dorothy Nyren, 1969.11

Daiches, David, 1949.10
"The Damnation of Theron Ware and Elmer Gantry," 1964.10
Daniel, Benne Bernice, 1963.5
Daniels, Howell, 1971.7
Danielson, Richard, 1925.14; 1926.17
David, Simone, 1939.7
Davidson, Donald, 1925.15; 1963.6
Davies, Horton, 1959.3
Davis, Elmer, 1927.15; 1934.23; 1935.12; 1938.13; 1974.5
Davis, Jack La Verne, 1968.1; 1971.8
Debs, Eugene, 1958.1

DeCasseres, Benjamin, 1931.17
Deegan, Dorothy Yost, 1951.23
de Kruif, Paul, 1924.6; 1925.34; 1932.8; 1945.21; 1955.17; 1962.4; 1963.18; 1964.18
Dell, Floyd, 1921.9, 16; 1922.30; 1924.7; 1927.14; 1933.10; 1964.21
Demmig, Charlotte, 1931.18
Dempsey, David, 1952.5-6
Derleth, August, 1959.4; 1963.7; 1971.15-16
"Le dernier roman de Sinclair Lewis," 1952.14
"A Descriptive Catalogue of Sinclair Lewis's Novels," 1976.9
De Villeneuve, R., 1937.4
De Voto, Bernard, 1933.11; 1934.24; 1936.14; 1944.2-4, 6; 1963.11
"Diarist of the Middle-Class Mind," 1947.12; 1958.3
Dickens, Charles, 1914.6; 1928.12; 1930.12-13; 1931.10, 26; 1951.41; 1952.21; 1953.7; 1958.1; 1960.13; 1970.9; 1971.23
Dickson, James K., 1945.8
Dinwiddie, Courtenay, 1925.16
D., K., 1921.6
Dobrée, Bonamy, 1934.25
Dodsworth, 1929.1-2, 4-6, 8, 11, 13, 16, 18-25, 27; 1930.18, 22; 1936.10; 1946.2; 1947.10; 1957.2; 1960.5, 10; 1962.9; 1964.16; 1966.10; 1968.2; 1969.2, 5, 7; 1970.12; 1971.6; 1972.10, 22; 1973.7
--film: 1936.6; 1949.18
--play: 1934.9-10, 14, 16, 18, 32-33, 36, 45, 49, 51; 1935.29; 1938.8
"Dodsworth and the Question of Art," 1971.6
"Dodsworth: Sinclair Lewis' Novel of Character," 1969.5
Dondore, Dorothy Anne, 1926.18
Dooley, David J., 1955.7; 1967.2; 1968.4
Dorothy and Red, 1963.23
"Dorothy Thompson," 1937.13

Dorothy Thompson: A Legend in Her Time, 1973.12
"Dorothy Thompson's Role in Sinclair Lewis' Break with Harcourt, Brace," 1971.22
Dos Passos, John, 1944.5; 1973.14
"Dottie and Red," 1938.15. See 1937.6.
Douglas, George H., 1970.6; 1972.9
Dounce, Harry Esty, 1926.19
Dowd, Wilbur J., 1933.12
"Do We Love Shaw's Abuse?" 1931.2
Downing, Francis, 1951.24
Dramatization of novels, 1927.7; 1928.8, 37; 1934.9-10, 14, 16, 18, 32-33, 36, 45, 49, 51; 1935.29; 1936.4, 7-8, 20, 22, 33-35; 1938.8; 1939.11; 1940.13
Dreiser, Theodore, 1920.5; 1921.11; 1930.4; 1931.7, 20; 1933.33; 1945.10; 1951.43; 1956.2; 1960.19; 1962.1, 9; 1964.12; 1976.1
"Dr. Evans and Arrowsmith," 1925.18
Drew, Elizabeth A., 1926.20
Drinkwater, John, 1924.8
"Dr. Zhivago and Babbitt," 1959.12
Du Bois, William, 1943.9; 1956.3
Duffus, R. L., 1935.13; 1955.8
Duffy, Charles, 1945.9; 1967.3
Duke, Maurice, 1969.12
Durtain, Luc, 1929.7
Dworkin, Rita, 1972.1

"The Earlier Lewis," 1934.15; 1957.3
Earnest, Ernest P., 1968.2; 1970.7
Eaton, Walter Prichard, 1935.14
"Echoes from 'Zenith': Reactions of American Businessmen to Babbitt," 1967.6
Edel, Leon, 1956.4
Edener, Wilfried, 1963.8
Edgar, Pelham, 1933.13

"The Education of a Rebel:
    Sinclair Lewis at Yale,"
    1955.12
Eggleston, Edward, 1921.13
Eicke, Gustav, 1939.8
Elgström, Anna Lenah, 1945.10
Eliot, George, 1921.5
Elmer Gantry, 1926.24; 1927.2-9,
    12-13, 15-17, 19-21, 23-25,
    27-29, 34, 37-42, 44-46;
    1928.8-9, 17-18, 34-35, 37;
    1929.14, 26; 1930.18; 1932.1;
    1935.18; 1946.2; 1951.14;
    1955.16, 18; 1956.6; 1959.3;
    1960.14; 1963.10; 1964.3-4,
    10, 13; 1967.11; 1968.10;
    1972.19
"Elmer Gantry and That Old Time
    Religion," 1969.13
"'Elmer Gantry' and the Church
    in America," 1927.34
Ely, Catherine Beach, 1921.7
Emerson, Haven, M.D., 1925.17;
    1968.4
Emerson, Ralph Waldo, 1938.26;
    1943.19
"English Countercheck Quarrelsome
    to Mr. Sinclair Lewis,"
    1922.7
"Enter Sinclair Lewis," 1938.21
"Epilogue: New Year's Eve,"
    1951.20
Erskine, John, 1931.19
"Europe Looks at Sinclair Lewis,"
    1931.10
"The Ex-Furnace Man," 1927.35-36
Exhibits, 1952.2, 5, 17; 1957.8;
    1960.4; 1969.33

Fadiman, Clifton, 1934.26;
    1935.15-16; 1938.14; 1940.12;
    1943.10; 1947.9-10; 1953.7;
    1955.9
"A Fairly Hard Week's Work:
    Main Street in the Class-
    room," 1974.20
Falke, Wayne C., 1967.4
"The Family in the Novels of
    Wharton, Faulkner, Cather,
    Lewis and Dreiser," 1971.28

Farber, Marjorie, 1945.11
Farrar, John C., 1922.12; 1924.1;
    1926.21-22
Farrell, James T., 1955.10;
    1976.5
"Fashions in Fiction," 1933.16
Faulkner, William, 1955.10;
    1976.10
Fay, Bernard, 1934.27
Feinberg, Leonard, 1946.3;
    1963.9
Feipel, Louis N., 1959.1
Feminism, 1933.21, 35; 1939.7;
    1951.23; 1962.12; 1963.12;
    1964.12; 1966.14; 1973.10.
    See The Job, Main Street and
    Ann Vickers.
"La Femme affranchie, d'après
    M. Sinclair Lewis," 1933.21
Fenton, Charles, 1959.5
Ferguson, Charles W., 1927.16
Ferrara, Cosmo, 1970.8
Fialka, Elaine, 1969.11
"The Fictionalized Biographies
    of Sinclair Lewis," 1970.21
Fife, Jim L., 1966.7
Figueira, Gaston, 1953.8
Fischer, Walther, 1931.20;
    1933.14
Fishbein, Morris, 1925.18;
    1932.8
Fisk, Earl E., 1924.8
Fitzgerald, F. Scott, 1921.9;
    1937.8; 1971.26
"Fitzgerald, 7; Lewis, 7; Cabell,
    12," 1937.3
Flanagan, Hallie, 1940.13
Flanagan, John T., 1947.11;
    1960.8
Flandrau, Charles Macomb, 1937.8
Flandrau, Grace, 1937.8
Flaubert, Gustave, 1922.24;
    1937.10; 1939.7; 1946.2;
    1958.1
Fleisher, Florence, 1922.13
Fleissner, Robert F., 1970.9-10;
    1971.9; 1972.10; 1973.2
Florey, Louis, 1933.3
Ford, Edwin H., 1937.5
Ford, Ford Madox, 1929.8; 1962.14
Ford, Harriet, 1921.3

"Foreword: The Revolt Against
    Gentility," 1964.8
"Foreword" to Dodsworth, 1947.10
"Form and Content in the Fiction
    of Sinclair Lewis," 1974.16
Forster, E. M., 1929.9-10;
    1932.9; 1936.15; 1962.14
Forsythe, Robert, 1936.16;
    1937.6-7; 1938.15
"Four American Impressions:
    Gertrude Stein, Paul Rosen-
    feld, Ring Lardner, Sinclair
    Lewis," 1922.2
Frank, Waldo, 1924.9; 1925.19;
    1926.23
Franklin, John, 1925.20
Frederic, Harold, 1934.29;
    1964.10
"Frederick Manfred Talks About
    Sinclair Lewis," 1970.15
Free Air, 1919.1-3; 1920.2;
    1924.10; 1964.5; 1969.14;
    1973.7
Friedman, Philip Allen, 1966.8;
    1971.10, 13
"From Babbitt to the Bomb,"
    1948.9
From Main Street to Stockholm,
    1952.1, 7, 9, 11, 16;
    1953.3, 17; 1958.3
"From Society to Babbittry:
    Lewis' Debt to Edith
    Wharton," 1960.16
Fulks, Clay, 1928.9
Fuller, John, 1964.9
"A Further Word on Sinclair
    Lewis' Prize-Consciousness,"
    1961.7
"The Future Significance of
    Sinclair Lewis," 1930.17
Fyvel, T. R., 1955.11; 1968.4

Gaines, Clarence H., 1925.21
Gale, Zona, 1921.16; 1922.30;
    1925.45; 1935.19
Gallup, Donald, 1954.5
Galsworthy, John, 1932.4
Gannett, Lewis, 1945.12;
    1949.11; 1951.26
Gardiner, Harold C., 1945.13;
    1951.27; 1972.11

Garland, Hamlin, 1955.5
Gaston, Edwin W., Jr., 1972.12
Gauss, Christian, 1931.21
Gay, R. M., 1922.14
Geismar, Maxwell, 1943.11;
    1947.12-13; 1952.7; 1953.9;
    1958.3; 1960.9; 1962.5, 14;
    1971.13
General assessments, 1933.31-32;
    1948.1, 3; 1951.7, 19-20, 32,
    37, 58; 1952.13, 20; 1955.2,
    10; 1969.11; 1970.17;
    1974.15
General critical studies, 1924.2;
    1925.10; 1926.20, 38;
    1927.9-10, 18, 26; 1928.19,
    28, 34; 1929.7, 17; 1930.12-
    13, 17, 20-21; 1931.11, 15,
    24-26, 32, 34; 1932.10, 12;
    1934.27; 1935.36; 1936.9,
    28, 30; 1937.9; 1939.12;
    1940.10; 1946.3, 5; 1947.12-
    13; 1951.30, 34, 40, 44;
    1953.8; 1954.9; 1956.9;
    1958.3; 1962.14; 1963.21;
    1964.7; 1967.2; 1969.30;
    1970.17, 21; 1971.10, 13;
    1972.2, 13; 1975.5
"The Genesis of Social Ideas in
    Sinclair Lewis," 1955.5
Genthe, Charles V., 1964.10
"George Babbitt: Mock-Hero of a
    Mock-Epic," 1966.5
"George Babbitt's Quest for
    Masculinity," 1969.25
Gerstenberger, Donna, 1961.3;
    1970.11
"Get to the Story!" 1951.18
"The Ghost of Jack London,"
    1931.38
Gibbs, Sir Philip, 1930.15
Gibbs, Wolcott, 1945.14
Gibson, Wilfrid, 1940.14
Gideon Planish, 1943.1-11, 13-
    18, 20-23; 1945.10
Gilenson, Boris A., 1959.6;
    1971.11; 1972.13
Gillis, Adolph, 1936.17
"Goblins in Winnemac: A Note as
    to Sinclair Lewis," 1930.12.
    See 1930.13.
Godfrey, Eleanor, 1935.17

The God-Seeker, 1949.1-8, 10,
    12-16, 19-23; 1959.3; 1973.5
Gohdes, Clarence, 1964.11
Goldsmith, Oliver, 1925.45
Goodman, Philip, 1966.1
"Gopher Prairie," 1922.19
Gordon, Donald, 1934.28
Gould, Gerald, 1925.22
Graeve, Oscar, 1931.22
Grant, Douglas, 1965.5
Grattan, C. Hartley, 1951.28
Gray, James, 1937.8; 1946.5
"The Great American Bitch,"
    1971.26
Grebstein, Sheldon Norman,
    1954.6-7; 1955.12; 1958.4;
    1959.7; 1962.6; 1968.4;
    1971.13
Greene, D. J., 1953.10
Greene, Donald, 1959.8
Green, Elizabeth Lay, 1925.23
Green, Paul, 1925.23
Grey, Zane, 1926.29
Griffin, Robert J., 1968.3-4
Gross, Barry, 1977.1
"The Growing Up of Sinclair
    Lewis," 1930.23
Grube, G. M. A., 1938.16
Grunwald, Henry Anatole, 1947.14
Guha-Thakurta, P., 1931.23
Gurko, Leo, 1943.12
Gurko, Miriam, 1943.12
Guthrie, Ramon, 1952.8-10;
    1960.10

Hackett, Alice Payne, 1945.15;
    1956.5; 1967.5; 1977.2
Hackett, Francis, 1917.12;
    1920.4; 1961.4
Haight, Anne Lyon, 1935.18
"'Hail, Hail, the Gang's All
    Here'--Twenty Years Late:
    Sinclair Lewis and the Revolt
    Against the 'Establishment,'"
    1972.12
Hakutani, Yoshinobu, 1964.12
Half a Loaf, 1931.29
Hamilton, Cosmo, 1933.15
Hand, Harry E., 1966.9
Hansen, Harry, 1933.16; 1947.15;
    1949.12

Harcourt, Alfred, 1951.29
Harkness, Samuel, 1926.24
Harmon, William E., 1926.25
Harrison, Oliver (Harrison
    Smith), 1925.24, 37
"(Harry) Sinclair Lewis (1885-
    1951)," 1969.33
Hart, H. W., 1949.13
Hart, James D., 1950.4; 1965.6
Hartley, L. P., 1926.26; 1927.17;
    1928.14; 1929.11
Hartwick, Harry, 1934.29
Hashiguchi, Yasuo, 1965.7
Hatcher, Harlan, 1935.19
Haworth, Jane L., 1974.6
Hawthorne, Nathaniel, 1938.26
Haycraft, Howard, 1942.3
Hazard, Lucy Lockwood, 1927.18;
    1968.4
Hazlitt, Henry, 1933.17; 1934.30
"The Heaven of Mean Streets,"
    1922.30
Heddon, Worth Tuttle, 1947.15
Heiney, Donald W., 1955.13;
    1958.5
Helleberg, Marilyn Morgan, 1968.5
Hemingway, Ernest, 1937.12;
    1944.5; 1945.10; 1955.10;
    1958.1; 1969.25; 1971.26;
    1976.2
Henderson, Robert W., 1947.16
Hendrick, George, 1961.3; 1970.11
Hendricks, King, 1965.8
Hergesheimer, Joseph, 1966.12
"The Heroines of Sinclair Lewis,"
    1947.25
Herron, Ima Honaker, 1939.9
"Hewing to the Line," 1931.14
"H. G. Wells and Sinclair Lewis:
    Friendship," 1962.7
Hicks, Granville, 1933.18;
    1934.31; 1935.20; 1936.18;
    1938.17; 1974.7
Hilfer, Anthony Channell, 1969.13;
    1971.13
Hill, John S., 1970.12
Hills, Walter, 1924.8
Hind, Charles Lewis, 1969.14
Hines, Thomas S., Jr., 1967.6
"Hints for Novelists," 1958.8
"The History of Their Books:
    III. Sinclair Lewis," 1929.17

"H. L. Mencken . . . and Sinclair
Lewis. . . ," 1956.9
"H. L. Mencken's Reviews of
Sinclair Lewis's Major
Novels," 1974.10; 1976.8
Hobson, Laura Z., 1947.15
Hoffman, Frederick J., 1951.30;
1955.14; 1971.13
Hohenberg, John, 1974.8
Hollis, C. Carroll, 1951.31;
1968.6
"The Hollow Note in Lewis's
Satire," 1974.22
Holman, C. Hugh, 1973.3
Holt, Edgar, 1931.24
"Honoré de Balzac and Sinclair
Lewis," 1927.1
Hopkins, F. M., 1938.18
Horton, Thomas D., 1939.10
Houston, Penelope, 1954.8
Howard, Brian, 1938.19
Howard, Leon, 1960.11
Howard, Sidney, 1934.9, 14, 16,
32-33, 36, 45, 51; 1936.23;
1937.1; 1938.8
"How Arrowsmith Was Written,"
1945.21
Howe, E. W., 1934.29; 1935.19
Howells, William Dean, 1950.3;
1953.11; 1956.9; 1966.9;
1970.10, 24
"How Good Is Sinclair Lewis?"
1948.3
"How It Was Done: Some Notes on
a Sinclair Lewis Manuscript,"
1954.11
"How Sinclair Lewis Works,"
1924.3
"How Sinclair Lewis Writes a
Novel," 1934.3
"How to Learn History from Sin-
clair Lewis and Other Uncom-
mon Sources," 1964.3
Hoyt, Besse T., 1933.19
H., R. S., 1925.25
Hubbell, Jay B., 1970.13; 1972.14
Huddleston, Sisley, 1928.15
Hughes, Rupert, 1956.2
Hughes, Serge, 1951.32
Hülsenbeck, Richard, 1931.25
Hunt, Frazier, 1938.20

Hutchens, John K., 1965.9
Hutchings, Winifred, 1936.19
"Hymns and Gospel-Songs in Elmer
Gantry," 1972.19

Ianni, Lawrence, 1971.12
Ibsen, Henrik, 1939.7
"Idealism in the Novels of
Sinclair Lewis," 1974.13
The Iliad, 1966.5
I'm a Stranger Here Myself,
1962.13
"The Impact of Satire on Fiction:
Studies in Norman Douglas,
Sinclair Lewis, Aldous Hux-
ley, Evelyn Waugh, and
George Orwell," 1955.7
"Impressions of Sinclair Lewis
with Some Letters," 1951.17
"In Another Country: The Revolt
from the Village," 1977.1
"The Incorruptible Sinclair
Lewis," 1951.41; 1957.4
"In Memoriam: Sinclair Lewis,"
1951.1
"In Memory of a Man from Main
Street," 1953.7
The Innocents, 1917.2, 4-6, 8,
11; 1945.8; 1964.5
"In Retrospect: Sinclair Lewis,"
1971.10
"An Interpreter of American
Life," 1925.30; 1962.14;
1968.4
Interviews, 1921.17; 1927.30;
1931.31; 1940.24; 1948.4;
1950.2; 1958.1
"An Intimate Glimpse of a Great
American Novel in the
Making," 1924.6
"Introduction" to Ann Vickers,
1962.12
"Introduction" to From Main
Street to Stockholm, 1952.16
"Introduction" to I'm a Stranger
Here Myself and Other Stories
by Sinclair Lewis, 1962.13
"Introduction" to It Can't Hap-
pen Here, 1961.11
"Introduction" to Lewis at
Zenith, 1961.12

"Introduction" to Main Street, 1946.8
"Introduction" to The Man From Main Street, 1953.11
Isaacs, Edith, J. R., 1934.33; 1935.21; 1936.20
Is "Elmer Gantry" True?, 1928.9
It Can't Happen Here, 1935.1-3, 7-10, 12-13, 15, 20, 24, 26-27, 32-34, 39, 41; 1936.1, 3-5, 7-8, 16, 18-20, 22, 24-25, 27-28, 31, 33-35; 1940.13; 1941.2; 1948.5; 1961.11; 1966.2, 11; 1973.11
"I Wrote a Biography," 1958.6

"Jack London's Use of Sinclair Lewis Plots Together with a Printing of Three of the Plots," 1953.15
Jack, Peter Monro, 1935.22; 1940.16
James, Henry, 1956.9; 1969.7
Jayhawker, 1934.13, 37, 50; 1935.4, 14, 21, 25
Jeffers, Robinson, 1971.18
Jenkins, Elizabeth, 1951.33
The Job, 1917.1, 3, 7, 9-10, 12; 1923.7; 1928.17
"John Bull and Sinclair Lewis," 1925.4
Jewett, Sarah Orne, 1921.13
Johnson, A. T., 1929.12
Johnson, Edgar, 1940.17
Johnson, Gerald W., 1951.34; 1954.9
Johnson, Merle, 1936.21; 1942.2
Jones, Howard Mumford, 1931.26; 1934.34; 1935.23; 1943.13; 1949.14; 1951.35
Jordan, Elizabeth, 1938.21

Kallapur, S. T., 1966.7
Kallsen, T. J., 1973.4
"A Kansan in Westchester," 1965.4; 1966.1
Karlfeldt, Erik Axel, 1930.16; 1931.27; 1933.20; 1937.11; 1968.4

Karsner, David, 1928.16
Kastner, Harold, 1951.36
Kazin, Alfred, 1942.2; 1961.5; 1962.14; 1971.13
Kearney, Patrick, 1928.8, 37
Kelley, Edith Summers, 1976.10
Kelley, H. Gilbert, 1943.14
Kennedy, W. P., 1925.26; 1968.4
Kern, Ben, 1976.7
Ketchum, Roland, 1936.17
Killinger, John, 1963.10
Kimbrough, E., 1934.35
Kingsblood Royal, 1947.1-6, 8-9, 15-19, 22-24, 26-31; 1948.2-3; 1954.4; 1957.6; 1960.19; 1962.1; 1966.9; 1971.4, 12; 1972.17; 1974.12; 1975.3; 1976.4
"Kingsblood Royal: A Revaluation," 1972.17
"Kingsblood Royal: Sinclair Lewis Writes a Best Seller on Negroes," 1947.18
Kirk, Clara Marburg, 1938.22
Kishler, Thomas C., 1965.10
Kittleson, J. Harold, 1969.15
"The Knight and the Pioneer: Europe and America in the Fiction of Sinclair Lewis," 1978.4
Knight, Grant C., 1961.6
"Knockers and Boosters: Sinclair Lewis," 1969.6
Knox, George, 1959.8
Kohler, Dayton, 1958.7
Kramer, Maurice, 1966.10; 1969.11
Kriesi, Hans, 1928.17
Kronenberger, Louis, 1929.13; 1938.23
Krutch, Joseph Wood, 1925.27; 1926.27; 1927.19; 1929.14; 1934.36-37; 1951.37; 1962.14; 1968.4
Kunitz, Stanley J., 1931.28; 1942.3

Labor novel, 1938.1; 1951.5;
  1952.8, 10; 1957.6; 1958.1,
  4
"The 'Labor Novel' that Sinclair
  Lewis Never Wrote," 1952.8.
  See 1952.10.
Land, Myrick, 1963.11
Lardner, Ring, 1922.2; 1973.3
"The Last Days of Sinclair
  Lewis," 1951.39
Lawrence, D. H., 1953.13;
  1968.10
Lea, James, 1973.5
Leary, Lewis, 1954.10; 1970.14
Leblanc, Thomas J., 1925.28
LeClaire, Lucien, 1954.11
Leech, Harper, 1925.29
Lerner, Max, 1936.22; 1939.11
"Let Main Street Alone!" 1921.13
"A Letter from Sauk Centre,"
  1960.7
Letters, 1951.17; 1952.7;
  1953.15; 1962.3, 7; 1963.24;
  1965.8; 1966.12; 1967.3;
  1969.12, 31, 33; 1972.4, 20;
  1975.2, 7, 9. See From Main
  Street to Stockholm.
"Letters of Sinclair Lewis to
  Joseph Hergesheimer," 1966.12
Le Verrier, Charles, 1933.21
Levidova, I. M., 1959.6
"Lewis," 1935.36; 1969.15
"Lewis and Marquand," 1960.1;
  1965.2
"Lewis and Svevo," 1971.14
Lewis and the theater, 1936.25;
  1937.4; 1938.4, 27; 1939.2;
  1940.24; 1946.9; 1958.9;
  1971.19
Lewis as lecturer, 1931.4-5;
  1937.7; 1955.1; 1963.5;
  1965.3; 1972.21
Lewis as popular novelist,
  1924.4; 1931.10; 1938.26;
  1945.15; 1946.1; 1947.21;
  1950.4; 1951.6; 1956.5;
  1967.5; 1974.2; 1977.2
Lewis as teacher, 1940.3;
  1951.56; 1961.19; 1969.28
"Lewis: Big Wind from Sauk
  Centre," 1960.17; 1972.23

Lewis, Claude, 1959.8-9
"Lewises/ Reporters at Large,"
  1934.5
"The Lewis Exhibition," 1952.17
"Lewis' Finicky Girls and Faith-
  ful Workers," 1963.12
Lewis, Grace Hegger, 1931.29;
  1939.5; 1951.38; 1955.15;
  1956.3-4, 7; 1958.6; 1960.4,
  12; 1972.5
"Lewis, [Harry] Sinclair," 1965.6
"Lewis Home Doubly Dedicated,"
  1969.3
Lewis, Jay, 1948.5
Lewisohn, Ludwig, 1920.5;
  1922.15; 1932.10; 1939.12;
  1971.13
Lewis, Robert W., 1972.15
"Lewis's Assessment of Carol
  Kennicott," 1974.11
"Lewis, Sinclair," 1931.28;
  1942.3; 1945.8; 1961.3;
  1969.11; 1970.11; 1970.20;
  1972.1; 1974.17; 1976.6;
  1977.4
"Lewis's Satire--A Negative
  Emphasis," 1966.3; 1971.13
"Lewis's 'Scarlet Sign':
  Accommodating to the Popular
  Market," 1967.8
"Lewis Travels Far," 1933.2
Libman, Valentina A., 1969.16
Liebert, Herman W., 1957.8
Light, Martin, 1960.13; 1961.7;
  1962.7; 1963.12; 1967.8;
  1971.13; 1973.16; 1975.5
Lillard, Richard G., 1967.1
Lingeman, Richard R., 1978.1
Linguistic analyses, 1938.32;
  1960.6; 1966.17-18; 1970.3;
  1974.1; 1976.12
Lippman, Walter, 1927.20; 1962.14
Literary influences on Lewis,
  1914.6; 1962.7; 1971.9
"A Literary Main Street," 1926.5
"Literary Personalities:
  1. Sinclair Lewis," 1932.13;
  1936.26; 1952.12. See 1958.9.
"Literary Personalities: Sin-
  clair Lewis," 1952.12. See
  1932.13.

"Literary Sign-Posts: Is the Nobel Prize an Insult?" 1931.36

"Literary Spotlight 12: Sinclair Lewis," 1922.8; 1924.1

"Literature and the 'American Way of Life,'" 1948.2

"The Literature of Revolt," 1950.3

Littell, Robert, 1922.16; 1927.21; 1971.13

"Littérature Étrangère: États-unis: Sinclair Lewis," 1931.9

"Les Littératures Étrangères: M. Sinclair Lewis et le Nouveau Roman Américain," 1931.35

Lockerbie, D. Bruce, 1964.13

Loeb, Harold, 1959.10

Loeb, Jacques, 1963.18

Loggins, Vernon, 1937.9

Loiseau, Jean, 1938.24; 1946.6

London, Jack, 1930.4; 1931.38; 1953.15; 1965.8

"London-Lewis Letters," 1965.8

"London Years," 1938.20

"Long Way to Gopher Prairie: Sinclair Lewis's Apprenticeship," 1947.11

Love, Glen A., 1973.7

Lovett, Robert Morss, 1921.8; 1925.30; 1935.24; 1962.14; 1968.4

Lowry, Helen Bullitt, 1921.9

Luccock, Halford E., 1934.38

Lüdeke, Henry, 1963.13

Lunden, Rolf, 1978.2

Lundkvist, Artur, 1939.13

Lundquist, James, 1969.17; 1970.15-18; 1972.16; 1973.8

Lynam, Hazel Palmer, 1934.39

Lynd, Helen, 1934.38

Lynd, Robert, 1934.38

MacAfee, Helen, 1926.28; 1933.22; 1934.40

MacAllum, T. W., 1938.25

McAlmon, Robert, 1970.22

McAlpin, Edwin A., 1928.18

McCarthy, John F., 1968.7

McCole, Camille, 1930.17

McCormick, Anne O'Hare, 1922.17

McCormick, John, 1971.14

McCullough, Sarah J., 1972.17

McDonald, Gerald D., 1963.14

McNally, William J., 1927.22

McS., J., 1933.23; 1934.41

McWilliams, Wilson Carey, 1973.9

Magill, Frank N., 1958.7; 1974.9

Maglin, Nan Bauer, 1973.10

Mailer, Norman, 1958.1

Mainsard, Joseph, 1930.18

Main Street, 1920.1, 3-7; 1921.1-5, 7-8, 10-13, 15-16; 1922.19, 22, 24, 31; 1923.6; 1924.5, 9; 1927.43; 1928.17-18; 1929.3; 1930.1, 11; 1934.29, 38; 1935.19; 1944.1; 1946.2, 8; 1947.11, 20; 1949.11; 1956.3; 1958.10; 1961.10, 12-13; 1962.10; 1963.20; 1964.21-22; 1965.1, 11; 1968.7; 1969.1, 9, 14, 24, 32; 1970.2, 6; 1971.18; 1972.6; 1973.6-7; 1974.6, 11, 14, 20; 1976.1, 10; 1977.1

"Main Street after Fifty Years," 1970.6

"Main Street and the Dust Bowl," 1944.1

"Main Street by Sinclair Lewis," 1963.20

"Main Street, Cass Timberlane, and Determinism," 1969.24

"'Main Street' Comes Into the Home," 1955.6

"Main Street in the Classroom: Another Approach," 1974.14

"The Main Street Mode in Selected Minor Southern Novels of the 1920's," 1976.10

"Main Street 1947," 1947.14

Main Street Notes, 1965.11

"Main Street--Plymouth Mass.," 1921.14

"Main Street Thirty-five Years Later," 1955.8

"Main Street Today," 1969.32

Mais, Stuart P. B., 1923.3
Manfred, Frederick F., 1954.12;
    1962.8; 1969.18; 1971.15-16
The Man From Main Street,
    1951.12; 1953.1-2, 4-5, 9,
    11, 14, 16; 1954.2, 8
Manly, John Matthews, 1929.15
Mann, Dorothea Laurance, 1926.29
Mansfield, J. B., 1922.18
Manson, Alexander, 1951.24, 39
Mantrap, 1926.3, 6, 8-10, 14-17,
    19, 21, 26-27, 29, 32, 34-37;
    1953.10; 1959.8; 1960.22;
    1964.5
Manuscripts and typescripts,
    1934.3; 1938.18; 1952.2;
    1954.5, 11; 1957.8; 1960.4;
    1975.2; 1977.4
The Man Who Knew Coolidge,
    1928.1-6, 10, 12-14, 20,
    22-25, 27, 29, 32-33;
    1953.12; 1968.6; 1970.2
"The Man Who Knew Lewis," 1928.26
"The Many Roles of Harry Lewis:
    A Study of Motive and Method
    in Creative Techniques,"
    1971.1
"A Map of Sinclair Lewis' United
    States. . . ," 1934.2
Maps and diagrams, 1931.21;
    1934.2-3; 1953.10; 1971.3
Marble, Annie Russell, 1928.19;
    1932.11
Marcus, Steven, 1963.15; 1964.14;
    1975.6
"Mark Schorer's Sinclair Lewis,"
    1971.8
Marks, John, 1940.18
"Mark Twain's The Gilded Age and
    Sinclair Lewis's Babbitt,"
    1972.7
Marquand, John P., 1960.1;
    1965.2
Marshall, Archibald, 1921.10;
    1922.19
Marshall, Margaret, 1947.17;
    1949.15
Marthaler, Sister M. Andre,
    1969.19; 1970.19
"Martin Arrowsmith and his
    Habitat," 1955.11; 1968.4

"Martin Arrowsmith: The Scientist
    as Hero," 1963.18; 1968.4
Masters, Edgar Lee, 1921.16;
    1922.31; 1925.45; 1973.3
Matheson, Terence J., 1974.10-12;
    1976.8
Matlowsky, Bernice D., 1951.40
Matthews, T. S., 1929.16; 1934.42
Maule, Harry E., 1953.11
Maurice, Arthur Bartlett, 1929.17
Mayberry, George, 1943.15
Mayer, Gary H., 1974.13
Mealand, Richard, 1945.16
"The Meaning of Literary Prizes,"
    1935.40
Measell, James S., 1976.9
Melton, John L., 1974.14
Melville, Arthur, 1923.4; 1926.30
"Memories of Fitzgerald, Lewis
    and Dreiser," 1958.9. See
    1932.13.
Mencken, H. L., 1921.11;
    1922.20-21; 1925.31;
    1926.31; 1927.14, 23;
    1928.20; 1929.18; 1931.30;
    1933.24; 1936.30; 1955.5;
    1958.7-8; 1960.15; 1961.13;
    1962.14; 1963.8; 1965.1, 3;
    1966.1; 1968.4; 1971.13;
    1972.2; 1974.10, 15
Mendelson, Moris O., 1972.18
The Merrill Checklist of Sinclair
    Lewis, 1970.16
The Merrill Guide to Sinclair
    Lewis, 1970.17
Michaud, Régis, 1928.21
Middletown, 1934.38
Milch, Robert J., 1964.15
Miller, Perry, 1951.41; 1952.11;
    1957.4
Miller, Wayne, 1947.18
Millett, Fred B., 1944.7
Millgate, Michael, 1962.9;
    1964.16
Milne, Gordon, 1966.11; 1977.3
Milton, John R., 1969.20
Miner, Ward L., 1955.19
"The Minnesota Backgrounds of
    Sinclair Lewis's Fiction,"
    1960.8

"A Minnesota Diary: Second
Thoughts on Babbitt, Main
Street, the Search for Home,"
1958.10
"The Minnesota Muse," 1937.8
Mitgang, Herbert, 1973.11
Mizener, Arthur, 1957.5
Moffitt, John C., 1936.4, 35
"The Monstrous Self-Deception of
Elmer Gantry," 1955.18. See
1956.6.
Monteiro, George, 1975.7
Moodie, Clara Lee Redwood,
1971.17; 1975.8
Moon, Bucklin, 1947.19
Moore, Geoffrey, 1959.11; 1962.14
Moore, James Benedict, 1960.14
Morand, Paul, 1930.7
Morgan, Louise, 1931.31
Morley-Mower, Geoffrey, 1975.9
Morris, Lloyd, 1938.26; 1947.20;
1949.16
Morrison, Elting E., 1951.42
Mortimer, Raymond, 1928.22;
1929.19
Mosher, John, 1936.23
Mott, Frank Luther, 1947.21
Mottram, Eric, 1971.18
Movies from novels, 1931.1;
1932.8; 1933.34; 1936.1, 3,
5-6, 16, 23; 1945.16; 1949.18
"Mr. and Mrs. Sinclair Lewis at
Home," 1937.6. See 1938.15.
"Mr. DeVoto and Mr. Sinclair
Lewis Call Each Other Fools
and Liars," 1963.11
"Mr. Lewis's America," 1931.26
"Mr. Sinclair Lewis," 1931.23
"Mr. Upton-Sinclair-Lewis,"
1961.18
"Mud Huts of Intellect," 1966.16
Muir, Edwin, 1925.32; 1926.32;
1927.24; 1968.4
Muir, John, 1940.19
Muller, Herbert J., 1937.10
Mumford, Lewis, 1931.32; 1932.12;
1962.14
Murry, John Middleton, 1936.24
Muzzey, David Saville, 1927.25
"My Life and Nine-Year Captivity
with Sinclair Lewis,"
1961.14; 1964.19

"Names in the Fiction of Sinclair
Lewis," 1962.2
Napier, James J., 1966.12
"Nathanael West, Sinclair Lewis,
Alexander Pope and Satiric
Contrasts," 1968.8
Nathan, George Jean, 1932.13;
1936.25-26; 1938.27;
1952.12; 1958.9; 1966.1;
1971.19
"The National Gadfly," 1947.20
"Nationalism and the Cultural
Battle: H. L. Mencken . . .
and Sinclair Lewis . . .,"
1936.30
"Le Nationalisme de Sinclair
Lewis," 1937.4
"The Naturalist," 1932.10;
1939.12
Neumann, Henry, 1926.33
"Never Meet an Author," 1957.7
Neville, Robert, 1963.16
Nevius, Blake, 1970.20
"New and Rather Revised 'Main
Street,'" 1921.6
"A New Look at an Old Street,"
1968.7
"A New Novelist," 1951.29
"New Pioneering on the Prairies:
Nature, Progress and the
Individual in the Novels of
Sinclair Lewis," 1973.7
"The New Realism: Sherwood
Anderson and Sinclair Lewis,"
1942.2; 1961.5; 1962.14;
1971.13
Niall, Brenda, 1969.22
Nichols, Beverley, 1921.12
Nichols, Elizabeth P., 1945.17
Nichols, James W., 1968.8
Nichols, Lewis, 1935.25
Nicholson, Meredith, 1921.13
"The 1945 Lectures: A Happy
Episode in Sinclair Lewis's
Life," 1972.21
"The Nobel Jury Judges America,"
1930.19
"The Nobel Lewis," 1937.11
Nobel Prize, 1930.3-6, 8-10, 14,
16, 19; 1931.2, 15-16, 20,
23-24, 27, 30, 33, 36-37;
1932.10-11, 14; 1933.20, 32;

(Nobel Prize) 1935.40; 1936.13;
   1937.3, 11; 1938.25; 1939.12;
   1951.43; 1957.1; 1959.7;
   1961.7, 16; 1964.8; 1966.4;
   1968.3; 1970.12; 1971.14;
   1976.2
"Nobel Prize for Literature:
   Goes to Sinclair Lewis for
   'Babbitt,'" 1930.6
"Nobel Prize in Literature,"
   1951.29
"Nobel Prize Oration," 1936.13
Norris, Frank, 1917.12
"A Note as to Sinclair Lewis,"
   1930.13. See 1930.12.
"Notes for Another Letter from
   Sauk Centre," 1960.2
"Notes on a Genius: Sinclair
   Lewis at his Best," 1954.14
"A Novelist with a Future,"
   1916.1
"The Novel of Disentanglement:
   A Thematic Study of Lewis's
   Babbitt, Bromfield's Mr.
   Smith and Updike's Rabbit,
   Run," 1967.4
"The Novel of the Future,"
   1966.2
"Novels from the Grub Street Days
   of Sinclair Lewis," 1923.7
"The Novels of Sinclair Lewis,"
   1931.24

Ober, William B., M.D., 1963.17;
   1968.4
Obituaries, 1951.1-2, 4, 6-7,
   10-11, 19, 25, 36-37
O'Brien, Kate, 1943.16
O'Connor, Richard, 1971.20
O'Dell, George E., 1922.22
O'Donnell, Norbert F., 1955.16
Ohara, Hirotada, 1962.10
O'Higgins, Harvey, 1921.3
"Old Dr. Alagash's Traveling
   Laboratory: Sinclair Lewis
   and the Bunko Artist,"
   1972.16
Oldham, Janet, 1959.12
O'Neill, Eugene, 1937.11; 1976.2

"On the Occasion of Sinclair
   Lewis' Burial," 1969.7
"Original Main Street Honors
   Lewis Memory," 1976.7
Ortiz, Alicia, 1949.17
Osborne, Lucy E., 1939.14
Osterling, Anders, 1951.43
Our Mr. Wrenn, 1914.1-8; 1923.7;
   1928.17; 1953.14; 1961.6;
   1962.7
"Our Photography: Sinclair
   Lewis," 1929.10; 1936.15;
   1962.14. See 1929.9.
Overton, Grant, 1925.33

Paley, Alan L., 1974.15
Palmer, Raymond H., 1930.19
Pandeya, S. M., 1974.16
"The Paper-Doll Characters of
   Sinclair Lewis' Arrowsmith,"
   1968.5
Parker, Dorothy, 1928.23; 1929.20
Park, Sue Simpson, 1967.9
Parodies of Lewis's works,
   1921.6, 14, 18; 1922.30;
   1923.8; 1928.26; 1945.14
Parrington, Vernon L., 1927.26;
   1930.20; 1962.14
Parrott, L. Marc, Jr., 1949.18
Pasternak, Boris, 1959.12
Paterson, Isabel, 1929.21;
   1934.43
Patrick, William Henry, 1941.3
Pattee, Fred Lewis, 1930.21;
   1937.11
Paul, Eliot, 1937.12
"Paul Morand Looks at Sinclair
   Lewis," 1930.7
Pavese, Cesare, 1951.44; 1970.21
Pearson, Edmund, 1927.27
"Perfiles: Dos escritores norte-
   americanos. 1, Sinclair
   Lewis. . . ," 1953.8
Peterkin, Julia, 1927.28
Petrullo, Helen Batchelor,
   1967.10; 1969.23-24;
   1971.21-23
Phelps, William Lyon, 1926.34;
   1930.22; 1931.33; 1933.25;
   1936.27; 1939.15

Photographs, 1914.1; 1925.8;
     1926.11; 1931.12, 37; 1932.2;
     1934.5; 1936.12; 1945.2, 7;
     1947.1, 31; 1948.9; 1950.1;
     1951.11; 1969.4
Piacentino, Edward J., 1976.10
Pickrel, Paul, 1951.45
Plato, 1939.4
Plomer, William, 1935.26
"The Point of View: Prizes,"
     1926.22
Poore, Charles, 1945.18; 1947.22
Pope, Alexander, 1965.10; 1968.8
"Popular Artists and Elite
     Standards: The Case of
     Sinclair Lewis," 1974.2
Porter, William Sidney, 1914.8
"Portrait de Sinclair Lewis:
     L'Américain à Rebrousse-
     poil," 1934.27
"Portrait of an American
     Citizen," 1922.20
"Portraits en Brochette:
     Sinclair Lewis," 1931.17
"Portraits of the Artist,"
     1951.24
"Postscript: Twenty Years of
     American Literature," 1964.8
"Post-War Realism," 1934.38
"The Power of Reality," 1965.13
Pownall, David E., 1974.17
"Practitioners, 1920-1960,"
     1977.3
Prescott, Orville, 1945.19;
     1947.23; 1952.13
Price, Lawrence Marsden, 1966.13
Priestley, J. B., 1960.15
Pringle, Henry F., 1928.24
Pritchett, V. S., 1934.44
"Prizes and Principles," 1926.7
Prodigal Parents, 1938.2, 5-7,
     9-14, 16-17, 19, 22-23, 26,
     28, 30-31, 34; 1960.17
"Profiles: In America's Image,"
     1925.19; 1926.23
"Profiles: The World and Sauk
     Center [sic]," 1934.48
"Prophecies," 1976.2
Prothro, James Warren, 1954.13
Ptomaine Street: The Tale of
     Warble Petticoat, 1921.18

Pugh, David G., 1975.10
Pugliatti, Paola, 1964.17
Pulitzer Prize, 1921.8; 1926.5,
     7, 12-13, 22, 25; 1927.30;
     1935.40; 1937.3; 1957.5;
     1961.7; 1966.15; 1974.8
"The Pulitzer Prizes," 1957.5
Pure, Simon, 1923.5

Quennell, Peter, 1933.26; 1935.27
Quinn, Arthur Hobson, 1936.28
Quivey, James R., 1969.25-26
Quixote, Don, 1973.6; 1975.5
"The Quixotic Motifs of Main
     Street," 1973.6
The Quixotic Vision of Sinclair
     Lewis, 1975.5

"Rare or Seldom-Seen Dust Jackets
     of American First Editions,"
     1973.1; 1974.4
Rascoe, Burton, 1922.23; 1925.34;
     1928.25; 1933.27
Rathe, Chuck, 1951.49; 1969.27;
     1971.24-25
Raymond, John, 1951.46
R., D., 1925.35; 1926.35
Realism, 1921.5, 15-16; 1922.31;
     1929.9-10, 12; 1931.9,
     14-15, 35; 1936.12; 1937.4,
     10; 1941.3; 1944.1; 1955.3-
     4; 1966.8; 1971.13; 1973.14;
     1977.3
"Realism in Contemporary American
     Literature: Notes on
     Dreiser, Anderson, Lewis,"
     1929.12
"Il Realismo di Babbitt,"
     1964.17
"The Redhead," 1973.9
"'Red' Lewis," 1932.2; 1938.1
Redlich, Monica, 1933.28
Redlich, Rosemarie, 1952.15
Redman, Ben Ray, 1940.20; 1947.24
"Red-Tempered Novelist," 1927.30
"A Reformer from Main Street,"
     1937.3
Reid, Forrest, 1938.28
"The Reincarnation of Holmes in
     Dr. Gottlieb," 1973.2

"Release Motif and Its Impact in Babbitt," 1969.26

Religion, 1927.34; 1932.1; 1935.28; 1959.3; 1960.14; 1963.8, 10; 1964.3-4, 10, 12; 1969.13. See Elmer Gantry.

Die Religionskritik in den Romanen von Sinclair Lewis, 1963.8

"Remarks upon a Once Glorious Epoch," 1955.2

Reputation
--Britain, 1925.4; 1926.16; 1930.5; 1931.4; 1936.24
--Europe, 1930.6, 15; 1931.10; 1934.27; 1938.32; 1951.1
--France, 1925.10; 1929.7; 1930.7; 1931.9, 35; 1932.1; 1934.27; 1937.4; 1938.24; 1946.2; 1951.15; 1955.19
--Germany, 1926.2; 1930.25; 1931.20, 25; 1933.14; 1938.32; 1960.18; 1966.13
--Italy, 1951.44; 1964.4; 1970.21
--Latin America, 1951.40; 1953.8; 1966.4
--Russia, 1946.7; 1948.2; 1953.6; 1954.4; 1959.6; 1962.1; 1969.16; 1971.11; 1972.13, 18
--Sweden, 1939.13; 1945.10; 1957.1

"Respectability Defied," 1951.59

"The Return of the Laureate: Sinclair Lewis in 1942," 1969.28

"Revision in Sinclair Lewis's The Man Who Knew Coolidge," 1953.12

"Revisions of Main Street; or, From 'Blood, Sweat, and Tears' to the Loss of a 'Literary Curiosity,'" 1974.6

"Revolt from the Frontier," 1930.21

"The 'Revolt from the Village' in American Fiction," 1925.45

"The Revolt from the Village: 1920," 1921.16; 1922.31

Reynolds, Horace, 1949.19; 1951.47

Rhodes, Eugene Manlove, 1966.7

Richardson, Lyon, 1953.12; 1955.17; 1968.4

Rickert, Edith L., 1929.15

Riddell, John, 1928.26

"The Riddle of Sauk Centre," 1956.7

Ridgway, William H., 1935.28; 1964.13

Riley, James Whitcomb, 1921.13

"The Rise of a Modern American Hero," 1966.9

Robbins, Frances Lamont, 1928.27; 1929.22

Robbins, J. Albert, 1977.4

Roberts, Carl Erik B., 1923.6

Roberts, Katherine, 1935.29

Robinson, Selma, 1933.29

Rogal, Samuel J., 1972.19

Rogers, Katharine M., 1966.14

Rolo, Charles J., 1951.48

"Romance and Mr. Babbitt," 1951.34; 1954.9

"Un Romancier Américain d'au-jourd'hui: M. Sinclair Lewis," 1925.10

Romanticism, 1926.14; 1959.11; 1962.14; 1963.4

Rosenberg, Charles E., 1963.18; 1968.4

Rosenfeld, Paul, 1922.2

Ross, Ishbel, 1970.22

Ross, Mary, 1927.29; 1929.23; 1933.30; 1935.30; 1940.21

Roth, Catherine, 1970.14

Roth, Russell, 1969.28

Rothwell, Kenneth S., 1960.16

Rourke, Constance, 1931.34; 1962.14

Rousseaux, André, 1952.14

"Rover Girl in Europe: The Story of Problem Girl Dorothy Thompson," 1940.1

Rowlette, Robert, 1972.20

Royster, Salibelle, 1964.18; 1965.11

Roz, Firmin, 1931.35

R., S. M., 1920.6

Russell, Frances Theresa, 1928.28; 1930.23

Ryan, Elizabeth Ann, 1947.25

Rylander, Edith, 1970.23

Sachs, Emanie N., 1976.10
"'The Sacred Rites of Pride': An Echo of 'The Rape of the Lock' in Babbitt," 1965.10
Saito, Mitsuru, 1968.9
"Salesman and Dream: Sinclair Lewis's Babbitt," 1969.22
Salisbury, William, 1932.14
Salpeter, Harry, 1927.30
"The Salvation of Sinclair Lewis," 1925.33
"Samuel Dodworth bereist Europa," 1933.14
Sanders, Marion K., 1973.12
Sargent, Marion S., 1970.24
Satire, 1924.4; 1927.31; 1932.4; 1933.13; 1939.10; 1942.2; 1943.12; 1944.6; 1946.3; 1951.59; 1955.7; 1958.5; 1960.15; 1962.14; 1963.9; 1965.10; 1966.3, 8, 17; 1967.10; 1968.1, 8; 1969.23; 1970.7; 1971.13, 21; 1973.8; 1974.16, 22; 1975.4
"Satire and Freedom: Sinclair Lewis, Nathanael West, and James Thurber," 1967.10
"Satire of Characterization in the Fiction of Sinclair Lewis," 1967.9
"The Satire of Sinclair Lewis," 1968.1
"Satirical Techniques in Sinclair Lewis's Works: Contrastive and Contradictory Expressions," 1966.17
Sats, Igor, 1946.7
Sauer, Philip Von Rohr, 1972.21
Sauk Centre, 1947.14; 1951.49; 1952.15; 1954.7; 1955.8; 1960.2-3, 7, 12, 20; 1969.3-4; 1971.24-25; 1976.7
"Sauk Centre Keeping Lewis Memory Warm," 1971.24. See 1971.25.
"The 'Sauk-Centricities' of Sinclair Lewis," 1954.3; 1959.2
Schary, Dore, 1963.19
Scherman, David E., 1952.15
Schier, Donald, 1963.20
Schmidt, Dolores Barracano, 1971.26

Schnittkind, Henry Thomas, 1938.29
"Schorer and Satire," 1955.16
Schorer, Mark, 1952.6; 1953.13-14; 1955.16, 18; 1956.6; 1958.10; 1961.8-17; 1962.8, 11-14; 1963.21-22; 1964.19-20; 1965.12; 1967.11; 1968.4, 10; 1969.29; 1971.8, 13, 15-16; 1972.22; 1974.18-19
Schreiber, Georges, 1936.29
Schriber, Mary Sue, 1971.27
Schroeder, Eric G., 1927.31
Schulberg, Budd, 1960.17; 1972.23
S., E., 1929.24
Selected Short Stories, 1935.5, 16-17, 22-23, 30
Seligmann, Herbert J., 1920.7
Serialization of novels, 1924.6; 1953.12; 1955.17; 1964.5; 1968.4; 1969.8
"The Serialized Novels of Sinclair Lewis," 1969.8
"The Serialized Novels of Sinclair Lewis: A Comparative Analysis of Periodical and Book," 1964.5
Seymour-Smith, Martin, 1973.13; 1976.11
"Shad Ampersand: A Novel of Time and The Writer, Tentatively Based on 'Cass Timberlane' . . . ," 1945.14
Shanks, Edwand, 1928.29
Shaw, Bernard, 1931.2; 1955.5
Shaw, Charles G., 1927.32; 1928.30
Sheean, Vincent, 1935.31; 1963.2, 16, 23-24; 1964.14
Shelton, Frank Wilsey, 1971.28
Shepard, Irving, 1965.8
Shepherd, Allen, 1974.20
Sherman, Stuart Pratt, 1921.8; 1922.5, 9, 24; 1925.36; 1927.33; 1968.4
"Sherwood Anderson and Sinclair Lewis," 1964.16. See 1962.9.
Sherwood, R. E., 1931.36
Shillito, Edward, 1927.34
"Shorter Fiction of Sinclair Lewis and the Novel-Anatomy," 1971.17

Short stories, 1962.13; 1967.8; 1971.17; 1972.24; 1975.1, 8. See Selected Short Stories; I'm a Stranger Here Myself.

"The Short Stories and Sinclair Lewis' Literary Development," 1975.8

Shrapnel, Norman, 1949.20

The Significance of Sinclair Lewis, 1922.24; 1927.33

Silhol, Robert, 1969.30

Simon, Tobin, 1972.24

"Sinclair Lewis," 1923.3; 1924.2, 4; 1927.9-10, 20; 1928.16, 19, 30, 36; 1930.8; 1931.11, 16, 18, 25, 30-31; 1933.11, 32; 1934.24; 1935.19; 1936.11, 14; 1937.2, 9; 1938.25; 1940.10, 23; 1941.4; 1944.7; 1946.2, 5; 1947.31; 1948.5; 1951.15, 19, 37, 44, 58; 1952.15; 1955.1, 13; 1958.4, 7; 1959.3; 1960.18; 1963.4, 7; 1966.1; 1967.12; 1968.3-4; 1969.14; 1970.21, 25; 1972.5; 1974.18; 1975.6

Sinclair Lewis, 1925.37; 1928.17; 1962.6; 1963.21, 25; 1964.6, 20; 1968.9; 1971.13, 20; 1973.8

Sinclair Lewis: A Biographical Sketch, 1933.31

"Sinclair Lewis: A Biographical Sketch," 1945.21

Sinclair Lewis: A Collection of Critical Essays, 1962.14

"Sinclair Lewis: A Comparison," 1946.4

Sinclair Lewis: A Critical Essay, 1932.6

"Sinclair Lewis, Actor," 1939.2

"Sinclair Lewis, a Few Reminiscences," 1952.18-19

"Sinclair Lewis: A Lost Romantic," 1959.11; 1962.14

"Sinclair Lewis: A Fontainebleau Memory," 1951.38

"Sinclair Lewis Again," 1948.1

"Sinclair Lewis--American Satirist and Novelist," 1925.8

"Sinclair Lewis: American Social Critic," 1954.6

Sinclair Lewis: An American Life, 1961.15

"Sinclair Lewis: An American Life," 1965.5

"Sinclair Lewis: An American Phenomenon," 1931.15

"Sinclair Lewis and Dreiser: A Study of Continuity and Development," 1964.10

"Sinclair Lewis and Floyd Dell: Two Views of the Midwest," 1964.21

"Sinclair Lewis and Rules," 1961.1

"Sinclair Lewis and Sherwood Anderson: A Study of Two Moralists," 1925.43

"Sinclair Lewis and the Average Man," 1928.21

"Sinclair Lewis and the Babbitt Warren," 1952.20

"Sinclair Lewis and the Drama of Dissociation," 1971.7

"Sinclair Lewis and the Fortress of Reality," 1955.3-4

"Sinclair Lewis and the Good Life," 1936.18

"Sinclair Lewis and the Hollow Center," 1966.10

"Sinclair Lewis and the Implied America," 1973.5

"Sinclair Lewis and the 'Labor Novel,'" 1952.10. See 1952.8.

"Sinclair Lewis and the Method of Half-Truths," 1956.6; 1962.14; 1963.22; 1968.10. See 1955.18.

"Sinclair Lewis and the Nobel Prize," 1931.27; 1959.7; 1961.16

"Sinclair Lewis and the Obscure Hero," 1962.9

"Sinclair Lewis and Theodore Dreiser," 1962.1

"Sinclair Lewis and Western Humor," 1970.2

"Sinclair Lewis and William Ridgway," 1964.13

Sinclair Lewis: An Exhibition, 1960.4

"Sinclair Lewis: A Portrait," 1954.12

"Sinclair Lewis: Apostle to the Philistines," 1952.3

"Sinclair Lewis: A Postscript," 1951.53

"Sinclair Lewis--A Pro-Jewish Stance," 1975.1

"Sinclair Lewis as a Prophet of Black Pride," 1971.12

"Sinclair Lewis as a Satirist," 1946.3

"Sinclair Lewis as a Young Publisher," 1961.17

"Sinclair Lewis, As Seen by an Average Reader," 1933.19

"Sinclair Lewis as Teacher," 1951.56

"Sinclair Lewis: Babbitt," 1969.29; 1971.13; 1974.19

"Sinclair Lewis: Babbitt (A Reconsideration)," 1967.7

Sinclair Lewis' Babbitt, 1965.15

"Sinclair Lewis' Babbitt," 1974.19

"Sinclair Lewis' Books in the Soviet Union," 1971.11

"Sinclair Lewis, Caliban, and the Federal Power," 1936.22; 1939.11

"Sinclair Lewis: Caricaturist of the Village Mind," 1969.13

"Sinclair Lewis: Crisis in the American Dream," 1964.7

"Sinclair Lewis, der Nobelpreis-dichter," 1931.20

"Sinclair Lewis, Dodsworth, and the Fallacy of Reputation," 1960.5

"Sinclair Lewis, Dodsworth, and the Nobel Prize," 1970.12

"Sinclair Lewis: 1885-1951," 1951.40

"Sinclair Lewis (1885-1951)," 1974.21

"Sinclair Lewis: Forgotten Hero," 1960.9

"Sinclair Lewis, 'Fundamental-ist,'" 1935.28

"Sinclair Lewis' Funeral," 1969.18

"Sinclair Lewis Gets the Job," 1947.32-33

"Sinclair Lewis Gör Come Back," 1945.10

"Sinclair Lewis: His Critics and the Public," 1938.26

"Sinclair Lewis: In Affirmation of Main Street," 1967.13

"The Sinclair Lewis Industry," 1927.45; 1928.38

"Sinclair Lewis in German," 1930.25

Sinclair Lewis Interprets America, 1932.9

"Sinclair Lewis Letter," 1967.3

"A Sinclair Lewis Letter to the Indianapolis News," 1972.20

A Sinclair Lewis Lexicon with a Critical Study of His Style and Method, 1976.12

"Sinclair Lewis: Main Street," 1948.11

"Sinclair Lewis: Main Street," 1965.1

"Sinclair Lewis Manuscripts in the Library of Congress Manuscript Division," 1975.2

"Sinclair Lewis' Minnesota Boyhood," 1954.7

"Sinclair Lewis: Mr. Babbitt's Dubious Victory," 1966.4

"Sinclair Lewis, Novelist and Speaker: A Comparison of Themes and Rhetorical Methods. . . ," 1963.5

"Sinclair Lewis on Public Speaking," 1935.11

"Sinclair Lewis on the Highway: An Unpublished Letter," 1969.12

Sinclair Lewis: Our Own Diogenes, 1927.26; 1930.20; 1962.14

"Sinclair Lewis Place, Vermont," 1934.35

"Sinclair Lewis, Plato, and the Regional Escape," 1939.4

"Sinclair Lewis Portfolio of Maps: Zenith to Winnemac," 1971.3

"Sinclair Lewis' Professor Gottlieb," 1948.6

"Sinclair Lewis: Remembrance of the Past," 1951.50-51

"Sinclair Lewis: Reviver of Character," 1968.6

"Sinclair Lewis: Satirist," 1936.17

"Sinclair Lewis's Attempts to Reform James Branch Cabell," 1975.9

"Sinclair Lewis's Condensation of Dickens's Bleak House," 1971.23

Sinclair Lewis's Dodsworth, Dramatized by Sidney Howard, 1934.32

"Sinclair Lewis's Gesture," 1926.12

"Sinclair Lewis's Good Intentions," 1937.7

"Sinclair Lewis's Kingsblood Royal: A Thesis Novel for the Forties," 1976.4

"Sinclair Lewis's Hornet's Nest," 1926.13

"Sinclair Lewis, 65 and Far from Main Street," 1950.2

"Sinclair Lewis's Plot Paradigms," 1974.3

"Sinclair Lewis's Sociological Imagination," 1970.5

"Sinclair Lewis Struts His Stuff," 1930.9

"Sinclair Lewis' Sunday School Class," 1926.24

"Sinclair Lewis's Unwritten Novel," 1958.4

"Sinclair Lewis's Zenith--Once Again," 1970.10

"Sinclair Lewis Talks of Writing --And Acting," 1940.24; 1946.9

"Sinclair Lewis: The Anti-Elk," 1933.15

"Sinclair Lewis: The Cosmic Bourjoyce," 1947.13; 1962.14; 1971.13

"Sinclair Lewis: The First American Winner of the Prize," 1932.11

"Sinclair Lewis: The Last of the Literary Liberals," 1934.19

"Sinclair Lewis: The Novelist Who 'Hated' Lecturing," 1965.3

"Sinclair Lewis: The Romantic Comedian as Realist Mimic," 1972.25

"Sinclair Lewis: The Russian View," 1953.6

"Sinclair Lewis: The Symbol of an Era," 1939.10

"Sinclair Lewis, the Voice of the New Age," 1938.29

Sinclair Lewis: 20th Century American Author and Nobel Prize Winner, 1974.15

Sinclair Lewis und das amerikanische Kultur- und Sprachbild, 1938.32

"Sinclair Lewis und die amerikanische Wirtschaft," 1935.38

Sinclair Lewis: Un Espiritu Libre Frente a la Sociedad Norteamericana, 1949.17

"Sinclair Lewis vs. His Education," 1931.21

"Sinclair Lewis Was Buried Here 20 Years Ago Today," 1971.25. See 1971.24.

Sinclair, May, 1922.25; 1971.13

Sinclair, Upton, 1922.26; 1927.35-36; 1930.4; 1956.1; 1961.18; 1971.13

Sinkler L'iuis, 1959.6

Skinner, Richard Dana, 1934.45

"Skoal for 'Red' Lewis," 1930.10

"Slap! Slap!" 1931.7

"S. L. Arrives," 1951.29

"Slick Nirvana," 1960.22

Sloper, L. A., 1935.32; 1938.30; 1940.22; 1943.17; 1945.20; 1947.27

Slosson, Preston William, 1930.24

Small town, 1920.4-5; 1921.13, 16; 1922.19, 30-31; 1925.45; 1926.18, 20; 1932.7; 1934.29; 1935.19; 1939.9; 1947.11;

1952.15; 1961.4; 1969.13;
1972.25; 1973.3; 1976.10;
1977.1. See <u>Main Street</u>.
Smith, Harrison, 1925.37;
1951.50-51; 1952.16; 1956.7
Smith, Mary Elinore, 1964.22
Smith, Thelma M., 1955.19
Social Criticism, 1925.10, 19;
1927.35-36; 1928.17, 21;
1930.24; 1931.13, 23;
1933.18, 33; 1936.11;
1938.24; 1939.10, 13;
1940.9, 23; 1943.19; 1946.5,
7; 1947.7, 20; 1949.17;
1950.3; 1952.3-4; 1954.6;
1955.5; 1959.11; 1960.9, 21;
1962.5-6; 1963.3-4, 21;
1964.1; 1965.13; 1967.12;
1968.4; 1969.6, 27; 1971.7;
1972.12, 18; 1973.8, 14
"Social Distance in Fiction,"
1929.3
"Society and the Novel," 1962.5
"Some Devices and Techniques of
Expression in the Works of
Sinclair Lewis," 1966.18
"Some Notes on Sinclair Lewis'
Funeral," 1962.8
"Some of the Working Peculiari-
ties of Sinclair Lewis,"
1933.3
"'Something Out of Dickens' in
Sinclair Lewis," 1970.9
"The Sophomores," 1970.7
"The Sordid or the Radiant Life,"
1928.18
Sorkin, Adam J., 1973.14
Soskin, William, 1938.31; 1943.18
Soule, George H., 1916.1
"The Sources of 'Elmer Gantry,'"
1960.14
"A Souvenir of Sinclair Lewis,"
1955.10; 1976.5
Spayd, Barbara, 1945.21
Spiller, Robert E., 1955.20
Spitz, Leon, 1948.6
Springer, Anne M., 1960.18
"Squandered Talents: Lewis,
Steinbeck, Hemingway,
O'Hara," 1952.13
S., R., 1934.46

Stallman, R. W., 1961.19
"Standardized America," 1922.26;
1971.13
Staples, Mary E., 1969.31
"States United: It Can't Happen
Here," 1940.13
Stearns, Harold, 1928.15
Steinbeck, John, 1944.1; 1958.1
Steiner, Arpad, 1930.25
Stein, Gertrude, 1922.2
Stevens, Alden, 1947.28
Stevens, Betty, 1956.8; 1957.6
Stewart, Donald Ogden, 1921.14
Stidger, William L., Dr., 1960.14
Stirling, Nora, 1970.25
Stolberg, Benjamin, 1935.33;
1941.4
Stone, Geoffrey, 1935.34
Storch, Willy, 1938.2
<u>Storm in the West</u>, 1963.1, 14,
19; 1964.2, 9, 11
Stout, Rex, 1947.29
Stovall, Floyd, 1943.19
Straton, John Roach, 1927.37;
1960.14
Straumann, Heinrich, 1965.13
Stribling, T. S., 1976.10
Strong, L. A. G., 1949.21
Strunsky, Simeon, 1925.38;
1928.31
Stuart, Henry Longan, 1923.7;
1925.39; 1926.36; 1928.32
Stuckey, W. J., 1966.15
<u>Studies in Babbitt</u>, 1971.13
"A Study of Characterization in
Sinclair Lewis's Fiction,"
1960.13
"A Study of Sinclair Lewis,"
1941.3
Suderman, Elmer, 1969.32
Svendsen, Werner, 1967.12
Svevo, Italo, 1971.14
Swados, Harvey, 1951.52
"Swedish Criticism 1920-1930:
The Reception of Sinclair
Lewis," 1957.1
<u>The Sweeping Wind</u>, 1962.4
Swinnerton, Frank, 1957.7

Taggard, Ernestine Kealoha, 1935.35

"A Talk with Vincent Sheean," 1963.16

"The Tangled Romance of Sinclair Lewis and Dorothy Thompson," 1963.24

Tanselle, G. Thomas, 1964.21

Tarkington, Booth, 1921.13; 1945.10; 1972.20; 1973.14

Taylor, Harvey, 1933.31

Taylor, Rachel Annand, 1927.38; 1928.33; 1929.25

Taylor, Robert H., 1957.8

Taylor, Stephen, 1938.25

Taylor, Walter Fuller, 1936.30; 1956.9

Techniques, 1929.9-10; 1935.11; 1946.3; 1962.2; 1963.5; 1964.5; 1966.8, 17-18; 1967.2; 1968.1; 1969.8; 1972.16; 1974.1, 3, 9; 1976.12

"Un Témoin des États-Unis: Le Romancier Sinclair Lewis," 1929.7

"Tendencies of the Modern Novel: III--America," 1933.33; 1934.47

"The Text: Sinclair Lewis's Babbitt," 1955.14; 1971.13

"Textual Variants in Sinclair

Thematic studies, 1938.24; 1960.5; 1965.13; 1967.4; 1969.5, 25-26; 1972.15

"Theodore Dreiser and the Nobel Prize," 1978.2

Thierry, James F., 1936.31

T., H. M., 1922.27

Thomas, J. D., 1960.19

Thomas, William, 1922.28

Thompson, Dorothy, 1931.37; 1937.13; 1939.1; 1940.1; 1951.5, 53; 1956.2; 1960.20; 1961.2; 1962.12; 1963.2, 16, 23-24; 1964.14; 1965.4; 1966.1; 1971.22; 1972.10; 1973.12

Thoreau, Henry David, 1938.26; 1958.1; 1965.1

Thorp, Merle, 1925.40-41

Thorp, Willard, 1960.21

"Three Americans: Exceedingly Personal Glimpses of Sinclair Lewis, Texas Guinan, and Clarence Darrow," 1927.32. See 1928.30.

"Three American Tragedies: Notes on the Responsibilities of Fiction," 1960.19

"Three Friends: Lewis, O'Neill, Dreiser," 1936.26

"Three Literary Men: A Memoir of Sinclair Lewis, Sherwood Anderson, and Edgar Lee Masters," 1959.4; 1963.7

Thurber, James, 1967.10; 1971.21

Tinker, Chauncey Brewster, 1952.17-19

T., M. I., 1943.20

Tolstoy, Leo, 1922.24

To Our Nobel Prize Winner: An Open Letter to Mr. Sinclair Lewis, 1932.14

Townsend, R. D., 1914.8; 1921.15; 1922.28; 1925.42; 1926.37

Toynbee, Philip, 1943.21

The Trail of the Hawk, 1915.1-6; 1923.7; 1973.7

Translations, 1925.10; 1930.7, 25; 1952.14; 1954.4; 1955.19; 1962.1; 1971.11

Tre Amerikaner: Dreiser--Lewis-- Anderson, 1939.13

Treaty Trip: An Abridgment of Dr. Claude Lewis's Journal . . . ., 1959.8

Trilling, Diana, 1943.22; 1945.22; 1978.3

Trounstine, John J., 1931.10

Turgenev, Ivan, 1922.24

Tuttleton, James W., 1972.25

Twain, Mark, 1928.12; 1938.26; 1941.4; 1972.7; 1973.3; 1974.2

"The Twenties: American," 1964.1

Twentieth Century Interpretations of Arrowsmith, 1968.4

"Two Early Manuscripts of Sin- clair Lewis," 1954.5

"Two Houses, Two Ways: The Florentine Villas of Lewis and Lawrence, Respectively," 1953.13; 1968.10

"The Two Main Streets of Sinclair
Lewis," 1943.12
"Two Views of the American
West," 1966.7
Les Tyrans Tragiques: Un Témoin
pathétique de notre temps:
Sinclair Lewis, 1969.30

"The Undeserved Degeneration of
'Babbitt,'" 1973.4
"The Unfortunate Failure of
Kingsblood Royal," 1974.12
Untermeyer, Louis, 1922.30
Updike, John, 1972.18

Van Doren, Carl, 1921.16; 1922.5,
31; 1925.43-44; 1927.39-40;
1929.26-27; 1933.31; 1934.2,
24, 27; 1935.36-37; 1936.32;
1940.23; 1946.8; 1968.4
Van Doren, Mark, 1925.44; 1927.41
Van Gelder, Robert, 1940.24;
1946.9
Van Nostrand, Albert, 1960.22
Veblen, Thorstein, 1955.5; 1965.1
Veiller, Bayard, 1927.7
Velte, F. Mowbray, 1933.32
Vernon, Grenville, 1936.33
"La Vie Conjugale aux États-Unis,
d'après Sinclair Lewis,"
1946.6
Viereck, George Sylvester,
1931.38
"A Village Radical Goes Home,"
1956.8
"A Village Radical: His Last
American Home," 1957.6
"The Village Virus," 1934.29
von Hibler, Leo, 1935.38
Vonnegut, Kurt, 1971.27
"'Vulgar Barnyard Illustrations'
in Elmer Gantry," 1972.8

Wagenaar, Dick, 1978.4
Wagenknecht, Edward, 1952.20
Wagstaffe, W. G., 1921.17
Walbridge, Earl F., 1951.54
Walcutt, Charles Child, 1966.16

Waldman, Milton, 1926.38;
1928.34; 1933.33; 1934.47
Walker, Franklin, 1953.15
Wallach, Ira, 1953.16

Walpole, Hugh, 1921.15; 1927.14
Walters, Raymond, Jr., 1961.20
"Walter White and Sinclair Lewis:
The History of a Literary
Friendship," 1975.3
Walton, Edith H., 1935.39
Wann, Louis, 1925.45
Ward, Alfred Charles, 1932.15
Ward, Christopher, 1923.8
Warfel, Harry R., 1951.55
Warren, Dale, 1954.14
"Waste Land," 1944.6
Waterman, Margaret, 1951.56
"The Way of Irony and Satire,"
1933.13
"The Way of Wizardry," 1924.5
Weeks, Edward, 1935.40-41;
1938.34; 1943.23; 1945.23;
1947.30; 1949.22; 1953.17
Wells, Carolyn, 1921.18
Wells, H. G., 1914.3, 8; 1922.14;
1925.39; 1955.5; 1957.7;
1958.1; 1962.7
West, Anthony, 1951.57
West Nathanael, 1967.10; 1968.8;
1971.21
West, Paul, 1965.14
West, Rebecca, 1922.31; 1927.42;
1928.35; 1962.14
West, Thomas Reed, 1967.13
Wharton, Don, 1937.13
Wharton, Edith, 1921.8; 1927.14,
43; 1957.5; 1960.16, 19;
1969.2
Wharton, Fred, 1951.58
"A Whartonian Woman in Dodsworth,"
1969.2
"When Lewis Walked Down Main
Street," 1960.12
When Roosevelt is Dictator . . .
A Reply to "Red" Lewis's
Novel . . ., 1936.31
"When Sinclair Lewis Wrote a
Sonnet in Three Minutes,
Fifty Seconds," 1951.22
Whicher, George F., 1951.59

Whipple, Leon, 1927.44
Whipple, T. K., 1925.46; 1928.36;
    1962.14; 1963.25; 1968.4;
    1971.13
White, E. B., 1928.37; 1933.34
White, George Leroy, Jr., 1937.14
"White Man Turns Negro," 1947.6
White, Walter, 1975.3
White, William Allen, 1927.31;
    1928.18
"Who Was Who," 1947.7
"Why Sinclair Lewis Got the Nobel
    Prize," 1930.16; 1931.27;
    1933.20; 1968.4
Williams, Michael, 1927.45;
    1928.38; 1933.35
Wilson, Arthur Herman, 1952.21
Wilson, Edmund, 1926.39; 1945.24;
    1952.22; 1956.10; 1962.14
Winans, Edward R., 1965.15
"Winesburg, Ohio and Main
    Street," 1962.10
Der Wirtschaftsgeist des
    Amerikaners im Spiegel von
    Sinclair Lewis' Romanen,
    1939.8
Witham, W. Tasker, 1947.31
With Love From Gracie, 1955.15
"With Sinclair Lewis in Darkest
    Saskatchewan," 1953.10
Wolfe, Linda, 1964.22
Wolfe, Thomas, 1958.1; 1976.10
"Women as Social Critics in
    Sister Carrie, Winesburg,
    Ohio, and Main Street,"
    1976.1
"Women in Three Sinclair Lewis
    Novels," 1973.10
Woodburn, John, 1949.23
Woodress, James, 1968.11; 1974.21
Woodward, William E., 1927.46;
    1934.48; 1947.32-33
Woolf, Samuel Johnson, 1932.16;
    1945.25
Woolf, Virginia, 1925.47; 1949.24

Work of Art, 1934.1-4, 6-7, 11,
    17, 19, 20-23, 25-26, 28-31,
    34, 40-44, 46
"The World of Sinclair Lewis,"
    1953.14
World So Wide, 1951.3, 8-9, 13,
    21, 26-28, 32-33, 35, 39,
    45-48, 52, 54, 57; 1952.14;
    1953.14; 1964.5; 1970.18
"World So Wide and Sinclair
    Lewis's Rewritten Life,"
    1970.18
Wray, Fay, 1939.2
Writing theory and practice,
    1924.3; 1931.21, 31; 1932.8;
    1933.3; 1934.3; 1940.24;
    1946.9; 1951.18; 1952.16;
    1954.12; 1955.1; 1960.1;
    1962.4
Wurster, Grace S., 1974.22
Wyatt, Euphemia Van Rensselaer,
    1934.49-50; 1936.34
Wylie, Philip, 1945.26

"Yale '09," 1939.3
Yoshida, Hiroshige, 1966.17-18;
    1976.12
Young, Filson, 1924.10
"The Young Mr. Lewis," 1928.28
Young, Stark, 1934.51; 1936.35
"You've Come a Long Way, Babbitt!
    From Zenith to Ilium,"
    1971.27

"Zenith Discusses 'Babbitt,'
    Epic of Pullmania," 1922.17
Zola, Emile, 1926.2